Religion
in Education: 3

The Religion in Education Series

a programme for professional development

in religious education and in church school education

is edited by

The Revd Dr William K. Kay

The Centre for Theology and Education

Trinity College

Carmarthen

and

The Revd Canon Professor Leslie J. Francis

Welsh National Centre for Religious Education

University of Wales, Bangor

The development of the series has been supported by grants from St Gabriel's Trust, Hockerill Educational Foundation, All Saints Educational Trust and St Luke's College Foundation. The collaborative nature of the project has been supported by a co-ordinating committee, including staff from the Church Colleges, Anglican Dioceses and The National Society: Ruth Ackroyd (University College Chester), the Revd Marian Carter (College of St Mark and St John, Plymouth), Dr Mark Chater (Bishop Grosseteste University College, Lincoln), the Revd Canon Professor Leslie J. Francis (Trinity College, Carmarthen), the Revd Dr John D. Gay (Culham College Institute, Abingdon), Dr Fred Hughes (Cheltenham and Gloucester College of HE), Dr Sheila Hunter (University College of St Martin's, Lancaster), the Revd Dr William K. Kay (Trinity College, Carmarthen), Dr Anna King (King Alfred's College, Winchester), David W. Lankshear (Secretary, The National Society, London), Ruth Mantin (Chichester Institute of HE), Carrie Mercier (College of Ripon and York St John, and National Society RE Centre, York), the Revd Canon David Peacock (Roehampton Institute, London), Dr Christine Pilkington (Christ Church, Canterbury), Gaynor Pollard (University College Chester), the Revd Canon Robin Protheroe (Diocesan Director of Education, Bristol), the Revd Alex M. Smith (Hope University College, Liverpool).

Religion
in Education: 3

Teaching about Christianity
Teaching about Judaism and Islam
Teaching about Hinduism, Buddhism and Sikhism
Research Methodology

edited by
William K. Kay
and
Leslie J. Francis

First published in 2000

Gracewing
2 Southern Avenue
Leominster
Herefordshire HR6 OQF

UK ISBN 0 85244 427 3

Typesetting by Anne Rees

Printed by Antony Rowe Ltd
Chippenham, Wiltshire, SN14 6LH

Contents

Foreword

The National Committee of Inquiry into Higher Education chaired by Sir Ron Dearing published its report in July 1997. Among its 93 recommendations (with a further 29 for Scotland!) are that the number of students, funded through loans, should rise and that a much greater proportion of the population should benefit from university level qualifications.

As part of these proposed changes, this is the third volume of a series designed to meet the needs of a growing number of people in Britain who are embarking on higher degrees in religion and education. When the working population needs constantly to be 're-skilled', distance learning provides the most painless method of progress. Learning materials come to your own home. You may work at your own pace. You can work in your own way. All you lack is the immediate stimulus of a lecturer or teacher and other students off whom you can bounce your ideas. So, to try to compensate for the lack of a teacher, most distance learning institutions provide a tutor, someone who is available to give technical and academic help.

To compensate for the lack of fellow students, there are various strategies, but whatever your college offers, a web site has been designed to use the capacities of the Internet to enhance the electronic presence of your resources. Contained within these pages and the resources of this project, then, are ideas which should make you a better teacher, lecturer, diocesan adviser, parent, governor or cleric.

This book is the outcome of an imaginative collaboration between representatives of the Anglican colleges in England and Wales and the church college trusts. In this connection, thanks should go to John Gay of Culham College Institute and to Ruth Ackroyd of University College Chester for their patient work in putting together the team and the funding that were necessary for all these materials to be written.

The work of editing these volumes has been undertaken within the Centre for Theology and Education at Trinity College, Carmarthen, a research centre stimulated by the Principal and Governors of the College specifically to facilitate developments of this nature. The editors record their gratitude to Diane Drayson, Mike Fearn, Anne Rees, Tony Rees and Mandy Robbins for their help in shaping the manuscript.

William K. Kay
Leslie J. Francis
January, 2000

Introduction

Overview

This book, the third in a planned set of four, contains four modules, each of which is broken down into three units. As they are presented there is clear progression within the modules. For example the module *Teaching about Christianity* starts with a sociological overview of religious communities in Britain and then moves from an engagement with specific Christian traditions in Britain to the way Christianity may be presented in the classroom, giving attention to the living expressions previously described and contextualised. The module *Teaching about Judaism and Islam* begins with historical outlines of these world religions before moving to consider contemporary debates caused by interaction with the modern world and, from there, to the teaching of both these religions in the classroom. Similarly, *Teaching about Hinduism, Buddhism and Sikhism* follows the pattern of moving from historical outlines through contemporary debates within the religions concerned to classroom practice. The module *Research Methodology* examines often highly influential examples of research in the field of religion or religious education. As the module title suggests the focus here is on the methods used by researchers. The module ends with a discussion of statistical terms and concepts before concluding with a practical introduction to SPSS, the foremost software package for psychological and social science data analysis.

Each unit, however, is written by a separate author and is to some extent independent of the others. Although we anticipate you would choose a pathway through this material that would lead you to work through all the units in a particular module consecutively, other options would also make sense. In other words, the materials given here are designed to be as flexible as possible within the constraints of a modern British degree at Master's level.

All the writers have been asked to write in a way that conforms to *Level M descriptors*. These descriptors express in a standardised way the 'operational contexts', 'cognitive activities' and 'transferable skills' which would normally be found in work at Master's degree level. In terms of evaluation, these descriptors require students to be able to weigh the strengths and weaknesses of alternative approaches and accurately assess and report on their own. For this reason the materials often include an outline of more than one standpoint on contentious issues. This allows student activities to be built into the text that encourage the evaluative process or, fulfilling another M level descriptor, to synthesise information and ideas so as to develop new approaches in new situations.

Similarly, since M level work requires 'depth of knowledge in complex and specialised areas', no concessions have been made to the detailed and sometimes demanding technical debates that the topics of these units cover. Moreover, M level asks students to be responsible within bounds of professional practice, to be autonomous in the use of resources and in the resolution of problems. We have sought to achieve the balance between supporting students and encouraging autonomy. Our pilot testing of the materials suggests we have been successful.

Many of the distance learning modules in the present series are free-standing. Nevertheless, it is not possible to pursue courses at this level without appropriate reference books but, to help you, and in the realisation that not all students will be able to obtain all books, we almost always include summaries of the texts to which you are pointed, so that you have at least an outline of what these texts say. The module on *Research Methodology* makes the reasonable assumption that, if you are serious about research, you will either have access to SPSS through a campus network or by purchasing a software version (for approximately £150) for use on your own computer.

In addition, many modules in the present series have been written with a view to the Readers edited by Francis and his collaborators and published by Gracewing. Each of these Readers contains about thirty original papers that have been carefully selected and reprinted from a wide range of journals across the world. The Readers therefore function like a miniature library and will save you many hours of tracking down important but out-of-the way literature. The Readers are:

- L.J. Francis and A. Thatcher (eds) (1990), *Christian Perspectives for Education*, Leominster, Gracewing.
- J. Astley and L.J. Francis (eds) (1992), *Christian Perspectives on Faith Development*, Leominster, Gracewing.
- L.J. Francis and D.W. Lankshear (eds) (1993), *Christian Perspectives on Church Schools*, Leominster, Gracewing.
- J. Astley and L.J. Francis (eds) (1994), *Critical Perspectives on Christian Education*, Leominster, Gracewing.
- J. Astley, L.J. Francis and C. Crowder (eds) (1996), *Theological Perspectives on Christian Formation*, Leominster, Gracewing.
- L.J. Francis, W.K. Kay and W.S. Campbell (eds) (1996), *Research in Religious Education*, Leominster, Gracewing.[1]

At the end of each unit, you will find a reference to the most helpful sections of the Readers and a full bibliography of other books either referred to by the author of the unit or to give you further lines of research on particular topics.

---

[1] This reader is different from the others in the sense that all its chapters are original and written specially for the book.

We recognise that distance learning students will be increasingly people who rely on electronic means of communication. The day of the 'electronic campus' has already arrived. Consultations by e-mail, the collection of resources using Internet search engines and video conferencing are being used by increasing numbers of students. *This project therefore has a web site specifically constructed to service its students and provide additional help for them.* Your college will be able to give you the information necessary to access the web site.

The next sections provide an overview of the modules in the order in which they appear and details of activities and assessment.

Teaching about Christianity

Unit A is designed to give an outline of the position of religions within British society as a whole. It is designed to set the scene for an appreciation of the place of Christianity, particularly, within this setting. It provides an historical overview of Christianity's numerical strength from the beginning of the nineteenth century and discusses the impact of secularisation on the position of the church within society. It contains statistical information that paints a big picture indicating, in many respects, the decline of Christianity. Congregations have dropped, the number of ministers has declined, religious solemnisations of marriages have weakened in relation to secular solemnisations and, by contrast, non-Trinitarian groups have increased in strength. In addition non-Christian religions have also flourished. The overall picture is that Christianity, while still numerically dominant, is in decline while other, still smaller, groups are growing. The unit ends with a discussion of sociological theories of religion and considers the possibility that religion may not, in actuality, be declining but is simply being displaced into other forms. It leaves the reader to draw his or her own conclusion about how the religious statistics should best be understood.

Unit B, after showing how Christianity itself has developed historically, has been designed to give detailed information, following on from the broad introduction provided by unit A, of five separate Christian traditions. Each tradition is treated in the same kind of way and readers are invited to attend a typical Sunday morning worship service after the basic features of each tradition have been described. Roman Catholicism begins this part of the unit and is followed by Orthodoxy, Methodism, the Salvation Army and black Pentecostalism. Each religious tradition is discussed objectively but sympathetically and the intention here is not only to provide readers with a living sense of these traditions but also to suggest what visitors, including school pupils, might expect to find if they were to make case studies of local expressions of these traditions within their own communities.

Unit C provides considerably more detail, using the work of Thomas Groome and the unifying concept of the Kingdom of God, about the teaching of Christianity. Dr Chater discusses issues of epistemology (the grounds and limits of human knowledge) and the ethical impact of learning about a religion with built-in moral demands. He considers recent major curriculum approaches: the Westhill project, Michael Grimmit's life-world curriculum, the conceptual model of Trevor Cooling, and Robert Jackson's ethnographic approach. He shows how each approach has made available its own pedagogic resources and invites the reader to reflect on teaching about Christianity and the way the various approaches might be evaluated.

Teaching about Judaism and Islam

Unit A places the history of Judaism and Islam side by side. It provides a brief outline of the history of the Jewish people, explaining why there is a Jewish diaspora and the importance of the State of Israel. It sketches out how first century Judaism developed from biblical Judaism and how rabbinic Judaism followed on. It outlines the rise of Hassidic Judaism and discusses the impact of the Enlightenment and the Holocaust. In relation to Islam the unit describes the life of the prophet Muhammad and the basic characteristics of the holy Qur'an. It shows how Islam spread in the centuries following, how Islamic law was constructed and how Islamic culture (especially in visual arts and architecture), shaped by its faith, flourished. It considers modern expressions of Islam across the world today.

Unit B, concentrating on contemporary issues in Judaism and Islam, considers first the dilemmas concerning the question of Jewish identity. Is Jewish identity conferred by birth, conversion, ethnicity or some other means? What are the major features of the Jewish religious calendar and how should they be celebrated and understood today? What dilemmas are likely to face Jews in the next few years? Is conservative or liberal Judaism likely to gain the upper hand and what will be the eventual impact of the Holocaust on Jewish theology? Can the position of women within conservative Judaism remain unaltered? With respect to Islam the unit describes the central beliefs and practices (the five pillars) of the Muslim community and shows the extent to which these may find institutional support within modern British society, particularly in the education system and also in respect of health care. It explores also the contrast between individualistic ethics within the secular society and the more communitarian ethics derived from a religious society where political and religious structures interlock. It considers Islamic sexual morality and the place of women.

Unit C turns attention to the teaching of these religions in the classroom, especially the British classroom. It seeks first to help readers clarify their own reasons for teaching these religions and describes which aspects of Judaism might be suitable for particular schools and syllabuses and at what stage they would best be introduced. It points out the variety of resources that are available to assist the teaching of Judaism and shows how a unit of work might be planned out and taught and how learning outcomes might be evaluated. The same procedure is followed in relation to Islam. The unit aims to be of practical value to practising teachers.

Teaching about Hinduism, Buddhism and Sikhism

Unit A, like the other units in this module, places three Indian religions - Hinduism, Buddhism and Sikhism - side by side. A third of each unit is devoted to each religion. Unit A is concerned with the historical development of all three religions. It engages with the issues surrounding the concept of Hinduism and the challenges it poses to western assumptions about religion. It explains the major characteristics of a Hindu worldview and its path of development over many thousands of years. An analogous process is followed in relation to Buddhism. The life and teaching of the historical Buddha are described and major features of Buddhist thought are introduced, particular attention being given to the differences between Theravada and Mahayana Buddhism. In relation to Sikhism the spiritual teaching of the gurus is introduced and the implications of these for issues of Sikh history and identity are sketched out.

Unit B explains contemporary forms of each religion giving particular attention to the British scene. Hindu ritual and social practice, iconography and mythology are outlined as they function today and contemporary debates within Hinduism about caste, women, ecology and attitudes to other faiths are discussed. With regard to Buddhism contemporary forms in Britain are described so the reader can appreciate the diversity of contemporary British Buddhism and discover how its philosophical debate is engaged with ecological issues. Modern Sikh religious practice is described, especially as it relates to questions of Sikh identity within a secular society. The unit shows how contemporary issues of authority, caste and identity impact upon the Sikh community and how life cycle rites are affected by the modern world.

Unit C turns attention to the teaching of these religions in the classroom, especially the British classroom. It seeks first to help readers clarify their own reasons for teaching these religions and describes which aspects of Hinduism might be suitable for particular schools and syllabuses and at what stage they would best be introduced. It points out the variety of resources that are available to assist the teaching of Hinduism and shows how a unit of work might be planned out and taught and how learning outcomes might be evaluated. The same procedure is followed in relation to Buddhism and Sikhism. The unit aims to be of practical value to practising teachers.

Research Methodology

Unit A offers a comprehensive review of the application of empirical research to the fields of religious education and church school studies. The major pieces of research in these areas in the 1960s and 1970s are introduced and described. Particular attention is paid to these researchers' methods in a way that allows the reader to discern the strengths, weaknesses and applicability of their various projects. By probing research techniques, and by asking the reader to put some of these into practice in a contemporary setting, the ability to apply research critically to current educational contexts is developed. This fruitful overview begins with the qualitative work of Harold Loukes, continues in the part-quantitative part-qualitative work of Ronald Goldman, visits the almost entirely quantitative work of Kenneth Hyde, Edwin Cox, Colin Alves and John Greer and assesses direct developments of this tradition by John Peatling and D. Linnet Smith and more indirect developments in the extensive attitude studies of Leslie J. Francis and E.B. Turner.

The first part of unit B takes the story forward through the 1990s. Again the major pieces of research are reviewed and their methods described and assessed. The ethnographic research of Robert Jackson is explored, the studies of religious experience by David Hay and of spirituality by Hay and Rebecca Nye are summarised and the work of Clive and Jane Erricker on children's worldviews is brought into focus. After the quantitative era in the 1980s, the 1990s have returned to a more qualitative approach.[2] The second part of unit B identifies a range of research topics in religious education and church school studies and illustrates how these topics have been approached from a range of empirical perspectives.

Unit C introduces key statistical concepts showing what they mean and how they may be applied. The notions of sample and sampling are discussed as well as more common terms like 'mean' and 'standard deviation'. Reliability and validity are explained and attitude measurement described. Levels of measurement are introduced so that different kinds of variables can be

---

[2] Unit C, Action Research, in the module *Method in Religious Education* in *Religion in Education 1* discusses qualitative research.

distinguished. The unit continues by introducing common statistical methods and gives worked examples showing the reader how to calculate simple and frequently used statistics like correlations, t-tests and chi-square. Finally the statistical software package, SPSS, is described and its basic workings explained. Readers are introduced to frequencies, analysis of variance, multiple regression and factor analysis. The unit ends with a research problem that might be answered using some or all of the methods described earlier in the unit.

Activities and assessment

Your assessment will be based on a piece of work carried out by you. The activities that punctuate these materials are not intended to be assessable, though in some cases your tutors may base an assessment around them. But your tutor will tell you *in advance* what your assessable assignment will be. Do not, however, treat the activities as an optional extra. They are designed to consolidate and deepen the learning process, to make you benefit more fully from the information and the processes laid before you.

Each activity is followed by a 'Comment' in which the unit's author has given an opinion on the kinds of things you might have thought or written in response to the stimulus you were given. The comment should be taken as just that, a comment, and not a definitive answer to the activity's stimulus.

All modules are broken into three units, A, B and C. All the activities are labelled by a letter and a number and indicated by double parallel lines in the margins. Activity A1 is the first in unit A, activity B3 is the third in unit B, and so on. The units themselves are broken into sections, each prefixed by the unit's identifying letter. A3 is the third section of unit A, B2 is the second section of unit B, and so on. This means that it is easy to refer to any part of a module in an assignment: *all you need is the module's name and a letter and a number*. For example, 'Kenneth Hyde' is found at A1 in the module *Research Methodology*.

Contributors

The twelve units in this book have been written by the following contributors.

- *Professor Brian Bocking* is Professor of the Study of Religions at the School of Oriental and African Studies, University of London.
- *Revd Marian Carter* is Tutor in Adult Theological Education at the College of St Mark and St John.

- *Dr Mark Chater* is Senior Lecturer in Religious Studies at Bishop Grosseteste University College and Course Leader of Religion in Contemporary Society
- *Rabbi Professor Dan Cohn-Sherbok* is Professor of Judaism at the University of Wales, Lampeter.
- *Lavina Cohn-Sherbok* is author of several books in the field of Judaism and Christianity.
- *Denise Cush* is Senior Lecturer in Religious Education and Study of Religions at Bath Spa University College.
- *Dr Wendy Dossett* is a Lecturer in Theology and Religious Studies at Trinity College, Carmarthen.
- *The Revd Canon Professor Leslie J. Francis* is Director of the Welsh National Centre for Religious Education and Professor of Practical Theology in the School of Theology and Religious Studies, University of Wales, Bangor.
- *Dr Mark Halstead* is Reader in Moral Education at the Faculty of Arts and Education, University of Plymouth.
- *The Revd Dr William K. Kay* is Senior Research Fellow at the Centre for Theology and Education, Trinity College, Carmarthen.
- *Dr Catherine Robinson* is Senior Lecturer in Study of Religions at Bath Spa University College.

The following people or organisations have also made significant contributions to the text of the unit B of the module *Teaching about Christianity*. In respect of Methodism: Revd John Haley, Dr Henry Rack and Revd Philip Richter; in respect of Roman Catholicism, The Right Revd Monsignor Dr Stephen Louden; in respect of the Salvation Army, staff at the William Booth Memorial Training College; in respect of Orthodoxy, Bishop Basil Osborne; in respect of black Pentecostalism, Revd Dr William K. Kay.

Activity symbols

This book is designed to be read interactively: there will be things you are asked to do while reading it. Sometimes you are asked simply to read a text, or re-read information given in the activity section, and then to think about it and write down what you think. At others the assumption is that you will work with a group of children or with a friend. Symbols are placed in the text's wide margin to alert you to the activity you will be asked to undertake.

Teaching about Christianity

Teaching about Christianity

Unit A

Society, Christian beliefs and practices: the large scale

Revd Dr William K. Kay

Centre for Theology and Education

Trinity College

Carmarthen

Contents

Introduction

Aims

After working through this unit you should be able to understand:

- the broad range of religious statistics available to describe religion;
- a typology of religious groups;
- how statistics depict religious groups in Britain;
- some of the social functions of religion;
- how religious statistics might be interpreted.

Overview

The whole of this module is entitled *Teaching about Christianity* and is therefore seen as existing in parallel with the modules in this volume entitled *Teaching about Hinduism, Buddhism and Sikhism* and *Teaching about Judaism and Islam*. But, since other modules and units in the *Religion in Education* series have been devoted to Christianity, the structure of this module is different. The first unit deals with current religious statistics in Britain, the second with selected Christian groups within Christianity and the third with teaching about Christianity in the classroom.

This unit guides you through the implications of these religious statistics and asks you to consider their meaning for yourself. In this way, this unit prepares you for a more detailed and less statistical exploration and appreciation of particular religious communities in the next unit.

A1 Religious classification

When you want to collect and interpret statistical data about the religious life of a country, you are confronted by the two preliminary questions:

- How should I classify religious groups?
- What statistics are available to me?

The classification of religious groups is complicated by the vast range of historical possibilities any comprehensive theory may expect to include. The most widely used system of classification begins with Max Weber's book, *The Protestant Ethic and the Spirit of Capitalism* (1930), where he introduced the distinction between a *church* and a *sect*. The church is 'a sort of trust foundation for supernatural ends, an institution including both the just and the unjust' (p 144) which, nevertheless, claims a universal validity and mission. A sect, on the other hand, is 'a believer's church' that is necessarily exclusive in its membership and frequently hostile to the outside world (see also Bainbridge, 1997, p 38f)[1].

This pair of categories has undergone refinement at the hands of subsequent writers. Yinger (1957) expanded the church category into two, the *universal church*, which has an international claim and appeal that transcends social and political boundaries, and the *ecclesia*, which is more limited in its scope and tends only to offer a social integration with the governing social class of a particular society, though, in theory, it may be open to all and sundry. At the other end of the scale the sect is divided into the *institutionalised sect*, which has had time to set up bureaucratic and other organisational support systems, and the *sect*, which is still socially unformed, though theologically it is exclusive and uncompromising in its claims. Between the ecclesia and the institutionalised sect is the *denomination*. The denomination is like a church in many respects except that it accepts the legitimacy of other similar religious groups. Whereas the church considers itself to offer the only way of salvation, even if this offer is tempered by less than stringent entry requirements, the denomination by definition recognises that other organised groups of Christians offer an equally valid path to God.

Some of these distinctions are easier to understand by using examples. The Roman Catholic church is the best instance of a universal church, while the Anglican church, especially in the nineteenth century, exemplified many elements of the ecclesia. Denominations are illustrated by Baptists and Methodists. Institutionalised sects might be demonstrated by Christadelphians or Jehovah's Witnesses. Sects pure and simple are less easy to pinpoint because, within a generation, they tend to set up the structures that make them institutionalised.

Finally, the *cult*, as a sociological phenomenon, is thought to be 'a loosely knit group organised around some common themes and interests but lacking any sharply defined and exclusive belief system' (Bruce, 1995, p 19).[2] Astrological groups are cultic in this sense. They are concerned to offer their members help to succeed in, or understand, society as a whole. Their doctrines are vague and offer no 'way of salvation'. Members drift in and out of

---

[1] The definition of a sect sometimes invokes its *origins* rather than its orientation or functions. Thus sects are sometimes thought of as schismatic deviations of established religious traditions. This definition, however, suffers from increasing irrelevancy as the founding of the sect recedes further and further into the past. For this reason I prefer a definition of a sect that relates to its current functions and attitudes.
[2] Some scholars define a cult by the cultural innovation it produces, but the problem with this definition is that it may be hard to distinguish cults from sects. The definitions used here seem clearer and easier to apply.

association and depend for their identification with sets of ideas and attitudes rather than with ritual practices.

Because this definition of a cult cuts against some of the darker connotations of the word found in the national press, it needs to be noted that cults *can* become closed and exercise sinister totalitarian control over the individuals who become members. This sort of regime very often breaks up families by preventing children keeping in contact with their parents.

The comparison between cults and sects is often drawn by reference to their attitude to the social world as a whole. Whereas the sect manifests a negative attitude to the social world, the cult need not do so. In this respect the sect is distinct from the church. The church is world-affirming, the sect is world-denying. The church accepts the social and political structure and works with it. The sect will often ignore social conventions. Jehovah's Witnesses, for instance, repudiate Christmas and military service. I have met members of the Exclusive Brethren who refuse to take part in the democratic process because to do so would be to identify with the 'world system'. On this principle, they do not vote in parliamentary or council elections.

Bryan Wilson (1963), in a discussion of the typology of sects, underlines his view that their defining criterion is their 'response to the world'. Any attempt to define them by reference to ideology and doctrine, he believes, is flawed by the inability of such attempts to cope with Christian and non-Christian sects in the same classificatory system. For this reason he enlarged the sect category by distinguishing between seven sect types: the conversionist, revolutionary, introversionist, manipulationist, thaumaturgical, reformist and utopian. Taken with the two church types, this expansion of the possible sect categories has given sociologists a comprehensive and flexible system for classifying most kinds of religious groups and orientations. But, although this theoretical work is valuable for coping with the many historical possibilities mentioned earlier, it remains true that, in discussions of the contemporary religious situation in Britain, the three main categories - church, denomination and sect - are the most useful.

Activity A1

Draw up a set of comparisons to show as clearly as you can the characteristics of the basic terms: church, sect and denomination.

Can you think of any modifications that might be made to this typology?

Comment on activity A1

You may have thought of the following points.

- A church is inclusive and sees itself as uniquely legitimate and universal.
- A sect is exclusive and sees itself as uniquely legitimate and universal.
- A denomination is inclusive and sees itself as pluralistically legitimate and often limited to a particular area.

Various modifications are possible. For instance, some writers (such as Currie, Gilbert and Horsley, 1977) add 'institutionalised sects' to the pattern and then describe such sects as exclusive and pluralistically legitimate. Bruce (1995) follows Currie, Gilbert and Horsley (1977) but, instead of the inclusive/exclusive criterion, uses the respectable/deviant criterion. Churches are respectable, sects are deviant, but this comes to the same thing as being inclusive/exclusive because respectability is conferred by inclusiveness and accommodation to cultural norms.

Thompson (1996) distinguishes between two kinds of church, two kinds of sect and two kinds of denomination by reference to theological criteria. He speaks of S1 sects, C1 churches and D1 denominations which hold to the historic truths of Christianity. S1 sects are Trinitarian, C1 churches hold to the Nicene creed and D1 denominations hold to traditional Christian positions. S9[3] sects reject the creeds and the historic churches, C2 churches permit a variety of belief positions and D2 denominations accommodate to the philosophies of the modern age. His point is that theological criteria are crucial to the proper understanding of sociological groupings and, indeed, that the original development of sociological classifications arose from a close study of the beliefs of the Christians in different historical circumstances.

A2 Collectable statistics

There are generally three kinds of statistics that might be used. The first kind is to do with *belonging* and the second is to do with *believing*. A third set reveals the institutional and financial strength of the church.

As you read them, you need to be aware that church attendance does not occur evenly over the United Kingdom. This means that it is important to notice where the figures are drawn from. We use 'United Kingdom' to refer to England, Scotland, Wales and Northern Ireland and 'Great Britain' to refer to England, Wales and Scotland.

---

[3] Thompson speaks of S9 sects rather than S2 sects to show that he regards these sects as being non or sub-Christian

Less care needs to be taken over the terms 'Nonconformist' and 'Free Churches' which are used interchangeably. Davie (1994) refers to Free Churches and Bruce to Nonconformists, but both quote from Brierley (1991) in reference to the same denominations. Originally Nonconformists were those who refused to subscribe to the 1662 Act of Uniformity but the wider use of the term is now to non-Anglican Protestants, even to those groups which cannot trace themselves back to 1662.

Finally, notice that the term 'Anglican' is not geographically limited. Anglicans in Great Britain include those attached to the established Church of England and the disestablished Church in Wales.

Belonging

Demographic statistics measure the number of persons admitted to a religious community by birth or infant baptism. These figures deal with formal conditions for entry and do not necessarily refer to voluntary religious practice.

Roll statistics are those applying to people who are duly qualified and who are 'sufficiently active in church life to have their names entered and retained on a membership or communicant roll or in similar church records' (Currie, Gilbert and Horsley, 1977, p 13). The Presbyterian communicant series and the Church of England electoral roll provide examples of these data. They give a general indication of religious practice.

Participation statistics show numbers of people attending a particular service. Easter communicant figures for the Church of England or Church of Scotland are good examples of these data.

Membership statistics show the number of church members within a denomination. The problem here, however, is that different denominations draw up membership conditions differently. While one group might have very strict requirements, another might have very lax requirements. At first reading the denomination with lax requirements might seem larger and more significant. One way to get round this problem is to use membership figures together with attendance figures. In general, groups with higher attendance than membership show strict membership conditions and groups with higher membership than attendance show lax membership conditions.

Attendance statistics are relatively straightforward provided that two points are observed. First, attendance can be rated on a frequency scale (daily, weekly, monthly etc.) or can be assessed by presence on a typical Sunday; it is this latter method which is used by Brierley (1989). Second, attendances are not equated with people. Thus, if a church has two morning services and some people attend twice, the *total* number of different people attending church that morning is fewer than the number of people counted as present at the two separate services.

Believing

The believing figures are more complex because many kinds of belief can be indicative of Christian commitment. People would be expected to have belief in God and in Christ, but they might also be expected to hold certain moral beliefs. Moreover, beliefs can be put together to form scales that measure attitudes. The figures we present later in this unit are largely self-explanatory, though the distinction between beliefs and attitudes needs to be elaborated.

There is a large literature on the subject of attitudes and their measurement (Thurstone and Chave, 1929; Guttman, 1944; Fishbein, 1963) which dates back to the 1920s. In general an attitude may be thought of as an evaluative disposition with an affective dimension or, to put this in more everyday speech, it is a tendency to be *for* or *against* something (the evaluative disposition) and it involves feelings as well as intellectual judgements. If you have a positive attitude to Chinese food, you will tend to think highly of it and to feel pleasure at the thought of eating it. A positive attitude, therefore, is linked with the likelihood of a matching action. Attitudes are made up of lots of beliefs about something and lots of evaluations of these beliefs. For this reason, attitudes tend to be broadly based and to be more stable than single free-standing beliefs or opinions. To take the example of an attitude to Chinese food again, this would be made up of beliefs about the healthiness of this food, its taste, its value for money and so on, and positive evaluations of all these beliefs.

Francis (1976) has constructed a scale that measures attitude toward Christianity among young people aged 8-16 years. This scale was constructed so as to conform to the most precise standards of social science procedure and rigorously tested to ensure that its statistical properties were robust (Kay and Francis, 1996). The scale has been used in more than a hundred studies, some of which are referred to here.

Institutional strength

Churches may be counted though care has to be taken to distinguish between branch works, daughter congregations and other off-shoots that growing churches produce. Sometimes care must also be taken to differentiate between buildings and congregations since some denominations have more buildings than congregations and others have more congregations than buildings.

Ministers may be counted though care has to be taken to distinguish between stipendiary and non-stipendiary, full and part-time, retired, missionary, itinerant and other kinds of ministers.

Income for charities is normally available for public inspection and is a useful indicator of the general strength of a denomination, but care must be taken to differentiate income from congregational collections, from investments and from tax or covenant rebates.

Activity A2

What sort of statistics do you think would be easiest to collect and why? What sort of statistics do you think would be most likely to be accurate and why? How might statistics be checked against each other to ensure their accuracy? What statistics are most meaningful?

Comment on activity A2

The easiest statistics to collect are those which are routinely collected by denominational groups. Every denomination, by virtue of the institutionalisation that contributes to the process of denominationalisation, has a list of its ministers. The same is true of denominational buildings. The denomination almost certainly holds a list of its properties. The income of charities (churches are considered as charities) is also reasonably easy to obtain because their accounts must be audited and available for scrutiny. The difficulty with financial statements, though, is that accounting procedures may vary so much between denominations as to make comparisons meaningless.

Denominational figures should be accurate provided that there is a good system in place for returning annual statistics to a central office. The system, however good it is, depends on efficient and accurate collectors at the local level. As a general rule of thumb, the smaller the number of things which have to be counted, the greater the accuracy should be. Counting ministers ought to be more accurate than counting church members.

Statistics can be compared against each other in many ways. Unless there is a period of change, there ought to be a year-on-year match, or at least constant ratio, between buildings and ministers. Similarly, there ought to be a constant ratio between church attendance and membership. Checks can also be made by comparing one year's figures with another. In general, one would expect all the figures profiling a denomination to rise and fall approximately together. Income would tend to fall as membership fell. Membership would fall as the number of ministers fell. The number of buildings would be reduced as the number of congregations dwindled. The catch here is that any recruitment or evangelistic drive would only gradually affect all the sets of figures. It is a moot point to decide whether a sudden rise in the number of ministers would lead eventually to a rise in attendance and membership or whether growing congregations would tend to precede additions to the ministerial list. Comparisons, then, *can* be useful for checking statistical trends provided decline or growth is steady.

The most meaningful statistics are a matter of opinion but it is arguable that because church attendance has the merit of signalling the Sunday-by-Sunday commitment of individuals to the church, these figures give the most likely measure of the impact of Christianity on society.

A3 What the belonging statistics show

In this section we are concerned to present some of the basic figures relevant to religion in Great Britain without extensive comment or interpretation. That will follow later.

First, we show the general and overall trends of church membership from 1800 to the present day. Then we look more closely at the figures from 1975-1995 by analysing them for trends over time and against the general population. As you look at the figures in table 1 you need to remember that the population of Great Britain rose steadily in the nearly two centuries we are considering. There were 6.7m people aged over 15 years in 1800 and this figure rose to 24.6m in 1900, to 36.6m in 1945 and to 41.2m in 1970 (Currie, Gilbert and Horsley, 1977, pp 65, 66). The final tables in this section match attendance against the age profile of the population so that it is possible to see the age groups where the church is especially strong and weak.

Figures also taken from Currie, Gilbert and Horsley (1977, p 25) show the size of church membership in thousands between 1800 and 1970. These are presented graphically in table 1 and figure 1.

Table 1: Church members in Great Britain, 1800-1970 (thousands)

	1800	1850	1900	1950	1970
Protestant	1101	2577	5056	5077	4311
Catholic	129	846	2016	3499	4829

Source: Currie, Gilbert and Horsley (1977, p 25)

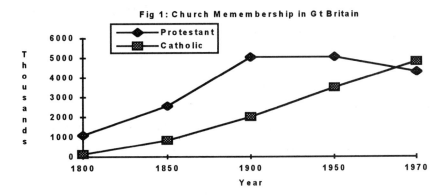

Fig 1: Church Memembership in Gt Britain

Table 1 and figure 1 show that church membership in Great Britain rose steadily throughout the Victorian nineteenth century. At the start of the twentieth century Protestant figures first levelled out and then, after the 1939-45 war, began to decline. Roman Catholic figures continued to rise without setback and now exceed those of the combined Protestant churches.

Statistical information on the strength of the churches from the mid-1970s to the mid-1990s is provided in a paper by Francis and Brierley (1997), drawing on data originally published in the *UK Christian Handbook*. These statistics are organised to discuss separately Trinitarian churches, non-Trinitarian groups, and other major world faiths.

Trinitarian churches

Table 2: Trinitarian churches: number of members 1975-1995

	1975	1980	1985	1990	1995
Anglican	2,297,571	2,180,108	2,016,593	1,870,429	1,718,500
Baptist	236,212	240,211	243,736	232,118	232,490
Roman Catholic	2,518,955	2,337,853	2,195,112	2,103,760	1,951,525
Independent	252,172	252,991	308,258	342,319	357,075
Methodist	596,406	540,348	500,702	475,440	437,950
Orthodox	196,850	203,140	223,686	265,918	286,700
Other Christian	155,835	138,948	127,632	129,823	131,330
Pentecostal	104,648	126,743	138,316	158,695	184,000
Presbyterian	1,641,520	1,505,290	1,384,997	1,288,505	1,195,305
TOTAL	8,000,169	7,525,632	7,139,032	6,867,007	6,494,875

Source: Francis and Brierley (1997)

In table 2 and all those of the same format which follow, the four largest groups of Independents are Brethren, Fellowship of Independent Evangelical Churches, Union of Welsh Independents and New/House Churches. The Other

Christian category includes seven Lutheran churches, the German Evangelical Synod, the Wesleyan Holiness Church and the Church of the Nazarene.

The figures in table 2 continue the story through to 1995, but they include Northern Ireland and so strengthen the overall Protestant figures. They agree, however, that the Roman Catholic church has overtaken the Anglican church. From the point of view of trends, they show that the Roman Catholic church, like the Anglican church from 1950, has begun to decline in membership. Only the Nonconformist church (which includes Baptists, Independents, Methodists and Pentecostals) has managed to grow slightly.

Table 3: Trinitarian churches: members as percentages of the 1975 figures

	1975	1980	1985	1990	1995
Anglican	100	95	88	81	75
Baptist	100	89	90	85	86
Roman Catholic	100	93	88	86	77
Independent	100	100	122	136	142
Methodist	100	91	84	80	73
Orthodox	100	103	114	135	146
Other Christian	100	89	82	83	84
Pentecostal	100	121	132	152	176
Presbyterian	100	92	84	78	73
TOTAL	100	94	87	87	81

Source: Francis and Brierley (1997)

Table 4: Trinitarian churches: members as percentages of population aged fifteen and over

	1975	1980	1985	1990	1995
Anglican	5.3	4.8	4.4	4.0	3.7
Baptist	0.5	0.5	0.5	0.5	0.5
Roman Catholic	5.8	5.1	4.8	4.6	4.2
Independent	0.6	0.6	0.7	0.7	0.8
Methodist	1.4	1.2	1.1	1.0	0.9
Orthodox	0.5	0.4	0.5	0.6	0.6
Other Christian	0.4	0.3	0.3	0.3	0.3
Pentecostal	0.2	0.3	0.3	0.3	0.4
Presbyterian	3.8	3.3	3.0	2.6	2.6
TOTAL	18.5	16.5	15.5	14.8	13.9

Source: Francis and Brierley (1997)

Table 3 shows the rate of change of church membership. The Anglican, Methodist and Presbyterian decline is most severe. The Pentecostal and Independent groups are largely charismatic in outlook and style of worship, and they demonstrate exceptional growth.

The bottom row of table 4 shows how, despite growth of the smaller groups in the previous table, the Trinitarian church's share of the adult population has continued to decline steadily since 1975, a decline that table 1 shows started after about 1950.

Table 5: Church members per 1000 of the adult population by UK region

	1975	1980	1985	1990
Northern Ireland	832	791	769	677
Scotland	378	346	327	301
Wales	233	206	175	165
England	143	128	114	111

Source: Brierley and Hiscock (1993, p 251)

Table 5 confirms the great regional variation in church membership across the United Kingdom. Northern Ireland and Scotland are very much more wedded to the church than England and Wales, and Wales is much less secular than England. These figures underline the need to specify from where religious statistics are taken before attempting to generalise their implications.

Table 6: Trinitarian ministers: numbers

	1975	1980	1985	1990	1995
Anglican	15,911	14,654	14,064	14,137	13,170
Baptist	2,418	2,469	2,648	2,803	2,984
Roman Catholic	8,892	8,854	8,408	7,980	7,643
Independent	1,575	1,483	2,022	2,786	2,915
Methodist	2,726	2,632	2,617	2,668	2,619
Orthodox	126	160	187	241	272
Other Christian	1,884	1,850	1,922	2,324	2,373
Pentecostal	1,605	2,243	2,580	3,359	3,780
Presbyterian	3,776	3,632	3,412	3,159	2,909
TOTAL	38,913	37,977	37,860	39,457	38,665

Source: Francis and Brierley (1997)

Table 7: Trinitarian members per minister

	1975	1980	1985	1990	1995
Anglican	144	149	143	132	130
Baptist	98	97	92	83	78
Roman Catholic	283	264	262	272	255
Independent	160	171	152	123	122
Methodist	219	205	191	178	167
Orthodox	1562	1270	1196	1103	1054
Other Christian	83	75	66	56	55
Pentecostal	65	57	54	47	49
Presbyterian	434	414	406	407	411
TOTAL	206	198	189	176	168

Source: Francis and Brierley (1997)

Tables 6 and 7 are informative on three counts. They show that the total number of Trinitarian ministers in the UK has remained almost static over the 1975-95 period. So, in view of the fall in the number of members revealed by table 2, the call to Christian ministry becomes proportionately more attractive. Second, there is a wide denominational variation in the ratio of ministers to members. Third, the Orthodox church, despite its growth, has a shortage of ministers and this suggests that the growth is due to immigration or cultural factors rather than to effective ministerial action. The two groups which have seen definite non-cultural church growth, the Independents and Pentecostals, have ratios similar to those of the Anglicans and Baptists. This supports the impression that the numbers of ministers a denomination fields is not as critical to its success as what these ministers actually do.

Table 8: Church membership and attendance (in millions), England, 1989 [4]

Denominational group	Members	Attendance
Nonconformist	1.17m	1.25m
Anglican	1.56m	1.14m
Roman Catholic	4.20m	1.30m
Orthodox	0.23m	0.009m
Total Christian	7.16m	3.71m
Total adult population	38.83m	38.83m
Attenders/members as % of population	18.44%	9.55%

Source: Brierley (1991, p 57)

---

[4] The figures were based on attendance on 'census Sunday' which was a mid-month Sunday in October.

From table 8 it can be seen that church attendance figures for England as a percentage of the total adult population are just under 10%. The Nonconformists' relative strength becomes evident here because, despite a membership of about 65% of that of the Roman Catholics, attendance is almost the same. And the relative weakness of the Anglican position is shown by a higher membership than the Nonconformists but a lower level of attendance.

Table 9: Church attendance and age, England, 1989 (%)

	Men	Women	Total
Under 15	13	15	14
15-29	8	10	9
20-29	5	8	6
30-44	7	10	9
45-64	8	12	10
65+	12	14	13
All age groups	9	12	10

Source: Brierley (1991, p 95)

Table 9 shows the percentage of men and women in each age band who attend church. What is striking about these percentages is that the church is best represented among the young and the old and that, in each band, women are more likely to be attenders than men.

Table 10: Church attendance and social class, Great Britain, 1991 (%)

Attendance	Non-manual	Manual
Fortnightly or more	16	12
Monthly to once a year	29	24
Less than once a year	3	4
Never	48	57
No answer	3	3

Source: 1991 British Social Attitudes Survey (Bruce, 1995, p 44)

Table 10 shows how a greater percentage of non-manual workers attend church and attend more frequently than manual workers. The middle class orientation of the church is demonstrable from these figures, a fact that would be even more evident if the table had separated social class and denomination (Kay and Francis, 1996, pp 62f).

Activity A3

> Look at the attendance and membership figures in table 8. Do you feel able to draw any conclusions about the relationship between membership and attendance?
>
> Look at table 5. Calculating the percentage drop 1975-90, in which part of the United Kingdom has church membership declined fastest?
>
> What do tables 2 and 8 suggest to you about the future strength of Nonconformity in relation to Anglicanism and Roman Catholicism?
>
> What do tables 9 and 10 suggest to you about the most and least likely people to be attending church?

Comment on activity A3

Table 8 shows membership and attendance figures for England alone. The relationship demonstrated would almost certainly be different for other parts of the United Kingdom. What they show, though, is that Nonconformist membership is held on stricter conditions than Anglican or Roman Catholic membership which is why Nonconformists have more attenders than members, and Anglican and Roman Catholics fewer attenders than members.

You will see from table 5 that the steepest rate of decline in church membership has taken place in Wales (1990 figures are 71% of 1975 figures), and this is followed by England (78%), Scotland (80%) and Northern Ireland (81%).

Tables 2 and 8, if the trends they identify continue, suggest that Nonconformist membership may eventually overtake Anglican membership and, again assuming the trends continue, Roman Catholic membership. Certainly, they suggest that Nonconformist *attendance* will overtake the attendance of the other two bodies.

Tables 9 and 10 suggest that the most likely people to be attending church are older women who are non-manual workers. Manual working men in their 20s are least likely to be attending church.

Non-Trinitarian groups

In the tables of this format which follow, the Others category includes 24 groups of which the best known are probably the Christadelphians and Unitarians.

Table 11: Non-Trinitarian groups: members

	1975	1980	1985	1990	1995
Jehovah's W	79,586	83,521	97,495	116,612	130,500
Mormons	99,830	114,458	132,810	149,000	140,000
Scientology	20,000	30,000	50,000	75,000	90,000
Others	139,488	125,911	117,615	110,418	102,600
TOTAL	338,904	353,890	397,920	451,030	463,100

Source: Francis and Brierley (1997)

Table 12: Non-Trinitarian groups: members as percentages of 1975 figures

	1975	1980	1985	1990	1995
Jehovah's W	100	105	123	147	164
Mormons	100	115	133	149	140
Scientology	100	150	250	375	450
Others	100	90	84	79	74
TOTAL	100	104	117	133	137

Source: Francis and Brierley (1997)

Table 13: Non-Trinitarian groups: members as percentages of population aged fifteen and over

	1975	1980	1985	1990	1995
Jehovah's W	0.2	0.2	0.2	0.2	0.3
Mormons	0.2	0.3	0.3	0.3	0.3
Scientology	0.0	0.1	0.1	0.2	0.2
Others	0.3	0.3	0.3	0.2	0.2
TOTAL	0.8	0.8	0.2	1.0	1.0

Source: Francis and Brierley (1997)

The three main non-Trinitarian groups (some might be classified as 'institutionalised sects') demonstrate steady growth in the years 1975-95. Overall they have grown to 137%, a figure which would be much higher if the Others had not declined. All the growing groups are noted for their active pursuit of new members, often exemplified by going door-to-door with their message. Nevertheless, as table 13 shows, the size of these religious groups relative to the population as a whole is small, amounting to no more than 1% of those over 15 years of age.

Other major world faiths

There are technical and political problems in the collection of data relating to non-Christian world faith communities in Britain. Technically these difficulties arise from the lack of a uniform definition of religious affiliation or membership. For instance some religious communities make the assumption that religious belonging is expressed by ethnicity whereas others, because of their ethnic variety, cannot and do not make this assumption. Moreover, membership is signified by initiatory rites, but these may be involuntary (as in the case of circumcision soon after birth) or voluntary (as in the case of *bar mitzvah*). Attendance figures are also problematised by variation in attendance rates associated with religious festivals. Do communities count attendance on ordinary days or special days? Politically these difficulties are associated with the tendency either to exaggerate figures to boost a religious profile in relation to the majority community or, alternatively, to reduce these figures so as to avoid appearing a threat to the majority community. Nevertheless, despite these caveats, the figures given here are often cited.

Table 14: Other major World Faiths represented in Britain: members

	1975	1980	1985	1990	1995
Buddhists	13,000	17,000	23,000	27,500	32,000
Hindus	100,000	120,000	130,000	140,000	145,000
Jews	111,000	110,915	109,150	108,400	108,000
Muslims	204,000	306,000	434,979	504,900	586,000
Sikhs	115,000	150,000	160,000	250,000	290,000
TOTAL	543,000	703,915	857,129	1,030,800	1,161,000

Source: Francis and Brierley (1997)

Table 15: Other major World Faiths: members as percentages of 1975 figures

	1975	1980	1985	1990	1995
Buddhist	100	131	177	212	246
Hindus	100	120	130	140	145
Jews	100	100	98	98	97
Muslims	100	150	213	247	287
Sikhs	100	130	139	217	252
TOTAL	100	130	158	190	214

Source: Francis and Brierley (1997)

Table 16: Other major World Faiths: members as percentages of population aged fifteen and over

	1975	1980	1985	1990	1995
Buddhist	0.0	0.0	0.0	0.1	0.1
Hindus	0.2	0.3	0.3	0.3	0.3
Jews	0.3	0.2	0.2	0.2	0.2
Muslims	0.5	0.7	0.9	1.1	1.3
Sikhs	0.3	0.3	0.3	0.5	0.6
TOTAL	1.3	1.6	1.9	2.2	2.5

Source: Francis and Brierley (1997)

Tables 14-16 show the major world faiths, apart from Judaism, have all increased substantially in the years 1975-95. Buddhist, Muslim and Sikh constituencies have more than doubled in size, while the growth of the Hindu constituency has kept pace or exceeded that of any Trinitarian church apart from the Pentecostals. As a percentage of the population over 15 years of age, the major world faiths amount to 2.5%.

Activity A4

Look at the figures in table 15 and work out whether the rate of growth or decline for each of the five world faiths has been consistent from year to year. You might find it easiest to do this by drawing a graph or by looking at the difference between each year's figures.

What reasons can you suggest for your figures? You may wish to look again at the figures in table 12 to help you interpret the figures in table 15.

Comment on activity A4

Tables 14 and 15 show that the Jewish group has declined slightly but consistently between 1975 and 1995 from 111,000 to 108,000. By way of contrast the Hindu and Buddhist groups have grown consistently over the same period of time.

The Muslim group has also accelerated upwards, but the rate of growth from 1985-95 is slower than 1975-85. Only the Sikh group shows a sudden jump in the period 1985-1990.

For the Jewish group, the even rate of decline suggests either an ageing community or a community being eroded in a slow and systematic way, either by emigration or assimilation.

For the Hindu, Buddhist and Muslim groups the steady growth suggests young communities growing by having children and keeping them in the faith.

For the Sikh community, the sudden growth between 1985-90 suggests either a period of immigration or a period of revitalisation.

Table 12 gives growth rates for Jehovah's Witnesses and Mormons, who are long established in Britain, and whose increase in size is by proselytisation and natural increase (that is, by retaining in the faith children born to members). Since these rates of increase - especially those of the Jehovah's Witnesses - are very constant, it is reasonable to suggest that some special factor accounts for the jump in the Sikh figures 1985-1990.

A4 What the believing statistics show

The next set of tables display some of the religious beliefs of the population. Again, these figures are taken from a mixture of sources and various age groups so that it is important to be careful when making comparisons. As with the previous section we start with the basic background statistics extending over as long a period of time as we can.

Table 17: Which of these statements comes closest to your beliefs?

	1947[5]	1957[6]	1963	1965[7]	1979	1981	1986	1989	1993
personal God	45%	41%	38%	43%	35%	36%	31%	30%	30%
spirit or lifeforce	39%	37%	33%	43%	41%	37%	41%	39%	40%
I don't know		16%	20%	12%	17%	15%	11%	19%	16%
no God or lifeforce		6%	9%	4%	8%	12%	16%	12%	14%

Source: Gallup, political and economic index[8]

[5] The first statement is identical in this year; the second is 'There is some sort of spirit or vital force which controls life'; the third is 'I am not sure that there is any sort of God or life force'. Sixteen percent responded affirmatively to the third statement.

[6] The wording here is almost identical to that used from 1963 onwards. The second statement is 'There is some sort of spirit/god or life force' and the fourth is 'Don't really think there is any sort of spirit/god or life force'.

[7] This column is taken from a survey made by Gallup on behalf of ABC Television. The sample of 2,211 was collected in London, the Midlands and the North i.e. England only. These figures are omitted from the line graph.

[8] These are quota samples. Personal communication.

The figures in table 17 come from a series of surveys carried out by the Gallup organisation on random samples in Great Britain since 1947. The questions asked and the way the samples were drawn did not change markedly (see footnotes to table) and this allows the trend over time to be accurately measured. Respondents were asked 'Which of these statements comes closest to your beliefs?':

- There is a personal God.
- There is some sort of spirit or lifeforce.
- I don't know what to think.
- I don't think there is any sort of spirit, God or lifeforce.

Figure 2 line graph of Gallup surveys 1967-93 based on table 17.

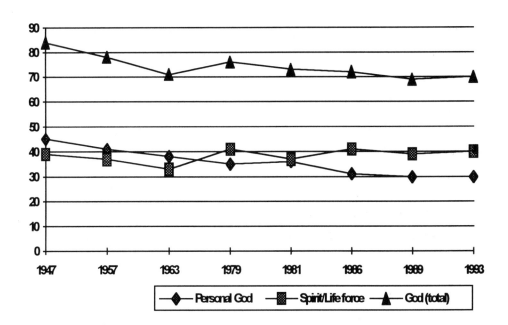

Table 18: belief in God (%) (13-15 year olds)

I believe in God	(%)
Agree or agree strongly	39
Not certain	35
Disagree or disagree strongly	26

Source: Francis and Kay (1995)

The figures in table 18 focus on young people and show how their belief in God is much lower than it is for the general population and how uncertainty is at a much higher level. If the long-term trends shown in table 17 are correct, many of the young people who are 'not certain' will come to a form of belief either in God or in a 'spirit or lifeforce'.   Whether any of the young people who are likely to change their minds join one of the growing groups shown in the earlier tables cannot be known for certain, but it seems probable that a general re-orientation towards spirituality, if it takes place, is going to be associated with institutional support.

The top line of table 17 shows that belief in a personal God in Great Britain has gradually diminished in a more or less consistent pattern in the years 1947-93.   The figures that buck the trend are those for 1965, but a reason for this can be attributed to the special nature of the sample for that year.   While the belief in a personal God has declined, belief in 'some sort of spirit or lifeforce' has remained remarkably consistent and, when the two top lines are added together, we see that around 70% of the British population believes in some sort of spiritual dimension to life, and has done so since 1979.   Meanwhile, the entirely materialistic view of the world, which rejects 'any sort of spirit, God or lifeforce', has gradually risen 1957-93.   The rise in materialism and the decline in acceptance of a spiritual dimension are roughly mirror images of each other because the 'don't knows' have remained at a fairly constant size.   The period since the end of the 1939-45 war may, as we shall see, be interpreted as one of consistent secularisation.   Such an interpretation would be supported by the figures describing church membership and attendance displayed earlier.

Table 19: Marriages in England and Wales by manner of solemnisation

	1902	1952	1962	1972	1980
All	261,750	349,308	347,732	426,241	406,000
Religious	218,989	242,531	244,630	232,107	204,000
Civil	42,761	106,777	103,102	194,134	202,000
% Civil	16.3	30.5	29.6	45.6	49.7

Source: Currie, Gilbert and Horsely (1977, p 224); 1980 figures from *Social Trends 1995*, table 11.11

The trend of figures shown in table 19 demonstrates an unmistakable shift away from religious solemnisation of marriage, yet the figures conceal an important factor which affects their interpretation: second marriages are much more likely than first marriages to use a civil form of solemnisation.   As second marriages increase, civil marriages as a percentage of all marriages automatically increase. In 1979, 89,000 of first marriages were solemnised in a civil marriage ceremony and 181,000 were solemnised in a religious marriage ceremony.   Of first marriages, then, 33% of the total were civil (*Social Trends 1995*, table 11.11).

Table 20: Percentage of live births baptised in Church of England 1902-1993

Year	%
1902	65
1927	71
1960	55
1970	47
1993	27

Source: Bruce (1995, p 59) taken from Brierley (1989); Brown (1994)

Table 20 also relates to a social function of religion and it shows, like table 19, that there is a general decline in the usage made of the services of the church in the standard rites of passage. Even in 1993, however, when the Church of England's membership comprised less than 4% of the population (table 4), many times this number of people wished their children to undergo baptism.

Activity A5

First, look at tables 17, 19 and 20. What is common to all these tables? Next, look at tables 19 and 20 and notice that they give figures for the year 1902, and the years 1960/62 and 1970/72. Either draw a graph of the six points in the range 1902-1972, comparing percentage of religious solemnisations with percentage of live births baptised (to do this, make the vertical axis refer to percentage and the horizontal axis to time) or alternatively, calculate the year on year percentage drop. What do you notice about the graph? What does it suggest to you?

Comment on activity A5

The figures relating to belief in God in table 17 drop in the years 1947-1993; the figures relating to religious solemnisation in table 19 drop in the years 1902-1980; the figures relating to baptism in the Church of England as a percentage of live births drop in the years 1902-1993. What is common to all the tables is that the measurement of religious belief and practice is in decline.

If you draw a graph you will see two nearly parallel lines. While there are 83% of religious marriages, there are 65% of live births baptised in the Church of England; while there are 70% of religious marriages, there are 55% of live births baptised; while there are 54% of religious marriages, there are 47% of live births baptised. What you will notice is that between 1902 and 1960/62 religious solemnisation of marriage and percentage of live births dropped at the same rate (70 is 84% of 83 and 55 is 84% of 65). Thereafter the rate of baptisms drops faster.

At first sight it looks as though what is happening is that baptisms were felt to be more important than religious solemnisation of marriage and that over the years this fringe of people who had religious solemnisations but did not care for child baptism grew smaller. This *may* be what is happening, but what prevents us being sure is that table 19 refers to religious marriages of *all* kinds (Christian, Jewish, and so on) and table 20 refers only to baptisms in the Church of England.

A5 What do the figures mean?

We consider first the problem of transformations and then a general interpretation of the figures. Do we see an inexorable process of secularisation and, if we do, what does this mean and imply?

Transformations

Difficulties with the description of the religious life of Britain arise from the ability of religious groups to shift categories. For example, there is a well-known tendency for sects to become denominations. Over time the anti-world and exclusivist orientation of the sect gradually becomes the pro-social and pluralist orientation of the denomination. The Evangelical Nonconformity of the early industrial age, for example, was a typically sectarian phenomenon, exclusive in attitude and social structure alike. Gradually, the 'tendency towards professionalism and institutional order' and the 'emergence of denominational characteristics in every aspect of Methodist life' were also found in the older Congregational and Baptist communities. The historically observed general path of development is therefore *from* sect *to* denomination. But there is also a path in the opposite direction *from* church *to* denomination which occurs as the universal claims of the church are implicitly relativised by the recognition of the validity of the new denominations. Thus Baptists and Anglicans might meet on the common ground of inter-denominational fellowship.

There are also other typically twentieth century transformations of religion that are more subtle and more controversial that affect the way religious statistics may be interpreted. Wilson (1976) argues that the shifting social basis for religion coupled with the accelerating pace of social change, has produced a crop of religious forms which, instead of transmitting the moral and cultural norms of an earlier age, pass on 'counter cultural' lifestyles, hedonistic attitudes and vigorously anti-moral opinions. In other words religions which used to be 'a vehicle of culture' providing 'guidelines for action' are now as transient as each generation and function only as the providers of 'symbolic communication' and 'creative consciousness' (pp 80, 115).

So we are left with the possibility that religion exists in a different form - transposed into a different key - but is essentially part of society. In connection with this possibility, we need to consider the social role of religion.

Social role of religion

Sociological study is the examination of society in all its aspects. One of the phenomena within society to which sociologists have for a long time given attention is religion. Religion is viewed from the angle of its function and from the angle of the social structures it supports (Mitchell, 1966). Religion functions to:

- mark the milestones in an individual life;
- give meaning to life;
- provide a rationale for morality;
- bind families or communities together through shared experiences.

According to a Marxist analysis, religion also functions to sedate the working class so that they will not rebel against their rulers ('religion is the opium of the people'[9]). Even a religious interpretation of religion considers that it serves particular functions. A Christian interpretation of Christianity is that it provides a total lifestyle that leads to God through Christ. Other religions also, in the main, would tolerate a functionalist description of themselves. To a greater or lesser extent they would see themselves as shaping or operating within society in order to bring people to a religious goal.

The social functions of religion are independent of the truth of religion. Nearly all religions have ceremonies, for example, linked with the birth of a child, or with death. These ceremonies appropriately mark the beginning and ending of life and there is little or no emotionally satisfying secular equivalent of them. By analysing the social function of religion, and laying it bare, there need be no intention of belittling or condemning religion. Religion's function can be objectively observed, even by participants within a religious tradition whose motivation is quite unconnected with a functionalist explanation. In other words, a mother may decide to have her child baptised because she feels that this is in some sense morally or religiously 'right'. Indeed, unless she is

---

[9] Karl Marx in the introduction to *Criticism of Hegel's Philosophy of Right*.

trained in sociology, she is unlikely to think of her child's baptism as having sociological significance.

Religion supports social structures by legitimating them and, in the case of religious institutions, creating them. Religion customarily legitimates the family, partly because religious truth is handed on within the family. Religion also supports churches, mosques, synagogues, monasteries and even the whole apparatus of government. Take away religion and there is little justification for government except patriotism or the power of physical coercion. For instance, the Roman empire in the first century went through periodic bouts of emperor worship (which led to the persecution of Christians, though that was not their prime purpose) as a means of unifying its disparate peoples.

The Christian teaching in Romans 13 that everyone should be subject to the authority of the state because all authority comes ultimately from God illustrates this point. Romans 13 endorses secular governmental structures, specifically the judicial system, and provides reasons why they should be obeyed.

Secularisation theory applied

The concept of secularisation, then, must be interpreted within the approach to religion that sociology adopts. David Martin's 1978 book *A General Theory of Secularization* stresses the growing apart of church and state, the uncoupling of their institutions and the emergence of what he calls a 'free market' of religion. The uncoupling of church and state ensures that the social structures of the state and the church are separate and distinct and that the state stands without needing the legitimation of the church. Martin's general theory is that the process of secularisation is linked with the economic substructure of society. In some countries a monopoly has existed (Catholicism in France), in others the free market has always reigned (the USA) and in others a mixed economy has become the norm (Great Britain). Religion becomes a product that is offered in the market place and functions as a leisure activity for consumers. Other leisure activities compete with religion and have equal validity. The pattern of secularisation follows the pattern of the market. Secularisation, in this view, is the turning of religion from a force for creating and legitimating social structures into a commodity and, because it is a commodity, its ability to provide a rationale for morality or to give meaning to life is relativised. Other commodities will provide other rationales and other meanings and the consumer is free to pick any philosophical package off the shelf. Choice is a matter of personal and private preference which may or may not be rational.

A more complicated theory of religion suggests that it offers *compensation* for the inability to realise material rewards and comforts. Stark and Bainbridge (1980, 1985, 1987) constructed a theory of religion based on 'exchange theory' which presumes that all, or nearly all, human interactions can be understood as a form of exchange. When confronted with the problems, tragedies or questions of life, the individual exchanges a deep-seated desire for meaning with an intellectual answer. But, where meanings are not obtainable because of the scope or difficulty of the question, the individual accepts a compensation by positing the existence of an explanation in a distant future or at the hands of a supernatural entity.

A further refinement of this theory has been put forward by Iannaccone (1992). Iannaccone argues for a 'rational choice theory' of religion by drawing a close parallel between economic activity and religious activity. Religions may be 'cheap' or 'expensive' depending on whether they make weak or strong demands on us. They may offer more or less to us by way of help in this life or promise for the future. People have to decide whether to accept an expensive religion that offers them a great deal or a cheap religion that offers less. Within the market place of religions in our present pluralist societies, people make rational choices between the religious products on offer.

This theory (and its refinement) has been extensively critiqued (Wallis and Bruce, 1992; Hamilton, 1995). It depends on the almost arbitrary interpretation of human life as fundamentally a form of exchange and it presumes that, in periods when no other rewards are available, religion will flourish most vigorously. At least, that is one suggestion, though another, put forward by Wallis and Bruce, is that there will be a 'persisting demand' for rewards and therefore a constant 'demand for credible intangible substitutes' which suggests that religion, even if it changes its forms, will continue to flourish at a constant level in society. Whatever the case, the large-scale data presented in this unit do not settle the matter. Material conditions in Britain have generally improved since 1800 and this would accord with the observed decline of religion but, at the same time, the disruption of family life, waves of unemployment and recession and two world wars have increased anxiety which would, presumably, lead to a desire for comforting religious answers, and a corresponding rise in religion. Bainbridge (1997, p 405f) has, indeed, drawn this conclusion, and presented empirical data showing that, when organised and traditional religious communities decline in the United States, new religious groups are most likely to arise. There is, in the preceding tables in this unit, some support for this view though a moment's thought will show that all kinds of factors, including immigration and better means of transport and communication, have a measure of responsibility for the pluralisation of the religious scene in Britain. Some of these issues are picked up again in the sections below.

A rather different account of secularisation comes from a study of the work of Weber, one of the founders of the sociological study of religion. Weber considered religion to have arisen as a means of explaining suffering in the world and to have been encouraged by a 'primitive mythology of nature' (Weber, 1915; quoted from 1969 source). Consequently religion retreats before modernism. As explanations of suffering (particularly illness) are made and as nature is better understood, the causes which gave rise to religion work against it. Modernity and technical control of the environment remove the mystery that religion explained. Moreover, religion is sustained by community, often religious community, and family. The arrival of industrialisation and urbanisation, which are themselves concomitants of modernity, strengthen the trend towards secularisation by dismantling religious community and diminishing families. Certainly, as a matter of historical record, the decline in religion, as recorded by the statistics given earlier in this unit, has been accompanied by a corresponding advance in technology and in huge urban areas. The Weberian explanation, therefore, helps to make sense of large-scale social and religious changes.

This explanation has been refined by Wilson (1976, 1982) in his account of 'societalization' which stresses the way the personal encounters of people living in communities have been replaced by anonymous transactions with machines or bureaucracies. We do not speak to the teller in the bank, we use a card machine in a wall; we do not meet insurance agents, we speak to answerphones. It is easy, then, to mark a birth or marriage by a similarly anonymous transaction, and religion loses its relevance. Accompanying the growth of bureaucracy, religion is challenged by the specialist. In the days of community, the minister of religion might be pastor, friend, counsellor and organiser of social events. In the days of society, the work of the minister is taken over by the professional counsellor and the officers of welfare agencies.

Is the secularisation theory correct?

Greeley (1973) has argued powerfully against both the theoretical and empirical account of secularisation. What modernity produces is not the marginalisation of religion, he contends, but its transformation. 'People will need religion as long as they need meaning' and whatever gives people their ultimate meanings is their religion. This attack in the main depends on a re-definition of religion. It was echoed by Lyon (1985) using historical examples. For example, the strongly Catholic nature of pre-Revolutionary France became the strongly rationalist, anti-clerical France of the Reign of Terror. God was dethroned by the guillotine and then reintroduced as the State. Religion was not displaced; it was relocated. A similar process was observable in Marxist

Russia. There the Tsar was executed and Christianity was forbidden. The icons of the church became merely historical relics. Lenin became an idealised Messianic figure leading everyone towards the millennium. After assassination in 1924, Lenin was embalmed and put on display in Red Square so that his 'presence' remained. Meanwhile his face was emblazoned on thousands of plaques and medallions which functioned like the icons of Christ in the days of the Tsar.

Berger (1970) in his influential book *A Rumour of Angels* questions secularisation on different grounds. The entire historical and philosophical process that has undermined the validity of religion by turning it into a merely human enterprise without any recourse to the supernatural or the divine may itself be undermined. This is because the historical and philosophical analysis assumes itself to be true and uninfluenced by its own cultural context. But this is not so. There is a double standard in assuming that 'the New Testament writers are... afflicted with false consciousness rooted in their time, but the contemporary analyst takes the consciousness of *his* time as an unmixed blessing. The electricity-users and radio-users are placed intellectually above the Apostle Paul' (p 58, original italics). This leads Berger to argue that anthropology can be the starting point for a revitalised theology. For example, a mother who takes a crying child in her arms during the night and offers comfort with the words 'Don't be afraid - everything is all right' is lying if the 'natural' is the only reality there is; but, if there is some elemental truth in the religious interpretation of existence, she is uttering a profound truth (p 73). From these, and other instances of life, Berger argues that 'it is possible to proceed from the faith that is rooted in experience to the act of faith that transcends the empirical sphere' (p 72).

Finally, it should be noted that the work of Stark and Bainbridge and of Iannaconne mentioned earlier, also effectively argues against secularisation since it posits a continuing ground for the continuance of religion in new or revitalised forms. Indeed, one of the main conclusions they draw from their position(s) is that, when the supply side of religion is increased (that is, when there are more religious possibilities available in society), religious activity will increase. As we shall see, none of this convinces those who contend that the real meaning of the picture presented by theory and statistics is that religion is on the decline in the contemporary world.

Re-statements of the secularisation theory

Gilbert (1994) is unconvinced by Greeley's arguments. He finds they lead to confusion and untestable theories. If, as those (such as Saunders, 1977) who support Greeley believe, every worldview or dominating concern that functions *like* a religion *is* a religion, then the meaning of religion dissolves into nothing-ness. Consumerism or Marxism or any powerful ideology become religions and religion cannot decline. Gilbert will have none of this, and contends that secularisation, as traditionally understood, is taking place, though he adds four modifications.

First, secularisation is a complex process that operates in different ways in different contexts. Secularisation is not the whole story about what is happening with religion, but it is one of its main parts.

Second, secularisation can never be anything other than a partial process. Because there can never be a completely modernised world where chance and accident are ruled out, there will always be room for the religious interpretation of events.

Third, the impact of secularisation on culture is segmental rather than general. Religion will be able to appeal *outside* the general stream of modernised culture, but it is unlikely to be able to find a solid place *within* the homogenised, media-influenced developed world.[10] Perhaps religious symbols will continue to have expressive functions rather than a shaping role in modern consciousness.

Fourth, secularisation is not necessarily irreversible because counter-cultural forces 'create or expand constituencies for traditional types of religiosity'.

Finally, to conclude this section, note that Wallis and Bruce (1992), as already mentioned, are also unconvinced by the de- or non-secularists.

Activity A6

Looking again at the figures you have studied earlier in this unit, what explanation for them seems to you to be most satisfactory? Do you accept the secularisation theory? Or do you think that it obscures what is really happening in the United Kingdom in respect of religion? Is Gilbert's comment on the secularisation thesis persuasive?

Comment on activity A6

You may feel that Greeley's position, or a modification of it, is tenable. You may have experience of a thriving Christian community and have personal religious experience of your own which seem to call into question the

---

[10] Gill (1993) draws on a less Euro-centric analysis to argue that the process of secularisation is not an inevitable accompaniment of urbanisation or modernity. The politics of the Middle East and the rise of religious fundamentalism - Christian, Islamic and Hindu - all point to the weakness of the secularisation thesis.

secularisation theory. You may also feel that the theory depends on the existence of an idealised religious past - perhaps the Victorian epoch, perhaps the period of Christian unity before the Reformation - from which the decline must be measured. And you may think this idealised past did not exist, that there was always religious non-observance or insincerity so that the situation today is probably not very different.

Yet, the figures for membership, attendance, religious solemnisation of marriage, baptism and belief in God all point in the same direction. They cohere as a set of statistics collected by separate people and organisations over a period of time. There is no reason to doubt their general accuracy, and so it seems reasonable to accept that there has been a decline in religion, in its practices, in its beliefs and in its place within society. The secularisation thesis offers a partial explanation of this based on the functions religion customarily fulfils. In order to test the secularisation thesis we should have to find a rural, and non-modern, society where religion is in decline and, conversely, a modern society where religion is in the ascendant. We may be able to find such societies (for example, it is possible to argue that ancient Rome became secular in the sense that many of its most prominent people did not accept classical mythology and religion), and we may think of occasions in the biblical record when the decline of religion in an ancient society took place just as markedly as has been observed in Britain in the last century.

Yet, even when this is said, it would appear that religious life within Britain is changing. There is both a shrinking of the Anglican and Roman Catholic churches, a growth of smaller charismatic, Pentecostal and independent churches and an increase in the size of non-Trinitarian groups and major world faiths. It is possible to argue that all these groups, to some extent or another, resist modernity as it has been previously defined. The key question, then, is whether their resistance to modernity is a rearguard action, or an indication that 'alternative lifestyles' are likely to become more prevalent in the future. The current data cannot answer this question. All we are entitled to say is that the historical durability of religion suggests that it can survive, even in an inhospitable climate.

Gilbert's qualification of secularisation theory seems reasonable and does allow for variations to exist within modern culture. He sees genuine secularisation (rather than simple transformation of religion and no secularisation) and, at the same time, limits to the process. These limits make room for unsecular pockets or components within society.

A6 Conclusion

It is important to notice what this unit has and has not covered. We have covered only one general religious belief within society as a whole, and this is belief in God. We have not considered quasi-religious beliefs like astrology or patterns of superstition. The background to religious belief and practice within Britain in the fullest possible picture would be set against the prevailing norms, what might be called the 'everyday popular and practical theology' of the British people. Such a background has not yet been fully drawn and awaits further empirical research.

We have not given any details of individual religious communities and congregations because that is the business of the next unit. We have shown the relative numerical strength of various religious constituencies and traced their rise and fall over time. We have identified trends and suggested how they might relate to each other. We have explained these trends in terms of secularisation theory and accepted the reasonableness of a functional explanation of religion. This explanation should not, and does not, explain religion completely. We do not wish to *reduce* religion to sociological theory as if sociological theory explains why religion exists or explains what religion explains. The Christian faith, like the other faiths reported on here, gives meaning and purpose to its adherents in ways quite outside the scope of sociological enquiry. Furthermore, even those aspects of public religion (like the use of the bible in law courts or prayers at the opening of Parliament) have been deliberately omitted from this unit because they say little about the impact of religion on ordinary life. Religious membership and attendance, on the other hand, say a great deal.

Readers

You will find relevant material in L.J. Francis and D.W. Lankshear (eds) (1993), *Christian Perspectives on Church Schools*, Leominster, Gracewing, chapters 3.1, 3.2 and 12.1 and in L.J. Francis and A. Thatcher (eds) (1990), *Christian Perspectives for Education*, Leominster, Gracewing, chapter 13.2.

Bibliography

Bainbridge, W.S. (1997), *The Sociology of Religious Movements*, London, Routledge.

Berger, P.L. (1970), *A Rumour of Angels: modern society and the rediscovery of the supernatural*, London, Allen Lane.

Brierley, P. (1989), *A Century of British Christianity: historical statistics 1900-1985*, Research Monograph 14, London, MARC Europe.

Brierley, P. (1991), *'Christian' England: what the English church census reveals*, London, MARC Europe.

Brierley, P. and Hiscock, V. (eds) (1993), *UK Christian Handbook 1994-5*, London, Christian Research Association.

Brown, A. (1994), Birth celebration without religion offered, *The Independent*, 23 July.

Bruce, S. (1995), *Religion in Modern Britain*, Oxford, Oxford University Press.

Currie, R., Gilbert, A. and Horsley, L. (1977), *Churches and Churchgoers: patterns of church growth in the British Isles since 1700*, Oxford, Clarendon Press.

Davie, G. (1994), *Religion in Britain since 1945: believing without belonging*, Oxford, Blackwell.

Fishbein, M. (1963), An investigation of the relationship between beliefs about an object and the attitude toward that object, *Human Relations*, 16, 233-240.

Francis, L.J. (1976), An enquiry into the concept 'Readiness for Religion', unpublished PhD dissertation, University of Cambridge.

Francis, L.J. and Brierley, P. (1997), The changing face of the British churches: 1975-1995, in W. Shaffir, (ed.), *Leaving Religion and Religious Life: patterns and dynamics*, Greenwich, Connecticut, JAI Press, pp 159-184.

Francis, L.J. and Kay, W.K. (1995), *Teenage Religion and Values*, Leominster, Gracewing.

Gilbert, A.D. (1994), Secularization and the future, in S. Gilley and W.J. Sheils (eds), *A History of Religion in Britain*, Oxford, Blackwell, pp 503-521.

Gill, R. (1993), *The Myth of the Empty Church*, London, SPCK.

Greeley, A.M. (1973), *Unsecular Man: the persistence of religion*, London, SCM.

Guttman, L. (1944), A basis for scaling qualitative data, *American Sociological Review*, 9, 139-150.

Hamilton, M.B. (1995), *The Sociology of Religion*, London, Routledge.

Iannaccone, L.R. (1992), Religious markets and the economics of religion, *Social Compass*, 39, 123-131.

Kay, W.K. and Francis, L.J. (1996), *Drift from the Churches*, Cardiff, University of Wales Press.

Lyon, D. (1985), *The Steeple's Shadow*, London, SPCK.

Martin, D. (1978), *A General Theory of Secularisation*, Oxford, Blackwell.

Mitchell, G.D. (1966), *Sociology: the study of social systems*, London, University Tutorial Press.

Saunders, T.G. (1977), *Secular Consciousness and National Conscience*, a report of a conference on secularisation held in Rome in 1976, quoted by Gilbert, A.D. (1994), Secularization and the future, in S. Gilley and W. J. Sheils (eds), *A History of Religion in Britain*, Oxford, Blackwell, pp 503-521.

Stark, R. and Bainbridge, W.S. (1980), Towards a theory of religion: religious commitment, *Journal for the Scientific Study of Religion*, 19, 114-28.

Stark, R. and Bainbridge, W.S. (1985), *The Future of Religion*, Berkeley, University of California Press.

Stark, R. and Bainbridge, W.S. (1987), *A Theory of Religion*, New York, Lang.

Thompson, M.J. (1996), An illustrated theology of churches and 'sects', unpublished PhD dissertation, University of Kent at Canterbury.

Thurstone, L.L. and Chave E.J. (1929), *The Measurement of Attitude*, Chicago, University of Chicago Press.

Wallis, R. and Bruce, S. (1992), Secularization: the orthodox model, in S. Bruce (ed.), *Religion and Modernization: sociologists and historians debate the secularisation thesis*, Oxford, Clarendon Press, pp 8-30.

Weber, M. (1930), *The Protestant Ethic and the Spirit of Capitalism*, London, Unwin University Books.

Weber, M. (1969/1915), Major features of world religions, in R. Robertson (ed.), *Sociology of Religion*, Harmondsworth, Penguin, pp 19-41.

Wilson, B.R. (1963), A typology of sects in a dynamic and comparative perspective, *Archives de Sociologie de Religion*, 16, 49-63.

Wilson, B.R. (1976), *Contemporary Transformations of Religion*, Oxford, Oxford University Press.

Wilson, B.R. (1982), *Religion in Sociological Perspective*, Oxford, Oxford University Press.

Yinger, J.M. (1957), *Religion, Society and the Individual*, New York, Macmillan.

Teaching about Christianity

Unit B

Society, Christian beliefs and practices: the small scale

The Revd Marian Carter

Centre for Christian Theology and Education

The University College of St Mark and St John

Plymouth

Contents

Introduction

Aims

After working through this unit you should be able to understand:

- historically-driven diversity within contemporary Christianity;
- how a typology of Christian congregations from case studies might be constructed;
- how Christian diversity might be educationally explored.

Overview

Using a form of case study this unit introduces you to the rich diversity of Christian congregations in Britain through the sociological categories of 'church', 'denomination' and 'sect'. Following an historical introduction to the church as a whole and to each Christian group individually a typical Sunday service is described to the visitor. To provide some comparability and to extend the analysis between them, each group is considered under the headings 'belonging', 'believing' and 'behaving'. At the end of this unit suggestions are made about ways the studies might be useful in the classroom.

Books relevant to each Christian group are listed at the end of the unit in the general bibliography. You might also wish to supplement the overview of Christianity as a whole by referring to the list of extra reading referred to in the section immediately preceding the bibliography.

B1 Diversity of Christian congregations

Unit A in this module invited you to the study of Christian beliefs and practices on a large scale. This unit invites you to look at the varied relatively local expressions of Christian belief (see Francis, 1996).

The 1988 Education Reform Act assumed that teaching about Christianity would occur at each Key Stage of the curriculum in England and Wales. Since church attendance is at a comparatively low level within Britain (see previous unit), it is reasonable to assume that pupils' experience of Christianity will be limited and may only amount to the kind of expressions of faith gained from the long-running television programme *Songs of Praise*. Partly to meet this problem the Chichester Project (Lutterworth) in the 1980s published a series of books that aimed to treat Christianity as a world religion (Erricker, 1995). It issued separate books on, for example, Christian communities and Christian worship in an effort to introduce pupils to a range of theological and cultural expressions of Christianity, and it often did so using examples from within Britain.

On the face of it there is a bewildering variety of Christian belief and practice in existence. There are Protestant and Catholic churches, but then there are varieties within Protestantism (for example Anglican, Baptist and Methodist) and within these varieties there are further variations (Hastings, 1991a). It would not be uncommon to distinguish between different types of Anglican (for instance, liberal or evangelical), and some of these types would be found in Methodist or Baptist congregations (Cooling, 1984).

Probably the best way to understand the development of Christianity is by looking at three basic factors:

- historical events;
- cultural variation;
- theological attitudes.

Historical events and *cultural variation* can be illustrated by the analogy of a river. If you imagine a river that starts from a single source and flows across a wide flat landscape, the depth and width of the river increases. After a thousand miles the river responds to the landscape and breaks into two streams. Five hundred miles later one of the streams comes to turbulent rapids and then a mountain and this causes it to break apart into two streams flowing to either side. There are now three streams all flowing in the same direction, but separated from each other. Each stream flows through a variety of landscapes. There is a jungle on the banks and the water supports suitable vegetation and aquatic life, and then there is a more temperate climate and the river passes houses, watermills and pastures. Each of the three streams responds to its environments separately and each is changed by them. A factory nearby discharges chemicals; a water purification unit takes chemicals out; a mill wheel slows the flow down; a damn builds up a huge reservoir supporting a large nearby town. The third stream is quite quickly broken up by islands and rocks and so subdivides further.

Imagine that the first division of the river (after a thousand years) is into Roman Catholic and Orthodox and that the second (after a further five hundred years), represented by the turbulence and the mountain, is the Reformation when the church split into its Protestant and Catholic streams. Later the Protestant stream splits and separates into the many varieties of Protestantism that exist. If we think of cultural variation, we might think of the different landscape through which the river runs so that, for instance, Catholicism in Europe is somewhat different from Catholicism in Mexico.

These three broad streams, Orthodox, Roman Catholic and Protestant, are basic to understanding Christianity. They show that there is a sense in which Orthodoxy is closer to Catholicism than it is to Protestantism and that the many subdivisions of Protestantism belong together even if some parts move across the landscape towards the other large rivers.

Theological attitudes are more difficult to express by an analogy. Instead think of political attitudes along an axis from 'progressive' to 'conservative'. These attitudes can then be applied to different elements of the political situation. Someone might be conservative with regard to the monarchy and progressive with regard to the reform of the House of Lords, or conservative with regard to the handling of public spending and progressive in relation to the legalisation of cannabis. Progressives want change; conservatives want to keep things as they are.

Theological attitudes can be similarly progressive and conservative. A Christian group might be conservative with regard to liturgy and progressive in its approach to homosexual relationships. Or, to take another example, a Christian group might be conservative in relation to the bible and conservative in its approach to liturgy but progressive in relation to the ministry of women. In other words, a variety of denominational profiles can be formed by applying different attitudes to the elements that comprise the beliefs and practices of particular churches.

To simplify an analysis of progressive and conservative attitudes three sources of authority within the church can be taken. Authority is usually thought to rest in:

- the scriptures;
- tradition;
- reason.

Each of these sources can be used to support change or the *status quo*. Thus *scripture* can be the lever that brings about change (as in the Reformation) or the wall that prevents change (as in some moral issues); *tradition* can likewise be a source of change (as in the Oxford Movement of the nineteenth century) or a ground for making no change (as in arguments about the ordination of women); *reason* can also be a force for change (as in liberal Christianity) or the method by which change is resisted (as in some forms of fundamentalism).

Given these factors, it is no surprise that we find lots of labels on church noticeboards: for instance, Protestant, Catholic, Baptist, Methodist, Reformed, and within churches lots of things taking place: Julian or charismatic prayer groups, healing meetings, organ or tambourine playing, solemn liturgies or exuberant dancing, ministers wearing vestments or ministers wearing jeans and trainers, completely black congregations or completely white congregations, robed choirs or casually dressed guitar-playing soloists, children participating joyfully or children kept quiet and in the background. And all this variety is matched by architectural variation as congregations meet in magnificent stone edifices or scout huts and community centres that smell of stale tobacco.

This profusion of Christian forms is expressed in the UK by many styles and types of church buildings. In 1992 there were 50,000 church buildings in the UK, one for every 940 adults (Bruce, 1995, p 30).

Activity B1

Collect a list of the names of all the places of worship in your area. You may wish to collect this list either from personal knowledge or by using the yellow pages in your local phone book. Locate each place of worship within the categories of church, denomination and sect discussed in unit A of this module. Why are there so many worshipping congregations? What difficulties might there be in using the typology church, denomination, sect?

Comment on activity B1

It is likely that the number of congregations surprised you. (The writer lives in a small city of 250,000 and such an exercise produced 192 listings!) You may have found a considerable number of sects. One reason for this may lie in the pluralisation and privatisation of religion in Britain. As religion becomes more personal and less of a public activity connected with major national festivals like Christmas, and as most religious opinions are thought to have equal validity by those who regard the matter superficially, the possibility of holding almost any spiritual viewpoint has become acceptable.

Difficulty in applying the church, denomination, sect typology arises from two main problems. First, the 'attitude to the world' that lies at the heart of the definition of sect is hard to assess simply by reference to buildings or advertisements. It is necessary to know about the inner workings of the group and its doctrinal emphases before this evaluation can be made. A simple listing of names provides insufficient evidence for this categorisation. Second, the distinction between church and denomination similarly rests on a doctrinal division between those groups that consider they combine a universal mission and sole access to the way of salvation and other groups that recognise the validity of their religious neighbours' theological positions.

B2 Historical overview

The first Christians were Jews within the Roman Empire. In many respects they were similar to other Jews, but simply believed that Jesus was the long-awaited Messiah. Gradually, Gentiles were added to the church and the lifestyle of Christians diverged from that of the Jews. For example Christians met together to worship on Sundays, the 'day of the Lord's resurrection' rather than on Saturdays, the Jewish Sabbath.

At first the Roman authority made no distinction between Christians and Jews (Acts 18.12f) with the result that Christians were given the same privileges as Jews. As Christianity became recognised as a separate religion, it ceased to be a permitted religion under Roman law and, under emperors who wished to unify the Roman Empire by creating religious uniformity, it suffered bouts of persecution that had the effect of shaping and ultimately strengthening it. With the conversion to Christianity of the Roman Emperor Constantine in 313 CE and his Edict of Toleration, the church moved into a different phase of existence. It was not only a permitted religion, but it also received the support of the state. Consequently the Bishop of Rome (the capital of the empire) and his successors became increasingly important. Attempts were made to standardise church organisation and worship but were never successful, even after 393 when Christianity became the only legal religion in the empire.

The Roman Empire was so vast that it eventually needed two administrative centres, one in the West, in Rome, and one in the East, in Byzantium or, as it was later called, Constantinople. Two theological cultures grew up in the two parts of the empire and this was compounded by linguistic preferences since the West spoke Latin and the East was more comfortable with Greek.

In 1054 the divergence between western and eastern Christianity was formalised. There were doctrinal disagreements between the two sees over the claims of the Pope, as the Bishop of Rome had then become. The West accepted the primacy and authority of the Pope. The East did not. But there was also a difference over the doctrine of the Trinity in that the East believed that the Spirit proceeded from the Father alone while the West believed the Spirit proceeded from the Father and the Son. The West came to be known as Roman Catholic and the East to be known as Orthodox. Subsequently, Orthodoxy developed along slightly different lines in Russia, the Balkans and Greece so that one may speak of Russian, Bulgarian or Greek Orthodoxy, but these differences are essentially administrative and liturgical rather than doctrinal (Hussey, 1986).

Byzantium fell to Islamic invaders in 1453 and so ceased to function as a Christian theological centre. The position of Rome was enhanced, but the church for which it was responsible had by now lost much of its earlier simplicity and spirituality. Various reform movements came into being, but only from 1521 onwards, when the Augustinian monk Martin Luther directly challenged papal authority, did these movements produce institutional, doctrinal and liturgical change. Subsequently, those who *protest*ed against papal rule became known as '*Protest*ants' and large sections of the church broke away from Roman jurisdiction, often along national lines. Much of Northern Europe and parts of the Netherlands and Britain became Protestant. These new churches rejected not only papal authority but also formulations of Catholic doctrine that minimised the role of individual faith in Christ's death as the basis for salvation. The Protestant churches simplified worship, re-wrote liturgies, abandoned such practices as the confessional, permitted the marriage of clergy, emphasised the authority of the bible over that of the Pope and denied the existence of purgatory. With the translation of the bible from Latin into the common languages of the people (for example, German after 1522; English after 1524), preaching grew in importance and Protestant congregations redesigned church architecture by placing the pulpit more centrally and by removing or diminishing representations of the Virgin Mary.

Protestantism itself subdivided in the following centuries. Sometimes a new leader brought a new set of churches into existence. John Wesley's preaching resulted in the Methodist Church and William Booth's in the Salvation Army. Sometimes insistence on the importance of a particular doctrine caused the appearance of a group of denominations (see Edwards, 1981). For instance, belief in the value of speaking in tongues led to the formation of Pentecostal churches.

In the rest of this unit, we will look at congregations belonging to various sections of the church in the British Isles. Each congregation is visited on a typical Sunday. The services are described and an attempt is made to draw out what it believes, how it creates a sense of belonging, what its people and ministers do and how they behave. The examples of congregational life are designed to make Christian variety plain while, at the same time, showing how this variety flows from underlying theological and historical sources.

B3 Case study approach

Christianity is a living faith and one way of understanding it is through watching how believers order their lives and worship. The diversity of practice can be discovered by making case studies of Christian congregations and focusing on the same areas in each case. The choice of issues used in this unit reflects the threefold typology of church, denomination and sect. For each congregation questions will be asked based on the distinctions made by Davie (1994) between:

- believing;
- belonging;
- behaving.

Each case study will be preceded by a brief introduction setting the historical context. The Church of England has deliberately been omitted as a case study since it is studied in other units.

Believing

To discover the beliefs of a congregation it is possible to look at its foundational or formative documents. These would include, for example, creeds and statements of faith such as the Anglican *Thirty-Nine Articles*, but these are likely to give the ideal rather than the actuality of what the congregation believes. Another way to discover beliefs is to look at buildings. What does the shape of a particular Christian building, its furnishings, artefacts and symbols say about what people believe? Answers to these questions will lead into other questions about the use of the building, for example, during worship. Again worship, its content and emphasis, give clues to the beliefs of the worshippers. Questions will be asked to discover how forms of worship in a tradition reflect the theology of that denomination and its concept(s) of authority.

Belonging

To discover who belongs we might look at how an individual becomes part of the community. At what age does this happen? How does it happen? What sort of people become part of the community and why? Is there any relationship between belonging and class, age, sex or race?

Behaving

To discover the practices of a particular community evidence may be found in the effect of the community on the larger community of society. Does the Christian community influence its own people in their life style? How? What effect does this have on the society at large? Is it world affirming or world denying? What is the function of religion?

B4 Roman Catholic Church

Historical context

The withdrawal of Roman forces and the official Roman political presence from Britain in 410 CE led to the disappearance of the cultural and political life of Roman Britain. It is unknown when Christianity first came to Britain, but there were tiny remnants of British Christian communities living among the Anglo-Saxons when Pope Gregory (590-604) sent the first missionaries to the Anglo-Saxons. Augustine, who led the missionaries, had to make his way to the River Severn to make contact with the leaders of the British church. By the beginning of the sixteenth century, within England and Wales, most people shared one faith. The changes arising from the subdivision and reconstruction of Christendom in the sixteenth century are detailed in history books as the Reformation, the Counter Reformation or the Catholic Reformation. The Reformation entailed the repudiation and even the physical destruction of some of the religious practices and buildings of the past. The compliance of the English people in the face of Henry VIII's injunctions is understandable but the rapidity of their compliance is a remaining puzzle. Catholics were excluded by penal laws from sitting in Parliament, from voting in parliamentary elections, and from bearing arms. Toleration for adherents to the old Catholic faith waxed and waned in the three succeeding centuries, yet the appointment between 1685 and 1688 of Apostolic Vicars in London, the Midlands and western districts ensured that a form of Catholic episcopal government was successfully maintained until the Restoration of the Hierarchy in 1850.

For close on two centuries, Roman Catholics continued to be a minority in a hostile environment (Archer, 1986). In 1700, Catholics probably numbered 5% of the population of 6 or 7 million yet, by 1780, their numbers had dwindled to 69,000. The influx in 1789 of 5,500 French clergy refugees from persecution in the French Revolution created further sympathy for English Catholics. In 1829 the Act of Emancipation restored to Catholics full rights as citizens, made them eligible for government office and allowed them to sit in Parliament. Catholics in England could breathe easily again.

The celibate Catholic clergy were dedicated and hardworking. Two notable Italian missionaries, Gentili and Barberi, preached with success and made many converts. Barberi received John Henry Newman into the Catholic Church in 1845. The Oxford Movement seemed to presage the early return of England to Roman Catholicism, but in spite of such Catholic hopes the expectation was not fulfilled. Instead, as a result of the potato famine of 1846-1847 there came from Ireland an enormous influx of destitute Irish. On the basis of the 1851 census return, it is estimated that Catholics then totalled 679,000 served by over 800 priests (Bossy, 1978). By 1964, possibly the recent high point of Catholicism in England, the officially estimated Catholic population was 3,824,000 in a total population of 44,000,000.

Hornsby-Smith (1991) identifies four distinct strands in the historical emergence of contemporary Catholicism:

- the very few recusant Catholics who can trace the continuity of their Catholicism from the pre-Reformation period (the term recusant was used of Catholics who suffered penal taxation and fines because of their refusal to attend Anglican services);
- converts to Roman Catholicism over the past 200 years;
- immigration since the late eighteenth century, especially the arrival of Irish immigrants;
- European refugees including 100,000 Poles fleeing the Communist take over of Eastern Europe after the Second World War.

As in Catholicism world-wide, so the already changing Catholicism in England was given impetus by the Second Vatican Council (1962-65) convened by Pope John XXIII (Hastings, 1991b). A key word was the Italian *aggiornamento* or bringing up to date. At parish level this took the following forms:

- mass in Latin was replaced by mass in English;
- the position of the altar was transposed so that the priest now faced the congregation;
- at mass, lay people took the role of reading the scriptures and the bidding prayers;
- the eucharist was again offered to the laity under the form both of bread and wine;
- more recently, lay men and women serve as 'extraordinary ministers of the eucharist';
- house masses were adopted in many parishes.

Lay liturgical participation and shifts in language signalled recovery of a less clerical and more egalitarian view of the church as the 'baptised people of God' which all but demanded:

- eucharistic concelebration by bishops and priests;

- the permanent diaconate;
- greater participation of lay people at various levels in the life of the church, for example, membership of bishops' advisory bodies.

Believing

St Mary Magdalene is a typical Roman Catholic church of the 1960s built on a new housing estate. Outside the church stands a notice board announcing the times of Sunday and weekday masses, as well as the time when the Sacrament of Reconciliation (previously called 'confession') is celebrated. The board displays the name, address and telephone number of the priests of the parish. Beside the notice board is a life-size crucifix. On entering the church porch or entrance area, hymn books, service books, Catholic newspapers and magazines are stacked on a table. Future events and advertisements are displayed on a notice board. There is a glass screen separating the porch area from the church proper. Advancing through a door from the porch into the body of the church, the pews (more usually called 'benches' by Catholics) are seen to be positioned to face a central altar. Unlike older churches, there is no pulpit but a lectern (reading stand) positioned to one side of the altar. The Blessed Sacrament (known by some Anglicans as the Reserved Sacrament) is kept in an often ornate, specially constructed, locked, metal container called a tabernacle, located about five feet from the ground and securely attached to the rear wall behind the altar. Hanging near the tabernacle burns a red light (sanctuary lamp) symbolising the presence of Christ in the eucharist (Catholics sometime refer to this as 'the real presence' of Christ; that Christ is really present in a sacramental way). We will return to this idea later.

To one side of the sanctuary (the open area surrounding the altar) a statue of Mary the mother of Jesus (more often called 'Our Lady' by Catholics) stands on a plinth, before which small votive candles, purchased by the faithful and symbolising prayer and devotion, are left to burn. Around the interior walls may be seen 14 carvings representing the condemnation and journey of Jesus to his crucifixion. These carvings are known as the 'stations of the cross' (Mark 15.1-4) and are found in older Catholic churches.

In St Mary Magdalene's church there are no confessional boxes. These are small rooms in which penitents kneel and confess their sins to a priest who is seated on the other side of a permanent dividing wall into which is set an openwork screen. Rather, in this church there is a room reserved to celebrate the Sacrament of Reconciliation and this gives parishioners, if they choose, opportunity to confess to the priest face-to-face.

The congregation attending mass is made up of obvious family groups, single people and couples of all ages. There is a preponderance of middle-aged and older men and women from a variety of racial groups. One is struck by how little notice appears to be taken of the noise made by the babies and young children. The service (mass) is led by a male priest. The vast majority of priests in the Catholic Church are celibate and they are addressed as 'Father'. There are no female priests in the Catholic Church. The priest is dressed in liturgical clothes (vestments) of the colour corresponding to the liturgical season. The topmost vestment is not unlike a South American 'poncho' and is called a chasuble. The colour may be white (major festivals of Easter and Christmas), purple (Advent and Lent), red (Palm Sunday and for martyrs' feasts) or green (throughout the year). In some churches the liturgical colour depicting the season of the Christian year appears as well on the cloth (fall) covering the lectern and the cloth covering the front of the altar (frontal). Lay people lead the singing; a trained lay scripture reader reads the scriptures from the lectern; members of the congregation carry the offertory gifts in procession to the altar; and a lay eucharistic minister assists the priest in the distribution of Holy Communion.

In many Catholic churches there is a daily celebration of mass, but the Sunday (Lord's Day) celebration is the most important and the one which most Catholics attend. The eucharistic service (mass) follows a set pattern. The confession and two scripture readings - one from the Old Testament, one from the New - are followed by the Gospel. Next, a homily based upon an exposition of the readings is preached by the priest. Recitation of the Nicene Creed is followed by bidding prayers. At this point a collection (offertory collection) is taken and these offerings, together with the gifts of bread and wine, are carried in procession to the altar and presented to the priest. The gifts are offered to God with formal prayers. The most solemn part of the mass, called the 'eucharistic prayer', follows. This includes the narrative of consecration, at which point it is believed the bread and wine are consecrated and Christ becomes really present among his people (1 Corinthians 11.23-27). This event may be highlighted by the ringing of a bell. Christ, now sacramentally present, is communicated to the people. Catholics believe they receive Christ at Communion. As Strange (1986, p 109) puts it:

> The host (bread) is not disguised flesh, the wine not camouflaged blood. Catholic eucharist is not a form of cannibalism. It is a sacrament. The whole of Christ is received, body, blood, soul and divinity, under either form.

Belonging

Membership of the Catholic Church is achieved through baptism (Matthew 28.19-20; Mark 16.16; Acts 2.41). The majority of Catholics become members of the church when they are infants. Babies may be baptised in a baptismal font, frequently situated near the door of the church, its position providing a symbol of entry to the church. Though the Orthodox Church and some Christian denominations believe that the correct way to baptise is by immersion, within the Catholic Church it is considered sufficient for valid baptism that water be poured over the head of the person being baptised while at the same time saying the baptismal formula 'I baptise you in the name of the Father and of the Son and of the Holy Spirit, Amen.' Besides water, the baptismal ceremony contains various symbols. Oil, a lighted candle, and a white garment are all used to signify the life of Christ in the newly baptised, who are told they now share in the priesthood, prophetic ministry and kingship of Christ. The parents and the godparents promise to 'bring the child up in the practice of the faith and to see that the Divine life which God has given is kept safe from the poison of sin'.

Christians believe that sacramental acts bring into effect the reality they signify. Catholics believe there are seven sacraments, channels of God's grace. The sacraments are baptism, confirmation, eucharist, penance, anointing of the sick, holy orders and marriage. These sacraments bring Christians to a share in the life, death and resurrection of Christ. 'What baptism, confirmation and eucharist initiate, penance purifies and marriage and holy orders define more specifically, while the ministry of salvation is expressed in the sacrament of the sick' (Strange, 1986, p 86). It is increasingly understood that becoming a Catholic or being a Catholic is to have made a positive choice. It is an affirmation of an acceptance of the calling to participate fully in the work of the whole 'People of God'. Rather than being seen as a given aspect of their cultural identity which is accepted passively, Catholics are invited to see their Catholic faith as the adoption of an active role requiring from them a positive commitment to the task of mission in the world. Membership of the People of God involves obligations as well as bestowing the right of being able to call Jesus their brother and God their Father. Continued adherence to the Catholic Church is now seen as membership through personal and considered choice; it is also voluntary religious commitment, not a passive, semi-cultural identity.

Behaving

Before the Second Vatican Council the Catholic Church saw herself as uniquely the One, Holy, Catholic and Apostolic Church founded by Christ and linked to the disciples (Matthew 16.13-20) through Apostolic Succession. Such an exclusive understanding of being the Church was replaced by a new understanding of her own nature which is more inclusive, encompassing the entire Christian community.

If the birth of Jesus reveals to us the true meaning of being human then Christian morality is a way of behaving which is most perfectly the outcome of lives rooted in Christ. People have to make decisions at various times in their lives. We can think of decisions that lead lives in one direction rather than another. Decisions, however, are not always consistently followed. For example, even loving husbands and wives can be unfaithful. Though they fall short of the ideal it does not necessarily cancel the choice they have made. To decide to be on the side of Christ, like other decisions people make, while it establishes a state of affairs, is no guarantee that the decision will never be broken. Catholic Christians believe that commitment to Christ can withstand very serious failings. Think of Peter the apostle denying Jesus (Matthew 26.69-75; Mark 14.66-72; Luke 22.56-62; John 18.17, 25-27). Little by little throughout life Christians try to reinforce their basic choice for Christ. Choices can still be made that conflict with that basic choice, yet the basic decision can remain intact.

Activity B2

From the material given and your reading, what belief is central to Roman Catholic identity and why?

Comment on activity B2

The emphasis is on forgiveness and redemption through participation in the celebration of the saving mystery of Jesus Christ. This sacramental liturgy mediates to the worshipping community the saving mysterious power of Christ's passion, resurrection and ascension. 'The whole Christian people, by virtue of their participation in Christ's priesthood, celebrate the liturgy, all liturgical services are celebration of the church, both people and clergy, and from it they derive as from its source the true Christian spirit' (Crichton, 1986). Crighton's words are found in more simplistic and direct form in these words of Mother Teresa of Calcutta (Dog, 1976, p 115):

> I cannot do without mass and Holy Communion. Without Jesus. If I can see Jesus in the appearance of bread then I will be able to see him in the broken bodies of the poor. That is why I need that oneness with Christ. If I have that deep faith in the eucharist, naturally I will be able to touch him in the broken bodies because he has said, I am the Living Bread.

The place given to Mary in the history and tradition of the church is often exaggerated and misunderstood, even by Catholics themselves.   The veneration of saints (individual Christians who have demonstrated some Christian virtue in an exemplary way) applies particularly to Mary the mother of Jesus who is called Mother of God (Luke 1.26-38; Galatians 4.4). 'As by her faith Mary gave birth to the Christ, so in her faith is she the model of every Christian' (Strange, 1986, p 187).   Both the gospels of Matthew and Luke appear to affirm plainly the virginal conception of Jesus (Matthew 1.18-20; Luke 1.31, 34-35).   Those who are not Catholics often confuse this, the virginal conception of Jesus, with the immaculate conception of Mary, which in fact refers to Mary's own conception in the womb of her mother which took place in the normal sexual manner.   It is worth referring to books written specifically on the subject of Mary or refer to an encyclopaedia to learn more fully the relevance of the position of Mary in Catholic theology.

B5 Orthodox Church

Historical context

The word 'Orthodox' has the double meaning of 'right belief' and 'right worship'.   The Orthodox Church believes that it has guarded this right belief and worship since the time of Jesus, through the era of the apostles and their successors and through the Church Councils (Ware, 1979).

Today within Orthodoxy there is no single central 'human' authority. Rather it is a family of churches, administratively separate but united by a common faith and way of life.   If there is an authority, it comes from tradition, from what was believed and practised by Christ and the apostles, for the Orthodox tradition also *includes* the bible, the creeds, the decrees of the Ecumenical Councils and the writings of the Church Fathers, the canons, the service books, the icons and the form of church government established in the early Christian centuries.   Yet tradition is not static.   It is understood as a living experience of the Holy Spirit in the church.   '"When the Spirit of truth has come, he will guide you into all truth" (John 16.13).   It is this divine promise that forms the basis of the Orthodox devotion to tradition' (Ware, 1963, p 207).

Central to Orthodox belief is the doctrine of the Trinity which speaks of God as transcendent mystery, above and beyond creation, yet everywhere present in the created world and finally at one with creation through the Incarnation of Christ and living in the individual by the Holy Spirit.   Matter itself has been made holy by the coming of Christ into it: 'through matter we have been saved', as one of the Fathers said. For this reason Orthodoxy has not been afraid of the physical side of life - indeed its parish priests are all expected to be married. Doctrinally and liturgically it has emphasised the resurrection of Christ and so has made Easter, rather than Christmas, the major festival of the church calendar (Walker and Carras, 1996).

Believing

In most Orthodox churches we note the shape of the building: it is square, topped by an onion shaped dome. The building's shape expresses the Orthodox Christian view of the world. The square is thought to represent correctness, equality and organisation. Standing together within the square people are called together and equal before God. The floor represents earth where the people are gathered. The four corners represent the four gospel writers, the ceiling represents heaven, the circle of the dome expresses the eternity of God - without beginning or end - and on the top of it there stands a cross.

Within the darkened interior of the church our senses are challenged by the perfume of incense, the sight of beautiful colours, mosaics, frescoes, icons and burning candles. The icons are stylised portraits of Christ or Mary or the saints that are painted on wood and sometimes adorned with precious metals. In front of them burn candles.

What strikes the visitor is that within the main part of the building there are no chairs or pews. The congregation is expected to stand throughout the lengthy but beautiful services. (There are a few benches at the side for the old and those with babies.) The icons are intended to help the worshipper realise that the worship of the church unites earth with heaven. Theologically, the icons are intended to be aids to worship so that the veneration given to the image passes to its prototype. When the worshipper first enters the church, he or she generally goes up to the main icons, kisses them and lights a candle on the candlestands beside them.

The nave, or central part of the church, is separated from the altar by the *iconostasis*, or wooden screen on which the main icons are placed. The iconostasis has three doors, one in front of the altar and one on either side. The iconostasis is understood symbolically as the dividing line between the church on earth (nave) and the church in heaven (altar). The altar is thought of variously as the holy of holies, the table of the last supper, Golgotha and the tomb. When, in the liturgy, the priest comes from the altar carrying the bible or the consecrated elements of communion to offer them to the worshippers, he is seen as coming from 'heaven' as Christ came, to offer illumination and salvation.

Worshippers make the sign of the cross many times in worship. With the first two fingers and thumb joined and the other two fingers folded down into the palm the believer touches his or her forehead, chest, right shoulder and left shoulder, drawing on him or herself the outline of a cross. When the hand is folded in this way, it represents the three Persons of the Trinity and the two natures of Christ.

There is only a single eucharistic service on Sunday, so that the whole community may gather (no celebrant may celebrate the eucharist more than once a day; neither can there be a celebration without laity present). Worship is personal but not individualistic. Private prayer is encouraged but the main source of strength is corporate worship. The highly skilled choir sings age-old tunes and chants without instrumental accompaniment and the congregation joins in from time to time.

The eucharist is celebrated each Sunday and on major fasts and saints' days. The service commemorates and makes present the events which took place at the Last Supper, passion and resurrection of Jesus but in its essence is a realisation, to the extent that this is possible for mankind, of the heavenly banquet that is the Kingdom of God. The service usually has two parts: the Liturgy of the Catechumens and the Liturgy of the Faithful. The Liturgy of the Catechumens begins with the choir singing Psalms, showing God's preparation in the Old Testament for the coming of Jesus. Prayers for various people and the needs of the church and the world are sung by the priest, and the choir responds 'Lord have mercy' after each short prayer. The worshipper is also praying silently with the priest repeating to himself 'Lord have mercy' and crossing himself. The climax of this part of the service comes with a procession through the main door in the iconostasis, led by the priest with the deacon carrying the bible which has been lying on the altar. During this the beatitudes, summaries of the gospel life, are sung. The bible procession is accompanied by servers with candles and incense. Lessons from the letters of the New Testament or the Acts of the Apostles are read, followed by the Gospel and a sermon.

The priest then returns behind the doors and the eucharist continues with the offering of bread and wine which are processed with candles and incense through the church, while the worshippers bow or kneel. The main doors are opened and the priest goes through and lays the gifts on the altar while the creed is said. The doors close while the priest offers thanks to God for sending Jesus, remembering the passion and looking forward to his coming again. The most sacred moment is the prayer that the Holy Spirit may come upon the worshippers and the gifts of bread and wine that they may become the body and blood of Christ. Again all bow in silence at this mystery. The priest prays for peace in our lives and the congregations sings or says together the Lord's prayer. The priest then breaks the consecrated bread (*doron*) into pieces, eats a small piece and drinks from the chalice. Then he comes through and those who have said they wish to receive communion come forward, but this is rarely a weekly participation since confession and fasting beforehand are required. The particles of consecrated bread are placed in the chalice and communion is administered with a spoon, even to babies. A blessing follows and the eucharist is over. Following this everyone, Orthodox or not, is invited to go to the priest, kiss the cross which he holds, and take a little piece of bread (*antidoron*), blessed but not consecrated, as a sign of fellowship and love. Now the worshippers greet one another. A meal may follow in another building, organised by members of the parish. Thus news is exchanged and culture, language and family are renewed.

The liturgy is the same each week: each Sunday is a 'little Easter'[1]. Orthodox religion is fundamentally liturgical, and doctrine is understood in the context of worship.

Belonging

The baby of Orthodox parents is baptised by being dipped naked in water three times in the name of the Trinity. The baby is then dressed in new white clothes provided by the godparents, symbolising the 'robe of light' which is received in baptism. The name of an Orthodox saint is given to the child, linking him or her with the traditions of holiness in the church. A little strand of the child's hair is cut off and this is symbolic of cutting oneself off from the world and the beginning of a new life. Chrismation or confirmation follows immediately after baptism. Special oil is used, blessed by the bishop. The priest anoints forehead, eyelids, nose, mouth, ears, chest, hands and feet with the sign of the cross, saying, 'the seal of the gift of the Holy Spirit'. This is a personal, sacramental Pentecost, and the baby thus becomes a full member of the church of the apostles. Holy Communion follows immediately. As Metropolitan Anthony of Sourozh, Head of the Russian Orthodox Church in Britain, said,

> When we receive Communion, I believe that God reaches out to us on the most primitive and simple level. A babe can receive a small particle of bread and a drop of wine, and with it be reached by God.

---

[1] Though Ware (1993, p 298) makes the point that there are twelve 'great feasts', each with their own liturgies, within the Orthodox Church, a far greater number than would be found in Anglicanism or Roman Catholicism.

Behaving

'Our social programme', said the Russian thinker Fedorov, 'is the dogma of the Trinity' (Ware, 1963, p 216). By this he meant that the relationships of Persons within the Trinity ought to be mirrored in the life of the church. Williams (1993) states that:

> the life of God is active only as a pattern of divine gift and relation and is known only when God freely draws us into this pattern through the *koinonia* of the church, established in Christ and constantly renewed and actualised in the Spirit.

Within Britain, Orthodox Christians follow a basic pattern of Sunday worship and parish activities. During Lent, the weeks leading up to Easter, the Orthodox usually fast or abstain from rich foods, often 'with a severity that has no parallel in western Christendom' (Ware, 1993, p 301). The Easter service itself is musically and visually beautiful. Candles are lit, the choir sings triumphant anthems and worshippers greet each other during the service with the words 'Christ is risen' to which the answer is, 'He is risen indeed!' and, on saying this, three kisses are exchanged. Afterwards, everyone goes to eat together and feast on eggs and meat that have been unavailable in the previous seven weeks of Lent.

There are no obvious signs of Orthodoxy in the day-to-day life of believers apart from the presence of an 'icon corner' at home, the saying of grace at meals, and morning and evening prayers. The effect of Orthodoxy has historically been to knit together the cultural life of its various peoples. In Russia and the former Yugoslavia, Orthodoxy when linked with political movements has fuelled patriotism and ethnic strife. The Orthodox, like Saint Paul, pray for the 'powers that be', 'that we, in their tranquillity, may lead a calm and peaceful life in all godliness and purity' (*Liturgy of St John Chrysostom*). Unfortunately, our political leaders are seldom tranquil. In Russia there has been almost no tradition of criticising government policy or of presenting an alternative ethical vision to that proposed by secular authority. The belief is that the saying and singing of the liturgy sanctifies the land and its peoples, a belief that gave rise in the days of the Czars to the concept of 'Holy Russia'. But in other parts of the world, for example in Serbia and Greece, a more critical stance vis-à-vis the state has been adopted.

Activity B3

Find out about icons and explain how and why they are important to Orthodoxy. Give attention both to theology and practice.

Comment on activity B3

Icons are stylised paintings of Christ, Mary or the saints. They are often painted on wood, though other materials are not forbidden, and are decorated with precious metal and even jewels. They create the unique appearance of the interior of an Orthodox church and are an expression of the Orthodox belief that its worship is a reflection of heaven. In heaven Christ is surrounded by the saints and worshipped by the heavenly powers. In church the icons represent Christ and the saints and the earthly worshippers stand before them.

The kissing of icons and the lighting of candles before them is indicative of respect, love and prayer. To kiss the hand of an icon of Christ is a symbolic act intended to express the desire of the worshipper to draw closer to Christ himself.

Icons in the Eastern Church were used from very early times, but in the eighth century they were at the centre of controversy. The Muslims, who had overrun more than half of the Byzantine Empire, were strongly opposed to the use of images of any kind, and it was perhaps in sympathy with their position that the emperor Leo III ordered the destruction of icons in 726. As a consequence civil disturbances broke out within the empire, as many Orthodox felt that the emperor and his supporters were threatening the very foundations of Christian faith in the Incarnation. The seventh and last Ecumenical Council in 787 proclaimed that icons were to be kept in churches and honoured with the same relative veneration as is shown to other material symbols, such as the Cross and the Book of the Gospels (see Ware, 1963, p 39). In the end, after many struggles and not a few martyrs, the opponents of the iconoclast emperors were victorious and, with the help of a distinction between veneration (offered to icons) and worship (offered to God alone), the use of icons was restored definitively in 843. Although the Church in the West accepted the decisions of the Seventh Ecumenical Council in 787, the use of icons never became widespread in the West, and this has no doubt contributed to the difference in style of worship found between the Orthodox and western Christians to this day. The use of icons is completely integrated into the worship of the Orthodox Church, where they are seen as 'windows onto eternity' and a gateway to the Kingdom.

B6 Methodist Church

Historical context

John Wesley (1703-91) was the son of an Anglican clergyman and a forceful, devout mother. Taught first at home and then at Charterhouse School he later went up to Christchurch College, Oxford. 'When I was about twenty-two' he records in his *Journal*, 'my father pressed me to enter into holy orders'. At the same time he began to read Kempis's *Christian Pattern* and to see 'that true religion was seated in the heart'. As a result he altered his entire lifestyle to seek 'inward holiness'. In addition to being serious, systematic and disciplined, he began, along with a group called 'The Holy Club', to carry out charitable acts like prison visiting. He soon became the club's leader. The rigour and methodical nature of his approach to life earned Wesley and his friends the nick name 'Methodists' which, becoming their official title, has remained ever since.

In 1735 Wesley sailed as a missionary to the American colonies. On the voyage across the Atlantic there was a violent life-threatening storm. Among the passengers was a group of Moravian missionaries who remained calm and their obvious faith began to persuade Wesley that he lacked 'that faith whereby alone we are saved'. Once in America he attempted unsuccessfully to convert the native American Indians and, in the process, annoyed other colonists by his sermons against slavery and alcohol. The real crisis was over his rigid churchmanship which alienated most of the settlers who were hardly the cream of society and had no desire to be 'Oxford Methodists'. Two years later he returned home. He later visited the Moravian colony in Germany and was impressed by what he saw. In 1738 he underwent his famous conversion at Aldersgate Street in London when, at a meeting where Luther's *Preface to the Epistle to the Romans* was read, Wesley recorded in his *Journal* that:

> I felt my heart strangely warmed. I felt I did trust Christ, Christ alone for salvation; and an assurance was given me that he had taken away *my* sins, even *mine*, and saved *me* from the law of sin and death[2].

From that time onward he devoted himself with single-minded devotion and untiring energy 'to promote as far as I am able vital practical religion'. From 1739 onward, after encouragement from George Whitefield and because the churches were beginning to close their doors to him, he preached in the open air, in market places, in graveyards, on common land and by roadsides, wherever a crowd would gather, the Gospel of Christ.

---

[2] The big question is whether 'assurance of salvation' and 'salvation' are one and the same. Wesley did not clarify this matter until much later in his life.

Wesley's converts were gathered into classes[3] and societies[4] for mutual support, prayer and study and, once it became clear that the work had grown too large for him to care for alone and that there were good speakers emerging among the Methodist believers, he put travelling lay preachers to work to teach and evangelise. He had no wish to begin a new denomination and would not have done so if the converts had all been willing to worship in their Anglican churches. Indeed he maintained that he lived and died in the Church of England. But many people, having been converted to active Christianity in Methodism, were reluctant to attend Anglican churches and preferred to receive teaching from lay preachers whom they trusted and who preached the gospel as they believed it. So, little by little, Methodist chapels or 'preaching houses' were built and, through Wesley's organisational ability, formed into what was effectively a denominational structure. Local societies were grouped into 'circuits' served by full-time travelling preachers who evolved into ordained ministers in the early nineteenth century. (Later, after Wesley's death, the circuits were grouped into 'Districts'.) From 1744 the organisation was guided and governed by an annual 'Conference' of travelling preachers under Wesley's control.

Wesley insisted that only those who had been ordained could administer the sacraments and so Methodists continued to receive communion from Anglican clergymen[5]. When the War of Independence (1775-83) disrupted relations with the American colonies, Wesley realised that he would have to take action to ensure that his converts there were properly looked after. Wesley took a critical decision and in 1784 ordained ministers and a 'Superintendent' for the churches in America. This, of course, was a radical step since, in the Church of England, only bishops may ordain; Wesley was therefore behaving like a bishop and was subsequently criticised for doing so. Nevertheless, having made America a special case, he soon treated Scotland in the same way. However he was horrified when the Americans named their Superintendents 'bishops'. Independent of Wesley, American Methodism has now become the largest part of world Methodism.

Once the ordinations had occurred, Methodism was never likely to merge back into the Anglican church in Wesley's lifetime or in the years immediately following his death (Davies, 1988). Methodism developed an increasingly self-sufficient and independent church life and the High Church Oxford Movement from the 1830s made even sympathetic Methodists feel that the Church of England was becoming doctrinally unsound. During the first half of the nineteenth century Methodism split into several separate

---

[3] Classes were small local groups, similar to modern housegroups.

[4] Religious societies were permitted by law. They were not as local as classes and not classified as churches.

[5] Wesley tried to find bishops who would ordain his lay preachers, but was rarely successful (Brown-Lawson, 1994, p. 343).

churches (such as the Wesleyan and Primitive Methodists). These divisions were seldom over doctrine but typically over ministerial versus lay control and over priority for orderly church life or free-ranging and often emotional evangelism. Almost all of these bodies reunited to form the Methodist Church in 1932. The current Methodist membership in the Great Britain is around 380,000, with a wider Community Roll of 1.24 million.

The Methodist revival, though it was driven by the ministry of John Wesley, was enriched by Charles, John's younger brother and an outstanding hymn-writer. Charles' hymns ('Amazing grace' or 'O for a thousand tongues') have become among the best known in the English language, and therefore in the world, and illustrate biblical themes, evangelical faith and conversion with a clarity that makes them aids to teaching as well as aids to worship.

Believing

Methodists call the buildings where they worship 'churches', though sometimes the older name of 'chapel' is used. The early chapels tend to be plain but may have a stained glass window. Within the worship area the only Christian symbol to be seen is usually a cross. Rows of chairs or pews face a pulpit and a table on which may be placed flowers or a bible. Behind this table is the pulpit and sometimes a gallery for a choir. The emphasis is on simplicity and on the central authority of the scriptures in public worship and exposition. Despite their basic similarity the buildings vary considerably, usually according to age. After the early chapels came the great Victorian preaching houses, and then the more gothic, liturgical style of the early years of the twentieth century gave way to the modern styles of the post-war years. The organ pipes are often a dominant feature representing the importance of congregational singing.

Sunday worship has a structure of hymns, extempore and written prayer, scripture readings, sometimes a psalm, sermon and offering. Worship is straightforward and dignified, frequently led by a Local Preacher. However, despite this dominant pattern of relatively 'free' worship, Wesley produced a book of services for the Methodists in America and there is a long tradition of liturgical services in Methodism. The so-called 'hymn sandwich' is an important liturgical form in its own right. After union in 1932 the *Book of Offices* (1936) was produced. The communion service which was widely used was very similar to the Anglican *Book of Common Prayer* (1662). The *Book of Offices* was replaced by the *Methodist Service Book* (1975). The *Methodist Worship Book* (1999) will replace that.

In addition to the bible itself and the historical creeds of the church, special Methodist emphases are found in Wesley's *Notes on the New Testament* and *Forty Four Sermons* which all Methodist preachers must read and to which they must give general assent. These writings emphasise that Christ died for everyone and that God's offer of salvation is made to everyone. Wesley's own theology was Arminian, that is, he did not believe that God predestined certain people to be saved and others to be damned. He believed that justification is by faith alone and that, when the gospel is presented, hearers are free to respond as they will. Once converted, believers should expect the Holy Spirit to give them a special assurance of their new relationship to God. The same Holy Spirit would then be expected to lead believers in a process of increasing holiness, or purification, towards 'Christian perfection' where individuals might reach entire love of God and of other human beings. Yet, it would be a theological mistake to think of such 'perfection' as sinless (Brown-Lawson, 1994). During the nineteenth and early twentieth centuries, however, though a version of Wesley's perfectionist teaching influenced 'holiness' sects and Pentecostalism, it became much less conspicuous among Methodists generally.

Belonging

The first stage of membership of the Methodist church is through baptism, and it is usual for babies to be baptised. When a person can take the promises of discipleship for him or herself, confirmation follows reception into 'full membership'. In the complicated social and economic changes that have taken place since the eighteenth century, the social status of typical Methodists has risen and, as with other older Christian groups, congregations in Britain now are predominantly middle class. In this respect Methodism has been transformed from being a 'sect' of the Anglican church to being a denomination.

Behaving

The nonconformist conscience is strong in the Methodism and is shown by the fact that the traditionally-minded minority will not drink alcohol or allow alcohol on church premises, and most would not gamble. Hard work is emphasised. This led to what came to be called the 'Protestant work ethic'. John Wesley (*Sermon on Riches*) commented:

> I fear, wherever riches have increased, the essence of religion has decreased in the same proportion. Therefore I do not see how it is possible, in the nature of things, for the renewal of true religion to continue long. For religion must

necessarily produce both industry and frugality, and these cannot but produce riches. But as riches increase, so will pride, anger and the love of the world in all its branches.

Sociologically, emphasis on hard work has led to financial prudence and so to social respectability and prosperity, and working class roots have been left behind. Equally, however, the ethical stance of Methodism - the positive side of the nonconformist conscience - has been found in commitment to social justice through political involvement in the Labour Movement and this has been translated into concerns for the rights of workers expressed through Trade Unionism. There is a historically well established link between Methodism and the organisation of working class culture (Thompson, 1980). In the modern era, it is still common for the Methodist Annual Conference to agree and publicise ethically-based statements on national issues. If necessary, these statements will criticise the government of the day, and Methodists feel that their non-established position, in contrast to that of Anglicans, gives a greater freedom to criticise the state without embarrassment. In the period of the seventeenth century, Anglicanism drew a parallel between the monarch and the bishop, both of whom represented rank and authority within their respective realms. Methodism by contrast sees itself as being egalitarian in its ecclesiastical stance and, as an evidence of this, would point to the election of a President of the (annual) Conference whose term of office lasts only for one year. In other words, no individual within Methodism can be thought to hold an ecclesiastical position permanently higher than everyone else. A large proportion of Methodist services are led by lay preachers and much of the church's life is sustained by a variety of lay officials.

In terms of practical and present activity Methodists have continued to target youth work and the social and spiritual needs of the inner city. As might be expected, commitment to justice and equality has led to the ordination of women and to specialist community work.

Holy Communion is becoming more important but still unlikely to be celebrated more frequently than once a month as a main Sunday service. Most communion services use the *Methodist Service Book* which is formal and similar to the Anglican prayer book. Individual cups containing non-alcoholic wine - a historical feature from the pledge of total abstinence - are used for communion, recognising the individual's discipleship (and that Methodism flourished at a time when there was also a great fear of catching tuberculosis). Communion is normally led by an ordained minister. Ministerial 'dress' for Sunday worship varies; many wear a suit and clerical collar, others wear cassock, Geneva gown and preaching bands, though because there is no rule, variety abounds.

Activity B4

Why in early Methodism were the working classes attracted to Methodism? Is class a factor in Methodism today?

Comment on activity B4

You may have commented on the respectability of the Anglican Church of Wesley's day. The Church of England was often seen as more suited to the upper classes, partly because of its literary style of worship and partly because, for example, seating in churches, when particular pews were reserved for the gentry, reflected the class structure of the country. Wesley regarded the gospel as being pertinent to the whole of the human race and therefore class, colour and nationality were irrelevant to its applicability. Moreover, the beginnings of the Industrial Revolution were associated with an increase in the size of cities and with a new and noticeable urban poverty housed in slums. Those who left their farm labouring and moved to the cities in search of factory work were often disappointed and, whereas farming communities could at least grow food and were relatively free of disease, the densely populated city areas were prone both to hunger and ill health. Wesley's Christianity, though it was fundamentally evangelical, drove him with almost equal zeal to attempt to improve the living conditions of urban workers. He took all kinds of direct action to ameliorate poverty, for example by setting up pharmacies to improve health. He was by no means applauded for what he did and his journals record that he was sometimes physically and verbally abused. Yet his drive towards the cities was eventually appreciated. In addition Wesley, unlike the traditional Anglicans, was not hampered by a parish structure that was poorly aligned to cope with new centres of population. Anglican churches were simply in the wrong place: they were in villages rather than at growing points of new cities.

Today Methodism is not very different from Anglicanism in its approach to the unchurched sections of the community. To this extent, Methodism *has* become more middle class and less evangelically concerned for the poor and, where Methodism works in cities, it often does so with a radical social purpose rather than with a directly evangelical agenda.

B7 Salvation Army Corps

Historical context

The Salvation Army was an off shoot of the Methodist Church and, in this respect, it was a sect but soon became a denomination. It was founded in 1865 as the Christian Mission by William Booth (1829-1912), an independent revivalist, working in an evangelistic capacity in east London, who began his ministry as a Methodist minister. On a July evening in 1865 William Booth returned to his east London home, having walked the streets, and announced to his wife, Catherine: 'I have found my destiny. I must take the gospel to the people of the East End.'

Once the mission became known as the Salvation Army in 1878 its growth was rapid. It turned military language to evangelistic purposes (for example, prayer was 'knee drill') and military ranks were adopted in the organisation's structure (for example, William Booth became 'General Booth').

Everywhere he looked Booth saw human and social needs crying out to be met. He published *In Darkest England, and the Way Out* to launch his 'Darkest England' scheme in 1890 on behalf of, as he saw it, 'A population sodden with drink, steeped in vice, eaten up by every social and physical malady. These are the denizens of Darkest England amidst whom my life has been spent.' Despite opposition and mockery, notably from the scurrilous Skeleton Army which was formed to break up Salvation Army meetings, Booth persevered in his urgent evangelistic social work. His scheme was designed to provide practical help to vagrants and unskilled people. He set up homes for those who were homeless, including released prisoners, and offered help to alcoholics. He also provided accommodation for single mothers and legal aid for the poor. There was vast public support for the programme; money was liberally subscribed and a large part of the scheme was carried out. In 1905, General Booth went through England and was received in state by the mayors and corporations of many towns. The fiery old man had become a revered person in English public life. After twenty years the Salvation Army was an accepted part of the religious scene and active on three continents.

The Salvation Army is now an integrated international Christian denomination working in more than one hundred countries. It is headed by an elected General. As its history would lead you to expect, it is both a church and a social service organisation.

In his final sermon in May 1912 William Booth declared:

> While women weep as they do now, I'll fight; while men go to prison, in and out, in and out, as they do now, I'll fight; while there is a drunkard left, while there is a poor lost girl upon the streets, while there remains one dark soul without the light of God, I'll fight - I'll fight to the very end.

Believing

Today a corps (church) building will be functional rather than ornate. Most modern buildings accommodate a weekly community programme as well as worship meetings. Military terms are not as readily used or as evident as in the past, though words on the outside of a building, such as 'Newtown Corps', can convey this emphasis. The main worship area may often have a central platform at one end with a reading desk (or pulpit), and a Mercy Seat (a long polished wooden bench) in front of the platform. Here people are invited to kneel on occasions for personal prayer. Some people make their conversion decision kneeling there. Sometimes a 'holiness table' with an open bible will be placed centrally near the Mercy Seat, as a reminder that the Salvation Army is a holiness movement. The platform is often used for music sections, such as the brass band and the songsters (choristers), though modern halls tend not to have raised platforms. Rows of chairs for the congregation face the platform.

Decoration is sparse: in a prominent place is the flag of yellow, red and blue woven into which is the motto 'Blood and Fire' reminding Salvationists of the blood of Jesus, who died for all, and the fire of the Holy Spirit. Very rarely there may be a picture of General Booth somewhere in the building, and flowers are placed on the holiness table for Sunday worship.

Other parts of the building may reflect services to the community, such as charity shop, coffee lounge, youth club, mothers and toddlers club.

Worship, in common with other churches, includes praise, prayer and bible readings, usually followed by a sermon which is often an exposition of the reading, though there is no official set form of worship. The meeting is planned by the officer who leads the worship. The service also often includes a 'testimony', which is an account of religious experience given by a member of the congregation. Following the sermon, listeners - and this will often include children and any visitors - may sometimes be invited to make a religious commitment and kneel at the Mercy Seat to pray. Traditionally the Sunday morning meeting was called the Holiness meeting, when Christian living was emphasised, and the Sunday evening meeting was termed the Salvation meeting, when conversion was emphasised, but this distinction has become blurred as attendance patterns have changed.

The informal style of worship enables everyone present to feel free to make a personal effort to contribute, though most may prefer to listen rather than make individual contributions.   General Frederick Coutts, a former international leader of the Army, has written: 'No contribution, whether of testimony or of prayer, becomes a private exercise in egoism, and the desire of the preacher is ever to speak "in demonstration of the Spirit"'.

The *International Spiritual Life Commission Report* (Salvation Army, 1998), in its explanation of worship, states:

> We affirm that God invites us to a meeting in which God is present, God speaks, and God acts. In our meetings we celebrate and experience the promised presence of Christ with his people. Christ crucified, risen and glorified is the focal point, the epicentre of our worship. We offer worship to the Father, through the Son, in the Spirit, in our own words, in acts which engage our whole being: body, soul and mind. We sing the ancient song of creation to its Creator, we sing the new song of the redeemed to their Redeemer. We hear proclaimed the word of redemption, the call to mission, and the promise of life in the Spirit.

Music plays a central part in the life of many Salvationists. General Booth said, 'Music is for the soul what wind is for the ship. Blowing her onwards in the direction in which she is steered' and memorably asked 'Why should the devil have all the best tunes?' Many corps have a brass band and songster brigade, as well as similar groups for children. Music draws on a wide range of sources, from the mediaeval church, classic Reformation hymns, the Wesleys, Isaac Watts, Philip Dodderidge and J.H. Newman, as well as songs by Salvationists and other modern songs.

An explicit feature of the Salvation Army is the absence of sacraments, which are not regarded as essential to salvation or Christian living. In the Victorian society in which the Salvation Army was born, drunkenness was rife among working classes and Booth decided teetotalism was essential. Even a sip of wine at communion might tempt a reformed alcoholic to return to drink, but this was not the main reason for not holding communion services. There were difficulties regarding the ministry of women (who played a prominent part in worship and leadership from the Salvation Army's earliest days), and a firm belief that 'no particular outward observance is necessary to inward grace'. With the movement growing rapidly and attracting many unchurched people, communion services ceased, though Salvationists have always been ready to (and frequently do) share in communion services in other churches. Similarly baptism is not practised so as to avoid possible arguments over its outward forms and theological meaning. (See Salvation Army, 1998.)

Following completion of the two-year validated training course at the William Booth Memorial Training College (in the UK), officers are commissioned as leaders ordained by God to minister in his name. Any individual congregation may be led by a man or a woman, or by a married couple jointly. The officer is given a rank based on length of service and level of responsibility, and husbands and wives are of the same rank. Both are commissioned, having left their original jobs in order to be trained. As befits the military style of the army, rather than choosing where they will serve, officers are sent by senior leaders to work where they are needed.

Belonging

Membership is open to all who make a public faith commitment. The babies of members are dedicated and parents make promises to bring up the child according to Christian teaching and Salvation Army principles. A colourful certificate is given to them to remind them of their responsibilities. Non-Salvationists are among those who attend meetings. Children may become junior soldiers from the age of seven upwards, making a simple promise to follow Jesus. At 14+ years of age, junior soldiers and converts of any age may become senior soldiers by affirming their faith in Christ and signing a 'Soldier's Covenant' that sets out the beliefs of the Salvation Army and requires a commitment to follow a particular Christian lifestyle, which includes an undertaking not to smoke or drink alcohol. This service of signing and swearing-in takes place beside the Salvation Army flag. It is always a special and significant occasion for the corps and for family and friends. The uniform is regarded as a Christian witness and is an optional evidence of membership. Officers usually wear it at all times when on duty. Soldiers who choose to wear uniform may wear it when engaged on Salvation Army activities, but not usually at other times.

At present, officers are expected to marry another officer, though the situation is being reviewed. Soldiers are free to marry as they choose.

Behaving

Worship and Christian witness cannot be divided without impoverishing both. The officer (minister) is responsible for serving members any time of day or night. He or she leads Sunday worship, organises daily activities, corps finance and property, cares for soldiers, teaches, and gives pastoral support and counsel. There is a small group of soldiers responsible for the nurture and discipline of the corps, and they make up the Pastoral Care Council. Discipline within the corps is considered important to give worthy witness to 'the world', but is now more co-operative than authoritarian.

Salvationists, both individually and corporately, seek to serve the community in which they live: no one in need is turned away by reason of religion, race or circumstance (Matthew 25.40). A weekly publication, *The War Cry,* is sold in the streets and public houses and elsewhere to spread the message of Christ. The annual Red Shield Appeal is a door-to-door collection in which members of the public usually give willingly, knowing that in times of national emergency the Salvation Army is there dispensing soup and blankets, and offering comfort and practical help. Hostels for the homeless and soup runs are operated in many cities and towns by the Salvation Army. The Salvation Army has continued to minister to the needs of the working class, though membership covers the whole social spectrum. Outdoor services still feature, with the brass band (or other music group) usually providing the attraction.

Activity B5

What clues do the building and its furniture give about believing within the Salvation Army community? What is characteristic of the Salvation Army?

Comment on activity B5

You may well note such features as:

- in the building there is plainness and simplicity that reflects the matter-of-factness, simplicity, ordinariness or the Christian life and, at the same time, the flag and other emblems that speak of being led by the Holy Spirit in a straightforward biblical faith;
- members coming from all walks of life but with an emphasis on working class and lower middle class;
- equality of men and women before God and in the congregation, regardless of rank or leadership;
- individual personal faith and commitment;
- uniform as sign of commitment and equality;
- emphasis on salvation and sins forgiven resulting in joyous assurance of God's presence in the individual's life and growth in holiness;
- absence of the traditional sacraments of believing or belonging used in other Christian communities, though other symbols are used;
- music as a strong element in both worship and social life;
- service to the community.

B8 Black Pentecostal Church

Historical context

Most Pentecostals trace their history back to a revival in Los Angeles in 1906. The first congregation[6] to be touched by the phenomenon of speaking in tongues, a hallmark of Pentecostalism, was led by the black preacher W.J. Seymour (1870-1922), the son of former slaves who raised him as a Baptist (Synan, 1988). Later, Seymour became an episcopal Methodist before accepting teaching which emphasised personal holiness following a crisis spiritual experience. After attending Charles Fox Parham's Bible School in Houston, Texas, Seymour accepted the view that speaking in tongues was the sign of receiving the Holy Spirit, though he himself did not enjoy the experience at this time. On being asked to visit a Holiness congregation in Los Angeles with the possibility of becoming its pastor, Seymour travelled west, but he was rejected because he preached from Acts 2.4 about the necessity of speaking in tongues. He then stayed for a while in Los Angeles in the home of a friend where he organised prayer meetings. After several weeks there was an outbreak of speaking in tongues at these meetings and this led to services being held in the garden and, when the crowds grew too great, to the hiring of an old stable/warehouse in Azusa Street. On April 14, 1906, Seymour held his first service there and four days later the San Francisco earthquake took place. The *Los Angeles Times* reported the damage and also that there was a 'weird babble of tongues' amid 'wild scenes' at the Azusa Street mission. These reports in the secular press had the effect of increasing the size of the meetings still further and, once the religious press had also detailed the phenomenon, numerous onlookers, visitors, enquirers and critics attended.

What they found was a loosely organised congregational centre that held meetings daily, was racially mixed and accepted the ministry of women. Seymour himself took the view that the church is 'one body' and that social divisions have no place in its activities or life. By the end of 1906 Seymour had designated his church the *Pacific Apostolic Faith Movement* and produced a periodical, *Apostolic Faith*, that rapidly reached a circulation of 50,000. For two years the revival continued, disseminating teaching about speaking in tongues, revitalising other congregations, stimulating missionary work, and witnessing powerfully to the reality of the inter-racial nature of the church to a racially segregated American society. All this was soon to end. After 1908 two of Seymour's team of ministers[7] left Los Angeles,

---

[6] Christian groups antecedent to the Church of God (Tennessee) reported speaking with tongues in the late 1880s but the phenomenon appears to have been sporadic and not to have affected a whole congregation.

[7] Clara Lum and Florence Crawford objected to Seymour's marriage to Jenny Moore.

taking with them the mailing list for the *Apostolic Faith* and thereby preventing Seymour's communication with the large group of people, in the States and overseas, who looked to him for leadership. In 1911 he suffered a further blow when W.H. Durham preached against his doctrinal position. Seymour had maintained that in order to speak in tongues it was necessary to be 'born again' and to be 'sanctified'. In other words, Seymour taught a three-stage process of Christian progress. Durham reduced this to two by arguing that sanctification and conversion should be seen together. Consequently, Seymour's dream of a single Pentecostal denomination of black and white Christians filled with the Holy Spirit came to an abrupt halt. By 1914 the Azusa Street church had become a black church with only an occasional white visitor. Seymour died in 1922 and his church building was eventually sold to clear a debt of unpaid taxes. The site where the church stood is still within the poorer area of Los Angeles, but from it all the main Pentecostal denominations can trace their origins (Synan, 1988, 1997). Today the Pentecostal and Charismatic movements amount to 500 million people, according to the latest estimates.

The Pentecostal movement began in Britain in 1907 and by 1924 had given rise to three new indigenous denominations, the Apostolic Church (influenced by but not connected with Seymour), the Elim Foursquare Pentecostal Alliance (now the Elim Pentecostal Church) and the Assemblies of God. In many respects these churches, though they were almost entirely white in membership, reflecting the predominant ethnicity of the British Isles until the 1950s, were similar to the black Pentecostal churches in the States and the Caribbean. In the 1950s, with the arrival of workers and their families from Jamaica and other West Indian islands, the Pentecostal churches might have been expected to benefit from the newcomers (Howard, 1987). But, sad to say, the white churches were often cold and unwelcoming and so the black population began to set up its own churches, sometimes linking with American black or black-led denominations (Arnold, 1992).

One of the earliest black Pentecostal churches to be established was the New Testament Church of God whose first public service was held at the YMCA in Wolverhampton in 1953 (Arnold, 1992, p 18)[8]. This denomination presently stands at 100+ congregations and 250+ ministers and it functions within or alongside the long established Church of God based in Tennessee. An episcopal structure of government is employed and it continues to have a strong holiness tradition.

---

[8] The original members of the New Testament Church of God had been members of the Church of God (Tennessee). After they had begun their denomination in 1953, they officially linked it with the Church of God in 1955. One of the factors which led to the establishment of black or black-led churches in the UK in the early 1950s was that the third World Pentecostal Conference was held in London in 1952 and this brought many visitors to the capital.

In the mid 1980s there were some 250 black-led Pentecostal organisations in Britain, mainly in the industrial conurbations, a total of 1,150 congregations with 67,600 worshippers meeting regularly. These Pentecostal groups then formed about 80% of the black-led congregations (MacRobert, 1989, pp 120-135). During the 1980s there has been a steady increase in the black and Asian population of the larger British cities and this has led to the formation of new Pentecostal or Charismatic groups. For example, the *Kingsway International Christian Centre* works mainly in London, particularly among the African and Asian communities and, since its senior pastor is a Nigerian of Islamic origin, the church's ministry is directed partly to this constituency. Its total number of adherents amounted to approximately 7000 in 1998, and the planned north-east London auditorium, seating 5000, is expected to accommodate the largest single congregation in the UK.

Central to the Pentecostal worldview is belief in the availability of the power of the supernatural world, the world of the Holy Spirit. Religion is an experience where the movement of the Spirit is to be felt and demonstrated within the worshipping community through the use of rhythm, music, swaying, dancing, clapping and more precisely through the manifestation of charismatic gifts (1 Corinthians 12). In some respects the African tradition has been transmitted through an oral narrative that has now been reworked in a Christian way. The black experience of slavery and oppression has been transposed by music and worship so that it reflects the biblical themes of Israel's deliverance from Egypt that is paralleled by the New Testament account of deliverance from sin (Exodus 15; Romans 6). A song like 'Steal away to Jesus' draws the listener into taking refuge from the pains and temptations of the world in the presence of Christ. The haunting melodies of 'Swing low, sweet chariot', pointing to an escape from this life, or of 'Were you there when they crucified my Lord?' making an emotional gospel appeal, would rouse a congregation's sense of God's love and judgement.

On a larger theological timescale the outpouring of the Spirit at the start of the twentieth century would be thought to indicate that the time of the return of Christ is drawing near (Hollenweger, 1969). The renewed arrival of the Spirit indicates that another phase of history has begun, like rain on a dry land. It indicates that harvest, a great endtime revival, is within reach.

Believing

Although they vary enormously in size, shape and prosperity it would be quite common to find an urban black-led Pentecostal church looking like a converted TA drill-hall. Many congregations rent accommodation from the private market, though sometimes they use a worship building belonging to another denomination. The particular community described here has its own building. On entering the vestibule there is a table on which are stacked hymn books and chorus sheets. A deacon hands out the books and shakes hands with everyone. Chairs in rows face a low platform on which stands a solid pulpit. A varied collection of musicians is assembled round a keyboard, and nearby is a group of lead singers who make use of hand-held microphones.

Worship has already begun. The musicians are leading singing, worshippers join in as they arrive. The formal service begins when the pastor stands up, greets everyone and announces a hymn. The service has a flexibility that allows for interruptions and contributions from the congregation, yet there is a pattern of hymns, songs, prayers and scripture readings that enables people to know roughly what to expect. The pastor speaks directly to the congregation and encourages them. 'Surely the Lord has done something for you this week' he says, 'come and tell us about it'. An elderly woman stands to tell the story of a problem in the life of her family that has been solved by an answered prayer, and this is met by spontaneous cries of 'Amen' or 'Hallelujah'. The congregation is encouraged to participate in the service as they feel guided by the Holy Spirit, and this may lead to visions or 'pictures' being shared with those present. More commonly there will be utterances in glossolalia (or tongues) given by one member of the congregation and interpretations of these given by another. The pastor listens carefully and usually broadens what has been shared so that it becomes an indication of what God is saying to the congregation as a whole. There will also often be a laying on of hands for healing or blessing.

In the New Testament Church of God the communion foot washing, following Jesus' example in the upper room at the Last Supper, will precede the actual 'breaking of bread'. In every respect, then, believing is focused on the person and work of Jesus.

The sermon is a central part of the service and the preacher may be expected to speak for at least forty minutes. It would be unheard of for a sermon to be read out from a prepared text. The topic is almost bound to be biblical and, if the service is one at which non-Christians are present, there will frequently be reference to the death of Christ and the blood of Christ given for sinners. Non-believers may be asked to respond by coming to the front for prayer or raising their hands to indicate that they have responded 'in their heart' to the gospel message. There is plenty of movement within the service - swaying during singing, clapping and sometimes dancing that all add up to an exuberant outpouring of faith.

The bible and its message are central to the lives and beliefs of Pentecostals. The methods and results of biblical scholarship are either not understood or are rejected by most Pentecostal people. The Pentecostal might take the view that 'the person with an experience is not at the mercy of the person with an argument', in other words that the experience of the love of God and of the power of the Holy Spirit are sufficient to sustain faith even against strong rational assaults on traditional Christian beliefs about the resurrection of Christ or the possibility of miracles happening today.

In this sense the bible is proclaimed as the living Word of God. It is interpreted as a text that is relevant for Christians today and 'more up to date than today's newspaper'; it is 'authoritative for faith and conduct'. Consequently the religious experiences described in the bible are considered to be ones that modern Christians may validly expect.

Belonging

Pentecostal churches all practise water baptism of adult believers and most offer the 'dedication' of children. People growing up in a Pentecostal church will have been dedicated as children and will then be expected to undergo water baptism in their early teens, at which point they will give a clear and public testimony about their experience of Christ. At some point after this, usually, a young Pentecostal would want to be 'baptised in the Spirit' and, in most denominations, he or she would expect to speak in other tongues.

Pentecostal churches often run Sunday schools or children's clubs as well as youth meetings, and those who grow up in them will learn to sing lively Christian songs, be taught to live a moral life which will include abstaining from pre-marital sex and drugs, and to give money to the church. Since Pentecostal churches have no other source of income than the earnings of their congregation, members are encouraged to tithe (that is, to give a tenth of what they earn) to help pay for the upkeep of buildings and for the salary of the pastor. Since, too, Pentecostal churches are often relatively new, they often have to pay mortgages on their buildings or on extensions to these buildings. Money, or the lack of it, can assume a greater prominence than is the case in more established denominations.

After baptism in water and the Holy Spirit many Pentecostal churches will formally welcome people into membership and this will usually enable believers to vote at church meetings. In recent years Pentecostal churches have become more obviously subject to British charity law and this law insists on annual accounts and some form of democratic involvement in the church's functioning. It would be a mistake, however, to think that most Pentecostals spend much time thinking of the 'business' side of church life which only rarely impinges on the large number of meetings that the church holds. There are usually two on Sunday, one or two midweek in the evening, perhaps a social gathering for older people during the day, as well as children's and youth clubs or alpha courses, Sunday school teachers' meetings, deacons' meetings and special occasional prayer meetings. A diligent Pentecostal devotes an enormous amount of time to church activities and must, as a consequence, live a disciplined life.

As part of their responsibilities as members of Pentecostal churches, Christians are encouraged to bring visitors to the services. The pattern of these services is arranged to make at least one of them, usually on Sunday nights, accessible to friends and visitors. For instance, in this service there may be no obvious charismatic gifts at work and the sermon may be shorter and assume less biblical knowledge so as to have greater appeal to newcomers.

The leadership within most congregations is male, though in many Pentecostal congregations there is no theological bar against female leadership. Indeed, the theological position that rejoices in the distribution of charismatic gifts to men and women equally could hardly deny the role of women's ministry, and therefore of female pastors[9]. Whatever the theology, however, males are more numerous than females in leadership positions, but in the main this derives from conservative social attitudes. Pentecostal churches certainly have female deacons and female preachers and more women may attend and participate in services than men.

In a black-led congregation most members tend to be black and this helps to give them affirmation and identity in a society that is marred by racism.

Behaving

The Pentecostal lifestyle, as we have said, tends to be caught up with congregation-related meetings. Not only are there meetings for prayer, worship and bible study, but also there are administrative meetings for deacons and church officers, and other kinds of meetings intended to preach to or teach children, youth or other members of the community. Thus there is a mixture between the disciplined requirement to attend meetings and the freedom that characterises the meetings themselves.

In daily life Pentecostals would be expected to show Christian love and Christian integrity and to try to 'witness' to friends and neighbours.

---

[9] Biblical titles like 'pastor' or 'evangelist' (Ephesians 4) are normally used to designate offices.

Pentecostalism, then, is strongly evangelistic as well as evangelical, and Pentecostals might well be found holding open air meetings on the streets of large cities or visiting prisons or taking services in old people's homes or schools.

In addition there is a tendency for Pentecostals to feel strongly about social and moral issues. Black-led Pentecostal churches will be aware of racism and engage in attempts to combat it, perhaps by the use of social programmes sponsored by local authorities or by letter writing campaigns or by organised community action. The balance between a gospel that concentrates on spiritual needs and a gospel that addresses this-worldly problems will vary between congregations and denominations.

Activity B6

What theological and sociological factors influence the style of the worship of the Black Pentecostal movement?

Comment on activity B6

Theologically Black Pentecostal churches, like white Pentecostal churches, are shaped by the importance they assign to the experience of the Holy Spirit. This experience is communal and individual, renewable and constant, outside of human control and accessible to the fervent seeker. It is above all an experience that denotes unpredictability and so allows almost anything to happen in a Pentecostal meeting provided that it is not immoral. People may clap or shout or fall over or laugh or speak in tongues or start to sing or pray out loud or interrupt the preacher or sit quietly.

In a more precise and theologically defined way, Pentecostal worship will also be shaped by the charismatic gifts listed in the Pauline epistles, notably by speaking in tongues, interpretation, prophecy and perhaps by healing (1 Corinthians 12.8-10). These gifts are often woven into the texture of worship, beautifying it and nudging it in one direction or another, while also adding a didactic element.

Sociologically, Black Pentecostal churches, like white Pentecostal churches, are shaped by the original poverty of their members (Parsons, 1993, 1994). The immigrants to Britain who arrived from the West Indies were not able to obtain well paid jobs and their churches were correspondingly small and architecturally unimpressive. The second and third generation of these families have, in some cases, improved their socio-economic status and this has led to an expectation of more intellectual preaching or worship. Yet, this is not always the case and there are relatively wealthy black Pentecostal churches, or churches with a substantial proportion of black Pentecostals, who expect their religion to be 'hot'.

Reading

Edwards (1997) is an up to date book which has a good index; Cush, Miles and Stylianides (1991) in a book that contains interviews with several members of various Christian traditions is helpful, and so is Pawlowsky (1994). For specialist topics Cross and Livingstone (1997) contains authoritative articles about all aspects of Christianity.

Bibliography

Archer, A. (1986), *The Two Catholic Churches: a study in oppression*, London, SCM.

Arnold, S.E. (1992), *From Scepticism to Hope*, Bramcote, Grove Books.

Bossy, J. (1978), *The English Catholic Community 1570-1850*, London, Darton, Longman and Todd.

Brown-Lawson, A. (1994), *John Wesley and the Anglican Evangelicals of the Eighteenth Century*, Cambridge, The Pentland Press.

Bruce, S, (1995), *Religion in Modern Britain*, Oxford, Oxford University Press.

Cooling, T. (1984), The evangelical Christian and RE, unpublished MA dissertation, Kings College, University of London.

Crichton, J.D. (1986), *A New Dictionary of Liturgy and Worship*, London, SCM.

Cross, F.L. and Livingstone, E.A. (1997*)*, *The Oxford Dictionary of the Christian Church* (third edition), Oxford, Oxford University Press.

Cush, D., Miles, C. and Stylianides, M. (1991), *Christians in Britain Today*, London, Hodder and Stoughton.

Davie, G. (1994), *Religion in Britain since 1945 - believing without belonging*, Oxford, Blackwell.

Davies, R.E. (1988), *Methodism*, London, Epworth Press.

Dog, D. (1976), *Mother Teresa*, London, Collins.

Edwards, D. (1981), *Christian England*, Glasgow, Fount Paperbacks.

Edwards, D. (1997), *Christianity: the first two thousand years*, London, Cassell.

Erricker, C. (ed.) (1995*), Teaching Christianity: a world religions approach,* London, Lutterworth Press.

Francis, L.J. (1996), *Church Watch: Christianity in the countryside,* London, SPCK.

Hastings, A. (1991a), *A History of English Christianity 1920-1990* (third edition), London, SCM.

Hastings, A. (ed.) (1991b), *Modern Catholicism, Vatican 2 and After,* London, SPCK.

Hollenweger, W.J. (1969), *The Pentecostals,* London, SCM.

Hornsby-Smith, M.P. (1991), *Roman Catholic beliefs in England - Customary Catholicism and transformation of religious authority,* Cambridge, Cambridge University Press.

Howard, V. (1987), A report on Afro-Caribbean Christianity in Britain, University of Leeds, Department of Religious Studies.

Hussey, J.M. (1990), *The Orthodox Church in the Byzantine Empire,* Oxford, Clarendon Paperbacks.

MacRobert, I. (1989), The new black-led churches in Britain, in P. Badham (ed.), *Religion, State, and Society in Modern Britain,* Lampeter, Edwin Mellen Press, pp 119-143.

Parsons G. (ed.) (1993), *The Growth of Religious Diversity: traditions,* Milton Keynes and London, Open University and Routledge.

Parsons G. (ed.) (1994), *The Growth of Religious Diversity: issues,* Milton Keynes and London, Open University and Routledge.

Pawlowsky, P. (1994), *Christianity: the basics,* London, SCM.

Salvation Army (1998), *International Spiritual Life Commission Report,* London, Salvation Army.

Strange, R. (1986), *The Catholic Faith,* Oxford, Oxford University Press.

Synan, H.V. (1988), W.J. Seymour, in S.M. Burgess, G.B. McGee and P.H. Alexander, *Dictionary of Pentecostal and Charismatic Movements,* Grand Rapids, Michigan, Regency, pp 778-781.

Synan, H.V. (1997), *The Holiness-Pentecostal Tradition: charismatic movements in the twentieth century,* Grand Rapids, Michigan, Eerdmans.

Thompson, E.P. (1980), *The Making of the English Working Class,* Harmondsworth, Penguin.

Walker A. and Carras C. (ed.) (1996), *Living Orthodoxy in the Modern World,* London, SPCK.

Ware, K. (1979), *The Orthodox Way,* London, Mowbray.

Ware K. (1963), *The Orthodox Church,* Harmondsworth, Penguin.

Williams, R.M. (1993), Eastern Orthodox theology, in A.E. McGrath (ed.), *Modern Christian Thought,* Oxford, Blackwell Publishers, pp 120-127.

Teaching about Christianity

Unit C

Classroom teaching

Dr Mark Chater

Bishop Grosseteste University College

Lincoln

Contents

Introduction

Aims

At the end of this unit you should have understood:

- the diversity of Christianity from the viewpoint of contemporary approaches to religious education;
- the perspectives Groome brings to these contemporary approaches to religious education;
- difficulties in distinguishing in practice between the learning from/learning about aims of religious education;
- strengths and weaknesses of approaches to religious education.

Overview

Any study of the education of children about Christianity must begin with a few questions of definition. This section will avoid going over ground covered in previous modules. It must, however, focus on two questions of definition.

First, we are considering here education about Christianity, not the wider movement of Christian education. While these activities may have some mutual affinities - especially in the areas of education in Christianity, and Christianity's acceptance or not of critical openness - they remain separate. It needs to be clear that the focus of our study here is the activity of teaching and learning about and from Christianity in the school classroom.

Second, we will be focusing on some questions and challenges which the Christian tradition presents to the educator. It will be argued that any teacher planning and presenting material on the Christian tradition must undertake some self-evaluation of their beliefs and attitudes towards it, in the interests of accuracy and integrity.

The word 'tradition' can suggest what Wilfred Cantwell Smith meant by it, that is, a living, evolving movement of thought, having change and process as one of its necessary conditions of life. Cantwell Smith (1978) prefers this term to 'religion' which is considered to suggest too much of the monolithic, the static. In this living, changing sense, then, Christianity is a tradition. On the other hand, as I suggest below following Küng, Christianity contains a core of ideas, doctrines and beliefs that have remained identifiably intact from its earliest times. Unless this had been the case there would be little to connect first century Christianity with its contemporary expressions. There is therefore a balance between change and continuity and it is this that makes Christianity such a rich and dynamic complex of life.

In this unit technical terms, but not names, have been italicised. This is because they have been transliterated from languages which do not use the Roman alphabet. There are a number of different ways of transliterating terms, and when using other written sources you need to be aware that you may come across different spellings.

C1 The river of Christianity

Hans Küng (1995), in his series entitled *The Religious Situation of Our Time*, suggests five 'paradigms' of Christianity. A paradigm may be understood as a model, or matrix of assumptions and insights. A paradigm of Christianity is how it understands itself as a whole; what language and thought-systems it uses to explain and express itself; how it relates to those outside the church.

The five paradigms span specific historical periods, but are also part of the contemporary expression of the tradition: all, therefore, are relevant to the learning of Christianity now. If we retain our analogy of the river taken from unit B, then Küng looks at particular parts of the river and identifies things flowing through it and, obviously, what is put in at the source is likely to emerge in various ways further upstream.

Paradigm one: the earliest Christian communities with their proclamation of Jesus Christ risen from the dead. The key figures are Peter and Paul. The context is the Roman Empire and a Hellenistic culture, resistant or hostile to the early Christian *Kerygma* or message. Several features of this period, including its liturgy, its strong evangelistic impulse, its relationship with a hostile culture and (in some fundamentalist churches) its expectation of the end-time, resonate with theologians and church leaders in the present, making reference to this paradigm a dominant and little questioned theological trait.

Paradigm two: the early church of the patristic period, namely the years leading up to the Councils of Nicea (325) and Chalcedon (451). The key figures are established bishops and theologians such as Athanasius. The context is the growing acceptance of the church and its heavy emphasis on the task of defining its teaching about Christ. The features of this period which are replicated in the present might include the internal processes of definition and clarification.

Paradigm three: the medieval period. The context is one in which Christian theology became ever more closely associated with the whole of learning and philosophy, and ecclesial power with the whole temporal nature of society, until there was - in the theological systems of the time - little to tell them apart. Key figures are scholars such as Thomas Aquinas, Grosseteste and Bonaventure: these and others resonate with the present period because of their fusing of divine revelation with human learning, in fields as diverse as philosophy, science and law. Those who wielded papal power, notably Gregory I and Innocent III, are key figures of the paradigm but the level and character of their political power is not much replicated in today's church.

Paradigm four: the Reformation. The context is one of theological and political struggle between rival theologies and churches with the emergence of reformed churches, and the reform and counter-reformation measures of the Roman Catholic Church. Key figures include Luther, Calvin, Cranmer and Knox who, whatever the historical reality of their theological beliefs, tend to resonate in the contemporary period as heroes resisting theological and ecclesial oppression. Reform and renewal are themes replicated in today's churches.

Paradigm five: the Enlightenment, Idealism and, we might add, modernism. The main development is the emergence of liberal theologies in response to enlightenment-based attacks on supernatural belief. Key theological figures include Schleiermacher and Bultmann: in our own time we could add to the list Robinson, Cupitt, Tracy and Küng.

Hans Küng argues that we are witnessing the emergence of a *sixth paradigm* of Christianity: this will be post-modern, ecumenical and inter-religious, responding to the calls of the young on issues such as environmental sustainability and justice, reaching out for a global ethic, exercising its sense of authority with due regard for individual belief and local variations, forging new positive relationships with psychology, politics, culture and the natural sciences.

What is the educational significance of Küng's theory of paradigms? In the historical development of the Christian tradition, Küng (1995, p 795) sees elements (both positive and negative) from each paradigm which affect our way of seeing Christianity, and of being Christian, in the contemporary period:

> For like a great river which has a modest beginning somewhere and has kept making new cuts through the emergent landscape, this religion has kept inserting itself into ever-new cultivated landscapes. In so doing it has experienced violent rejections and undergone revolutions, indeed has itself often caused new shifts in world history. But mustn't we also see here the stream of goodness, mercy, readiness to help, care, which flows from the source, from the gospel, through history? Granted an infinite amount of debris, flotsam, silt and rubbish has been collected on the long way through the centuries. But has the water at the spring really become fully polluted, as many say?

We suggest that the teaching of and about Christianity today needs, in its planning phase, to take account of the way the paradigms represent different historical epochs. Ideally, we want pupils to gain an overview of all the paradigms, of the whole river, and so a balanced and accurate portrayal of the entire tradition: but more, it may also help to give the Christian curriculum a dynamic towards new evolutions in the Christian tradition which, while keeping certain key and core beliefs remarkably unchanged introduces a sense of expectancy about the adaptability of Christianity to whatever landscape the future creates.

The truth of the Christian tradition

Küng's reflection on paradigms leads him to a defence of Christianity's dynamic truth, seen in Jesus Christ and his cause. This he holds while still calling for peace and dialogue between the religions and ideologies for the sake of world peace. The question of the objective truth about Christianity, and its position in relation to other world religions claiming revelation, is still of importance for those engaged in teaching about it. On this point, the personal beliefs of the teacher cannot but affect his or her approach. Broadly speaking, teachers whose theological position on revelation is exclusivist (that is, who hold Jesus Christ to be the unique and summative form of revelation of God) must own some questions and methodological reservations when planning and presenting material on Christianity. According to Rodger (1982, p 121):

> Thus Christians witness to their faith as much by their voluntary restraint in the classroom as by their open proclamation.

This enables them to step outside their beliefs for the sake of gospel charity; while those whose position is relativist (that is, holding Jesus Christ to be but one among many incarnations or images of God, whether divinely revealed or expressed by the human spirit) have some obligation to accept the unique claims for Jesus made by the Christian tradition, and to communicate these for the sake of accuracy.

As teachers about Christianity we need, therefore, an honest theological self-evaluation which enables us to place ourselves on its theological and political spectrums. By this means, whether conservative or liberal in our theological orientation, we can see ourselves contextually in the light of Christianity's historical development through various paradigms. We can also begin to evaluate the likely effect of our own beliefs about Christianity's truth and uniqueness and, when all that is done, to take appropriate remedial action. Thus we become learners as much as teachers and compensate for and complete our own particularity in a pedagogical reflection of Christianity which has theological and historical integrity.

Activity C1

Your experience of planning and presenting Christianity will have raised some or all of these questions in your mind. Attempt an honest self-evaluation of your theological position, if you wish using the spectrums and Küng's paradigms as a framework, and discuss how this may have affected your educational approach to the Christian tradition.

Comment on activity C1

Other spectrums may have occurred to you for addition to the graph: where, for instance, does the question of women in the church, and the growing body of feminist theological writing, feature? It may belong in either the theological or political spectrums, or else the importance of this theology may require its own spectrum. Where do urban and rural differences feature? They certainly throw up considerably distinctive ministry needs and theological perspectives in dioceses all over the world. Ought they to form a part of a fourth, social spectrum? Also, the variations between Christianity as lived in the child's immediate community, in the British Isles as a whole (Scottish, Welsh, Irish and Black forms, to name but a few), in Europe and globally (Asian, Latino and African theologies) must all be borne in mind.

C2 Educating about Christianity

In this section we will deal with issues relating to the activity of teaching about Christianity. While several of these issues ought to be familiar to you (for instance, they will have occurred to you if you have been in regular practice as a teacher, or else they will have been rehearsed in other modules of this course) they must be given a direct look here to see the way in which they impact on the teaching of Christianity particularly.

In the first part, *Interpreting Christianity*, we will deal with issues of hermeneutics and the Christian interpretation of the world. The second part, *Knowing Christianity*, looks at epistemological questions and asks how the pupil is supposed to know, or know about, this religion. Thirdly, in *Planning Christianity*, we discuss the issues which arise when we look at particular schemes of planning.

Interpreting Christianity

How is Christianity to be interpreted? This is more than a question of the backgrounds and beliefs of the pupils. Just as Muslims feel that Islam needs to be learned in an Islamic way, so the Christian tradition has certain characteristics which suggest it be learned in particular ways. In this part, we shall look at the work of Thomas Groome (1991) to discover some of these characteristics.

Groome suggests nine hermeneutical criteria for the teaching of or about Christianity. These vary in importance - the first, for instance, intentionally dominates the others - and are perhaps not all easy to justify. They will not all be enumerated and described here: instead, we will look at Groome's argument for a way of educationally opening up Christianity which reflects Christian priorities. The overall function of the criteria is to set a framework for how Christianity (its texts, rituals, doctrines and so on) is to be so interpreted and experienced by the teacher and learner that its deepest insights and highest priorities are faithfully accounted for.

The Kingdom of God forms the first criterion (Groome uses the phrase 'reign of God' in preference). This is a priority as a set of values and as an end-point for all Christian educational endeavour. According to Groome, Christian teachers and learners already have an inbuilt existential awareness of the kingdom; their churches are communities of witness and struggle for the kingdom and against values which contradict it. Educators should, therefore, approach every aspect of the Christian tradition with this kingdom priority uppermost in mind. Also, aspects of the Christian tradition which do not reflect kingdom values are less authentic and should not be written out but should be presented as less at the heart of the tradition.

If we look for a more clearly defined notion of an 'existential awareness of the kingdom', then the most obvious place to turn is the New Testament. Here there is a tension between present and future: the kingdom is now-and-not-yet. The kingdom is found where Christ is. He embodies it, is its king and, by his ministry, brings it into the present. The gospels record how Jesus began by calling people to repentance and announcing the coming of the kingdom which, as people were healed and taught, was seen in action (Mark 1.15; Luke 4.43; Matthew 12.28; Luke 22.18). Even in the present, though, the kingdom may be concealed as an inner treasure, a personal possession and a state of being before God (Luke 17.21; Romans 14.17). The kingdom also has a future aspect in the expectation that Christ himself will return to bring in an era of peace and righteousness. Whether this expectation is understood literally, as many Christians believe, or metaphorically as referring to the improvement in social and political conditions through the mediation of the church, does not affect its relevance to the way Christianity is lived. The prayer, 'your kingdom come', shows how Christians are continually looking with hope for a better future. They bring a request to God for a new era where the old order is superseded and where the kind of life brought about by Christ's ministry is seen perpetually.

To ensure this, teachers need to apply other hermeneutical principles, making themselves aware of their own experience and that of their learners. Further, they must employ a 'hermeneutic of retrieval' which recovers and prioritises the most life-giving aspects of the tradition together with a 'hermeneutic of suspicion' which uncovers and identifies as false those aspects of the tradition which are distortive of its central truths and insights (Groome, 1991, p 230ff). This may be paraphrased as retrieving and presenting what is most liberating and positive in the gospel while rejecting what is oppressive or negative in the church's tradition. It must be stressed that Groome nowhere advocates censorship, neither is he interested in a fig-leaf pedagogy which hides the Christian tradition's worst characteristics. For example, anti-Semitism and colonialism are part of the Christian story but plainly contrary to its original vision of love and justice (these examples are mine, not Groome's). The hermeneutic of retrieval emphasises the vision of love and justice; the hermeneutic of suspicion tells the story of the persecutions and colonisations, but invites the learner to recognise their destructiveness and to turn against those values.

There may be a question about whether educators outside the Christian fold can subscribe to such practice. Certainly there is a concern among all non-confessionalists that each religious tradition be understood in its own right and according to its own way of defining itself: this concern should surely apply to Christianity no less.

For Groome, the priority of the kingdom impels Christian educators in the direction of lived commitment to it; he therefore argues for a 'creative commitment' which is faithful to the tradition and works itself out in personal and social action (Groome, 1991, p 235ff). For him, any experience of studying Christianity which stops short of an active response to Christ in the context of contemporary social realities would not be complete. Again, there may be non-confessional reservations about the application of these criteria. While not wishing to undermine any Christian child's commitment, non-confessionalists may well baulk at fostering a spirit of active commitment as an intentional part of their programme for all pupils. Nevertheless, the reality for Christians is that Christ calls for discipleship, and there must be a way in which learners of and about Christianity experience and interpret this existential reality.

The challenges of interpreting Christianity authentically and freely will beset every practitioner. This brief discussion of Groome's demanding and detailed criteria serves to let us see the problem in sharp focus. This supports the emphasis of learning *from* Christianity and not just *about* it. One of the prime concerns of the Warwick project (mentioned later) is the issue of the interpretation and representation of religion in the school curriculum.

Knowing Christianity

Epistemology is usually defined as a theory of knowledge, and for our purposes here it is an attempt to be clear about the way(s) in which the young learner will encounter (know, know of, know about) Christianity. The question of whether religious knowledge of any sort is possible is not addressed here, since assumptions of that sort are normally made and shared in the world of religious educators; but a discussion of that preliminary and basic point may be seen in *Knowledge and the Curriculum* by Paul Hirst (1974) and in *The Psychology of Religious Knowing* by Fraser Watts and Mark Williams (1988). This part will ask questions about the form such religious knowing in Christianity should take, and will invite Christianity to offer answers.

Thomas Groome is a major Christian contributor to epistemological work as it affects religious education. In his 1991 work he offers a definition of knowing as conation, an act of the whole person engaging mind, emotions and will. These three faculties form a pedagogical unity to such an extent that knowing becomes inseparable from being. He traces the roots of conation to Christian, pre-Christian and post-Christian sources, but is deeply critical of the Christian and enlightenment traditions for their failure to define knowledge in this broad sense.

Groome shares with Grimmitt (1987) and several others a strong critique of the enlightenment-based way of knowing which has exclusively elevated to normative status a paradigm of knowledge based upon objectivity, rationality and empirical information. Their argument suggests that this form of knowledge, important in itself, becomes a distortion of knowing and of the knower when it is offered as the only, or most important, form. Personal forms of knowledge, based on experience, emotion and intuitive insight, are offered by, among others, feminist philosophers as a humanising antidote to the extremes of technical rationality. How does this debate affect the teaching of Christianity? One answer to this question must be that it supports the notion that pupils are not only to learn *about* Christianity as a more objectivist phenomenological approach would insist.

The understanding of Christianity, Groome and Grimmitt argue, is dependent not solely on information about it but on a personal encounter with it. Here Groome and Grimmitt differ, Groome offering a model of education as personal renewal through an encounter with the spirit of Christ in the Christian tradition, and Grimmitt offering a less ambitious model in which pupils question and examine their own response but are not necessarily existentially transformed by what they know. Transformational responses by pupils may sometimes be legitimate, but should not be sought or expected by the teacher[1]. Aspects of moral education may affect not only what the pupil thinks, feels or does, but who he or she actually is. A pupil response which includes commitment of some sort is, once again, becoming thinkable in non-confessional religious education, provided it is not commitment of the narrow sort.

A consideration of the nature of Christianity adds strength to this argument. Part of the Christian church's *raison d'être* is evangelism in response to the commission of Matthew 28. A characteristic part of the four gospels, in their presentation of Jesus' message, is their emphasis on the desirability of an immediate positive response to him (Mark 1.16ff, Matthew 12.46ff). Knowing, in the gospels, is an intensely personal act, as the discourses in, for instance, John 6 make clear. The climactic events of the gospels, the Resurrection and subsequent appearances, are a vivid encounter with the mystery of the risen Christ, which must surely be understood in terms which go beyond the descriptive or propositional but reach further into the emotions, as the example of Mary Magdalene, Peter and the others shows. It would be a bold educator who could claim that no such considerations should enter the epistemological framework of the teacher and learner in their dealings with Christianity.

In the light of these theoretical concerns, practitioners might look critically at courses and resources on Christianity, evaluating the extent to which aims and tasks invite learners to involve themselves fully in learning. One critical perspective on textbooks and videos is that they can take a strongly descriptive approach. Adherents of a faith are described in print, or caught on film, going through ritual duties. Although there is explanation of the meanings, there is sometimes little evidence of a mature ownership of faith or any interest in dialoguing with, challenging or sharing personally with the reader or viewer. It is as if the adherent lives faith in terms of duty, habit and received belief, operating at relatively low developmental levels, such as Fowler's second (mythical literal) and third (synthetic-conventional) stages. Surely both the Christian tradition and the capacities of the pupil call for a deeper, fuller model of knowing than this: and if a model of knowing with one's whole being is put into action, so much the richer will be the religious education process, and the encounter with Christianity.

---

[1] This sentence might seem to deny the aim of learning *from*. The problem is not seeking a transformational response, but seeking a *particular type* of transformational response (such as becoming a Christian).

C3 Planning Christianity

Planning Christian material so that it reflects the full complexity and possibilities of the tradition forms the focus of this part of our work. We shall be looking at the ways Christianity has been treated and organised in three contemporary works on religious education: the Westhill Project books and photopacks (Read *et al*, 1986 and 1987a-e, and Becher, 1995), the life-world curriculum of Michael Grimmitt (1987) and the ethnographic model of Robert Jackson (1997) and the Warwick RE Project (1996a-f).

The Westhill Project

A major initiative of the late 1980s and still in use in many primary and secondary schools, the Westhill Project materials aimed to give coherent structure and progression to religious education for pupils aged 5 to 16, reflecting the four Key Stages of the national curriculum and covering, initially, Christianity, Islam and Judaism. Further materials on Hinduism and on Black Christianity followed in later years. This chapter will make use of the materials in later sections. Taking a look at the materials and noting their structure and approach would, accordingly, be advisable background work.

Although steeped in the non-confessional tradition, the authors of the materials advise against any approach which so dissects a religion that it ceases to be a religion and becomes merely an object of scientific study: while use of analytical tools is important, experience and reflection must also play a part (Read *et al*, 1986, p vi). There is, thus, an element of knowing with one's whole being in the implied epistemological position of the authors.

For planning purposes, the project material divides Christianity into four constituent parts: personal life, family life, community life and public life. Personal life mentions prayer, morality, the sense of vocation and pilgrimage. Family life deals with the celebration of major festivals, family devotions, rituals and ceremonies. Community life again embraces festivals, but also deals with ecclesial issues such as evangelism, pastoral care, social welfare and worship. Public life includes state-church relations, pressure groups and varied forms of Christian experience from the Charismatic Movement through Mormons and Jehovah's Witnesses to Christian action against racism and nuclear weapons. Family and community life are represented substantially in the books for Key Stages 1, 2 and 3; personal life is introduced in Key Stage 2 and returned to at Key Stage 3; public life is a major theme of Key Stage 4. The emphasis, as the child grows through the stages, is thus organised to move from immediate family and community surroundings, which are crucial for infants but remain important throughout, towards inner personal life and outward public life, roughly reflecting the interests which may be anticipated in early and middle adolescence. There is, then, a systematic attempt at fitting the Christian tradition into a developmental schema. The extent to which this is viable and can be said to do justice to a religious tradition is an issue for your own reflection.

Grimmitt's life-world curriculum

Grimmitt (1987) expounds a developmental and human rationale for religious education: in other words, he argues an ideology and a formal approach based upon what we know of children's unfolding needs, concerns, interests and sense of human identity. His work on the adolescent life-world curriculum breaks new ground, identifying the ultimate questions arising from adolescent reflection on human experience. For instance Grimmitt (1987, p 274) writes:

> Is there order, meaning and purpose in my life? Should there be? Why, why not? Should I decide on goals? How do I decide on them?

Not that Grimmitt claims an adolescent would naturally frame the questions in these words, but these (and others) are the issues identified as existentially preoccupying them. Grimmitt takes these issues and arranges them across a grid of contexts (family, community, plural society, world-wide community) bearing a resemblance to the four parts in the Westhill project material (see above). The importance and originality of Grimmitt's schema, however, is his creation of a firm psychological and human base for the systematic and existential study of a religion. Building on this base, he takes each religion in turn and devises an essential minimum of concepts which match the adolescent learner's questions and concerns. Thus his treatment of Christianity organises key concepts in a planning sequence from 'Christians growing together in the family' through to 'Christians believing together in the world-wide community' (1987, p 289ff). The planning sequence is not theological, in other words, not based on a biblical plan of salvation (Old and New Testaments) nor on credal formulae such as Father, Son and Holy Spirit: it is an essentially human and psychological sequence based on a theory of the development of the learner. The same human basis is used for the planning of all the religions (1987, p 299ff).

Questions may be asked about the applicability of this schema. Whether it fits all the religions equally well, whether Christianity in particular is appropriately treated, and whether it is sufficiently flexible, are issues on which you may wish to reflect.

The conceptual approach

An approach which resonates with Groome's concern to open up Christianity in a way that reflects Christian priorities, and Küng's concern to reflect the relationship between the defining features of Christianity which are constant down the ages and their expression in varying cultural milieu, is the conceptual approach. This became influential in the 1990s and is reflected in the *Teaching RE* series published by the Christian Education Movement (see particularly 1993c, 1993d) and the publications of the Stapleford Project (see Cooling, 1994a, 1997). The Stapleford Project has produced a wide range of resources for teaching Christianity in school religious education, including its magazine for primary schools called *Cracking RE*. The approach is incorporated in Model 2 of the Model Syllabuses for RE published by the Government's School Curriculum and Assessment Authority (1994) and in the BBC *Pathways of Belief* series of programmes on Christianity.

The conceptual approach draws on the work of the psychologist Jerome Bruner, and in particular the following three main assertions:

- the key to understanding any subject is to identify and teach its structural concepts, that is, those concepts which make sense of and give meaning to all the information learnt in the subject;
- it is possible to teach any concept to any child at any age;
- to do this the concepts have to be translated into a form that makes sense in the child's world of experience and is appropriate to the child's stage of development.

In relation to teaching Christianity, this means that the curriculum should be structured around the key theological concepts such as *Incarnation* and *Trinity*, which are what define the meaning and significance of all the information about Christianity that we might require our pupils to learn. In contrast to Grimmitt above the curriculum is therefore structured around a basic creed. The conceptual approach is therefore a challenge to the prevalent philosophy, based on the work of Ronald Goldman (1964), that it is not appropriate to teach abstract theological concepts to children until secondary school.

Considerable emphasis is given in the approach to the process of translating abstract theological concepts into forms that make sense to the child. The process involves identifying concepts in the child's world of experience which act as parallels to the theological concept and then using these to initiate the pupil into an understanding of the theological concept. This process is sometimes called *building bridges* and is very similar at this point to the work done in the ethnographic approach (see below). Doing this well is one of the defining features of successful teaching. The art is to design learning activities which are effective in facilitating this translation process.

A key feature of this approach is the aspiration that pupils feel and respond to the challenge that is presented by the basic message of Christianity. However this is not confessional as it is recognised that many of the pupils may respond from within a non-Christian or even non-religious framework which does not embrace the 'truth' of the Christian message. The freedom to respond in a way that respects one's own religious integrity is integral to an approach which is appropriate for the school classroom.

A fundamental question to ask of this approach is whether it is a distortion of the Christian faith to seek to represent it through a theological essence. Some would argue that the diversity of Christian experience means that any approach built on teaching a theological essence is inevitably going to create stereotypes. This is a particular concern of our next approach.

Jackson's ethnographic model

A new breakthrough in the planning of religious education is seen in Robert Jackson (1997, p 50). Motivated early on by a desire to move the phenomenological model on into a new phase, Jackson recognises the ambiguity and elusiveness of religious traditions: they are 'organic, internally diverse and more complex than "belief systems"'.

This applies to Christianity as much as to the rest. Jackson therefore wishes the learner to approach religions not as systems of thought but as experiences on the ground and in individual and communal life. Elements of the Westhill and Grimmitt approaches are seen here, but are taken further in the direction of individuals and communities shaping the reality of religious life.

The ethnographic element of his work borrows a model of cultural study and applies it to curricular religious education. According to this application of the model, concepts of a religion are formed not on the basis of theoretical study but on the immediate 'text' of the lives of individuals and communities both inside the religious tradition and outside it. The emphasis is on personal narratives rather than abstract generalisations, experience rather than received habit, people rather than systems. Jackson suggests that, as with the Westhill Project, books be called 'Christians' rather than 'Christianity'. The overall intended result is a more vivid encounter with a religion, taking into account the cultural reality of the religion itself and of the learner.

There can be little doubting the originality and importance of this interpretative approach, but can Christianity be approached in this new way? Alive to the possible charge of relativism, Jackson argues that his approach must embrace a certain epistemological openness, and must guard against the comfortable avoidance of controversial issues (1997, p 122ff). Another danger discussed by Jackson is the possibility that his approach reduces religious systems to personal or communal experience. While not denying the existence or importance of religious systems, he suggests that, as social constructs, they do not constitute all that there is to see (1997, p 126ff).

There are, perhaps, features of contemporary Christianity - its decline in numerical support (see unit A in this module) and its bewildering variety of forms (see this unit, above) - which would become, if anything, more elusive when seen through an ethnographic approach. How, for instance, is the British learner to encounter the full richness of Orthodox liturgy through personal narrative? Or how is the witness of Christians in previous, crucially formative struggles, such as the Roman persecution, the Soviet persecution, the civil rights and anti-Apartheid movements, to be encountered without resort to traditional texts? Other, generic issues facing all religions including Christianity also suggest themselves: will a local, personal and narrative account of religious life give an accurate enough idea of the reality of a religious tradition? Is there a suggestion of post-modern rejection of the very notion of the objective life and strength of a religious tradition lying beyond individual experience? These and other questions should form part of our reflections on the curricular planning of Christianity.

Activity C2

How is Christianity to be interpreted, known and planned for in the classroom? Christians may wish to argue that Christianity must be interpreted, known and planned for according to Christian principles: a contrary argument is that the tradition must submit itself to purely educational procedures. Write a letter to teachers outlining your hopes for how the tradition can be most authentically represented. Bear in mind:

- its interpretation (hermeneutics), that is, what parts of the tradition should be presented, and what response is called for;
- its model of knowledge (epistemology), that is, the ways in which pupils will encounter it;
- the planning process which best represents the richness of the tradition.

Comment on activity C2

Writing a letter is a personal activity and so I have not attempted to show you how it should be done. No doubt your letter will be influenced by your own experience of Christianity and of teaching. No doubt you will have your own ideas about what is most important for pupils to understand and appreciate. My own emphases are contained in the bullet points above.

C4 Planning teaching about Christianity

In this section we will look at the teaching of Christian beliefs, worship and practices. Why have these three areas been demarcated? Would it not be better to approach Christianity as a unified whole? Contemporary theories of theological education usually favour holistic approaches, whether uniting many sub-disciplines (Farley, 1995, p 255) or integrating technical theological competence with a variety of life experiences (Schussler Fiorenza, 1995, p 267). Furthermore, in terms of the primitive Christian message, its sense of itself, a unity of belief with action, or theology with practical experience, seems paramount (see, for example, Matthew 7.21).

In organising Christianity into facets such as belief, worship and practices, there is no intention to fragment theological study, or to dichotomise Christian theology from practice. This is done for pragmatic purposes because pupils can respond, from early ages, to simple organised pieces of learning about what Christians think, how they pray and what they do. It is considered crucial, therefore, that if teaching is organised under such headings, the teacher be aware of the profound theological and Christian connections between the three categories, and make these connections explicit for the learner whenever possible. Therefore it is hoped that these form a coherent whole.

These three facets of Christianity are dealt with through four contemporary practical approaches to religious education: the Westhill Project (Read *et al*, 1986, 1987a-e,), the Christian Education Movement (1990, 1991a-b, 1993a-d, 1994a-b, 1997a-b), the Stapleford Project (Cooling, 1994a, 1997; Wright 1995a and 1995b; and the magazine *Cracking RE*) and the interpretative ethnographic approach of the Warwick RE Project (Jackson, Barratt and Everington, 1994, 1997; and Warwick RE Project, 1996a-f). In addition reference is made to the Chichester Project (Rankin, 1982a-d, 1984a-c, 1985, 1986) which remains important because it was the first to treat Christianity as a world religion showing regional and denominational variation. Each approach is briefly analysed below. When you have familiarised yourself with these approaches and the associated resources, you will be asked to gain some practical experience of using them in the classroom; and you will need to use your reflections on this experience in order to evaluate the extent to which the approaches succeed in meeting the challenges set out earlier in this unit.

The *Westhill Project* books and photopack on Christianity are designed for pupils from age 5 to 16. Each pupil book relates to a Key Stage: for example, *Christians 1* is for pupils in Key Stage 1, and so on. No assumptions are made about the teacher's or the pupil's acceptance of the Christian religion now or in the future.

The *Chichester Project* materials are designed to support secondary pupils in their study of Christianity as a world religion, and to promote understanding and sensitivity but not consent. The books use a combination of prose analysis, punctuated by pictures, cartoons and excerpts from documents to focus on an aspect of Christian belief, worship or practice.

The *Christian Education Movement* materials are designed to support primary and secondary teachers in planning good quality religious education which is sensitive, effective and enjoyable. There are two categories of material: the earlier series, entitled *Exploring A Theme*, and the more recent *Teaching RE*. Both series work by taking an implicit or explicit theme and suggesting areas of content, practical approaches and resources. The teacher has to adapt the material for the classroom.

The *Stapleford Project* has published over 30 different books on teaching Christianity based on a conceptual approach. The major representative texts for secondary schools are Wright (1995a and 1995b). For primary schools the best representation of the Project's approach is in the magazine *Cracking RE*. The approach is non-confessional, relying particularly on the use of 'owning and grounding' language (an idea originally propagated by the Westhill Project).

The *interpretative approach* developed by Robert Jackson and others is based upon a concept of religion as personally and communally experienced, and seen through the eyes of its practitioners and its students. The theoretical foundation of this work (Jackson, 1997) supports the Warwick Project materials, some of which are in print (Jackson, Barratt and Everington, 1994; Warwick RE Project, 1996a-f; Robson, 1995; Mercier, 1996). The materials are narrative and pupil-centred, focusing on an individual child's experience of his or her faith and its community. As with other materials, these provide a resource but still require the teacher to plan and create appropriate contexts.

Materials on beliefs, worship and practice

The approaches discussed above have distinctive presuppositions about Christianity, and about educational method, which mark them out from each other. The Westhill and Chichester Project materials share a commitment to a neutral approach, not advocating Christianity; CEM and Stapleford Project material stand closer to Christianity; the interpretative approach developed by Robert Jackson breaks new ground in starting with the practitioner's subjective experience. You will be able to sample and evaluate these distinctive styles.

This section shows what exact materials can be accessed and used for teaching the three facets of Christian belief, worship and practice. For convenience the references are arranged under the subheadings of the five approaches already discussed.

Christian beliefs in the Westhill Project

Key Stage 1: Read *et al* (1987a), *Christians 1*, people's varying beliefs are implied, pp 3-6.

Key Stage 2: Read *et al* (1987b), *Christians 2*, beliefs about Jesus, pp 5-15.

Key Stage 3: Read *et al* (1987c), *Christians 3*, beliefs about Jesus, God, the Trinity, the sacraments and the church, pp 6-23.

Key Stage 4: Read *et al* (1987d), *Christians 4*, beliefs about the church, pp 37-46.

Christian beliefs in the Chichester Project

Key Stage 3-4: Rankin (1982b), vol. 3, *Christian Experience*, Rankin (1982d), vol. 4, *Jesus*, and Rankin (1984c), vol. 5 *Exploring the Bible*.

Christian beliefs in the Stapleford Project

Key Stage 1: Thacker (1995), *The Hafferee Hand Book*.

Key Stage 2: *Cracking RE*, Spring 1997, Autumn 1997.

Key Stage 3: Wright (1995a, 1995b), *Key Christian Beliefs*.

Christian beliefs in the Christian Education Movement material

Key Stage 1-2: Christian Education Movement (1997a), *Teaching RE: the bible 5-11*.

Key Stage 3-4: Christian Education Movement (1997b), *Teaching RE: the bible 11-16*.

Christian beliefs in the Interpretative Approach

Key Stage 1: Warwick RE Project (1996e), *Meeting Christians Book 1*.

Key Stage 2: Warwick RE Project (1996f), *Meeting Christians Book 2*.

Key Stage 3: Robson (1995), *Interpreting Religions: Christians*.

Christian worship in the Westhill Project

Key Stage 1: Read *et al* (1987a), *Christians 1*, places where Christians meet, pp 7-22.

Key Stage 2: Read *et al* (1987b), *Christians 2*, major festivals and styles of worship, pp 16-39.

Key Stage 4: Read *et al* (1987d), *Christians 4*, spirituality, including prayer in formal liturgies, conversion experiences, and Christian views of life, pp 47-59.

Christian worship in the Chichester Project

Key Stage 3-4: Rankin (1982c), volume 1, *Christian Worship*, Rankin, (1984a), volume 7, *Christmas & Easter*, and Rankin (1985), volume 9, *The Eucharist*.

Christian worship in the Stapleford Project

Key Stage 1: Thacker (1995), *The Hafferee Hand Book*.

Key Stage 2: Cooling (1992), *Christianity Topic Book 3*.

Key Stage 3: Wright (1995a, 1995b), *Key Christian Beliefs*.

Christian worship in the Christian Education Movement materials

Key Stage 1-2: Christian Education Movement (1993c), *Teaching RE: Easter 5-11*.

Key Stage 3-4: Christian Education Movement (1993d), *Teaching RE: Easter 11-16*.

Christian worship in the Interpretative Approach

Key Stage 1: Warwick RE Project (1996d), *Lucy's Sunday*.

Key Stage 3: Robson (1995), *Interpreting Religions: Christians*.

Christian practices in the Westhill Project

Key Stage 1: Read *et al* (1987a), *Christians 1*, helping other people, pp 23-27.

Key Stage 2: Read *et al* (1987b), *Christians 2*, marriage and family life, pp 40-47.

Key Stage 3: Read *et al* (1987c), *Christians 3*, personal and social action on belonging to the church, on vocations and on moral issues, pp 44-62.

Key Stage 4: Read *et al* (1987d), *Christians 4*, Christians in public life, including issues of poverty, abortion, nuclear war and apartheid, pp 7-36.

Christian practices in the Chichester Project

Key Stage 3-4: Rankin (1982a), vol. 2, *Christian Communities*, and Rankin (1984b) vol. 8, *Christian Ethics*.

Christian practices in the Stapleford Project

Key Stage 1: Thacker (1995), *The Hafferee Hand Book*.

Key Stage 2: *Cracking RE*, Summer 1998.

Key Stage 3: Wright (1995a, 1995b), *Key Christian Beliefs*.

Christian practices in the Christian Education Movement materials

Key Stage 3: Robson (1995), *Interpreting Religions: Christians*.

Christian practices in the Interpretative Approach

Key Stage 2: Warwick RE Project (1996f), *Meeting Christians Book 2*.

Activity C3

The purpose of this task is related to praxis: that is, to help you have a vision of good practice in teaching about Christianity. In order to engage in this process, we ask you to begin by reflecting on the resources and approaches itemised above.

Review and make critical notes on a selection of the resources identified above. They will be available in resource centres, schools bookshops specialising in education, and some theological bookshops such as SPCK. As you review the resources, reflect on:

- the coverage of Christianity as a plural religion: are the different denominational branches, the theological and political varieties clearly enough in evidence?
- the coverage of Christianity as a global religion: is Christian worship and practice in third-world, base-community, ethnic minority and persecuted contexts visible?
- the unity of belief, worship and practice: how easily can connections be made by pupil and teacher between these facets of Christian experience?
- the learning outcome expected in the resources: often, educational materials about Christianity will resist asking for any personal response from the pupil. What evidence is there, in these resources, of structured opportunities for pupils to have a real encounter with the claims of Christianity? What form does it take? Does it bear any resemblance with

Groome's priority for the reign of God and for action and reflection towards the reign of God?

Comment on activity C3

Comment on this activity is given in the form of three examples, reviewing Christian belief in the Chichester Project, Christian worship in the Westhill Project, and Christian practices in the interpretative approach.

Christian beliefs in the Chichester Project

The Chichester Project volume 3, *Christian Experience* (Rankin, 1982b) takes aspects of the human experience of living the Christian life. Aspects of this experience are used as chapter headings: the chapters then use cartoons, excerpts from fiction or church history, and connecting prose analysis to raise issues and explain beliefs.

There is a genuine attempt to portray Christian experience in denominationally plural terms: excerpts are taken from literature about Luther and about a Roman Catholic order of nuns. There does not seem to be any coverage of experience in the Orthodox tradition. Theological and political pluralism is implicit in a chapter which looks at Mother Teresa and Camillo Torres. The tasks are certainly thought-provoking, but rarely do they ask pupils to analyse differences and similarities between forms of Christianity.

The power of the literary extracts is complemented with an unassuming commentary which gently invites deep reflection. Among the formal pupil tasks, *Ask yourself* activities focus on the pupil's understanding; *Further activities* explore and probe more deeply and could, in the hands of a gifted teacher fostering positive and thoughtful relationships, form the basis of more challenging reflection and action. But the book as a whole never confronts pupils openly with the challenges of radical Christian living.

Christian worship in the Westhill Project

The Westhill Project's pupil book on Christianity at Key Stage 1, *Christians 1* (Read et al, 1987a) offers infants a lively and personal look at worship through the experience of two children (see pp 14-22). This is done through the eyes of Jane, a Christian girl, and her two Muslim friends Shanaz and Chetna. The children's experience of the physical surroundings and the main events in worship is well recounted; there is also mention of several crucial features of Christian worship, including prayer, hymns, a collection, a bible reading and a Sunday school. The significance of these features is not drawn out, but their importance is indicated.

The commentary and questions (pp18ff) give further information and invite children to share their experience of visiting a church for worship. Singing, praying and rituals are explained in terms of their underlying beliefs and the Christian experience of them.

There are elements of diversity hinted at, but not much developed. Variant beliefs and practices with regard to eucharist, for instance, are only gently indicated by the sentence which explains that for many Christians it is their most important ritual. Clearly there is a belief that any further development of denominational or theological differences would be inappropriate at this level.

The language is studiously neutral: 'Christians believe that God listens... they remember Jesus...' (pp 20-21). Aside from the story of Jane and her friends, there is little that is personal. Moments of singing, or silent communication or rituals which might exist in the child's imaginative experience are not used as ways into concepts of hymn-singing, prayer and ritual.

Christian practices in the interpretative approach

The Warwick RE Project's book for pupils at Key Stage 2, *Meeting Christians Book 2* (1996e) offers a pupil's eye view of Christian living through the use of Christian 'insiders' - children of the same age as the learner, interviewed at length in the preparation of the series (Jackson, 1997, p 107). Connections are frequently made between experience and worship, and Christian values come out in the quoted comments of the 'insiders'. For instance, links are made between the commitment implied by the Roman Catholic sacrament of confirmation and the practical service of work for charitable agencies such as CAFOD. The concept of Christian practice is presented in a pupil-centred and accessible way.

Pupils are not directly invited to respond through action; they are, however, asked to place themselves alongside the experience, action and attitudes of the Christian 'insiders' they are studying, in order to demonstrate understanding of their Christian living. The extent to which this successfully challenges learners in this very practical dimension of Christianity may well depend on the teacher's commitment and ability to take the extra step of confronting her/his own children with the demands and challenges of Christian commitment.

C5 Reflecting on teaching about Christianity

Having sampled material from the four sources (the Westhill, Chichester and Warwick projects, and the Christian Education Movement) you are now about to plan, teach and evaluate some aspects of Christianity using an appropriate combination of the sources. As you begin this section, you need to bear in mind the following points.

- Your teaching about Christianity needs to be appropriate to the age and ability of the pupils and the context in which they are learning. If you are not working in a school yourself, your approach to a school (or other context of learning) needs to include careful consideration of, and adaptation to, its syllabus and ethos.

- The results of your work with pupils can be carefully measured against your original aims and against the concerns and issues explored in sections C1 and C2 of this unit. It is this careful measurement which will provide you with the analytical material you need for completing the unit.

- Your choice of school (or other context for learning), and your identification of aims and content, will need to be carefully discussed with your tutor for this unit before you proceed further.

This section now provides an example of one particular approach to teaching about Christianity. This approach involves the three clear stages of planning, implementing and evaluating.

Planning the approach

The following example concentrates on belief and is based on the Christian Education Movement (1997b), *Teaching RE: the bible 11-16.*

Topic: The bible with secondary pupils (Year 7 or 8).

Aim: To introduce the concept of the bible as Word of God.

Objectives: The pupils will be:

- able to explain a range of different Christian beliefs about the bible;
- able to identify the differences and similarities between the Christian beliefs;
- invited to talk about, and commit themselves to, their own beliefs about the bible.

Content: The idea that Christians share a reverence for the message of the bible, believe it to be revelation in some way, and look to it for important answers, should be complemented with the rich variety of attitudes to biblical truth (literal and mythical) and to the exact sense in which the bible speaks to Christians (through worship, individual reading, or in its main themes).

Approach: The following six activities will be employed.

- Pupils will be asked to write and share in pairs a phrase summing up their belief about what the bible is. Stimulus words may be used.

- Using the four 'bubbles' in Christian Education Movement (1997b, p 8), pupils will be asked to express in their own words what the four characters believe.
- In groups, pupils will have the task of matching the four comments with the quotations from scripture on p 9.
- In discussion, pupils will be asked to identify what is different and what is the same between the comments.
- Pupils will be asked to identify how their beliefs have changed through this exercise, and to express in their own words their feelings about the bible.
- A ritual may be used to allow pupils to express their commitment.

Resources: The following resources will be needed:

- *Teaching RE: the bible 11-16* (Christian Education Movement, 1997b);
- pencil and paper for each pupil.

Implementing the approach

When putting the lessons into practice, pay particular attention to the aims and objectives, and try to take time as soon as possible afterwards in order to reflect on the extent to which you were successful in achieving them.

Evaluating the approach

After you have taught the two or three lessons on Christianity, evaluate the lesson itself: did it achieve what you intended? This will lead you on to a consideration of the aims, objectives and content, and you will need to make a critical evaluation of your own approach. Use the following questions to guide you.

- Was an adequate variety of Christian beliefs/worship/practices covered, bearing in mind the level?
- Were pupils given exposure to Christianity in various cultural, theological and geographical forms?
- Was there any expectation that pupils might respond to Christian beliefs and claims using their own commitment and/or action?

These considerations should lead you on again to wider issues, including the following:

- Can children gain an accurate theological grasp of Christianity in its many forms?
- To what extent can beliefs be handled in the classroom in ways which are appropriate to the dynamic of the Christian message in the classroom?

Activity C4

Plan, implement and evaluate two or three pieces of teaching about Christianity along the lines explained above. In your evaluation, consider those basic principles of teaching about Christianity which informed our work in sections C1 and C2 of this unit.

Make sure that you plan at this level of detail. In particular, if you are not used to teaching, notice the function of the aim and the objectives: the aim gives an overall sense of what the teacher is trying to achieve in the lesson; whereas the objectives identify more precisely what smaller, detailed things the pupils ought to be able to achieve by the end of the lesson.

Begin your detailed planning only when you have identified the school or other place in which you intend to do this work, and have established agreement on the level of the class, the topic outline and other important factors. If possible, your two or three pieces of teaching should cover aspects of Christian beliefs, worship and practices.

Comment on activity C4

Can your experience be understood in the following terms? Here are three teachers' comments on their experience. First on the difficulty and consolations of the process, Richards (1994, p 8) writes as follows.

> My journey has not been without frustration and tears, but, as for most teachers I know, it has been sparked by the generosity of colleagues and above all by the good humour, common sense and honesty of the young people I love to be with.

Next, on the orientation of the process towards Christian values associated with the reign of God, Schipani (1995, p 305) makes the following point.

> 'Believing' and 'doing' must be brought together in a mutually influencing dynamic relationship. Consistent teaching principles must also be included together with the question of the place and the roles of educators as servant leaders; in other words, educators must educate for freedom, peace and justice, by educating in freedom and peace, and justly.

And finally on the role and commitment of the teacher, Rankin (1984, Preface) makes the following point.

> Some might conclude that the teacher with Christian convictions has to suppress them. This is not the case. Indeed the teacher's convictions can often become a valuable source for students trying to discover some of the things that it means to be a Christian. This should not, however, contradict the principle which leaves students free.

Readers

You will find relevant material in J. Astley and L.J. Francis (eds) (1996), *Christian Theology and Religious Education: connections and contradictions*, London, SPCK.

Bibliography

Becher, V. (1995), *Black Christians: black church traditions in Britain*, Birmingham, Westhill RE Centre.

Christian Education Movement (1990), *Exploring A Theme: the environment*, Derby, CEM.

Christian Education Movement (1991a), *Exploring A Theme: when Christians meet*, Derby, CEM.

Christian Education Movement (1991b), *Exploring A Theme: water*, Derby, CEM.

Christian Education Movement (1993a), *Teaching RE: harvest 5-11*, Derby, CEM.

Christian Education Movement (1993b), *Teaching RE: harvest 11-16*, Derby, CEM.

Christian Education Movement (1993c), *Teaching RE: Easter 5-11*, Derby, CEM.

Christian Education Movement (1993d), *Teaching RE: Easter 11-16*, Derby, CEM.

Christian Education Movement (1994a), *Teaching RE: Pentecost 5-11*, Derby, CEM.

Christian Education Movement (1994b), *Teaching RE: Pentecost, 11-16*, Derby, CEM.

Christian Education Movement (1997a), *Teaching RE: the bible 5-11*, Derby, CEM.

Christian Education Movement (1997b), *Teaching RE: the bible 11-16*, Derby, CEM.

Cooling, M. (1992), *Christianity Topic Book Three*, Norwich, RMEP.

Cooling, T. (1994), *Concept Cracking: exploring Christian beliefs in school*, Nottingham, Stapleford Project.

Cooling, T. (1997), Theology goes to school: the story of the Stapleford Project, *Journal of Christian Education*, 40, 1, 47-60.

Farley, E. (1995), The Structure of Theological Study, in Gill, R. (ed.), *Readings in Modern Theology*, London, SPCK, pp 255-266.

Goldman, R.J. (1964), *Religious Thinking from Childhood to Adolescence*, London, Routledge and Kegan Paul.

Grimmitt, M. (1987), *Religious Education and Human Development*, Great Wakering, McCrimmons.

Groome, T. (1991), *Sharing Faith: a comprehensive guide to religious education and pastoral care*, San Francisco, Harper.

Hirst, P. (1974), *Knowledge and the Curriculum*, London, Routledge and Kegan Paul.

Jackson, R. (1997), *Religious Education: an interpretative approach*, London, Hodder and Stoughton.

Jackson, R., Barratt, M. and Everington, J. (1994), *Bridges to Religions: teacher's resource book*, Oxford, Heinemann.

Küng, H. (1995), *Christianity: its essence and history*, London, SCM Press.

Mercier, S.C. (1996), *Interpreting Religions: Muslims*, Oxford, Heinemann.

Palmer, M. (1991), *What Should We Teach? Christians and education in a pluralist world*, Geneva, World Council of Churches, 1993.

Rankin, J. (ed.) (1982a), *The Chichester Project: Christian communities*, Cambridge, Lutterworth Press.

Rankin, J. (ed.) (1982b), *The Chichester Project: Christian experience*, Cambridge, Lutterworth Press.

Rankin, J. (ed.) (1982c), *The Chichester Project: Christian worship*, Cambridge, Lutterworth Press.

Rankin, J. (ed.) (1982d), *The Chichester Project: Jesus*, Cambridge, Lutterworth Press.

Rankin, J. (ed.) (1984a), *The Chichester Project: Christmas and Easter*, Cambridge, Lutterworth Press.

Rankin, J. (ed.) (1984b), *The Chichester Project : Christian ethics*, Cambridge, Lutterworth Press.

Rankin, J. (ed.) (1984c), *The Chichester Project: exploring the bible*, Cambridge, Lutterworth Press.

Rankin, J. (ed.) (1985), *The Chichester Project: the eucharist*, Cambridge, Lutterworth Press.

Rankin, J. (ed.) (1986), *The Chichester Project: Christianity*, Cambridge, Lutterworth Press.

Read, G. *et al* (1986), *Westhill Project RE 5-16: Christianity: teacher's manual*, Cheltenham, Stanley Thornes.

Read, G. *et al* (1987a), *Westhill Project RE 5-16: Christians 1*, Cheltenham, Stanley Thornes.

Read, G. *et al* (1987b), *Westhill Project RE 5-16: Christians 2*, Cheltenham, Stanley Thornes.

Read, G. *et al* (1987c), *Westhill Project RE 5-16: Christians 3*, Cheltenham, Stanley Thornes.

Read, G. *et al* (1987d), *Westhill Project RE 5-16: Christians 4*, Cheltenham, Stanley Thornes.

Read, G. *et al* (1987e), *Westhill Project RE 5-16: Christians photopack*, Cheltenham, Stanley Thornes.

Richards, C. (1994), *Who Would A Teacher Be?* London, Darton, Longman and Todd.

Robson, G. (1995), *Interpreting Religions: Christians*, Oxford, Heinemann.

Rodger, A. (1982), *Education and Faith in an Open Society*, Edinburgh, Handsel Press.

Schipani, D. (1995), Liberation theology and religious education, in R. Miller (ed.), *Theologies of Religious Education*, Birmingham, Alabama, Religious Education Press, pp 286-313.

School Curriculum and Assessment Authority (1994), *Model Two: questions and teachings*, London, SCAA.

Schussler Fiorenza, E. (1995), Commitment and Critical Enquiry, in Gill, R. (ed.), *Readings in Modern Theology*, London, SPCK, pp 267-277.

Smith, W.C. (1978), *The Meaning and End of Religion*, London, SPCK.

Thacker, H. (1995), *The Haffertee Handbook*, Oxford, Lion.

Warwick RE Project (1996a), *Bridges to Religions: teacher's resource book Key Stage 1*, Oxford, Heinemann.

Warwick RE Project (1996b), *Bridges to Religions: teacher's resource book Lower Key Stage 2*, Oxford, Heinemann.

Warwick RE Project (1996c), *Bridges to Religions: teacher's resource book upper key stage 2*, Oxford, Heinemann.

Warwick RE Project (1996d), *Lucy's Sunday*, Oxford, Heinemann.

Warwick RE Project (1996e), *Meeting Christians Book 1*, Oxford, Heinemann.

Warwick RE Project (1996f), *Meeting Christians Book 2*, Oxford, Heinemann.

Watts, F. and Williams, M. (1988), *The Psychology of Religious Knowing*, London, Cassell.

Wright, C. (1995a), *Key Christian Beliefs*, Oxford, Lion.

Wright, C. (1995b), *Key Christian Beliefs: teacher handbook and photocopy master*, Oxford, Lion.

Teaching about Judaism and Islam

Teaching about Judaism and Islam

Unit A

Historical outlines

Rabbi Professor Dan Cohn-Sherbok

Lavinia Cohn-Sherbok

Department of Theology and Religious Studies

University of Wales, Lampeter

and

Dr J. Mark Halstead

Rolle Faculty of Education

University of Plymouth

Contents

Introduction

The units in this module are constructed differently from most of the other modules. In this unit we present two separate sections offering historical outlines of Judaism and Islam. Each section is preceded by its own aims, but the recommended reading and the bibliography for all the sections are put at the end of the unit. Part A1 concerns Judaism and part A2 concerns Islam.

The second unit in the module uses the same method of placing the two religions in historical order, first Judaism then Islam, and deals with contemporary practices and current debates in the each religion. The third unit, again using the same method, presents ideas for teaching each religion in the classroom. The module invites you to work through both religions starting with this unit and with the older of the two, Judaism, and then to follow their development, their adjustment to the modern world and in the contemporary issues that occupy them. If you want to follow only one of the religions, then all you have to do is to select the relevant parts of the three units. Yet, we think that trying to work on a broad front will enrich you, because there are similarities between these two monotheistic religions and the challenges they present to modern readers.

A1 Judaism

Aims

After working through part A1 of this unit, you should be able to:

- understand the outline of the history of the Jewish people;
- explain why there are Jewish communities all over the world;
- understand the importance of the State of Israel to Jews today.

Overview

This part of the unit provides you with a brief overview of the history of the Jews from biblical times until the present day. Judaism is an historical religion and Jews understand themselves and their beliefs in the context of God revealing himself in and through historical events. Since both Christianity and Islam grew out of this Jewish understanding of God, it is important that you have some familiarity with the early beliefs of the Jews. At the same time, you must remember that Judaism is a living religion and that Jewish history and thought continued after the time of Jesus and Muhammad. The ground which is covered in this unit is vast, therefore the information presented is inevitably partial and selective. It does, however, focus on the issues which will help you understand the background to the diversity which is to be found in the Jewish community today.

Hebrew is the sacred language of the Jews. It is still used for worship and it has been revived to become the language of the modern State of Israel. At the time of Jesus, however, and for several centuries after, the everyday language of the Jewish people was Aramaic, a later dialect of Hebrew, and this is the language of the Talmud, the great compendium of Jewish law. In addition, the Jews of Eastern Europe spoke Yiddish, a language based on German but written in Hebrew letters, while the Jews of Islamic countries used Ladino. In the following units, all foreign words are translated; they should be pronounced phonetically, since they are transliterated from a different script.

Biblical Judaism

Most Christians are familiar with the Hebrew scriptures - or the Old Testament as they call the collection. At the outset it is important to stress that most Jews do believe that the scriptures record their own history, that they themselves are the physical descendants of the group of Semitic tribes who were enslaved in Egypt and who were led to freedom in the Promised Land (present-day Israel) by the prophet Moses. Furthermore, Orthodox Jews accept as a matter of faith that the first five books of the scriptures (Genesis, Exodus, Leviticus, Numbers and Deuteronomy) were directly dictated to Moses by God. Collectively the five books are known as the Torah, which can be translated as 'law' or 'teaching'.

This hypothesis, that the Torah was written down by Moses, has been called into question since the sixteenth century. There are notable stylistic differences within the text; certain stories are duplicated (see Genesis 12 and Genesis 26); there are various anachronisms (such as the list of the kings of Edom in Genesis 36); there are inconsistencies (such as the different orders of creation in Genesis 1 and 2) and, perhaps most strikingly, God is called by different names. Sometimes God is known as JHWH; this name is never articulated by Jews and it is translated in the English text as 'the LORD'. Other times God is known as Elohim, which is translated into English as 'God'.

This has led biblical scholars to conjecture that the five books are the product of several different sources. The best-known exposition of this theory is that of the two nineteenth century German scholars, Karl Heinrich Graf and Julius Wellhausen. Known as the Documentary Hypothesis, the theory suggests that the earliest source, known as J (because it calls God JHWH) originated in southern Israel in the ninth century BCE. The second source is thought to have come from the north in the eighth century BCE; it is known as E because God here is Elohim. The D source, which is mainly to be found in the Book of Deuteronomy, was probably composed in the seventh century BCE and the P source, which is primarily concerned with priestly ritual may have had its origin in the sixth century BCE (Drane, 1983).

Nonetheless Orthodox Jews continue to believe that the Torah was given directly by God and that consequently all its laws must be obeyed in their entirety. Altogether there are 613 laws in the Torah. These cover both general ethical precepts ('You shall not steal'), specific prohibitions ('You shall not muzzle the ox as he treads the grain'), detailed dietary laws ('You shall not seethe the kid in its mother's milk') and precise ritual instruction ('You shall sacrifice one kid of the goats for a sin offering and two lambs of the first year for a sacrifice of peace offerings').

The Jews divide the rest of the scriptures into Prophecy (Nevi'im in Hebrew) and Writings (Ketuvim). Although these are considered to have been inspired by God, they are not thought to have been directly dictated by God. They cover the history of the Jewish people from their conquest of the Promised Land, the establishment of an independent kingdom under Saul, David and Solomon, the later division of the kingdom, the destruction of the ten northern tribes by the Assyrians and the conquest of the southern tribes by the Babylonians. The story ends with the return of the Jews to the land in the fifth century BCE after seventy years in exile, and the rebuilding of the Temple in Jerusalem. There are also books of poetry, aphorisms and prophecy, all of which provide commentary on the historical events experienced by the Jewish people (Blenkinsopp, 1977).

Activity A1

Briefly outline the various ways in which Torah is of importance within traditional Judaism.

Comment on activity A1

The reason for this activity was to enable you to explain the status of the Torah in the Jewish religion. This is a vast task and a great many books have been devoted to it by eminent scholars. However you should have been able to identify the following issues.

- The term Torah is used in several different ways by Jews. It can refer to the first five books of the Hebrew scriptures. It can mean the whole corpus of Jewish law, both written and oral, and it can be used to describe the whole traditional Jewish way of life.

- The scroll on which the Torah (in the sense of the first five books) is written is the most sacred object in the synagogue. The reading from the Torah Scroll forms a central part of the Jewish liturgy and it is described as the 'tree of life to those who grasp it'. Thus the Torah is the central revelation of Judaism, parallel to the Qur'an in Islam or Jesus himself in Christianity.

- The fact that its authorship has been called into question by modern biblical scholars is irrelevant to Orthodox Jews. It has, however, made Reform movements within Judaism possible.

- Because the Torah is believed to be divinely inspired, all parts are of equal worth. It is just as important to the traditional Jew to keep the details of the food laws as it is to avoid theft and covetousness. It is important to stress that the reason for keeping the laws is because they are commanded by God. It is nothing to do with personal health or maintaining community solidarity.

First century Judaism

The New Testament is the product of the Christian Church and its constituent books were written in the late first and early second centuries CE. By that time the Temple in Jerusalem, the central shrine of the Jews, had been destroyed by the Romans in their crushing of the Jewish rebellion after 70 CE. Jesus himself, who was a practising Jew, lived earlier, at a time when the Temple was still standing and the Jews enjoyed a privileged religious status in the Roman Empire.

We know a great deal of the religious life of early first century Jews, partly from the New Testament, partly from the writings of the Jewish historian Josephus who lived through the rebellion and partly from the recently discovered Dead Sea Scrolls. In addition, later rabbinic writings record many details of the traditional Temple ritual (Sandmel, 1978).

The New Testament mentions both Pharisees and Sadducees. Josephus also describes them and he mentions another religious party whom he calls the Essenes. This seems to have been a monastic sect whose members regarded themselves as the last of the righteous ones of Israel. They expected that the last days were soon to dawn and, in preparation, they withdrew themselves from society. The Dead Sea Scrolls, which were found in caves near Qumran, were produced by a community that shared many of the Essene characteristics described by Josephus.

The Sadducees were a small, aristocratic group of hereditary priests. They were responsible for organising and maintaining the worship in the Jerusalem Temple. This involved daily animal sacrifices and regular annual festivals. Their leader was the High Priest who had a political as well as a religious role. Although the Sadducees accepted the authority of the Hebrew scriptures, they did not allow further oral interpretation of the text. Consequently they did not believe in doctrines such as the resurrection of the dead, or personal immortality, because they are not clearly stated.

According to Josephus, it was not the Sadducees but the Pharisees who enjoyed the support of the people. The New Testament presents a highly biased, negative view of this group, but it should be set against the rabbinic picture as shown in the later Mishnah and Talmud (see below). They are described as scribes and sages and they were skilled in the study and interpretation of scripture. They did not in any way want to destroy the Temple and its rituals since they saw them as given by God, but they regarded themselves, rather than the hereditary priests, as the moral leaders of Israel and they saw their role as explaining the relevance of the law to the problems of everyday life.

The centre of the Pharisees' activity was the synagogue. By the first century, every Jewish settlement had a synagogue, a place where the people could congregate to study the law. It is probable that the institution first started in Babylon in the sixth century BCE, during the period of the Exile. The Temple had been destroyed in 586 BCE, and the local synagogue became the place where the Jewish faith was kept alive while the ritual sacrifices were in abeyance. Even when the Temple was rebuilt in the fifth century BCE, the synagogue survived as the local centre of education and worship (Gilbert, 1988).

Rabbinic Judaism

The destruction of the Temple in Jerusalem in 70 CE was a disaster for the Jewish people. It removed the central focus of their worship. Sacrifices for the redemption of sin could no longer be offered because the Book of Deuteronomy teaches that sacrifice could only be performed in the one place. The Sadducees, the hereditary priests, lost the reason for their existence and it seemed as if the Jewish religion, like so many other cults in the ancient world, would soon disappear.

Its survival was the result of the activity of the Pharisees. According to the tradition, during the very siege of Jerusalem a prominent sage, one Johanan ben Zakkai, received permission to set up an academy for the study of Jewish law in

Javneh. Under Johanan's successor, Gamaliel II, the official Jewish court, the Sanhedrin, was re-established. This body was dedicated to the discussion of Jewish law and practice. Scholars came from far and wide to listen to and to share in the deliberations. It was during this period that the canon of scripture was agreed, a regular pattern of daily prayer organised and some of the old Temple rituals adapted for use in the local synagogues.

By the third century CE, the oral interpretation of the law had become extremely complex. It was felt that some form of codification was necessary. This fell to Judah ha-Nasi (the prince) who was the president of the Sanhedrin at that time. His work is known as the Mishnah (literally oral law). It records the debates on such subjects as agriculture, festivals, marriage, divorce, criminal law, Temple ritual and ritual purity. The minority view was always expressed first, as in 'Rabbi Johanan says...' and the final decision is set down as a collective agreement 'but the sages declare...'.

The Mishnah proved to be a solid foundation on which further discussion could be based. Israel was not the only site of academies. Many Jews had remained behind in Babylon after the exile of the sixth century BCE and there was a vibrant community there. In the third century CE, important academies were established and there was constant travelling between the various centres. By the end of the fourth century, scholars in Israel gathered together the oral teachings based on the framework of Judah ha-Nasi's Mishnah. Similarly another great work was being produced in Babylonia at the end of the sixth century. These are known as the Jerusalem and the Babylonian Talmud respectively. The latter in particular is a massive work of approximately two and a half million words. In modern editions, the Mishnah is printed in the centre of the page and the later commentary (the Gemara) is set around it, so it is clear how the discussions developed. The Talmud has been compared with a great ocean, with inexhaustible depths. To this day it remains the cornerstone of Jewish education. For the pious Jew, study is a life-long commitment and the Talmud is a never-ending source of information, guidance, challenge and fascination.

Dispersion

Jews lived in Babylonia from the time of the exile (sixth century BCE). By the first century, there were Jewish communities in the major trading towns throughout the Roman Empire. They remained separate from their non-Jewish neighbours by their insistence on keeping the Sabbath (the seventh day of rest) and by their distinctive food laws and ritual practices. In most places under the Romans, the Jews maintained a harmonious relationship and were given various privileges in recognition of their religious duties.

By the sixth century CE, Christianity had become the dominant religion of the Roman Empire and Jews suffered many civil disabilities under Christian rule. However, Babylonia largely remained outside the influence of the Church and the academies there continued their activities. In the seventh century, Muhammad in Arabia hoped to convert the Jews to his own vision of Allah, the one true God, and his role as prophet. The Jews refused to accept him and Muhammad turned against them.

Nevertheless, in the subsequent centuries Jewish communities often did well under Islamic rule. Provided they accepted the political reality of the Islamic state, they were guaranteed exemption from military service and they enjoyed judicial autonomy and religious tolerance. They did have to pay an extra tax and to wear distinctive clothing, but this had the effect of drawing the community together and helping to preserve their special identity. Because there was a free movement of peoples in the empire, the Jews could trade freely, establish new centres and the legal decisions of the academies could be spread throughout the Jewish world. By the tenth century, there were flourishing communities throughout North Africa, Arabia, Israel and, particularly, Spain (Gilbert, 1988).

Things were not so happy in Christian Europe. Christianity emerged as a sect within Judaism and the Christians believed that they had inherited the rights and privileges of the true Israel. The New Testament in various places contrasts the Jews' blindness with Jesus' enlightenment, and the blame for the death of Jesus is laid squarely on the upper echelons of the Jewish community. Some modern New Testament scholars have pointed out that this anti-Jewish bias infused the Gospel traditions for political reasons: it was not sensible to accuse the all-powerful Romans of murdering the saviour of the universe. Nonetheless, this Christian hatred has caused untold suffering for the Jewish people (Gilbert, 1988).

During the First Crusade in the eleventh century, Jews were massacred in the Rhinelands. As early as 1144, Jews were accused of using the blood of Christian children in making Passover unleavened bread, and this libel spread throughout Europe. The Jews were forced out of trade by the restrictive practices of the Christian guilds; they were not allowed to own land and they were compelled to turn to money lending, which was a forbidden activity for Christians. In 1290, the entire Jewish community was expelled from England. At the time of the Black Death, Jews were publicly accused of poisoning wells. Finally in 1492, after the Christian conquest of Muslim Spain, all Jews were expelled from Spanish soil. The great Iberian community was scattered. The exception to this catalogue of persecution was Poland. Here the Jews were actively encouraged to settle, to manage the estates of the noblemen and to engage in trade (Parkes, 1976).

Activity A2

Explore why you think Jews tended to have an easier time in Muslim than in Christian lands.

Comments on activity A2

You may have thought about the following factors:

- Parts of the New Testament have a strong anti-Jewish bias. Jews are identified with unjust Roman provincial government and are perceived as blind and obstinate in their rejection of Christ.
- Islam, unlike Christianity, is based on a direct written revelation and lays the same emphasis on law.
- The restrictive practices of the guilds and the Christian prohibition against usury forced the Jews into a necessary, but highly unpopular, occupation.
- Islam teaches tolerance towards the 'Peoples of the Book' (namely Christians and Jews), in contrast to the exclusivist view of salvation in Christianity.

Rise of Hasidism

By the later Middle Ages, it was recognised that there were two different groups of Jews in the world: those who had their origin in Spain and the Islamic countries and those who came from Christian Europe. This division still exists today. The former are known as the Sephardim and the latter as the Ashkenazim. They have different liturgies and slightly different customs. The Ashkenazim, in particular, were known for their piety, their strict adherence to the Torah and for their talmudic scholarship (Katz, 1961).

Large communities grew up in Eastern Europe because the rulers of Poland and Lithuania provided a secure base for communal existence. However, in 1648 the Cossacks, under their leader Bogdan Chmielnicki, rebelled against the Polish gentry. Large numbers of Jews were murdered as they were perceived as serving the interests of the nobility. There were further disturbances in the 1730s and 40s and an entire Jewish village was butchered in 1768. Increasingly the Jews of Poland began to look for a different form of Judaism.

The founder of the new religious movement was Israel ben Eliezer, known as the Baal Sem Tov (Master of the Good Name). With a group of disciples, he encouraged ordinary Jews to have an intense mystical relationship with God. He taught that serving God should be an occasion for joy and he encouraged his followers to sing and dance during worship and to make every aspect of daily life a form of devotion. His followers became known as the Hasidim (pious ones) and, after his death, the movement spread throughout Poland and beyond (Dawidowicz, 1966).

The Hasidim follow a particular leader, known as a Zaddik (righteous one). He is their mentor and he is seen as the channel through which God's grace flows to earth. By observing the Zaddik, the individual Hasid can see how God should be worshipped. There are several Hasidic groups today. Most of them, since the destruction of European Jewry in the Holocaust, are based in the United States. The Zaddik of each group is a direct descendant of one of the Baal Shem Tov's original disciples. Even today they hold court, give mass audiences and offer individual advice. Hasidim are distinctive in their appearance. The men characteristically wear black hats, black suits and sport beards and side-curls. Their wives dress modestly and are encouraged to have large families. Perhaps the easiest way to catch a glimpse of their culture is through the novels of Chaim Potok, such as *The Promise* (1969) or *My Name is Asher Lev* (1972).

By no means all the Jews of Eastern Europe followed the Hasidic way. The traditional rabbis (teachers) fought back and continued to insist that the way to God was through the painstaking study of the law. They disapproved of the exuberance of the new movement, believing that it undermined serious scholarship. Today, however, assimilation and secularism threaten the community. In general the Hasidim are admired by the Orthodox as dedicated religious Jews.

Enlightenment and Reform

Meanwhile times were changing in Western Europe. Increasingly Jews were tolerated and came to be regarded as full citizens of their countries. For example, the revolutionary National Assembly of France in 1789 issued a declaration proclaiming that all men are born and remain free and that no religious group should be persecuted provided that they keep the law. In 1791 full citizenship rights were granted to all French Jews. It happened rather later in Germany, but by 1871 Jews were recognised as citizens of the Reich in every respect (Katz, 1973).

Meanwhile, in the Jewish community itself, there was a feeling that Jews must feel comfortable in the modern world. In the mid nineteenth century an important scholar, Moses Mendelssohn, translated the first five books of the scriptures into German and wrote a commentary giving a rational explanation for the laws of the Torah. Jewish schools were opened which offered a secular as well as a religious education and young Jews gladly took on the re- sponsibilities of political citizenship as well as those of their religious heritage.

Jews were no longer insulated from mainstream western civilisation and many felt that the traditional forms of worship were irrelevant and unseemly. The first Reform temple was built in Seesen in the early nineteenth century. Services included choral singing, hymns and prayers in German as well as the traditional Hebrew, and much of the old liturgy was cut. So, for example, the prayers for the coming of the Messiah and the restoration of Zion were removed because it was felt that there should be no possibility of a conflict of political interest. Similarly these Reform groups were influenced by the findings of modern biblical scholars and many rejected the belief that the Torah was divinely inspired in every respect. As a result they felt free to modify the traditional dietary laws and even to work on Saturdays.

The movement spread throughout Western Europe. The west London Synagogue for Reform Jews, for example, was founded in England in 1841. At the same time, immigrants also took it to the United States. The first conference of American rabbis took place in Philadelphia in 1869, and in 1875 the first American rabbinical seminary was founded. Then in 1885 a group of American rabbis declared the principles of their movement. While accepting that the moral laws of the Torah were binding for all time, only rituals which were seen to be spiritually edifying were retained. The dietary laws and the laws of ritual purity were rejected as anachronistic and, instead of looking for a future Messiah, Reform Jews were urged to establish peace and justice in the here and now (Meyer, 1988).

Traditional Jews were horrified by these developments and formed their own organisations. At the same time, up until the First World War, the old way of life in Eastern Europe continued largely untouched by these modern movements.

Holocaust

Between 1881 and 1921, the Jews of Eastern Europe suffered a series of violent attacks. Anti-Semitism became official state policy in Russia. It was a time of political turmoil and violent outbreaks were linked to nationalist outbursts. The Czars did little to protect their Jewish subjects and increasingly the Jews of Lithuania, Poland and Russia looked to the United States as the place where they could settle and live in peace. Western European Jewry, however, felt secure. In the First World War, Jews fought in the armies of both sides and the Jews of Germany, in particular, felt part of the fabric of German society.

The rise of National Socialism changed all this. Between 1930 and 1933, over six million people were unemployed in Germany. Hitler's message of intense German patriotism, coupled with virulent anti-Semitism, appealed to the hard-pressed German people. In his book *Mein Kampf* (*My Struggle*), Hitler taught that the Germans had lost the war as a result of the treachery of German socialists, liberals and pacifists. The Russian revolution was a Jewish Bolshevik plot. He maintained that the Jews were parasitical vermin who were determined to contaminate the blood of the Aryan, German, race.

Once the Nazi party gained power in 1933, a series of anti-Jewish measures were introduced. All sexual liaisons between Jews and non-Jews were classified as crimes against the state. All Jewish communal bodies were put under the control of the Gestapo and there were a series of attacks on Jewish people and their property. In response, Jews desperately tried to leave Germany, but it was not easy. There was a world-wide economic depression at the time. The United States and other western nations were reluctant to add to their unemployment problems and to accept new citizens. People did what they could, sometimes even sending their children out of the country by themselves. All too many, however, were compelled to stay.

Once war was declared, emigration became impossible. The Germans invaded Poland in 1939 and in every conquered town the large Jewish population was compelled to take part in a vast work programme. By 1941, when Hitler had moved into Russia, troops were rounding up Jews in their thousands and shooting them. In the following year, at a secret conference, the Final Solution came into being. Six death camps were built at Chelmno, Auschwitz, Sobibor, Majdanek, Treblinka and Belzek. There Jews were systematically transported. The young and fit were selected for work - for a time. The elderly and the helpless were gassed immediately.

The figures speak for themselves. Hitler's intention was undoubtedly to destroy world Jewry. In Europe he nearly succeeded. It has been estimated that 90% of the Jewish population of Poland, Estonia, Latvia, Lithuania, Germany and Austria were murdered and 70% of that of the Ukraine, occupied Russia, Belgium, Yugoslavia, Romania and Norway. Probably about six million died and the old Jewish life of Eastern Europe was destroyed for ever (Dawidowicz, 1975).

The State of Israel

Through the vicissitudes of history, the dream of returning to the Promised Land remained an essential part of Jewish consciousness. Every year, during the Passover meal, the participants promise themselves 'Next year in Jerusalem!' After the first outbreak of violence against the Jews in Russia in 1882, several thousand left for Palestine and started small Jewish settlements there. However, the real founder of the Zionist movement was Theodor Herzl

(1860-1904), an Austrian journalist. In 1896, in his book *Der Judenstaat* (*The Jewish State*), he advocated the founding of a Jewish state as a refuge against anti-Semitic attack. The following year he convened the First Zionist Congress in Basle and the World Zionist Organisation was founded. For the rest of his short life, Herzl worked tirelessly to build up international support for the project (O'Brian, 1986).

From its earliest days there were different parties within the movement. The World Zionist Organization was essentially secular in orientation and, in response, the Mizrachi party was founded, which was to become the religious wing of the movement. Meanwhile there was a steady stream of settlement in the land and, by the end of the First World War, the Jewish community in Palestine numbered approximately 90,000 people; by 1929, it had increased to 160,000. Increasingly the Arab population of Palestine became unhappy with this flood of immigrants.

At this stage the British government was administering the land. Although the British had declared sympathy for Zionist aspirations in the Balfour Declaration of 1917, they used their power to cut down on Jewish settlement. In 1937 a Royal Commission advocated the division of the land into a Jewish and an Arab state, but this was rejected in a government White Paper in 1939. In any event, war broke out and there was no further possibility of further emigration for the duration. Once the full enormity of the Holocaust had been revealed in 1945, the international community was in a quandary. The war had left thousands of destitute displaced persons. Their non-Jewish friends and neighbours had betrayed them and there was nothing for them in their old homes. What was to be done? The then President of the United States, Harry S. Truman, was anxious to secure the Jewish vote in the forthcoming elections and was, in any case, personally sympathetic to Zionism. In late 1947 it was agreed in the United Nations that Palestine should be partitioned into a Jewish and an Arab state. The Arabs were not prepared to accept this, but after a series of Jewish military successes, on 14th May 1948 the independence of the Jewish State of Israel was formally declared.

This was not the end of the story. War broke out again between Jew and Arab in 1954, in 1967 and in 1973. Nonetheless Israel has survived. By its laws all Jews are entitled to settle and make their home there. It is regarded as a permanent place of safety in the event of another holocaust and it commands the loyalty of the world-wide Jewish community. Indeed, today, support for the State of Israel is one of the major factors in Jewish self-understanding (Laqueur, 1976).

Activity A3

Explain the loyalty of the Jewish community today to the modern State of Israel.

Comments on activity A3

Again this is a huge subject and members of the Jewish community themselves will give very different answers - explaining why the different political parties in Israel have different aspirations for the land and have different attitudes towards the present peace initiatives. Nonetheless a number of crucial factors will have emerged:

- The land was promised by God to Abraham and to Moses for all time. Thus Orthodox Jews feel that the Jews have a right to all the land specified in the Book of Genesis.
- A longing for the Promised Land has been enshrined in the liturgy and possession of the land is seen as God's will for the Jews.
- The long history of anti-Semitism has led Jews to believe that they will only be safe if they have a land of their own like other nations.
- The Holocaust was the pivotal event which convinced Jews of all persuasions, even the most assimilated, that a Jewish State was a necessity.

A2 Islam

Aims

After working through part A2 of this unit, you should:

- have some knowledge of the historical origins of Islam and its place in the modern world;
- be aware of the importance of the Prophet Muhammad, the Holy Qur'an and the shari'a (divine law) within Islam;
- have some understanding of the influences that have affected contemporary relations between Islam and the West;
- be able to appreciate some aspects of Muslim culture.

Overview

This part of the unit begins with a description of the life and times of the Prophet Muhammad and of the revelations he received which were transcribed as the Holy Qur'an. This is followed by a discussion of the rapid growth of Islam as a major world religion and the establishment of a number of Muslim empires. The centrality of divine law (shari'a) in Islamic civilisation is stressed, and examples are given of some of the main features of Islamic culture. The unit concludes with an overview of the contemporary Muslim world and a discussion of the relationship between Islam and the West.

Christian bias?

There are four main kinds of Christian writings about Islam. First, there is an extensive tradition of polemic against Islam; in earlier centuries, Muhammad was likely to be described as a false prophet or anti-Christ, but nowadays criticism tends to focus on the 'fanatical' or 'uncompromising' nature of Islam. Second, there is the proselytising tradition, where the point of learning about Islam is simply to facilitate the successful preaching of the gospel to Muslims (see, for example, Marsh, 1975). Third, there is what might be called the Christian orientalist approach, in which Islam is studied with meticulous scholarship, but scholarship which takes for granted the superiority of western values such as the critical study of religion, so that conclusions are reached which are in serious conflict with Islamic perspectives (cf. Said, 1978). Finally, there are those Christians (such as Bishop Kenneth Cragg, 1956) who approach Islam in a spirit of humility, recognising that in spite of doctrinal differences they may have much to learn from Islamic spirituality and devotion. The author of this unit seeks to adopt this fourth approach. He has studied Islam and interacted closely with Muslims for over thirty years, and he writes from a position of deep respect for the faith of Islam. The unit is written in a desire to help readers to share this respect, and to understand the religion as if through the eyes of a believer.

What is Islam?

'Islam' is an Arabic word meaning surrender or submission, and a 'Muslim' is one who submits to the divine will. Both words derive from the same root (slm) as the Arabic word for peace and well-being (*salaam*), and the name Islam thus implies an acceptance of the belief that true peace can be attained only through submission to the will of God. At the very heart of Islam therefore are values which are antithetical to the contemporary western values of personal and moral autonomy, self-worth and self-fulfilment.

Muslims believe that Islam is the original and natural religion of the whole of humanity, and that the religion taught by Muhammad and based on the revelations contained in the Qur'an is simply a re-expression of the one true religion which God revealed through a series of prophets since the beginning of the world. On a Muslim worldview, human beings, though the summit of God's creation, are forgetful and prone to go astray and therefore in need of the guidance provided by divine revelation. Since the earlier revelations were distorted or corrupted over time, God sent the 'seal of the Prophets', Muhammad, to re-establish the one true religion. Humans are free to choose or reject this religion, but their eternal destiny depends on their choice.

For Muslims, there is no distinction between sacred and secular, for religion covers every aspect of life. Religion, as Muslims never tire of saying, is an entire way of life. This approach to religion has several consequences, including the following:

- Muslim philosophers, theologians and jurists have attempted to systematise a comprehensive code of law based on Islamic sources which provides guidance for every aspect of life. The shari'a (religious law) is therefore at the very heart of life in Islam.
- Islamic culture and civilisation can only be understood from a religious perspective.
- Local customs, rituals and traditions are permeated by religion and their continuation is justified in religious terms, even where their links with Qur'anic teaching are tenuous.
- The term 'Islam' has come to apply not only to belief in the eternal truths revealed by God, but also to the society which embodies these beliefs in practice.
- Muslims believe that, since their religion is universal, it must be capable of meeting all the demands of contemporary life. However, Muslims have sometimes had difficulties responding to the vast expansion of knowledge that has occurred in the increasingly secular West in recent times. One response has been the 'Islamization of knowledge' (see International Institute of Islamic Thought, 1989).

Arabic is the sacred language for Muslims since it was the mother tongue of the Prophet Muhammad and the language in which the Holy Qur'an was revealed. All Muslims therefore, irrespective of their mother tongue, are expected to use Arabic in their prayers and to read the Qur'an in the original language. There are various systems of transliterating Arabic words into English, and readers will sometimes find Muhammad written as Mohamet, the Qur'an as the Koran and Makka as Mecca. The English meaning of all Arabic words appearing in this unit is given in brackets the first time the term is used. Useful glossaries are contained in several of the readers listed above.

The Islamic calendar dates from the *hijra* (migration) of the Prophet Muhammad and his companions from Makka to Medina on 16 July 622.

However, in accordance with Qur'anic teaching, the Islamic year is made up of twelve lunar months of either 29 or 30 days, and so is eleven days shorter than the western solar year. This means that Islamic festivals and the month of fasting do not start on the same date on the western calendar each year, but move gradually backwards through the seasons. It also means that a person who is 70 years old according to the Islamic calendar is not as old as a 70 year-old in the West (you may care to work out by how much!). The year 2000 in the Gregorian calendar corresponds to 1420-1 AH (Anno Hegirae).

The Prophet Muhammad

It is very dangerous to draw parallels between the position of Muhammad in relation to Islam and the position of Jesus in relation to Christianity. Muslims do not consider Muhammad divine, and do not worship him in any circumstances. He had no superhuman characteristics, and his humanity is seen in the fact that he engaged in trade, married (several times), had a household, had children, led his followers into battle and on pilgrimage, died and was buried. But for Muslims he is at the same time the seal of the prophets, chosen by God to convey God's final message to the world, and the prototype of human perfection, an example to all believers of moral, religious, domestic, social and political virtue.

Muhammad was born in Makka in north-western Arabia in or around the year 570. Makka was an important trading city, a focal point for inter-tribal quarrels and a centre of pilgrimage. Most of the inhabitants were polytheists, worshipping a variety of deities including al-Manat (the goddess of fate), al-Uzza (the goddess of love) and Allat (a mother goddess), but there were also Jewish and Christian minorities. We do not know much about Muhammad's early life. He was orphaned at the age of six and brought up by his uncle Abu Talib. He seems to have developed an early reputation as a trustworthy negotiator and trader, and worked as an agent for a wealthy widow, Khadijah, whom in due course he married. They had six children. As he grew older, he spent an increasing amount of time in prayer and meditation in the mountains around Makka.

In the year 610, at the age of about 40, Muhammad was meditating in a cave on Mount Hira when he received his first divine revelation. The angel Jibra'il (Gabriel) appeared to him, proclaiming him God's messenger and commanding him to recite a message from God (the lines of which now form the first part of Surah 96 of the Qur'an). At first he was terrified and full of doubts but gradually, reassured by his wife Khadijah, he accepted his calling. From this time until his death in the year 632 he continued to receive messages which he believed were direct revelations from God. He memorised the messages, as did his close followers. Some were written down straight away by his followers (he himself was illiterate) and others were put into writing after his death.

By the year 613 he began to preach openly, proclaiming the oneness of God, the moral responsibility of humans to obey God, and the Day of Judgement. His preaching gained a mixed reception: some accepted his message and became Muslims, but many abused and ridiculed him and his followers. As he became more powerful in Makka, so opposition to him intensified, and when he was invited to migrate with his followers to Yathrib (later called Medina), he readily accepted. The migration in the year 622 marks the turning point in the development of Islam, because many of the citizens of Yathrib became Muslims and the first Muslim community thus came into being. Over the next few years, a series of raids, skirmishes and battles took place between the Muslims and the Makkans, many of them led by Muhammad himself, until finally, in the year 630, the Makkans were defeated and Muhammad returned in triumph to Makka. Many Makkans now chose to become Muslims, and Muhammad purged the ancient shrine of the Ka'ba of its idols and proclaimed Makka to be the sacred city of Islam. By the time of his death in the year 632, Muhammad was the most powerful statesman and military leader in Arabia, and widely accepted as the Prophet of God.

Judged from a contemporary western perspective, Muhammad may be criticised for his patriarchal values, his personal polygamy, his military and political connivance, and his severity against some of his Jewish opponents. But for Muslims such criticisms are totally irrelevant. Muhammad was God's messenger, the last in a long line of prophets. In his lifetime he was admired for his justice and piety, and it was his compelling personality which enabled him to achieve so much in integrating the social, the political and the spiritual into a unified whole. More than that, for Muslims across the ages he has been the perfect exemplar, the one whose piety and virtues all believers must seek to emulate. It was this belief which led Muslims in the years after his death to collect every possible *hadith* (narrative of Muhammad's words and actions), and the resulting body of *sunna* (traditions of the Prophet) became the next most important source of Islamic law after the Qur'an itself.

The Holy Qur'an

The word 'Qur'an' is the Arabic for 'recitation', and it is a collection of all the revelations received by Muhammad during his lifetime. The Qur'an occupies a place in Islam very similar to that occupied by Jesus in Christianity. Muslims believe it is literally the Word of God and that it embodies God's final and complete message to humans. Muhammad is thus in no sense the author of the

Qur'an - he simply recited the words which God chose to reveal to people through him. Muslims therefore treat the Qur'an with the utmost respect.

The final version of the Qur'an was put together some years after Muhammad's death. It consists of 114 surahs (chapters), but apart from the first surah, Al-Fatihah (The Opening), which is recited in all prayers, the surahs are arranged neither chronologically nor by subject matter, but according to length, with the longest placed first. Scholars have distinguished the shorter, Makkan surahs, which describe the oneness of God, human responsibility, the Day of Judgement and Heaven and Hell, from the longer, Madinan surahs which contain more detailed rules for living. Muslim scholarship is concerned with exposition, not textual criticism. To discuss the historical influences on the development of the religious ideas in the Qur'an, as attempted by some non-Muslim scholars, is worse than incoherent - it is blasphemous, since there are no historical influences on the Word of God.

Many Muslims agree that the poetic style and rhythms of the Qur'an are incomparable in their beauty, and it is capable of arousing the highest emotions in people. This in itself is taken as proof of its divine origin. No translation can capture the full meaning, the beauty and the spiritual depths of the Qur'an; indeed, for Muslims, a translation of the Qur'an is not the Qur'an at all, but an interpretation, though it may be useful for the purposes of study. For all ritual purposes, such as prayer, chanting, recitation and memorisation, the Arabic text must be used, even though Arabic is not the mother tongue of the majority of Muslims in the world today.

In addition to setting out the central religious beliefs of Islam and the religious and moral duties of Muslims, the Qur'an contains stories from the lives of the prophets, lists of legal injunctions and proscriptions, proverbial expressions, invective against the enemies of Islam, guidance on relations with Jews and Christians and declamations on the folly of human perversity and the reality of God's mercy.

There are numerous 'translations' of the Qur'an available for the English reader, the most readily available being:

- A. Yusuf Ali, *The Holy Qur'an: Text, translation and commentary* (Leicester: the Islamic Foundation, 1975).
- A.J. Arberry, *The Koran Interpreted* (Oxford University Press, 1964) - an attempt to recapture the poetic force of the original Arabic.
- N.J. Dawood, *The Koran* (Penguin, 1959) - note that the surahs are rearranged in this version for literary effect.
- M. Pickthall, *The Meaning of the Glorious Koran* (Mentor, 1953)   an English writer who became a Muslim.

But be warned: the Qur'an is not an 'easy read' for the westerner. Thomas Carlisle (1906), who was far from unsympathetic to Islam, called the Qur'an a 'wearisome, confused jumble'; Ninian Smart (1977), in more tempered language, called it 'structurally diffuse'. It may be best to begin by reading a particular story, such as the story of Joseph in Surah 12, or by studying a theme such as the mercy of God or the Day of Judgement, for which a concordance, index or other guide will be needed.

Activity A4

Read the main sections of the Qur'an that refer to Jesus (Surah 3: 45-59; Surah 4: 156-9; Surah 5: 17, 46, 75, 110-8; Surah 6: 85; Surah 9: 30; Surah 19: 22-33; Surah 43: 59, 63-4), and compare the teaching of the Qur'an about Jesus with Christian belief.

Comment on activity A4

You will have noted in particular that the Qur'an rejects the doctrines of the Trinity, the incarnation and the divinity of Jesus, but presents Jesus as the greatest prophet before Muhammad. The crucifixion, death and resurrection of Jesus are rejected, since the Qur'an states that God intervened at the last moment to save him from death. An alternative version of the virgin birth to the biblical one is provided. The ideas of atonement and justification by faith in Jesus are also rejected.

Spread of Islam

After the death of Muhammad, a *khalifa* (successor) was chosen from his closest companions: Abu Bakr, and on his death, Umar, and then Uthman. The fourth khalifa (from 656-661) was Ali, Muhammad's cousin who had married his daughter Fatima. The thirty years after the death of Muhammad were a time of great military expansion by the Muslims. At first the tribes who deserted Islam after Muhammad's death were subjugated, and soon all Arabia was conquered. The Muslims then turned their attention to the Byzantine Empire to the north and the Sassanian Empire to the east. By 661 the Levant, Iraq and Persia had been conquered and major advances had been made into North Africa. After the murder of Ali, the caliphate moved to the Umayyad family, who made their capital Damascus and continued the military expansion. By the year 750, the whole of North Africa was conquered and the Muslims had moved into Spain, while in the east the conquests stretched to the borders of India. The Muslim conquerors treated their new empire generously, reducing taxes and allowing Christians and Jews to worship as they wished.

Many of the conquered people turned to Islam, though there appear to have been few attempts to force them to do so. In the year 750 the Umayyads were overthrown by the descendants of Muhammad's uncle Abbas, and the Abbasid caliphate, with its capital in Baghdad, continued for the next 500 years. This period saw the flowering of Muslim culture in terms of philosophy, theology, science, medicine, mathematics and poetry. Gradually the empire disintegrated as a result of Turkish invasions, the crusades, the establishment of alternative caliphates and power struggles between different leaders. Nevertheless, religion continued to provide a unifying force in the Muslim civilisation, particularly in terms of the dominance of the Arabic language, the universal acceptance of the Pillars of Islam, the religious basis of the legal structure and the important links between religion and cultural expression.

As the Islamic Arab empire gradually lost power, five new Muslim empires emerged:

- the Moorish Empire in Spain and North Africa;
- the Ottoman Empire, which ruled Eastern Europe, the Middle East, Arabia and most of North Africa;
- the Uzbek Empire, which ruled the Muslim republics of the former Soviet Union, together with part of China;
- the Mughal Empire, which ruled the Indian subcontinent, Burma and Malaysia;
- the Safavid Empire, which ruled Iran and parts of Afghanistan.

These were probably the most civilised areas of the world in the later Middle Ages (see Ahmed, 1993, chapter 3), and were noted among other things for their culture, learning, the splendour of their courts and their spectacular architectural achievements, all done in the name of Islam. Islam also thrived in Indonesia, Mongolia and several sub-Saharan African states. But the empires gradually declined. The Moors were driven out of Spain in 1492, and the North African territories were gradually taken over by the Ottomans. The Ottoman Empire was weakened by Napoleon's successes in Egypt, though it limped on until the First World War, continuing to give the Muslim world a focal point in the person of the Sultan. The Russians gradually conquered the Uzbek Empire. The Mughal Empire was weakened by Safavid attacks and was eventually absorbed into the British Empire. The Safavid Empire was weakened by constant wars on the western, northern and eastern borders.

Islamic law (Shari'a)

It has already been noted that law occupies a much more central place in the Islamic worldview than it does in Christianity, and that Islamic law has provided a major unifying force throughout the world of Islam. In contrast to western thinking, law and morality are coterminous in Islam, and both are dependent on religion. There is thus no distinction between sinful and unlawful behaviour. As Schacht (1974, p 392) points out, 'Islamic law is the totality of God's commands that regulate the life of every Muslim in all its aspects.' The Arabic word for (religious) law is *shari'a*, which implies the road which all Muslims should follow. Islamic law pays equal attention to private and public domains, and sets out religious duties for the individual and the community as well as political and economic rules, social manners, moral obligations, inheritance laws, transactional laws and rules for family life.

The shari'a is derived from four main sources. The principal authority is the Qur'an, since this is the Word of God Himself. The next most important source is the hadith, the authoritative accounts of Muhammad's words and actions, since, as we have seen, Muhammad is viewed as the best example for humans to follow and his advice and guidance is the next best thing to divine guidance. The third source is *qiyas* (reasoning by analogy and precedent) and the fourth *ijma'* (the consensus of the *'ulama*, the leaders of the community who are well versed in Islamic religious and legal values). There is some debate as to whether a fifth source, *ijtihad*, is permissible any longer (*ijtihad* means the exercise of individual judgement on a new matter in accordance with divine law). This is because Islamic law is now crystallised into four major schools of law which emerged during the Abbasid period: the Maliki, the Hanafi, the Shafi'i and the Hanbali (there are further schools of law accepted by the Shi'ites). In the main, the differences between these schools are subtle and technical, and are often more to do with geographical than ideological differences.

In contrast to western law, where an act is either lawful or unlawful, Islamic law classifies all actions into five categories:

- Obligatory actions include belief in God and in Muhammad as his prophet, performance of the five pillars of Islam, *jihad* (fighting in the cause of Allah) when Islam is under threat, modesty and decency in clothing, care of children, reverence to parents, male circumcision.
- Commendable actions include hospitality, generosity, charity and the equitable distribution of wealth and the saying of *du'a* (non-obligatory) prayers.
- Permitted actions include private ownership of wealth and property, trade in order to gain a fair profit, the wearing of silk and jewellery by women, marriage to Jewish or Christian women, marrying up to four wives - subject to certain conditions, and a wide range of activities on which no specific guidance is given.
- Discouraged actions include celibacy, personal extravagance, divorce and visiting the graves of saints.

- Forbidden actions include murder, compulsion in religion, theft, hoarding wealth and taking interest, gambling, rape, premarital or extramarital sexual relations including homosexual practices, nudity, drinking alcohol, and the consumption of pig products or any meat which is not *halal* (ritually clean); the law is stringently enforced with canonical punishments which may seem severe by western standards, for example, apostasy is punishable by death, theft by the amputation of the hand and the consumption of alcohol by 80 lashes.

Another difference between western and Islamic law is that while western law adapts to changing social values and circumstances, Islamic law, because it is the embodiment of the divine will, is considered unchangeable. Traditionally, the law was administered in each town by a *qadi*, an appointed judge, who listened to evidence, assessed guilt and ordered punishment, consulting a *mufti* (professional expert on law) where appropriate. There was no jury and no court of appeal. However, the impact of western civilisation has brought about many changes. Three trends in particular have emerged in modern times. First, many Muslim countries have adopted western legal codes for criminal, civil and commercial laws, relegating the shari'a to family and religious matters. Second, there has more recently been a resurgence of interest in applying the shari'a in its entirety in Muslim countries. Third, some prominent Muslims have suggested that the door of *ijtihad*[1] should be thrown open again, so that experts in Islamic law can exercise personal judgement and discretion in a way that is appropriate for life in the contemporary Muslim world.

Muslim Culture

There is only room here to mention a tiny fraction of the cultural achievements of the Islamic world. In the domain of the visual arts, a very different hierarchy has prevailed from that of the West. At the top of the hierarchy are architecture and calligraphy, while decorated crafts such as pottery, metalwork, wood-carving, rug-making and other textiles occupy the middle ground, and paintings such as the stylised miniatures that illustrate Persian and Indian books come at the bottom, while because of Islamic condemnation of idolatry, sculpture and oil paintings are virtually non-existent. Tames (1982, p 77) hardly exaggerates when he says that 'theologically speaking, figural artists were ranked with dealers in stray dogs'. Architecture and calligraphy are so important because of their direct links with religion. The finest examples of Muslim architecture are almost invariably mosques (the Taj Mahal and the

---

[1] A legal term indicating that people are allowed to exercise personal judgement in contentious legal matters.

mausoleum of Tamerlane at Samarkand being notable exceptions): these include the Great Mosque of Cordoba, the Dome of the Rock, the Shah Mosque at Isfahan and the Sultan Hasan Mosque in Cairo. The prestigious place of calligraphy in the visual arts results from the belief that the Qur'an is literally the Word of God, so that wherever the Qur'an was written, whether to decorate the walls of mosques or in bound volumes, there was a desire to make the words as visually attractive and harmonious as possible. Tiles, decorative metalwork and wood carving, particularly using abstract geometrical motifs and the arabesque, were used to embellish mosques, and the almost universal use of the prayer rug among Muslims helped to maintain carpets as one of the most important visual arts in Islam. Beyond these tangible links with religion, however, lies an important spiritual dimension (cf. Nasr, 1987a); Burckhardt (1976) calls Islamic art 'essentially contemplative', with the endless visual rhythms of elaborate decoration or formal garden reflecting the rhythms of prayer or the underlying harmonies and repetitions of the created universe. Undoubtedly for Muslims it is religion which unifies and harmonises the artistic designs and techniques which have been drawn from a wide variety of sources.

The same principles apply in the non-visual arts. For example, music which has a religious function, such as the cantillation of the Qur'an and the call to prayer, is accorded very high status (though Muslims do not call these activities music at all: see Halstead, 1994, p 147), whereas other forms of music, even where these attain a very high degree of technical proficiency, tend to be viewed as at best a frivolous luxury, at worst a dangerously sensuous activity associated with dancing and wine-drinking. Similarly, lyrical poetry and story-telling in verse and prose are a great skill in the Muslim world, but even such rich gems as *The Arabian Nights* are not generally held in high esteem. Sufis (Islamic mystics), on the other hand, have raised the profile of the non-visual arts by imbuing them with spiritual significance; thus erotic poetry, for example, is interpreted as symbolising the soul's desire for union with God. Most of the greatest Muslim poets, including Nizami, Rumi, Hafiz, Sadi, Jami, and Fuzuli, were influenced by Sufi thinking (see Kritzeck, 1964). Another important Sufi was the theologian al-Ghazali, who took it upon himself to challenge what he saw as the basic unbelief underpinning the work of Muslim philosophers such as al-Kindi, al-Farabi and Ibn Sina (cf. Leaman, 1985).

The particular interest of Muslim scholars in mathematics can also be traced to religion: they needed to work out exactly the right times for prayer and the exact direction of Makka, and also needed ways of sharing out inheritances in accordance with the complex rules of the shari'a. Though the so-called Arabic numerals were actually invented in India, it was Muslims who worked out the full system of decimal calculation, and the word 'zero' comes from Arabic. Muslims also virtually invented algebra (another Arabic term) and trigonometry.

The Abbasids established a great library, Bait al-Hikma, in Baghdad in which the writings of ancient Greece, India and Persia were translated into Arabic. Muslim scholars then built on the scientific knowledge contained in these writings, particularly in the areas of medicine, geography and astronomy (Nasr, 1987b). Ibn Sina (d. 1037) discovered meningitis and studied epidemics. Al-Razi (d. 925) successfully distinguished between smallpox and measles. Both wrote medical encyclopaedias which remained standard works for centuries. Others carried out research into eye diseases, the use of drugs and herbs and the importance of diet. Al-Khwarizmi (d. 846) was a famous astronomer who also compiled the first Arabic atlas. Umar Khayyam (d. 1123), famous in the West as author of the *Rubaiyat* translated by Edward Fitzgerald, was a court astronomer who also reformed the calendar. Some of the first observatories were built in the Muslim world (Nasr, 1987b, pp 80-88). However, the driving force behind Islamic scientists was rarely the pursuit of knowledge for its own sake or for the sake of economic ends, but rather the desire to see order and beauty in the structure of the created universe and to understand its spiritual significance (Nasr, 1976).

Activity A5

Outline some of the ways in which the arts in Islam reinforce the religious worldview.

Comment on activity A5

Artistic creativity is not an autonomous activity in Islam, for all artistic activity comes under divine law. Certain artistic forms, therefore, such as sculpture and many kinds of music, remain undeveloped in Islam because they are proscribed in the shari'a. On the other hand, the desire to give one's time and skill to create something beautiful or useful in keeping with divine law is a form of worship. In a sense, both art and science in Islam have the same goal: to become more aware of the order, patterns and rhythms of the universe God created, so that one may understand and worship God more fully and serve God's purposes in the world. Muslims (in particular Sufis) use literature and other art forms to give expression to the deepest yearnings of their soul.

Contemporary Muslim world

In the present day, about 20% of the world's population is Muslim, which makes Islam the world's second largest religion after Christianity. The *umma* (worldwide Muslim community) is united by religion, and the political, social and economic aspects of the life of the community are all deeply coloured by religion. Traditionally, the umma is divided into two regions: *dar al-Islam* (the territory of Islam) and *dar al-harb* (the territory of war).

Dar al-Islam refers to those parts of the world where Muslims are in the majority, and where Islam (in theory at least) directs personal and social life and political and legal structures. The twentieth century has seen the collapse of empires and the growth of nation states in the Muslim world as elsewhere, and various forms of Islamic nationalism have emerged. There are currently about fifty Muslim nations. In addition to all the Arab states of the Middle East and North Africa, Islam is the majority religion in two European countries (Albania and The Republic of Bosnia and Herzegovina), in several countries of Asia (Turkey, Iran, Afghanistan, Pakistan, Bangladesh, Malaysia, Indonesia and Brunei, plus six of the recently independent former Soviet republics) and in several sub-Saharan countries (including Senegal, Guinea, Mali, Niger, Chad, the Gambia, Mauritania, Nigeria, Somalia and Sudan). In many parts of dar al-Islam, however, national loyalties are very much subordinate to loyalty to Islam and, contrary to western expectations, there seems to be growing pressure in many Muslim countries for social, legal and political structures to be brought more into line with Islamic beliefs and values.

Dar al-harb refers mainly to ideological rather than literal warfare, for in territories where Muslims are not in the majority they are involved in a twofold struggle: to defend their right to practise their religion freely and to convince non-Muslims of the truth of Islam. The first but not the second may sometimes lead to military activity as seen, for example, in the resistance of the Afghani mujahidin to Soviet forces or in the resistance to what some Muslims see as American attempts at ideological world domination. Muslim minorities are found in every country of the world. There are substantial numbers of Muslims in China and India, and significant minorities in some African countries including Tanzania and South Africa. Migration, mainly in the last century, has led to growing numbers of Muslims in western countries. Precise numbers are not available, but according to some estimates it is likely that there are five million Muslims in the USA (Haddad, 1991), three million in France and two-and-a-half million in Germany. There are also significant numbers of Muslims in Eastern Europe (Nonneman, Niblock and Szajkowski, 1996).

Sectarianism is not a major problem among Muslims, and differences between groups do not by and large impair their sense of belonging to the umma, the worldwide Muslim community. The main division in Islam is between Sunnis, who form the large majority of Muslims, and Shi'ites, who make up 10-12% of the Muslim community. Sunnis, whom we may call orthodox Muslims, take their name from their adherence to the *sunna*, the traditions of the Prophet Mohammed and the example set by him. Under the Sunni umbrella are a number of reform movements, such as the zealous Wahhabis who are dominant in Saudi Arabia. The Shi'ites, who take their name from *Shi'at Ali* (the party or faction of Ali) differ from the Sunnis in a number of details of doctrine and practice. In particular, they believe in a line of twelve imams succeeding Muhammad, the first being his son-in-law, Ali, and all the rest being descendants of Muhammad and Ali. After the twelfth imam, the leadership of the Shi'ite community passed to specially trained religious leaders known as ayatollahs. Shi'ites have additional festivals such as Al' Ashura which celebrates the death of Ali's son Husayn, and make additional pilgrimages to Shi'ite shrines such as Karbala and Najaf. There are certain differences between Shi'ite and Sunni law, for example, Shi'ite law permits temporary marriage (for a fuller list of the differences between Shi'ites and Sunnis, see Watton, 1993, pp 121-125). Most Muslims in Iran are Shi'ite, and there are also significant Shi'ite communities in Iraq, Azerbaijan, Bahrain, Kuwait, Afghanistan, Lebanon and India. There are numerous Shi'ite sects, including the Druzes, in Lebanon and Syria, the Zaidis who recognise only four imams, and the Isma'ilis who uphold the claims of Isma'il as the seventh imam. The Isma'ilis established the Fatimid caliphate in North Africa in the tenth and eleventh centuries, which was responsible for the establishment of al-Azhar University. The Nizaris, a branch of the Isma'ilis, are led by the Aga Khan, who is recognised by his followers as the forty-ninth imam.

Islam has also given rise to a number of religions which are not recognised as part of the Islamic umma. These include the Baha'i religion, founded in Iran in the mid-nineteenth century by Bab and his disciple Baha'ullah; the Ahmadiyya movement founded towards the end of the nineteenth century by Mirza Ghulam Ahmad in Qadian, Punjab; and the Nation of Islam, founded as a black separatist movement by Wali Fard Mohammed and Elijah Mohammed in the USA in the early twentieth century.

Sufis (Islamic mystics) do not belong to a separate sect in Islam, though their practices (if not their beliefs) may be unorthodox. They emphasise the importance of inner spiritual experience and the need for self-abandonment in the individual quest for union with God. The famous theologian al-Ghazali did much to ensure that Sufism was accepted within orthodox Islam. As already noted, much Muslim poetry is the product of Sufi thought, and Sufis are also respected as sources of folk-wisdom (cf. Idies Shah, 1964).

Muslims and the West

Muslims may have ambivalent attitudes to the West. The political imperialism of the nineteenth century has now vanished, but many Muslim countries are still ruled by a western educated élite who are often considered out of touch with the religious values of the ordinary people. The material success of the West is sometimes admired, and western technological progress has generally been welcomed in Muslim countries (and has necessarily had a big impact), yet Muslims remain suspicious of western values like secularism and individualism and of what they see as western cultural imperialism. At the same time Muslims often find themselves the target of a growing western antipathy.

With the decline of the perceived threat to the West from the Soviet bloc, it has been suggested that Islam has emerged in the western consciousness as the foremost challenger to western security and values. This perception has been justified by militant activities and kidnappings carried out by Islamic extremists including the Lebanese Hezbollah; by the *fatwa* (legal judgement) issued by the late Ayatollah Khomeini condemning Salman Rushdie to death; and by the perceived military threat first of Gadaffi's Libya, then of Khomeini's Iran and most recently of Saddam Hussein's Iraq. As a result, a strong anti-Islamic bias has developed in the western media in recent years. Islam has been portrayed increasingly as a religion of irrational 'fundamentalism' and fanatical book-burning, where free speech is suppressed and women oppressed. For example, writing in the *Sunday Telegraph* on 3 February 1991, Peregrine Worsthorne used the occasion of the Gulf War to provide a wholesale condemnation of Islam: 'Islam, once a great civilisation worthy of being argued with... has degenerated into a primitive enemy fit only to be sensibly subjugated. But if they want a *jihad*, let them have it.' Perhaps he forgot momentarily that Britain and the western alliance were at that very moment fighting *on the same side* as several Muslim countries. But such animosity has deep roots both historically (going back to the Crusades and beyond) and theologically (centring on the mutually exclusive claims of Christianity and Islam). In such a context, many Muslims in the West unsurprisingly consider their position precarious.

In spite of these factors, Akbar Ahmed (1993, p 206) concludes *Living Islam* on a positive note, suggesting that 'the confrontation between Islam and the West can be one of great stimulation to both sides'. If both sides are prepared to shed prejudices, abandon stereotypes, listen to each other, strive for empathy and understanding, and try to avoid imposing their own intellectual frame on the other, then the exchange of ideas will be mutually enriching.

Activity A6

In order to embark on the process of seeing the world through the eyes of others, this task is to list some of the main western values which are likely to be viewed as problematic from an Islamic perspective.

Comment on activity A6

Some of the things you could have mentioned include the following:

- Religious commitment tends to be seen in the West as a matter of personal choice, in which the state has little or no interest.
- Public institutions tend to be secular in structure and ethos.
- Moral values are based not on revealed truth but on rationally justifiable principles.
- Individual freedom is a crucial value, which is taken to legitimate a wide diversity of beliefs and behaviour.
- The dominant critical-speculative method of modern science requires all beliefs to be held in a way which is open to critical challenge and debate.
- Education is not based on authority, but on the development of critical rationality and personal and moral autonomy.

Readers

For Judaism

You will find four books particularly helpful in your study of this unit:

Cohn-Sherbok, D. and Cohn-Sherbok, L. (1994), *A Short History of Judaism*, Oxford, Oneworld.

de Lange, N. (1984), *An Atlas of the Jewish World*, London, Phaidon Press.

Johnson, P. (1987), *A History of the Jews*, London, Weidenfeld and Nicolson.

Sirat, C. (1995), *History of Jewish Philosophy in the Middle Ages*, Cambridge, Cambridge University Press.

For Islam

Introductory texts which may be of help in your study of this unit include:

Ahmed, A.S. (1993), *Living Islam*, London, BBC Books.

Armstrong, K. (1991), *Muhammad: a western attempt to understand Islam*, London, Victor Gollancz.

Azzam, S. (ed.) (1982), *Islam and Contemporary Society*, London, Longman.

Lings, M. (1983), *Muhammad*, London, Allen and Unwin.

Nasr, S.H. (1966), *Ideals and Realities of Islam*, London, Allen and Unwin.

Nigosian, S. (1987), *Islam: the way of submission*, London, Crucible.

Bibliography

For Judaism

Blenkinsopp, J. (1977), *Prophecy and Canon: a contribution to the study of Jewish origins*, London, University of Notre Dame Press.

Dawidowicz, L.S. (1966), *The Golden Tradition*, London, Holt Rinehart and Winston.

Dawidowicz, L.S. (1975), *The War Against the Jews*, London, Holt Rinehart and Winston.

Drane, J. (1983), *The Old Testament Story*, Oxford, Lion.

Gilbert, M. (1988), *Jewish History Atlas*, London, Weidenfeld and Nicolson.

Laqueur, W.A. (1976), *A History of Zionism*, New York, Schocken.

Katz, J. (1961), *Out of the Ghetto*, Cambridge, Massachusetts, Harvard University Press.

Katz, J. (1973), *Tradition and Crisis: Jewish society at the end of the middle ages*, New York, Free Press.

Meyer, M. (1988), *Response to Modernity: a history of the reform movement in Judaism*, Oxford, Oxford University Press.

O'Brian, C.C. (1986), *The Siege: the saga of Israel and Zionism*, London, Weidenfeld and Nicholson.

Parkes, J. (1976), *The Jew in the Mediaeval Community*, London, Harmon Press.

Potok, C. (1969), *The Promise*, New York, Fawcett Crest.

Potok, C. (1972), *My Name is Asher Lev*, Harmondsworth, Penguin.

Sandmel, S. (1978), *Judaism and Christian Beginnings*, Oxford, Oxford University Press.

For Islam

Ahmed, A.S. (1992), *Postmodernism and Islam: predicament and promise*, London, Routledge.

Ahmed, A.S. (1993), *Living Islam*, London, BBC Books.

Burckhardt, T. (1976), *Art of Islam: language and meaning*, London, World of Islam Festival Publishing Co.

Carlyle, T. (1906), *On Heroes, Hero Worship and the Heroic in History*, London, Dent.

Cragg, K. (1956), *The Call of the Minaret*, Oxford, Oxford University Press.

Haddad, Y.Y. (1991), *The Muslims of America*, New York, Oxford University Press.

Halstead, J.M. (1994), Muslim attitudes to music in schools, *British Journal of Music Education*, 11, 143-156.

International Institute of Islamic Thought (1989), *Islamization of Knowledge: general principles and work plan*, Herndon, Virginia, IIIT.

Kritzeck, J. (ed.) (1964), *Anthology of Islamic Literature*, Harmondsworth, Penguin.

Leaman, O. (1985), *An Introduction to Medieval Islamic Philosophy*, Cambridge, Cambridge University Press.

Marsh, C.R. (1975), *Share your Faith with a Muslim*, Chicago, Moody Press.

Nasr, S.H. (1976), *Islamic Science: an illustrated study*, London, World of Islam Festival Publishing Co.

Nasr, S.H. (1987a), *Islamic Art and Spirituality*, Ipswich, Golgonooza Press.

Nasr, S.H. (1987b), *Science and Civilisation in Islam*, (second edition), Cambridge, Islamic Texts Society.

Nonneman, G., Niblock, T. and Szajkowski, B. (eds) (1996), *Muslim Communities in the New Europe*, Reading, Ithaca Press.

Said, E.W. (1978), *Orientalism*, London, Routledge and Kegan Paul.

Schacht, J. (1974), *The Legacy of Islam*, Oxford, Oxford University Press.

Shah, I. (1964), *The Sufis*, London, Cape.

Smart, N. (1977), *Background to the Long Search*, London, BBC Books.

Tames, R. (1982), *Approaches to Islam*, London, John Murray.

Watton, V.W. (1993), *Islam*, London, Hodder and Stoughton.

Teaching about Judaism and Islam

Unit B

Contemporary practice and current debates

Rabbi Professor Dan Cohn-Sherbok

Lavinia Cohn-Sherbok

Department of Theology and Religious Studies

University of Wales, Lampeter

and

Dr J. Mark Halstead

Rolle Faculty of Education

University of Plymouth

Contents

Introduction

We have put side by side, in consecutive sections in this unit, outlines of the contemporary practice and current debates within Judaism and Islam. Each section is preceded by its own aims, but the recommended reading and the bibliography for both sections are put at the end of the unit. Part B1 relates to Judaism and part B2 relates to Islam.

B1 Judaism

Aims

After working through part B1 of this unit, you should be able to:

- understand the dilemmas concerning the question, 'Who is a Jew?';
- gain an appreciation of the divisions in the modern Jewish community;
- become aware of the major festivals in the Jewish calendar;
- appreciate the dilemmas facing Jews in the future.

Overview

This unit offers an overview of some of the central features of the Jewish faith. Beginning with an examination of the dilemmas surrounding the issue of Jewish identity, the discussion focuses on the various denominations in the Jewish world today. From Orthodoxy to Humanistic Judaism, Jews are divided amongst themselves over both belief and practice. Nonetheless, the community is united in its allegiance to the Jewish heritage, although these sub-groups interpret it in a variety of ways. Of particular importance are the role of the synagogue, and the observance of festival, fasts and life-cycle events. Although there is no overarching framework for Jewish existence, it is still possible to depict the everyday lifestyle of Jews in modern society. The unit concludes with an examination of Jewish living in the future, highlighting some of the central issues facing Jewry today.

Who is a Jew?

In previous centuries, the definition of Jewishness was clear: a person is Jewish if his or her mother is Jewish, or if the person's mother had converted to Judaism. In other words, maternal descent or conversion defined Jewishness.

In addition, a person who was not born Jewish could become a Jew if converted in the proper manner. Before the time of the Enlightenment in the nineteenth century, Judaism was hence a unified religious system. Jews lived apart from their Gentile neighbours, and came into contact only in superficial ways. Intermarriage was forbidden, and the community was an integrated whole. The question 'Who is a Jew?' never arose. In the modern world, however, the issue has become highly complex.

In the past Jewish identity was understood in religious terms. If Jewish individuals converted to another faith, the secular authorities ceased to regard them as Jewish - they were free to become full citizens and were not subject to the same restrictions that applied to Jews. In Nazi Germany, on the other hand, such religious identification gave way to racial categorisation. The Nazis viewed anyone with one Jewish grandparent as a non-Aryan regardless of their religious convictions. Hence in the 1930s there were many individuals in Germany who saw themselves as practising Christians and were not accepted by the Jewish community as Jews. Yet, they shared the same fate as the Jewish people in the Holocaust. Similarly, in Russia today, because the government understands Jewishness in ethnic terms, there are thousands of individuals who are deemed as Jewish even though they have no religious background and are the offspring of marriages between Jewish men and non-Jewish women. In the eyes of the Orthodox, such an individual is not a Jew, but has 'Jew' written in his or her passport.

The situation is even more complicated in the United States as well as the countries of the British Commonwealth. Increasingly intermarriage between Jews and Gentiles has become widespread. In addition, men are more likely to marry out than women, which raises the problem of the status of offspring of such a union. Traditionally such children would be viewed as non-Jewish since they do not have a Jewish mother. In order to resolve this dilemma, the Reform and Conservative movements have encouraged the non-Jewish spouse to convert. As a result, in many American cities as much as two-fifths of non-Orthodox synagogue membership is made up of couples in which one partner is a convert. These converted Jews and their children are accepted within their own communities as Jewish - but not by the Orthodox establishment. Because the non-Orthodox do not even pretend to keep the body of Jewish law, the Orthodox regard such conversions as invalid and insist that such individuals are Gentiles.

Faced with such difficulties, the Reform movement has adopted a new approach to the problem of Jewish identity. In 1983 their rabbinical association, the Central Conference of American Rabbis, passed a motion that any child of a mixed marriage is under presumption of Jewish status. This means that even if the Gentile mother does not convert, the child is regarded as Jewish as long as he or she undergoes appropriate and timely public and formal acts of identification as a Jew. The Orthodox were outraged by this change in Jewish law, but this criterion of Jewishness is now widely accepted in Reform quarters. Thus, there is considerable uncertainty within and without the Jewish community concerning Jewish status. The debate about who is a Jew has divided the Jewish people into warring factions (Sacks, 1993).

Denominations in the Jewish community

In the modern world, the Jewish community has fragmented in a variety of sub-groups. Beginning with the most traditional form of the Jewish faith, Orthodox Judaism is based on the belief that the Torah was given by God to Moses on Mount Sinai. In consequence, the Orthodox see themselves as true to the tradition. This belief has enormous practical consequence on their day to day life. Not only are they bound by biblical law, they are also faithful to the rabbinical interpretation of scripture. Yet, despite such uniformity of belief and practice, there is considerable disagreement between the various factions within the Orthodox world. The strictly Orthodox, for example, view modern Orthodoxy as making too many concessions to modernity. Nonetheless, all Orthodox Jews are united in the conviction that the Torah was given directly by God to Moses. In addition, they remain hostile to the moral liberal interpretations of Judaism.

A distinct sub-group within the world of Orthodox Judaism is Hasidic Judaism. The word *hasidim* means 'the pious', and Hasidic Jews are known for their spiritual devotion. The men are immediately recognisable: they are bearded and wear side-curls which are twisted and tucked behind their ears. These Jews are invariably dressed in black - large black hat worn over small black skull-cap, black jacket, plain black trousers and black shoes and socks. This movement arose in the early nineteenth century in Eastern Europe as a reaction against the sterility of traditional Orthodoxy. In recent times, however, Hasidic Jews have made common cause with Orthodoxy. Although they support different institutions and have a different liturgy, they are united in their abhorrence of the more radical forms of Jewish life.

Among religious Jews, the great divide is between these various Orthodox branches and the non-Orthodox. Non-Orthodox Judaism arose in response to Jewish participation in secular civilisation. Increasingly, western Jews were uncomfortable with the traditional forms of Jewish existence. Initially reformers sought to change the forms of Jewish worship; in time, traditional belief and practice came under attack. Currently Reform Judaism is one of the largest branches of Judaism world-wide, championing the need for adaptation of the tradition to modern life.

Alongside Reform, Conservative Judaism arose as a reaction to what were perceived as the radical excesses of the Reform movement: it stands midway between the certainties of Orthodoxy and the liberties of Reform. Adherents of this approach contend that Judaism has changed through the centuries and that the ultimate source of authority must be the Jewish people themselves. According to Conservative Judaism, some aspects of the tradition are permanent, whereas others are only meaningful at certain periods. Today Conservative Judaism is the largest movement in the United States with branches in other parts of the world.

In addition to these major movements, two smaller non-theistic groups have arisen in the United States in recent years. Founded by the Jewish theologian, Mordecai Kaplan, Reconstructionist Judaism grew out of Conservative Judaism. In Kaplan's view, Judaism is a religious civilisation rather than a divinely revealed religion. Like Conservative Judaism, Reconstructionism retains many traditional Jewish practices, but differs from its parent movement in explaining its beliefs in this-worldly terms. Today the movement supports its own rabbinical college and has established a network of synagogues.

Paralleling Reconstructionist Judaism, Humanistic Judaism rejects the belief in a supernatural deity. Founded by Sherwin Wine, the movement extols the humanistic aspects of Judaism while abandoning traditional theism. Hence the manifesto of the Humanistic Federation proclaims: 'The natural universe stands on its own, requiring no supernatural intervention... Judaism, as the civilisation of the Jews, is a human creation.' Today there are approximately forty thousand Humanistic Jews and the movement has established an international network (Wertheimer, 1993).

Activity B1

Suggest reasons why Strict Orthodoxy is the only growing religious movement within the Jewish community. The reason for this activity is to enable you to discuss the vibrant growth of the Strictly Orthodox community in relation to other sectors of the community. This will require a knowledge of the various non-Orthodox movements, as well as the various sub-groups within Orthodox Judaism.

Comment on activity B1

In this discussion, you should have been able to isolate the following issues:

First, Orthodoxy is an umbrella term for several distinct movements: Strict Orthodoxy, Modern Orthodoxy and Hasidism. There are crucial differences of approach between these different movements that have given rise to conflict over a wide range of subjects. These differences should be attended to when discussing the growth of those who regard themselves as Strictly Orthodox.

Second, the strength of the various non-Orthodox groupings vary: attention should be paid to the relative size and importance of these groups, particularly in the United States which has the largest Jewish population in the world.

Third, since the time of the Enlightenment in the early nineteenth century, Jews have assimilated into the societies in which they live. The Strictly Orthodox, on the other hand, seek to retain traditional ways. You should be aware of the various ways in which Jews have assimilated and the reaction of the Strictly Orthodox to these developments.

Fourth, Strictly Orthodox Jews seek to exert control over the marriages of those who belong to this grouping, and to direct the education of the young in conformity with Jewish life. It is important to explore the ways in which such marriages are arranged and childbirth regulated so as to ensure the growth of the community.

Synagogue

The synagogue emerged as a central institution of Judaism during the Babylonian captivity that took place in the sixth century BCE. Since sacrifice was only permitted in the Jerusalem Temple, there was a need for a place where Jews could meet together for prayer and study. Increasingly Jewish life revolved around the synagogue, and eventually when the Romans destroyed the Temple in the first century, the synagogue came to play a central role in Jewish life.

There are no laws regarding the building of the synagogue; in general, its architectural features echo the tastes of the time. Medieval synagogues in Europe, for example, were built in the Romanesque or Gothic style; in Poland synagogues were built of wood; revivalists buildings were created in the nineteenth century; and in contemporary society many synagogues are designed in line with modernism. Today synagogues serve as community centres as well as places of worship and study: in addition to a sanctuary, they contain meeting rooms, classrooms, kitchens, libraries and administrative offices. The regular staff usually includes a rabbi, a cantor as well as educational director, and secretaries. Families pay substantial sums to belong, and the rabbis are directly employed by an elected board of lay members.

As far as the sanctuary is concerned, there are a number of elements that parallel both the ancient sanctuary and Temple. The focus of the building is the Ark that symbolises the Holy of Holies. Just as the Ark of the Covenant contained the tablets of the Ten Commandments, so the synagogue Ark contains the Torah scroll. When the doors of the Ark are opened, and scrolls are removed and replaced, the congregation stands as a sign of respect. It is considered an honour to be invited to open or close the doors, as it is to be asked to read from the Torah scroll.

A lamp hangs in front of the Ark that symbolises the light that burnt perpetually in the Temple sanctuary. In the centre of the building or alongside one wall is a raised platform which is used for the reading of the Torah scroll and from the scriptures, for the leading of prayers, and for the sermon. The worshippers sit or stand, facing the Ark, and follow the service in the prayer books. In Orthodox synagogues men and women sit separately so that the men are not distracted. Conservative and Reform Judaism, however, have abolished separate seating and families sit together. There must be at least ten men for a liturgical service to take place in an Orthodox synagogue. Attendance is viewed as meritorious, yet synagogues are rarely full except for the High Holiday Services during the New Year and the Day of Atonement. Nonetheless, the synagogue remains the central focus of Jewish life.

Festivals and fasts

Unlike the secular year, the Jewish year follows a lunar calendar, thus Jewish festivals do not occur on the same date every year. The following is an overview of some of the major festivals and fasts:

Season	Month	Date	Festival
Autumn	Tishri	1-2	New Year (Rosh Hashanah)
		1-10	Ten Days of Repentance
		3	Fast of Gedaliah
		10	Day of Atonement (Yom Kippur)
		15-21	Sukkot
	Marshevan		
	Kislev	25-2/3	Hanukkah
Winter	Tevet	10	Fast of Tevet
	Shevat	15	New Year for Trees
	Adar	14	Purim
Spring	Nisan	15-22	Passover

	Iyyar	5	Israel Independence Day
		18	Lag Ba-Omer
	Shivan	6-7	Shavuot
Summer	Tammuz	17	Fast of Tammuz
	Av	9	Fast of Av

Rosh Hashanah: The New Year Festival inaugurates the beginning of the spiritual year. It is observed for two days.

Ten Days of Repentance: This period begins with Rosh Hashanah and concludes with Yom Kippur. It is a time for religious reflection and penitence.

Fast of Gedaliah: This fast commemorates the assassination of Gedaliah, the Governor of the Jews appointed by Nebuchadnezzar.

Yom Kippur: The Day of Atonement is the most solemn day of the Jewish year. Jews are commanded to fast and atone for their sins.

Sukkot: This festival commemorates God's protection of the Israelites in the wilderness. Booths are built during this festival to symbolise the temporary shelter used by the Israelites in their wanderings.

Hanukkah: The festival is celebrated for eight days. It commemorates the re-dedication of the Temple by Judah Maccabee after the Seleucids were defeated in 165 BCE.

Fast of Tevet: This day commemorates the siege of Jerusalem by Nebuchadnezzar.

New Year for Trees: This festival is celebrated in Israel by the planting of trees.

Purim: This festival commemorates the defeat of Haman's plot to destroy the Jewish people.

Passover: This eight-day festival commemorates God's redemption of the Israelites from Egyptian bondage. It is also referred to as the Festival of Unleavened Bread; this term refers to the unleavened bread that the Israelites baked in their hurried departure.

Israel Independence Day: This holiday commemorates the proclamation of Israel's independence on 5 Iyyar, 1948.

Lag Ba-Omer: The period between Passover and Shavuot was frequently a time of tragedy. During the time of the sage Akiva, a plague occurred among his disciples and only ceased on 18 Iyyar. This day became known as the Scholar's Feast. The Day is a day of joy. In Israel pilgrims go to Meron where the scholar Simeon ben Yochai is buried.

Shavuot: This festival is celebrated after seven weeks have been counted from the bringing of the Omer on the second day of Passover. It commemorates the giving of the Torah on Mount Sinai.

Fast of Tammuz: This fast day commemorates the day when the walls of Jerusalem were breached by the Romans as well as other disasters.

Fast of Av: This fast commemorates the day on which the First Temple was destroyed by Nebuchadnezzar, and the Second Temple by Titus.

Life cycle events

The first commandment in the Hebrew scriptures is: 'Be fruitful and multiply' (Genesis 1.28). Having children is thus a divinely prescribed way of life. According to tradition, a woman was viewed as ritually unclean for seven days after giving birth to a boy and fourteen days for a girl. The first time the Torah is read after the birth of a girl, the father is called up in honour of the birth. For boys the circumcision ceremony is a sign of the covenant, a ritual believed to go back to the time of the first Jew, Abraham. In Genesis (17.10-12), God decreed:

> This is my covenant which you shall keep, between me and you and your descendants after you: Every male among you shall be circumcised... and it shall be a sign of the covenant between me and you... He that is eight days old among you shall be circumcised, every male throughout your generations.

Another law regarding boys is also scripturally based. The book of Exodus records that 'The Lord said to Moses: Consecrate to me all the first-born, whatever is the first to open the womb among the people of Israel, both of man and beast is mine' (Exodus 13.1-2). This is understood to mean that every first child who happens to be male must be redeemed from a priest. During this ceremony the baby is formally brought into the room, and the father gives him to a priest. He then makes a declaration. The priest then states that the father may redeem the child. This ancient practice still takes place among the Orthodox, but it has been largely abandoned by the non-Orthodox groupings.

Jewish law also stipulates that parents have an obligation to educate their children. In the book of Deuteronomy (6.7), God said about the commandments:

> You shall teach them diligently to your children, and shall talk of them when you sit in your house and when you walk by the way and when you sit down and when you rise.

In the Orthodox world, the religious education of boys is a fundamental duty: a rigorous programme of learning takes place from the earliest age. In the non-Orthodox world, religious education generally takes place alongside secular schooling in the afternoons after school or on weekends.

At the age of thirteen a boy attains Jewish adulthood; this transition is marked by the bar mitzvah ceremony. It is customary for a boy to be called up during the Sabbath service to recite the Torah blessings, chant some verses from the weekly reading and the reading from the prophets. In the tradition, girls are viewed as having reached religious maturity at the age of twelve, but there is no legal obligation for the occasion to be marked in any particular way. Today, however, a ceremony for girls - bat mitzvah - has been introduced in both the Orthodox and non-Orthodox communities.

Marriage marks a crucial stage in adulthood. In biblical times, weddings took place in two stages. The first element was betrothal; the second was the wedding proper. In modern times, these two elements have been combined. In Orthodox ceremonies, a formal contract, the *ketubah*, is completed, and the bride and groom, together with their parents, all stand under the marriage canopy. Prayers are recited and both bride and groom drink from a wine cup. The bridegroom then puts the wedding ring on the bride's finger with the traditional words of consecration. In non-Orthodox congregations, variants of the traditional marriage service are used.

The Jewish tradition also determines the procedure for burial and mourning. According to Jewish law, the body must be buried as soon as possible after death. It is considered a righteous act to sit with the body, which is subsequently taken from the house to the funeral parlour where it is washed. Among the Orthodox this task is accomplished by a burial society, *Chevra Kadisha*. A funeral service is then held, and the body buried. A period of mourning, *shiva*, then takes place. Among the non-Orthodox, modifications to these traditional practices take place.

Everyday Jewish living

The daily life of an Orthodox Jew is circumscribed by the 613 commandments given in scripture. These laws, and the rabbinic elaboration of this code, serve as the framework for daily living. Men are obliged to keep all these commandments, whereas women are exempt from positive laws that must be fulfilled at a particular time.

Beginning with the morning service, men are obliged to gather for prayer in the synagogue. Ten men are required for a full service. Later in the day they assemble for the afternoon and evening services. These three acts of worship are intended to correspond with the times sacrifices were offered in the Temple. Services also take place on the Sabbath and for festivals. Among the non-Orthodox, various modifications to this pattern of worship have been adopted.

Among Orthodox Jews it is customary to say the Shema prayer on rising in the morning and when going to bed at night. In addition, strictly observant Jews put on phylacteries (*tefillin*) for morning prayer: these consist of boxes attached to straps. One is placed over the head and the other is wound round the left arm. The reason for putting on phylacteries is to fulfil the commandment that God's words should be 'as a sign upon your hand and they shall be as frontlets between your eyes. And you shall write them on the doorposts of your house and on your gates' (Deuteronomy 6.8-9). To fulfil the latter part of this command, Jews are obliged to place a mezuzah (a small box containing parchment) on the right-hand doorpost of the house. Strictly Orthodox Jews also put a mezuzah on the doorpost of nearly every room in the house. It is unusual for non-Orthodox Jews to put on tefillin, but the practice of placing mezuzahs on the doorpost of a house is universal within the Jewish community.

Within Jewish life, there are also laws related to clothing. One of the most recognisable signs of masculine Orthodox dress is the yarmulke (skull cap). This is worn at all times as a sign of respect. Non-Orthodox Jews also frequently wear yarmulkes when praying. According to the book of Leviticus, it is forbidden to cut the corners of the beard (Leviticus 19.27); this biblical verse was interpreted to mean that Jews should not shave, but it was permissible to clip facial hair. Another element of Orthodox appearance is *tzizit* (fringes). Orthodox men wear an undergarment with fringes on the four corners known as a *tallit katan*. Similar fringes are put on the four corners of the prayer shawl (*tallit gadol*) which is worn in the synagogue during the morning service. A final law related to clothing concerns the mixture of cloth which is forbidden by Deuteronomy (Deuteronomy 22.11). While the Orthodox scrupulously follow these practices, they have largely lapsed with the non-Orthodox world, with the exception of wearing fringes on the prayer shawl.

Turning to forbidden foods, scripture stipulates a host of laws regarding ritual purity. The book of Deuteronomy, for example, specifies that for an animal to be permitted as food, it must have a cloven hoof and chew the cud (Deuteronomy 14.6). Pigs are thus forbidden as are many other types of animals. Further, the creature must be slaughtered in a particular way. Because of the prohibition against eating blood, this law involves getting rid of as much as possible from the carcass. A *shohet* (Jewish ritual slaughterer) then kills the animal in a prescribed manner.

According to Jewish law, it is not permitted to eat meat and dairy products together. The biblical injunction, 'You shall not boil a kid in its mother's milk' (Exodus 23.19) has been interpreted to mean that neither meat nor poultry may be mixed with anything made from milk. In order to carry out these food laws, it is necessary to have a kosher kitchen. It is commonly assumed that the laws of ritual purity developed due to health considerations, but it is possible that the laws of *kashrut* developed in this fashion. In any event, there is a wide range of observance among both the Orthodox and non-Orthodox of this legislation.

In the modern world Jewish family life is extolled. Although divorce is permitted, the tradition has always valued married life. It is said that the Jewish community has few broken families, low levels of delinquency, high standards of education and strong bonds between the generations. Because of her domestic duties, a woman is not expected to perform all the positive, time-bound commandments. She does not have to wear fringes or put on phylacteries, nor does she have an obligation to attend religious services. If she does go to services she is not part of the daily *minyan*. Her obligations are instead to care for the members of her family and to ensure that her children are educated.

Activity B2

How have Jewish laws and customs ensured the continued separate identity of the Jewish people?

Comment on activity B2

You may have thought of the following issues:

First, Jewish law is of ancient origin. It may appear outmoded in the modern world yet it served an important function in the past. By keeping God's laws as recorded in scripture and developed by the rabbis, Jews have been able to sustain their identity through the centuries. In concrete ways it distinguished them from their neighbours.

Second, biblical legislation, unlike secular law, is based on revelation. This means that it is binding on all future generations and cannot be changed to meet altered circumstances.

Third, as Jewish law is revealed, new movements (like Reform, Conservative or Reconstructionist Judaism) which seek to alter the law are regarded as subversive. This explains hostility between Orthodox and non-Orthodox.

Fourth, if much Jewish law is abandoned, it is difficult to see what is distinctive about a modernised Jewish way of life. In what respects is it different from the lifestyle of any other faith? How are Jews different from Gentiles if laws and customs are set aside?

Fifth, despite the above, is it possible to retain anachronistic and arguably untenable opinions simply because they make Jews identifiable?

The future hope

According to traditional Judaism, the Messiah will usher in a period of redemption. He will initiate peace in the world and promote justice and teach Torah. In addition, the Messiah will right all wrongs and bring a state of healing to the earth. Further, it is he who will restore the twelve tribes to the Promised Land and establish his righteous kingdom for all time. Besides looking for a return to the Promised Land in a future golden age, many Jews also hope for personal immortality. This belief arose late in the history of Judaism. Possibly as a result of Persian influence during and after the exile in Babylon in the sixth century BCE, Jews came to believe in the eventual resurrection of the dead.

According to rabbinic Judaism, the world to come is divided into several stages. First there is the time of messianic redemption. According to the Talmud, the messianic age is to take place on earth after a period of decline and misery, and will result in a complete fulfilment of every human wish. Peace will reign throughout nature; Jerusalem will be rebuilt; and at the close of this era, the dead will be resurrected and rejoined with their souls. Those who are judged righteous will enter into heaven, which is portrayed in various ways in rabbinic sources, and portrayed in glorious terms:

> There are five chambers for the various classes of the righteous. The first is...
> the habitation of non-Jews who become true and devoted converts to Judaism...
> The second is... the habitation of the penitents. The third chamber... contains
> the best of heaven and earth... The fourth chamber is inhabited by those who
> have suffered for the sake of their religion... The fifth chamber is built of
> precious stones and... is inhabited by the Messiah of David, Elijah and the
> Messiah of Ephraim.

Conversely, those who are judged wicked will be condemned to eternal punishment:

> Some sinners were suspended by their eyelids, some by their ears, some by
> their hands and some by their tongues... These sinners were punished in this
> way because they swore falsely, profaned the Sabbath and the Holy Days,
> despised the sages, called their neighbours by unseemly nicknames, wronged
> the orphan and the widow and bore false witness.

In the modern period, however, the Jewish community has largely abandoned these beliefs. Traditional Jewish eschatology has lost its force for a large number of Jews. Given this shift in Jewish life, what is the Jewish hope for the future? The Strictly Orthodox continue to wait for God's anointed, the

Messiah, who will bring in the messianic age (Jacobs, 1973). Today, however, the Strictly Orthodox are a small minority of the Jewish people. For the rest, the answer is less straightforward. The non-Orthodox movements have largely retained the doctrines of the messianic age and the immortality of the soul, but the messianic age is perceived as the result of human endeavour and the soul does not have to confront the possibility of eternal torment (Jacob, 1983).

Very many Jews go still further. They no longer expect any form of messianic deliverance. They do not anticipate that God will ever make his presence known in the world, and they have lost all belief in personal immortality. For many of these individuals, the creation of the state of Israel has taken the place of messianic deliverance. For others, Jewish survival has become an end in itself. Hitler succeeded in murdering a third of world Jewry. It has become a matter of principle that he should not, fifty years later, succeed in finishing the job. For such individuals, it is essential that the Jewish people survive into the next century (Rubenstein and Roth, 1987).

Dilemmas facing Judaism

Over the last two hundred years Jewry has entered the mainstream of western society, and no longer are Jews restricted to a ghetto existence. Such a transformation of Jewish life has profoundly altered the nature of the Jewish faith. In the past Judaism was essentially a unified structure embracing different interpretations of the same tradition. But the modern period has witnessed the fragmentation of the Jewish community into a variety of sub-groups. After nearly four millennia, Jewry faces new difficulties.

First, and arguably most importantly, Jews must ask themselves what they should make of the greatest tragedy of modern Jewish history - the destruction of six million of their number by the Nazis. If the God of Israel is an all-powerful, omniscient, benevolent father who loves his children, how could he have allowed such an event to take place? If there is a divine providential scheme, what is the purpose of this slaughter of the chosen people? These haunting questions will not disappear, and individual Jews will not find it easy to escape from this religious dilemma (Cohn-Sherbock, 1996).

Related to the problem of religious belief is the dilemma of observance. Today Orthodoxy claims the largest number of adherents, yet the majority of those who profess allegiance to Orthodox Judaism do not live by the Code of Jewish Law. Instead, each individual feels free to choose for himself or herself which of the multitude of laws are spiritually relevant. This is so also within the other branches of Judaism. For most Jews the legal tradition has lost its hold on Jewish consciousness. The bulk of rituals and observances appear anachronistic and burdensome. This situation raises serious questions about the status of Jewish law and its application to modern Jewish life (Jacobs, 1973; Sacks, 1993).

In this connection, there is also considerable confusion about the scripture. According to Orthodox belief God gave the Five Books of Moses to Moses on Mount Sinai. This act of revelation provides the basis for the legal system as well as Jewish belief. Many modern Orthodox adherents pay lip-service to this conviction, but in their daily lives illustrate that such a belief has little if any relevance. They fail to live up to the legal requirements as prescribed in scripture and are agnostic about the nature and activity of God. The gap between traditional belief and contemporary views is even greater in the non-Orthodox branches of Judaism. Here there is a general acceptance of the findings of biblical scholarship. Thus Jews today will need to determine what role the Torah should play in their everyday lives.

Another serious dilemma facing the Jewish community concerns the position of women. This issue has become one of the most pressing problems in the Jewish world as many Jewish women are attempting to reshape their personal lives as well as public institutions in the light of modern feminism. According to these women, traditional Jewish law discriminates against them by exempting women from the obligations to observe positive time-bound commandments as well as from participating in public prayer, Torah reading and traditional study. Such discrimination, they argue, extends to a variety of other areas of Jewish life. Orthodox Judaism will need to heed these voices, and reconsider the role of women in contemporary Jewish life (Adler, 1998).

All of these dilemmas about the nature of Judaism in modern society are in varying degrees related to the fundamental issue of assimilation. Prior to the Enlightenment, Jews did not have full citizenship rights of the countries in which they lived. Nevertheless they were able to regulate their own affairs through an organised structure of self-government. Today, however, this state of affairs has dramatically altered. Jews are now free to choose where to live, whom to marry, and what career to follow. The increasing number of mixed marriages testifies to the changed circumstances in which Jewry finds itself. As Jews stand on the threshold of a new millennium, answers must urgently be found to the perplexing problems confronting world Jewry (Wertheimer, 1993).

Activity B3

How far is it possible to define the 'essence' of Judaism and does this have any bearing on the question 'Who is a Jew?'

Comment on activity B3

For centuries Jews have wrestled with this issue, arriving at a variety of answers. Some have sought to find the essence of Judaism in religious belief; others have emphasised the importance of the law in trying to define the nature of Judaism. Yet this is an elusive topic, evoking a wide range of responses. Nonetheless, the following crucial factors should be stressed.

First, Judaism is not a credal faith; in the liturgy there is no parallel to the creed. In addition, Jews have not debated with each other about correct belief in the same way that Christians have. For this reason Jews have generally not been concerned with formulating a systematic theology. Instead, fervent debate has taken place concerning the meaning of the law.

Second, nonetheless, Maimonides and others have made various attempts to formulate the central principles of the Jewish faith. Maimonides' formulation of the Thirteen Principles of the Jewish Faith has generally been viewed as authoritative within the Orthodox community.

Third, in the Middle Ages, however, other scholars disagreed with Maimonides; these thinkers formulated a different set of central tenets of the faith.

Fourth, for non-Orthodox Jews, Maimoinides' Principles of the Jewish Faith are irrelevant. Instead of subscribing to these beliefs, reformers and others contend that Jewish religious conviction must be changed in the modern world. Thus, it has become increasingly difficult to isolate the essence of Judaism.

Fifth, the confusion about the essence of Judaism has created further confusion about Jewish status. If it is no longer possible to isolate the essence of Judaism, how is one to ascertain the criteria for Jewishness?

B2 Islam

Aims

After working through part B2 of this unit, you should:

- have some knowledge of the distinctive beliefs and practices of Muslims;
- have some understanding of the nature of Islamic spirituality;
- be able to appreciate some of the difficulties and dilemmas facing Muslims living in Britain and the western world;
- be aware of Muslim attitudes to and debates about education, family life and gender issues.

Overview

This unit begins by describing the central beliefs and practices of Islam and the main religious obligations. The role of the mosque in the life of Muslims and the major Islamic festivals is examined. To counterbalance this emphasis on the public dimensions of Islamic religious life, the concept of Islamic spirituality is also explored. In the second half of the unit, attention turns to the difficulties and dilemmas facing Muslims living in Britain and other western countries. Current debates include the education of Muslim children, the nature of family life and the place of women in contemporary society.

Since Muslims number over one billion worldwide, a wide diversity of attitudes and practices is inevitable, and it is almost impossible to make generalisations that are universally applicable. Students should therefore be wary of statements which begin 'Muslims think...' or 'The Muslim attitude to this is...'. Nor does labelling help: terms such as 'Muslim fundamentalists' or 'liberal Muslims' are western inventions, and carry little meaning for Muslims themselves. When this unit moves from a discussion of Islamic teaching to an examination of contemporary practice, therefore, the approach adopted follows orthodox ('Sunni') Islam as far as possible, but this should not be taken to imply that all Muslims conform to this path or follow a single set of practices.

Basic beliefs

The Qur'an states that 'true piety is this: to believe in Allah, the last day, the angels, the book and the prophets' (Qur'an 2:171), and these may be taken as the five central beliefs in Islam (cf. Nasr, 1987; Sarwar, 1989; Rippon, 1990-3).

Allah

Allah is the Arabic name for the one true God, the God who is also worshipped by Jews and Christians. However, the stringent monotheism of Islam allows no place for belief in the Trinity or in the divinity of Jesus. The oneness (*tawhid*) of Allah is *the* central doctrine of Islam, and is so important that it has repercussions on the whole of life: relationships between men and women, between humans and the natural world, and between the physical and spiritual world, should reflect this harmonious unity (*tawhid*) which belongs to Allah. Finite human beings cannot grasp the fullness of the mystery of Allah, but have been given a list of the 'ninety-nine most beautiful names of Allah' which symbolise his attributes (see Nigosian, 1987, pp 143-4 for a full list). When Muslims recite these names (sometimes running their fingers three times through a string of thirty-three beads), they remind themselves of Allah's sovereignty over all affairs. Allah is the Creator and Sustainer of the universe, and he is Eternally-existent, All-knowing, All-wise and All-powerful. He is the Judge who punishes the unfaithful but is the Merciful and Compassionate to the penitent, and it is through understanding his attributes that individuals come to understand the nature of moral virtues such as mercy, justice, truth, righteousness, generosity and wisdom. The destiny of every creature is already known and predetermined by Allah; indeed, nothing can happen without the will of Allah - though this does not mean that from a human perspective people do not have the freedom to choose their path in life. The appropriate choice for the believer is complete surrender to the will of Allah, so that the purpose of existence, which is to worship Allah, may be fulfilled in every area of life.

The last day

Life after death (*akhira*) is a central Islamic belief which puts the uncertainty of life on earth into perspective. Prior to the Last Day, there will be cataclysmic events on earth, accompanied by the appearance of the 'Guided One' (*mahdi*) and other signs. On the Last Day itself, a physical resurrection will take place and all individuals will be judged according to their deeds. The faithful will be rewarded with heaven, which is often described as a place of exotic physical delights, and the unfaithful punished in hell. The influence of Islamic eschatology can be seen in numerous Christian writings, including Dante's *Divina Commedia*.

The angels

Angels are the messengers of Allah, winged, sexless, immortal beings. Whereas humans were created out of clay or dust, the angels were created out of light and inhabit the invisible world, though they can take human form. Prominent among the angels are Gabriel (*Jibra'il*), Michael (*Mika'il*), Israfil (who will blow the last trump) and Izra'il (the angel of death). Other angels record the deeds and thoughts of each human being, receive their souls at the moment of death and witness for or against them at the day of judgement. The leader of the rebellious angels is Satan (*shaitan* or *iblis*), who refused the command of Allah to bow down to Adam after the creation, and he leads humans astray. Angels should not be confused with genii (*jinn*), mortal but generally invisible beings created from fire, who may inhabit trees, waste places or ruins, may take various shapes, and may interact, sometimes mischievously, with human beings.

The book

Islam proclaims that Allah has sent messages through prophets to all parts of the world throughout history, revealing himself and offering guidance on how to live. Sacred books are the transcripts of these messages. Earlier scriptures mentioned in the Qur'an are the scroll (*suhuf*) revealed to Abraham, the Torah (*tawrah*) revealed to Moses, the Psalms (*zabur*) revealed to David and the Gospel (*injil*) revealed to Jesus. All these revealed books are believed to contain the same basic message (and Jews and Christians are thus called the 'people of the book'), but Islam teaches that the earlier messages were distorted or corrupted over time and are no longer reliable. Only the Qur'an, Allah's final revelation to humanity, retains its original purity and authenticity and thus it should be accepted as superseding the earlier scriptures. For Muslims, therefore, belief in the Book means an acceptance of the Qur'an as literally the words of Allah and as the most comprehensive source of knowledge and guidance for believers. Inevitably any copy of the Qur'an is treated with the greatest respect by Muslims. In style, content and emotional impact, it is considered inimitable and untranslatable, and although Arabic is not the mother tongue of five-sixths of the world's Muslims they are expected to read the Qur'an in Arabic and use verses from it in the five daily prayers. Many seek to memorise the whole book by heart. The Qur'an is not poetry, nor a narrative, nor a philosophical treatise with a coherently developed argument; to Muslims it is far more than any of these: it is divine truth, describing the nature of Allah, the purpose of creation, human destiny, human responsibilities and notions of good and evil.

The prophets

Since the beginning of creation Allah has sent prophets or messengers to guide people in the right path. The essential message of all the prophets is the same: Worship Allah, the only true God. Muslim tradition says that there have been 124,000 prophets, but only 25 are mentioned by name in the Qur'an. Of these, Adam is the first and Muhammad is the last, the Seal of the Prophets, through whom Allah's final message to humanity was revealed. Muslims consider Jesus a prophet, next in importance only to Muhammad. It is normal practice in Islam to add the phrase 'Peace be upon him' after the mention of the name of a prophet.

The Five Pillars of Islam

The five basic duties that Muslims are obliged to perform are known as the five pillars of Islam. They are the declaration of faith (*shahadah*), prayer (*salah*), fasting (*sawm*), welfare contributions (*zakat*) and pilgrimage (*hajj*). These five duties comprise the formal side of worship in Islam, though in a broader sense any action of daily life which is carried out in accordance with Islamic law is also considered a form of worship.

The declaration of faith

The public declaration, 'I bear witness that there is no god but Allah and Muhammad is the Prophet of Allah', spoken in Arabic, is all that is needed for a person to be accepted legally as a Muslim. However, belief in Allah implies a desire to worship him, and belief in Muhammad's prophethood implies an acceptance of the message he brought (the Qur'an) and of the guidance he offered on how to live a holy life. The declaration of faith also forms part of the call to prayer.

Prayer

Regular prayer is at the heart of worship in Islam, and tradition requires five prayers a day: at dawn, noon, mid-afternoon, evening and night. In Muslim countries the call to prayer made from the minaret of a mosque reminds Muslims that it is time to pray. They are allowed to pray in public or in private, at home, in a mosque or wherever they happen to be, but most other aspects of prayer are closely prescribed. Ritual purification precedes the actual prayer, involving the washing of hands, mouth, nostrils, face, arms, head, ears, neck and feet; earth or sand may be used for the ritual cleansing if water is not available. Footwear is removed, and the worshipper must stand on a clean spot (hence a prayer mat is commonly used), facing the Ka'ba in Makka. The prayer itself consists of a repeated pattern of words and gestures. The four basic positions are standing, bowing, prostrating and sitting, and the words spoken include passages from the Qur'an and other expressions of praise, submission and supplication. Prayers are normally spoken in Arabic. Children are encouraged to pray as soon as they can, though prayers are not obligatory before puberty. In addition to the prescribed prayers, devout Muslims will offer further prayers, especially during festivals, when fasting, at times of danger or at funerals. The main value of prayer lies in the spiritual discipline involved, the symbolic expression of devotion and submission to Allah, and the sense of belonging to a community of believers all worshipping Allah together. The name of Allah is also regularly invoked in daily life: before starting to do anything, Muslims may say *bismillah ar-rahman ar-rahim* (in the name of Allah the Compassionate, the Merciful); when finishing an action, they may say *alhamdulillah* (praise be to Allah); when talking of the future, they may say *insha' Allah* (if Allah permits); and they may say *masha' Allah* (what Allah has willed) to express acceptance of any outcome.

Fasting

Adult Muslims are obliged to fast for the entire month of Ramadan, the ninth month of the Muslim calendar. Fasting involves abstaining completely from food, drink, smoking and sexual activity from dawn to sunset; normal life is resumed from sunset to dawn. The sick, pregnant women, nursing mothers, soldiers and travellers are exempt, but are encouraged to make up any missed days when they are able to. Fasting is not an act of penance or asceticism, but a spiritual discipline: it involves putting Allah before one's immediate physical needs, controlling one's passions and learning to empathise with the poor and hungry. Muslims are also encouraged to offer special prayers and Qur'anic recitations during Ramadan.

Welfare contributions

These are compulsory payments that Muslims should make at the end of every lunar year for the purposes of helping the poor and needy, orphans, slaves, prisoners, debtors and travellers and for other worthy charitable or religious causes. The payment is generally calculated at one-fortieth of a person's wealth, though the rate varies for cattle, agricultural produce and the produce of mines. The welfare contributions are a collective duty for Muslims, which symbolise the importance of caring for others and the rejection of the selfish pursuit of wealth. In fact, Islam teaches that wealth and property are held on trust from Allah, and in making such payments Muslims are fulfilling the terms of the trust. Additional individual acts of charity are also encouraged.

Pilgrimage

All physically able Muslims who can afford to do so are expected to perform the pilgrimage to the holy shrine of the Ka'ba in Makka once in their lifetime. The Ka'ba is the focus of prayer for Muslims, a one-storey building within the Grand Mosque of Makka; Muslims believe it was originally built by Adam, and was rebuilt by Abraham and Ishmael, and believe it is the oldest shrine built for the worship of the one true God. The pilgrimage is performed in the second week of the twelfth month of the Muslim calendar, and at this time up to two million people from all walks of life and from all around the world converge on Makka. The pilgrimage lasts several days and involves a number of symbolic rituals, but for those taking part it is a major spiritual experience in their lives. It is also an important way of strengthening the links between the different communities and groups in Islam. At the start of the pilgrimage, men put on sandals and two sheets of unsewn white cloth in place of their ordinary clothes; this symbolises purity and the equality of all believers. Women wear ordinary clothes, but must not wear a veil. Pilgrims must not have conjugal relations, carry arms, use perfume, harm animals, break or uproot plants or even cut their hair or clip their nails before the end of the pilgrimage. The rituals they perform include walking round the Ka'ba seven times, special prayers and meditations, stoning three pillars that represent Satan and re-enacting various incidents from the lives of Adam and Eve, Abraham, Hagar and Ishmael, including the sacrifice of an animal in commemoration of the famous sacrifice offered by Abraham.

Activity B4

On the basis of what you have read so far, what do you think is the purpose of existence according to Islamic teaching?

Comment on activity B4

At the heart of Islamic teaching is the belief that the purpose of human existence is to worship Allah. Worship involves total submission to him and living in accordance with his will. Worship includes not only the formal practices listed above as the five pillars of Islam, but every aspect of life which is lived according to Allah's creative purposes. Thus the pursuit of knowledge, the cultivation of the land, political activity and sexual relations can all be examples of worship if they are carried out in accordance with the divine will, as revealed in the Qur'an and the other sources of the divine law (shari'a). Worship also includes the development of Islamic virtues, and seeing this life as a preparation for the life to come.

Festivals

Islamic festivals are occasions of public thanksgiving and celebration, but also times of spiritual significance for individuals. There are two obligatory religious festivals, Id al-Fitr and Id al-Adha, and a number of other optional or cultural ones (von Grunebaum, 1976). All the festivals are dated according to the Islamic lunar calendar, and thus have no fixed date on the western solar calendar.

Id al-Fitr comes immediately after the end of Ramadan, and is a time for giving thanks for the fast, almsgiving and special prayers in the open air. It is a public holiday in Muslim countries, and is celebrated by wearing best clothes and perfume, giving presents to children, sending greetings cards, visiting friends and relatives and eating special food. The celebrations may last for two or three days.

Id al-Adha runs from the 10th to the 12th of Dhu 'l-Hijjah (the twelfth month in the Muslim calendar) and thus coincides with the time of pilgrimage. After special prayers, Muslims who can afford it sacrifice an animal, such as a goat, sheep, cow or camel, sharing the meat among relatives, neighbours and the poor. This commemorates Abraham's willingness to sacrifice his son (Ishmael, not Isaac) at Allah's command.

Other festivals include:

- 10 Muharram (1st month): 'Ashurah (creation of Adam, also birthday of

Abraham and Jesus; Shi'ites also celebrate the deaths of Hasan and Husain, the Prophet's grandsons);

- 12 Rabi' al-Awwal (3rd month): Milad al-Nabi (Birthday of the Prophet Muhammad);
- 27 Rajab (7th month): Lailat al-Miraj (the Night of Ascension);
- 15 Sha'ban (8th month): Lailat al-Bara'at (the Night when Fate is Decided);
- 27 Ramadan (9th month): Lailat al-Qadr (the Night of Power).

There are several other festivals that are celebrated only in certain parts of the Muslim world, or only by minority groups.

The mosque

From the first mosque built by the Prophet and his followers in Medina, mosques have developed into the most dramatic and elaborate architectural form in Islam. Styles vary from region to region throughout the world, but there are certain features that all mosques share, particularly the minaret, the facilities for washing, the courtyard and the prayer hall. The minaret is the tall thin tower from which the *muezzin* makes the call to prayer five times a day. The facilities for ritual washing may be a simple row of taps or a much more elaborate series of fountains. The courtyard serves as a gathering place for worshippers. The prayer hall itself has no pictures or images and no furniture except carpets; the direction of prayer (the *qibla*) is marked by an empty arch (the *mihrab*) on one of the walls of the hall. There is usually a pulpit with steps (the *minbar*), from which the prayer leader (the *imam*) delivers the Friday sermon. In some mosques there is a separate section or room set aside for women. In addition, there may be other smaller rooms used for teaching. Many mosques are buildings of considerable grandeur, with gold domes, carvings, rows of columns and elaborate decorations using calligraphy and arabesque designs. The endowment of a mosque is considered to be a particularly meritorious use of wealth.

Mosques are used for meetings, for teaching, for meditation, but above all for prayer. While any of the daily prayers *may* be offered in a mosque, the noon prayer on Friday is a time when all adult male Muslims are expected to join congregational prayers in the mosque (female attendance is not compulsory, and may depend on local custom). Thus Friday, while not a day of rest in the formal sense of the Jewish Sabbath or the Christian Sunday, is a time when normal business activities are suspended for a couple of hours or perhaps a half-day. For the formal prayers, worshippers stand in rows behind the imam, and follow his lead in the ritual movements and recitations. After the prayers the imam delivers a sermon which may be on a moral, social or political theme, and the assembly concludes with further prayers.

Muslim spirituality

A distinction is sometimes drawn between 'being a Muslim' and 'being Muslim'. The former may be a matter of external cultural identity, whereas the latter implies being on a spiritual journey, searching for inner meaning, striving to perfect one's personal submission to Allah. The metaphor of the journey is contained in two key terms: *shari'a* literally means the broad highway and is the name, as already noted, for Islamic law, which integrates political, social and economic rules into a harmonious religious worldview, as well as providing guidance on how individuals should live their lives; *tariqa* literally means the narrow path and refers to the individual's spiritual growth. Muslim mystics (*sufis*) emphasise the pursuit of spiritual enlightenment, the knowledge of hidden reality, loss of self and union with Allah. Numerous Sufi orders have grown up in the Muslim world offering different rituals and disciplines as a route to inner illumination. Some people have seen a tension between the public and private dimensions of Islam, but al-Ghazali, the eleventh century theologian, philosopher and mystic, has argued that the external rules of Islam and the inner experience are mutually supportive (Nasr, 1987).

An important dimension of spirituality in Islam is the development of a balanced life of virtue. Islam does not teach the doctrine of original sin, or antagonism between flesh and spirit. Rather, it teaches that physical pleasures which are enjoyed in line with Allah's divine will (as revealed in the shari'a) reinforce our thankfulness and love of Allah, so that body and soul exist in harmony and unity. Individuals who submit completely to the divine will become instruments of Allah's will on earth and will exemplify characteristics such as humility, fear of Allah, generosity, sincerity, honesty, justice, truthfulness, kindness, forgiveness, hospitality, modesty, purity, patience, brotherliness and a determination to resist evil (Ashraf, 1988, Part Three).

Muslim family life

Birth and childhood

Islam teaches that the birth of a child is a blessing from Allah, and that the parents are responsible for nurturing the child in the faith. The Prophet taught that all children are born Muslims and it is their parents who make them follow other religions or none. As soon as a baby is born, the call to prayer is recited in its ears so that the first words it hears are the name of Allah and the declaration of faith. Usually on the seventh day there is a naming ceremony: the child's hair is cut (and the weight of the hair in gold is given to charity), and an animal is sacrificed, the meat being shared between the family, relatives and neighbours, and the poor. Male circumcision is a universal practice among

Muslims, a custom traced back to Abraham, and is usually carried out early in a boy's life. Female circumcision was a pre-Islamic practice in some Muslim countries, and although it is not sanctioned in Islam, it is still practised in some parts of Africa and the Middle East. Early childhood is a time of considerable freedom for Muslim children, but children also learn about their religious duties both by direct teaching and by the example set by their parents. The family is the context where children are educated in character and the virtues (*adab*): they learn such things as respect for parents and elders, thankfulness, courtesy, compassion, kindness, patience and consideration for others.

Teenage years

By the age of twelve or thirteen children are considered old enough to carry out the religious duties of an adult. They are expected to work hard at school and to take their share of family responsibilities at home. The use of alcohol, drugs and artificial stimulants is not permitted unless prescribed by a doctor. Sexual relations of any kind are strictly forbidden before marriage, and a girl's loss of virginity would be considered to bring dishonour on the whole family; for this reason there is no dating or free mixing of the sexes after puberty. This also explains Muslim support for single-sex education at secondary level. Respect for parents should continue throughout life, and children are expected to care for their parents in old age. It is clear that Muslim teenagers brought up in the West may be exposed to a quite different set of values at school or among their non-Muslim peers (Halstead, 1994).

Marriage

All Muslims are expected to marry and to find spiritual, physical and emotional support within marriage; celibacy and same-sex relations are considered to frustrate God's creative purposes. The family (which in Islam means the extended family) is the cornerstone of the social structure of Islam. Pre-marital love is not a pre-requisite for marriage, and marriages are usually arranged by parents, though the persons to be married should always have the right to veto any arrangements. Marriage is a social and religious contract in which husband and wife have complementary duties, the man providing protection and financial support for the family and leadership outside the home, and the woman making decisions relating to the home and family. Women are free to work only if this does not interfere with their primary responsibilities towards the family. Sexual relations are regarded as a blessing from Allah which bind the couple together in love, but extra-marital relations are strictly forbidden. Divorce is permitted, though there is a saying of the Prophet that describes it as the worst of the things that are not actually forbidden. Men are allowed to have up to four wives so long as they are all treated equally (though polyandry is forbidden), but monogamy is the norm throughout the Muslim world.

Death

The key significance of death for Muslims is that after death there is no further chance to rectify one's errors or ask Allah for forgiveness before the Day of Judgement. Friends and relatives will therefore do all they can to support the faith of the dying person. After death, the body is washed, shrouded in new white cloth, prayed over in a mosque or open space, and then buried, resting on its right side facing Makka. Further prayers complete the ritual. Excessive mourning is discouraged, and elaborate gravestones or monuments should not be prepared (though this rule has not always been followed, as may be judged from the Taj Mahal, a tomb built by the Muslim ruler Shah Jahan to commemorate his wife).

Current debates on education

Muslims in Britain find themselves at the meeting point of two quite different cultures and worldviews (Lewis, 1994; Joly, 1995). Islam provides a clearly defined framework of public values enshrined in divine law, and Muslim culture and community life is shaped largely by religious belief; in the broader society, however, religious commitment is a matter of personal choice, most institutions are secular, and a wide diversity of moral and cultural practice is accepted. These conflicting values potentially generate tensions wherever Muslims interact with the broader society, for example, in the health care system, in the economic domain, in the judicial system and above all in education (Halstead, 1994).

Islam has a long-standing tradition of respect for education, but the ultimate goal of education in Islam is to nurture children in the faith, to make them good Muslims (Halstead, 1995). Liberal educational goals such as the development of critical rationality and personal and moral autonomy do not make much sense from an Islamic perspective. Many Muslims may give higher priority to the preservation of cultural identity than to the achievement of social integration, but liberal educators generally claim that it is not the role of the school to reinforce the cultural identity of the home. However, Muslim parents often look to education as a way of solving the social and economic problems they face (such as poor qualifications, high unemployment, poor housing, racism and religious prejudice) and of ensuring a better economic future for their children (Halstead, 1988).

To sum up, many Muslim parents have two major educational aspirations for their children. The first is to enable their children to enjoy all the benefits of life in Britain, competing in the employment market on an equal footing with non-Muslims and sharing the material advantages of modern scientific and technological progress. The second is to encourage commitment to Islamic values and the Islamic way of life, which will help to shape the identity of Muslim children, give them a rootedness and stability as they grow up and provide the foundation for a harmonious Muslim community in years to come. These two aspirations would be catered for most clearly in state-funded Muslim schools (Halstead, 1986), but the option of sending their children to such schools is not available for most Muslim parents, since by 1998 state-funding had been approved for only two Muslim schools, one in London and one in Birmingham.

Activity B5

Examine the pros and cons which may be advanced in the case for giving state funding to Muslim schools.

Comment on activity B5

Among the pros you may have mentioned:

- equality of treatment with other religious groups including Anglicans, Roman Catholics and Jews;
- the provision of a high quality general education while at the same time preserving the religious identity of the Muslim community;
- consistency between the values of home and school;
- symbolic recognition of the right to Muslim self-determination.

Among the cons you may have mentioned:

- the danger of ghettoising Muslims, thus isolating them from the broader society;
- the potential damage to the processes of social integration and mutual understanding between different cultural groups and the possibility of provoking a racist backlash;
- the belief that it is not the place of the school to reinforce the specific cultural commitments of minority groups, but rather that schools should free pupils from the constraints of the present and the particular and help them to grow towards personal autonomy.

The majority of Muslim parents in Britain have to choose between sending their children to a fee-paying, independent, separate Muslim school, or sending them to a regular state-funded church or county school, supplemented perhaps by attendance at a mosque school in the evenings or at weekends. The independent Muslim schools are generally small and under-resourced with poor quality accommodation and facilities and poorly qualified staff; and the fees, although generally low, put a strain on the limited income of the average parent. Currently about two percent of Muslim children in Britain attend such schools. The vast majority attend the local church or county schools. Their parents recognise that they will be exposed to un-Islamic values in both the overt and the hidden curriculum, but hope that the example set at home, together with the Islamic education provided after school hours in mosques, will counteract the influence of the state school. In fact, few parents are completely happy with this compromise, since it makes a distinction between religious and non-religious learning which is alien to the spirit of Islam, and although the education provided in mosques may compare unfavourably with state-funded education in terms of resources and pedagogy, the state school may insist on practices that are incompatible with Islam. Consequently, for over twenty years Muslim parents have been campaigning for concessions in the state school which will stop their children from being put in the position where they are expected to act in a way that is contrary to their faith. The main Muslim demands include:

- the retention of single-sex schooling as an option for Muslim girls;
- permission for Muslim girls to wear trousers instead of skirts for school uniform and to wear tracksuits for sporting activities;
- permission for Muslim children to be absent from school during the religious holidays of Id al-Fitr and Id al-Adha;
- the provision of *halal* meat (that is, meat slaughtered in accordance with Islamic teaching) for school dinners for Muslim children;
- facilities for Islamic prayers within schools;
- Muslim representation on school governing bodies and other committees;
- sensitivity in other areas, including school worship, swimming, dancing, certain forms of art and music, and the use of raffles in fund-raising.

Many of these demands have been met by local authorities where there are considerable numbers of Muslim children, and they are generally welcomed as a genuine attempt to meet the needs of Muslim children within the framework of the common school and to show respect for the cultural and religious beliefs of Muslims.

Current debates on women

The position of women in Islam probably generates more debate than any other topic (Mernissi, 1991). It is widely assumed in the West that Muslim women are 'prisoners of domesticity', being 'stifled by oppressive dress and other customs' and treated as 'second-class citizens'. These views are supported sometimes by mythology, such as the belief that a Muslim woman always has to walk five paces behind her husband, sometimes by reference to the strict dress codes in certain Muslim cultural traditions, and sometimes by reference to selected quotations from the Qur'an, such as male authority over women (2:228) and men's right to beat their wives (4:34). Some western feminists have gone further, treating Muslim societies as archetypal examples of patriarchal structures, and claiming that Muslim men deny women control over their own bodies and insist on single sex education so that they can keep women in a subordinate role.

The Muslim response is that it is in the West, not in Islam, that women are exploited both sexually and economically, and that modesty of dress, for example, is not so much about patriarchal domination as about creating a context where sexual harassment is less likely to occur and where women are valued for their personalities, thoughts, emotions and behaviour rather than for their physical attributes. In Islam, it is claimed, women are treated with respect, and this is regularly emphasised in the Qur'an (for example, 4:19). Women are recognised as the spiritual equals of men, having the same religious duties and rewards (3:195), but this is not considered incompatible with differentiated social roles based on partnership rather than competition. In addition, Muslim women were allowed to keep their own property after marriage and to inherit property from male relatives over a thousand years before English women gained similar legal rights.

The debate involves many different points of view, and is made more complex by the number of different issues involved (including legal status, education, division of labour and sexual mores), by the discrepancy that sometimes exists between Islamic teaching and actual practice and by the social and cultural diversity between countries and different ways of life (nomads, villagers, city-dwellers). It is worth noting that the debate is not only between western and Islamic values, but also goes on within Islam. Fatima Mernissi, for example, claims that women had higher status in the time of the Prophet than today and argues for a return to the original values of Islam (1991). Muslim feminists generally reject both western stereotypes of Muslim women as passive and docile and a belief in the superior liberating values of western feminism; instead they are seeking recognition of the right of Muslim women to find their own identity and future within an Islamic framework if they choose (cf. Halstead, 1991).

Activity B6

What do you think are the main difficulties facing Muslims living in Britain and the West?

Comment on activity B6

You may have considered any of the following:

- religious prejudice and misunderstanding, often resulting from an ignorance of Islam, and racism;
- the unfavourable image of Islam which is often presented in the media;
- poverty and high levels of unemployment;
- the difficulties faced in the place of employment, including taking time off for the daily prayers and the extended Friday noon prayer, taking holidays on Islamic festivals, wearing the headscarf (*hijab*);
- the difficulties encountered in following Islamic law (for example, relating to food, clothing and the separation of the sexes) in public institutions such as schools, swimming baths and hospitals;
- direct and indirect discrimination in many areas of life;
- the lack of adequate representation in parliament and other public decision-making bodies;
- the difficulty of maintaining the Islamic ban on receiving or paying interest;
- poor quality and overcrowded housing, generally in inner-city districts;
- low levels of educational qualifications;
- the impact of television and other media which introduce non-Islamic values and lifestyles into the home;
- language difficulties, including an inadequate grasp of English among older Muslims and the difficulty of maintaining the mother tongue among younger Muslims;
- immigration problems, which sometimes keep families apart;
- the struggle to maintain their identity under a dominant value system quite different from their own.

Readers

For Judaism

There are several important introductory books which will be of help in your study of this area including:

Cohn-Sherbok, L. and Cohn-Sherbok, D. (1997), *A Short Introduction to Judaism*, Oxford, Oneworld.
Jacobs, L. (1987), *The Book of Jewish Practice*, New York, Behrman House.
Jacobs, L. (1995), *The Jewish Religion*, Oxford, Oxford University Press.
Magonet, J. (1998), *The Explorer's Guide to Judaism*, London, Hodder and Stoughton.

Siegel, R., Strassfield, M., Strassfield, S. (eds) (1973), *The Jewish Catalogue*, Philadelphia, Pennsylvania, The Jewish Publication Society of America.

Wouk, H. (1968), *This is my God*, New York, Doubleday.

For Islam

Introductory texts that may be of help in your study of this unit include:

Haeri, S.F. (1993), *The Elements of Islam*, Shaftesbury, Element.

Lewis, P. (1994), *Islamic Britain: religion, politics and identity among British Muslims*, London, I. B. Tauris.

Nigosian, S. (1987), *Islam: the way of submission*, London, Crucible.

Sarwar, G. (1989), *Islam: beliefs and teachings*, London, Muslim Educational Trust.

Tames, R. (1982), *Approaches to Islam*, London, John Murray.

Watton, V.W. (1993), *Islam*, London, Hodder and Stoughton.

Bibliography

For Judaism

Adler, R. (1998), *Engendering Judaism*, Philadelphia, JPS.

Cohn-Sherbock, D. (1996), *A Concise Encyclopaedia of Judaism*, Oxford, Oneworld.

Jacob, W. (ed.) (1983), *American Reform Responsa*, Cincinnati, CCAR Press.

Jacobs, L. (1973), *A Jewish Theology*, London, Darton, Longman and Todd.

Rubenstein, R.L. and Roth, J.K. (1987), *Approaches to Auschwitz*, London, SCM.

Sacks, J. (1993), *One People*, London, Lettman Library.

Wertheimer, J. (1993), *A People Divided*, New York, Basic Books.

For Islam

Ashraf, S.A. (1988), *Islam: Teacher's Manual*, London, Mary Glasgow.

Halstead, J.M. (1986), *The Case for Muslim Voluntary-Aided Schools: some philosophical reflections*, Cambridge, Islamic Academy.

Halstead, J.M. (1988), *Education, Justice and Cultural Diversity*, London, Falmer Press.

Halstead, J.M. (1991), Radical feminism, Islam and the single-sex school debate, *Gender and Education*, 3, 263-278.

Halstead, J.M. (1994), Between two cultures? Muslim children in a western liberal society, *Children and Society*, 8, 312-326.

Halstead, J.M. (1995), Towards a unified view of Muslim education, *Islam and Christian-Muslim Relations*, 6, 25-43.

Joly, D. (1995), *Britannia's Crescent: making a place for Muslims in British society*, Aldershot, Avebury.

Lewis, P. (1994), *Islamic Britain: religion, politics and identity among British Muslims*, London, I.B. Tauris.

Mernissi, F. (1991), *Women and Islam: an historical and theological enquiry*, Oxford, Blackwell.

Nasr, S.H. (ed.) (1987), *Islamic Spirituality: foundations*, London, Routledge and Kegan Paul.

Nigosian, S. (1987), *Islam: the way of submission*, London, Crucible.

Rippon, A. (1990-3), *Muslims: their religious beliefs and practices* (two volumes), London, Routledge.

Sarwar, G. (1989), *Islam: beliefs and teachings*, London, Muslim Educational Trust.

Von Grunebaum, G.E. (1976), *Muhammadan Festivals*, London, Curzon Press.

Teaching about Judaism and Islam

Unit C

Classroom teaching

Rabbi Professor Dan Cohn-Sherbok

Lavinia Cohn-Sherbok

Department of Theology and Religious Studies

University of Wales, Lampeter

and

Dr J. Mark Halstead

Rolle Faculty of Education

University of Plymouth

Contents

Introduction

We have put side by side, in consecutive sections in this unit, suggestions for the teaching of Judaism and Islam. Each section is preceded by its own aims, but the recommended reading and the bibliography for both sections are put at the end of the unit. Part C1 relates to Judaism and part C2 relates to Islam.

C1 Judaism

Aims

After working through part C1 of this unit you should be able to:

- explain why you have chosen to teach Judaism and be in a position to justify this choice to governors, parents, colleagues and pupils;
- analyse your own approach to the teaching of Judaism - whether you are going to approach the subject phenomenologically or whether you are teaching it in the context of a confessional approach to religion;
- decide which aspects of Judaism can be most usefully taught in your particular school and at what stage in the curriculum these aspects should be introduced;
- locate a variety of resources to assist in the teaching of Judaism;
- plan and execute a unit of work on Judaism for at least one age group, making use of whatever resources are available and employing a whole range of teaching and learning skills;
- assess the learning outcomes of your unit of work and evaluate the success of your teaching methods.

Overview

This section discusses teaching Judaism in county schools and then in church schools. Attention is then drawn to confronting anti-Semitism and stereotyping. Sections are devoted to teaching Judaism in the primary school and in the secondary school.

Teaching Judaism in county schools

It is generally agreed that in county schools, world religions should be taught phenomenologically; in other words, the child should be helped to understand what it means to have religious commitment, without any previous assumptions being made about his or her own beliefs. The situation is obviously different in denominational schools. The phenomenological approach is usefully discussed in such works as:

- Read, G., Rudge, J. and Howarth, R.B. (1986), *How Do I Teach RE?*, London, Mary Glasgow Publications.
- Watson, B. (1993), *The Effective Teaching of RE*, London, Longman.

After Christianity, Judaism is probably the religion in which religious education teachers feel most confident. They will already be familiar with the outline of the Old Testament; they will know something of the historical and religious background to the life of Jesus; it is probable that they will already have some acquaintance with some Jewish people and they may have heard lectures and talks on the radio and television from such leaders as Chief Rabbi Jonathan Sacks, Rabbi Lionel Blue, Rabbi Julia Neuberger and the late Rabbi Hugo Gryn. However, there are pitfalls. The New Testament is not a reliable source for information on modern-day Jewish practices and contains a strong anti-Jewish polemic. By no means all Jews in Britain today practise their religion and, in fact, some know very little about it. It is too often associated with the world of their grandparents, with immigration, hardship and poverty. However well-meaning, such assimilated Jews are unlikely to give a vivid picture of the fullness of the Jewish tradition.

On the other hand, the Jewish religion does lend itself easily to the phenomenological approach. Smart (1989) identifies seven main dimensions of religion and all can be illustrated in the Jewish tradition. The ritual element is found in the rich daily and festival liturgy; the experiential can be identified in the prophetic experiences and the mystical tradition; stories of biblical and rabbinic heroes reflect the narrative dimension; the doctrinal element is to be found in the teaching about the Torah and in the various identified principles of the Jewish faith; the huge complexity of the Torah and Talmud are expressions of the legal and ethical dimension; the Jewish community itself with its various divisions illustrates the social dimension and, despite the destruction of the Holocaust, there are synagogues, manuscripts and a whole array of religious artefacts to demonstrate the material element. Over a number of years, all these elements can be represented at a level suitable to the age of the child.

However, a word of caution must be sounded. The phenomenological approach has been criticised on the grounds that complete objectivity in any subject is impossible and that it is, in any case, undesirable. All religious education teachers need to think about this problem seriously. It is particularly acute in the case of Judaism, when there is already some familiarity with the material and there is a long cultural and religious history of anti-Semitism.

Teaching Judaism in church schools

The situation of religious education teachers in church schools is somewhat different. The fact that parents have chosen to place their children in such a school may imply that they are looking for a more confessional approach to the material. However, parents may decide on a church school for a variety of reasons, not least because the discipline is thought to be better and (less Christian still) a bias in admission policy in favour of churchgoers is likely to result in a more middle-class clientele.

Useful examples of plans of work for a confessional approach to religious education can be found in such books as:

- Byrne, A. and Malone, C. (1992), *Here I Am: a Religious Education Programme for Primary Schools*, London, HarperCollins (gives a Roman Catholic slant).
- Lohan, R. and McClure, M. (1988), *Weaving the Web; a Modular Programme of Religious Education*, Glasgow, Collins.
- Groome, T. (1991), *Sharing Faith: the way of shared praxis*, San Francisco, California, Harper (gives an American slant).

These schemes start with the child's own experience of religion and from there the child is encouraged to reflect, to learn more and to incorporate the Christian vision into his or her own worldview.

Because Judaism is in a special relationship to Christianity, this approach does have certain problems. In the *Here I Am* scheme, which is built round the four activities of 'recognise', 'reflect', 'respect' and 'relate', there is an attempt to introduce stories from other faiths in the 'relate' category. The problem is that Judaism has traditionally been taught by Christians as a negative creed against which the truths of Christianity shine forth. So, for example, the Jews were waiting for a long-promised saviour. Jesus was God's saviour, but the Jews were so blind that they did not accept him, even though he himself was a Jew. It was left to the outcasts and sinners, the non-Jews and foreigners to recognise the Lord of Life.

Sensitive teachers will immediately see the dangers in this approach, yet it is quite difficult to avoid, particularly since the New Testament itself continually emphasises the obtuseness of the Jewish people. The problem is far less acute with other religions in that Jesus did not, as a matter of history, preach to the peoples of the Indian sub-continent or the Arabian peninsular. Some very evangelical teachers can avoid the difficulty (following Paul's line in the Epistle to the Romans), maintaining that the Jews' rejection of the Christian message was part of God's plan for the eventual salvation of the whole world. Still the implication for the intelligent child must be that the Christians are right and therefore the Jews are in serious error.

The confessional approach to religious education has, in any case, been criticised as being incompatible with the basic aims of a liberal education. There is a considerable, and interesting, debate on this. Nevertheless, within the context of a church school following one of the Diocesan Syllabi, it seems an appropriate approach, provided that the particular difficulties of teaching Judaism in an explicitly Christian context are confronted.

Confronting anti-Semitism and stereotyping

Another problem of teaching Judaism concerns the child's own pre-conceived notions. The stereotype that all Jews are mean and avaricious is still current in British society. Children may, quite unselfconsciously, accuse each other of being 'Jewish' when they are complaining of some classmate's minor lapse in generosity. They may also have heard the expression 'to Jew him down', meaning to strike a hard bargain. This stereotype goes back a very long way: it is essential background, for example, to understanding Shakespeare's *Merchant of Venice* and, still more, Marlowe's *Jew of Malta*.

Less obviously offensive, but equally insidious, is the notion that all Jews are clever and, as a result, most Jews are rich. In fact any categorisation which labels all members of an ethnic or religious group with a particular quality must be seen as essentially dehumanising. It is also probable, in this pluralist era, that there will be children of Jewish origin within the school. Not only are these stereotypes hurtful, they may also bear little relationship to the circumstances of these children's lives.

The religious education teacher may feel that this is not really a problem for religious education lessons. It more properly belongs to the realm of social studies or personal and moral education. Nonetheless this stereotype will get in the way of an understanding of Judaism as a living tradition. In addition it perpetuates the age-old Christian conviction that the Jew is sinisterly different as a human being, that he belongs to a world of dark, foreign, crooked machination while the Christian earns his living honestly by the sweat of his brow. This contrast was made much of in the Nazi propaganda in the 1930s and 40s and is by no means dead today. For a general introduction to the all-pervasiveness of anti-Semitism in Christian society, see:

- Cohn-Sherbok, D. (1997), *The Crucified Jew* (second edition), Grand Rapids, Michigan, Eerdmans.
- Wistrich, R.S. (1992), *Anti-Semitism*, London, Mandarin.

These preconceived notions must be confronted in ways appropriate to the age of the children concerned. In class, the children should explore how the stereotype of Jewish avarice occurred. This involves showing how the Jews were excluded from mainstream society, how they were kept out of the craft guilds and trading organisations and why usury was forbidden to Christians. Most children today have a post office or building society savings account. They all have the experience of lending money on interest! It should also be recognised that Judaism, with its emphasis on studying the Torah, is an intellectual culture and thus academic rather than physical prowess tends to be encouraged. However, it should be emphasised that there have been some world-class Jewish sportspeople - the swimmer Mark Spitz is an obvious example. Similarly, although there may be some Jews, as there are many non-Jews, who are less than generous, at the same time a look at any synagogue or Jewish charity indicates a very high level of giving within the community. Time spent in the classroom exploring these kinds of issues will do much to encourage greater open-mindedness towards the Jewish people and their religion.

Activity C1

Plan work either for a sixth form class or for an adult discussion group on anti-Semitism. The session should last for about fifty minutes and should include a reading (perhaps from Cohn-Sherbok or Wistrich, see above) to act as a stimulus. The group should address the following questions:

- Is anti-Semitism fundamentally a racial or a religious prejudice?
- Is Christianity necessarily anti-Semitic?
- Has the increased secularism of the present age lessened the feelings of discrimination against the Jews?
- Has the creation of the State of Israel made a difference?
- Does the fact that Jews are not immediately visible in society protect them against discrimination?
- Is there any evidence of anti-Semitism in Britain today?

If there is a Jewish member of the group, he or she might be willing to share personal experience.

Comment on activity C1

The purpose of this exercise is to examine, at first hand, the feelings of educated, modern Britons towards the Jewish people. You may, as result, feel that anti-Semitism is a dead issue. On the other hand, you may have been surprised at some of the generalisations made (all Jews are clever with money) or attitudes expressed (Jews should forgive and forget about the Holocaust).

In any event, it should throw some light on the background thinking of your pupils in school and help you prepare your lessons with this in mind.

Learning about and learning from Judaism

Even teachers who are determined to take a strict phenomenological approach to Judaism, will find that they are teaching more than the facts. Both of the SCAA Model Syllabi set attainment targets for each Key Stage and these demand that the student 'learns from' the religion as well as 'learns about' it. This means that the material must be presented in such a way that the pupil is encouraged to reflect on his or her own experience. Discussing religion, any religion, involves pondering such questions as those of morality, of the ultimate nature of reality, of personal feelings, of human relationships and of the nature of community ties. Thus children who learn about Judaism should not only achieve a broad general knowledge of the basic tenets and practices of the Jewish community, he or she should also have used the opportunity to consider his or her own stance to the questions raised.

There are many attitudes within Judaism that are foreign to the average, British, secularly educated child. The notion of being the chosen people and the clearly differentiated roles for men and women within the community are two obvious examples. Neither issue is easy to explain without distortion. It is vitally important that the teachers themselves understand that there are many different attitudes even among practising Jews to these questions and that the views of the very Orthodox are almost diametrically opposite to those of the Reform or Liberal. In any event, in order that the material is neither over-simplified nor trivialised, it is crucial that the child is encouraged to see that a religious tradition is not monolithic. It is not enough to say that Jews believe this or that. Just as they know that their own parents and teachers have differing opinions within a general consensus, so children should be encouraged to see that there is the same variety within other religious communities. This raises a great many interesting questions on the extent of tolerance, which could profitably be explored in the classroom.

In any event, many Agreed and Diocesan Syllabi introduce religions thematically rather than systematically. Thus the same aspects of a number of religions are studied together. So, for example, under the category 'holy books', the class might explore the Old Testament, the New Testament, the Talmud, the Qur'an, the Upanishads and so on. There is much to be said for this approach, particularly for younger children, since it is concrete, tangible and relatively value-free. On the other hand, it is open to distortion. The Jew has a different attitude to the Talmud from that of a Muslim to the Qur'an. At the same time, the teacher has difficult decisions as to how much to introduce and when. To a great extent it must depend on the age and ability level of the children concerned as well as their own religious backgrounds and the resources that are available within the school and local community.

Experiencing Judaism

Judaism is not a missionary religion. For both historical and theological reasons, Jews do not want to make converts. Salvation is available to any non-Jew who serves the One God, provided that he or she avoids idolatry, murder, theft and sexual immorality. The Jew, on the other hand, has to keep all the 613 commandments of the Torah as well as all the interpretations thereof. Thus it is, arguably, a disadvantage to be a Jew and the Jewish establishment sees no point in encouraging converts. This means that Jews will invite non-Jews to their homes and synagogues, but only on the clear understanding that they are there as outsiders. It is like visiting a family. Guests are welcomed and enjoyed, but they will never be part of the inner circle.

In many ways, this makes the task of helping children experience Judaism easier. There is no fear, as there may be in exposing children to evangelical Christians, that attempts will be made to convert them. In addition, the Jewish community is very anxious that non-Jews should know something about Judaism and that the traditional barriers of suspicion and fear should be overcome.

Most big towns, for example, have a branch of the Council of Christians and Jews. This is an organisation in which Jews and Christians can come together to meet each other and to learn about each other's faiths. Many religious education teachers enjoy the talks and exhibitions and their teaching is enriched by them. Local branches will often provide a list of speakers who are willing to come into schools to talk to children about aspects of Judaism. Thus, when the children are doing a unit of work on festivals, it is not impossible to find someone who will go through a modified Passover meal with a class, demonstrating the symbolic food and explaining the significance of the Exodus story for the Jewish community.

The local rabbi is also often willing to act as a resource. It is not realistic to take children to an Orthodox synagogue service. In the first place, the boys and girls have to sit separately in the synagogue and, all too often, the girls can see very little up in a balcony. The service is very long and it is almost entirely in Hebrew. In addition, the major service is on Saturday morning and most older schoolchildren have Saturday jobs. A Reform service is a little more accessible. Men and women sit together and some of the liturgy is in English, but it is still too much for most students. However, most pupils would enjoy a visit to a synagogue during the week and these can be arranged.

Elements of Judaism can also be experienced in the classroom. Jewish ritual objects, such as Hanukkah candlesticks, prayer shawls, prayer books, Passover plates, matzah (unleavened bread) and skull caps can all be purchased in synagogue gift shops or from the Jewish Memorial Council, Woburn House, Upper Woburn Place, London WC1H OEP. There are several excellent films and film strips. Older students can be encouraged to read Jewish novels, such as those of Chaim Potok or Harry Kellerman, and many thousands of children have come to grips with the enormity of the Holocaust through the diary of Anne Frank.

Activity C2

Making use of Ninian Smart's seven dimensions of religion, identify which dimensions can reasonably be explored in the classroom at the following levels: early juniors, top juniors, early secondary, middle secondary.

Comment on activity C2

You may have decided to focus on the mythological dimension (the stories) for the early juniors who are as yet unable to understand abstract thinking. By the middle secondary level, however, they should be able to cope with the doctrinal dimension and would find the mythological level too childish. The top juniors and the early secondary level might be able to come to terms with the experiential dimension and, with varying degrees of understanding, the ethical dimension.

You may, however, feel uncomfortable with the whole approach. There seems little point in learning about the Passover meal for example if it is only explored on the level of mythology. It is only comprehensible if the doctrinal and social dimensions are also explored. It is not helpful to explore the synagogue from a material dimension if the social and ritual dimensions are completely ignored. In other words, you have probably asked yourself whether it is really useful to separate the dimensions from each other. This, of course, does not invalidate the phenomenological approach, but it does mean that it must be treated with a degree of sophistication.

Judaism in the primary school

The introduction of a national curriculum with its sets of attainment targets has encouraged a flow of new books on the teaching of religious education. The primary school teacher may find the following particularly helpful:

- Bastide, D. (ed.) (1987), *Religious Education 5-12*, London, Falmer Press.
- Bastide, D. (ed.) (1992), *Good Practice in Primary RE*, London, Falmer Press.
- Erricker C. (ed.) (1993), *Teaching World Religions*, Oxford, Heinemann.
- Jackson, R. and Starkings, R. (1990), *The Junior RE Handbook*, Cheltenham, Thornes.
- Lazenby, D. (1993), *Eggshells and Thunderbolts: religious education and Christianity in the classroom*, London, BBC Educational and Culham College Institute.

Different aspects of Judaism and different approaches to teaching and learning are suitable for children of different ages. Among Strictly Orthodox Jews, children of five or six are considered to be capable of starting Hebrew, of studying the basic stories of the scriptures and of learning the prayers of the daily liturgy. Only at the age of twelve or thirteen are children thought to be ready to tackle the intricacies of Talmud argument.

Religious education in the church or county primary school will be less ambitious. The following are very brief suggestions for suitable topic areas within the Jewish tradition.

Key Stage 1

- The life of Moses, particularly concentrating on his birth story, his adoption by Pharaoh's daughter, his new life as a herdsman away from Egypt and his subsequent sense of mission. This should encourage reflection on personal identity, the child's position in his or her own birth and/or adopted family and the role of brothers and sisters. Later in the unit, the problems of going from being rich to being very poor can be explored. How difficult would the child find it to give up his or her own favourite possessions? They should then be encouraged to reflect about leaving home, at what stage adulthood begins and how people decide what they are going to do with their lives. The story should be continually referred back to the child's own experiences and that of his or her own family members.
- Many biblical stories are suitable for craft exercises (Noah's ark is an obvious example). These activities are much enjoyed and the moral of the story can be brought out clearly in each case.

Key Stage 2

- At this level, children are responsive to group activities. A unit on the festivals of the religions of the world could last throughout the year. Thus in the winter term, they could think about new beginnings with the Jewish New Year, the harvest festival of Sukkot (which involves building a booth and decorating it) and the Hanukkah story with the lighting of the Hanukkah menorah. During the spring term, the Purim story could be acted out and the festival of Passover explained with an accompanying modified Seder meal. Then, in the summer, the festival of Weeks (Shavuoth) could be explored with work on the Ten Commandments. Obviously, the children will be able to find similarities with the festivals of other religions and they should be encouraged to make such connections. Information about Jewish festivals is provided by Wood (1995), while Barnett (1984) concentrates on the wider issues of Jewish families in Britain.

Judaism in the secondary school

In the early years of the secondary school, the children grow and change into young people. The move from a small primary to a large secondary school can be bewildering and overwhelming. For many it is their first experience of meeting large numbers of their contemporaries from different areas and different backgrounds. In addition, psychologists recognise that this is the age when children become capable of going beyond the concrete and can begin to sustain serious abstract thinking. Thus it is a time of change and excitement and it is accompanied by the whole emotional and physical turmoil of adolescence.

Key Stage 3

- Children at this stage are profoundly interested in moral questions, thus it would be appropriate to embark on a unit of work on Jewish law. Worksheets can be prepared on the Ten Commandments, from various passages from Leviticus or Deuteronomy, from the Sayings of the Fathers in the Mishnah and even from condensed passages in the Talmud (Cohen, 1975, and Montefiore and Lowe, 1974, provide useful anthologies). From there discussion can range onto the necessity of rules within society, appropriate sanctions and the place of self-discipline.
- This may be an appropriate time to discuss with children religious prejudice and to introduce the Holocaust. Parallels should be drawn with other acts of genocide (sadly the children may already be familiar with the situation in such countries as the Republic of Bosnia Herzegovina, Rwanda and Indonesia through the daily newspapers). Probably the best way to help

children reach some understanding of the events of the Holocaust is through the stories of young people who lived through it. *The Diary of Anne Frank* is the most famous example, but there are many other memoirs which will aid empathy; many of these are edited for children. Again the Jewish Memorial Council is a rich source of supply.

Key Stage 4

- At this stage, the curriculum is dominated by the demands of the public examination system. Many boards offer Judaism as a full paper option or it is studied as part of an aspects of world religion paper. In any event, the boards themselves outline full syllabi and offer suggestions for class text books, for school library books and for books for teacher reading. The course may well include a visit to a synagogue and/or one of the local Jewish museums. One excellent text book is Pilkington (1991).
- More difficult is the weekly religious studies slot for those not taking religious studies for GCSE. All too often, the students themselves regard such lessons as a waste of time, taking them away from their 'more important' examination work. Probably it is best to favour an issue based, rather than a content based, course. Judaism, in common with the other great religions of the world, has a great deal to say on issues of personal morality, on the environment and on the building of a just society, and fourteen to sixteen year olds are always ready to explore such matters.

Judaism in the sixth form

More and more young people are continuing their education beyond the statutory school-leaving age. For many, the final two years prove to be the richest educational experience of their lives, with smaller classes, subjects of their own choosing and committed, dedicated teachers. At this level the curriculum is largely dominated by the demands of higher education; achieving the necessary grades to go on to the chosen next stage is the overarching goal. Religious studies will be included in the programme as one of two options; it may be taken as a full A or AS level, often one of the three which will provide the usual passport to higher education; alternatively it will be part of a general studies programme, which is designed as a counter to the over-specialisation of a traditional sixth form course.

- An Advanced Level Religious Studies course offers many options. There are papers on the Old Testament, the New Testament, Church History, Philosophy of Religion and World Religions. Most boards offer the alternative of a complete paper on Judaism, which covers both the history and the practices of the Jewish faith. No Hebrew is necessary, but the final examination questions are challenging and a high level of knowledge and analysis is required. The candidate is expected to be conversant not only with the traditional beliefs and rituals of Jews in the past, but also how Judaism is practised today. Thus it is essential that the students have some contact with the Jewish community and that their knowledge comes from experience as well as from books. Again the local Council of Christians and Jews will prove a helpful resource and will let the teacher know what lectures, expeditions and celebrations are occurring in the neighbourhood. There is no doubt that this is an easier option for students who live in big towns where there is a vibrant Jewish community. Also, in the case of schools which take a strictly phenomenological approach to Jewish studies, there may well be Jewish students in the class whose experience will be particularly enriching to the group.

- Many schools and colleges attempt to offer a sixth form general studies course in addition to the examination classes. This will have the same problems as any non-examination course - the students will perceive it as 'less important' than their other studies. To counter this, some schools enter their students for the JMB General Studies AS level. In any event, a unit in world religions is an obvious component. This could be pursued either thematically (ideas of the divine, religious art, worship in the world's religions) or by studying one religion as a whole. If the latter approach is adopted, the course may emerge as a highly modified version of the A level syllabus. Another alternative is to integrate world religions into current affairs teaching. Understanding the conflict between Jew and Muslim in the Middle East requires a knowledge of modern Jewish and Arab history. Similarly a study of the re-emergence of fascism in Eastern Europe demands some understanding of the Nazi period.

Activity C3

Plan a unit of work on Judaism that will last at least half a term (minimum six sessions). Write up your unit, including all the relevant contextual information.

Comment on activity C3

You should have taken into account the following factors:

- the type of school, whether church or county, comprehensive or selective and its catchment area;
- the age group of the pupils;
- the requirements of the examination syllabus or the relevant Agreed Syllabus;

- the arrangements for the assessment of the unit in your particular school;
- the learning objectives of the unit;
- the resources required, including the possibility of outside visitors or trips;
- your own teaching strategies.

Ideally you should use the unit in your own school. After it is finished, evaluate its success. The following questions may help you:

- Was the unit suitable for the age and ability of the pupils?
- Were both the most able and the least able pupils in the class challenged and absorbed?
- Did the pupils learn something from Judaism as well as something about it?
- Would a practising Jew have been satisfied with your treatment of the subjects under discussion?
- Was your assessment strategy effective? What exactly were you testing?
- Did the unit have anything to contribute to cross-curricular links?
- Did the unit contribute to the spiritual and moral development of the pupils?
- Did your pupils enjoy it?

C2 Islam

Aims

After working through part C2 of this unit you should:

- have clarified your own reasons for teaching children about Islam and be able to justify the aims of such teaching if questions about it are raised by pupils, parents, colleagues or governors;
- have reflected on which approaches and methods for the teaching of Islam are most appropriate to your own school, and on the key stages at which the different elements of Islam should be introduced;
- be aware of a range of resources which could be used to support the teaching of Islam in schools;
- be able to set learning objectives and plan, carry through, assess and evaluate a unit of work on Islam for a chosen age group.

Overview

This is the second section of this unit and it deals entirely with Islam. It follows a roughly similar pattern to that adopted by the previous section by suggesting ways you might approach Islam in the classroom in maintained schools and pointing you to some of the resources you might use.

Why teach about Islam?

Contemporary Britain is a culturally diverse society, and if children are to be prepared adequately for life in such a society they need to learn about the diversity of cultures in Britain. Since Muslims are the largest religious minority in Britain today, it makes sense that children should be taught about their faith and culture. But developing children's knowledge and understanding of Islam and other religions and cultures is not enough to ensure a harmonious society in the future. Children also need to develop positive attitudes and values, such as respect for those whose beliefs differ from their own, openness to a variety of ways of looking at the world and a willingness to see diversity as a source of enrichment. Children need to be freed from inherited biases and from the arrogance and insensitivity which a narrow, monocultural education can bring. If they never get beyond the framework of their own culture and beliefs, they are less likely to develop lively, enquiring minds, imagination, a critical faculty, intellectual humility, the capacity for reflection, self-criticism or the ability to form independent judgements. The study of Islam and other religions is thus central to the liberal vision of what education fundamentally is about.

Islam is the religion of one-fifth of the world's population. For Muslims all over the world, their religion is a way of life that provides answers to the deepest questions about human existence and purpose. The lives of individuals and of whole societies have been shaped by the teachings of Islam. A person could hardly be considered educated who knows nothing of the religious beliefs and traditions of Muslims or the perspectives on life which Islam offers.

Islam has made a rich contribution to human history. If it is part of children's education to learn about the great human achievements of the past, then they need to study, among other things, the contribution that Islam and Islamic civilisations have made (and continue to make) to culture, politics, social organisation, the arts, the sciences and other areas of human experience.

Any serious study of Islam will force the non-Muslim student to think about questions relating to human existence from new perspectives. These questions include the relationship between law and morality, the spiritual side of life, the distinction between religious and non-religious domains of life, the possibility of personal autonomy and the way religion can affect the life of an individual. As Jackson (1997, pp 129-134) points out, understanding and reflection are inseparable in the interpretative process which he sees as a central aim of religious education.

Activity C4

List the main aims of teaching Islam to non-Muslim students under the following headings: skills, attitudes, concepts, knowledge.

Comment on activity C4

You may have identified the following issues:

- *Skills*: to develop the motivation and skill of pupils to learn from the study of Muslim beliefs and values, so that they can reflect more effectively on their own relationships, spiritual and moral values, feelings, commitments and worldviews;
- *Attitudes*: to help pupils to develop openness, sensitivity and respect towards Muslims and others whose beliefs differ from their own, a willingness to try to see the world through the eyes of others, and a recognition of their inter-relatedness with others;
- *Concepts*: to enrich pupils' understanding of key religious concepts such as prayer, revelation, prophethood, pilgrimage and worship;
- *Knowledge*: to extend pupils' knowledge and understanding of Islam as one of the world's main religions, including the beliefs, traditions and lifestyles of Muslims and the contribution Islam has made to world civilisation.

Confronting Islamophobia

One of the important contributions that religious education can make in a multicultural society is to help people to understand each other and to break down fear and prejudice. The deep-seated prejudice and discrimination which many Muslims experience in the West has been highlighted in a publication by the Runnymede Trust (1997), *Islamophobia: a challenge for us all*. The rather cumbersome term 'Islamophobia' has gained currency recently as a way of referring to the fear and hatred of Islam and the consequent suspicion and dislike of all Muslims. The Runnymede Trust claims that such fear and dislike have existed in western countries for centuries, but have become more explicit, more extreme and more dangerous in the last twenty years. The evidence of Islamophobia is seen in violence against Muslims (physical assaults, vandalising of property, verbal abuse); in exclusion from positions of political and economic power and influence; in discrimination in areas such as employment, health and education; in the prejudice witnessed all too frequently in the media and in everyday conversation; and in the stereotyping of all Muslims as medieval fundamentalists, barbaric terrorists, fanatical book-burners and oppressors of women.

Because Islamophobia is now so widespread in Britain (as in other western countries), children may come to school with many negative images and preconceived notions about Islam and Muslims. Providing accurate information about the religion and its followers is an important first step in combating prejudice and stereotyping (for they thrive on ignorance). But, as the Cohn-Sherboks point out in connection with anti-Semitism, this is only the first step. The negative images must be confronted head-on, the stereotypes challenged in ways appropriate to the age of the children concerned, and the injustice of the prejudice, discrimination and social exclusion highlighted, otherwise they will hinder children from developing a sympathetic understanding of Islam as a way of life followed by many millions of people.

The Runnymede Trust report points out that Islamophobic attitudes may sometimes be found within Christian organisations, though Christian leaders have generally been anxious to 'dissociate themselves from the bigotry expressed in the name of Christianity' and the Archbishop of Canterbury in particular has spoken of the need for Muslims and Christians 'to choose to walk together in harmony' (Runnymede Trust, 1997, pp 54-5). Church schools have an important part to play in promoting this harmony.

Teaching Islam in church schools

While county schools, particularly those which adopt a phenomenological approach to religious education, are more likely to be comparatively even-handed in teaching a variety of world religions, this is not necessarily the case with church schools. The latter may see Christian nurture as the main purpose of religious education and may therefore adopt a Christian confessional approach, encouraging children to incorporate a Christian vision into their own worldview. This may leave comparatively little time within religious education for the teaching of Islam and other non-Christian faiths, and it may also raise questions about how such faiths will be approached.

Muslims have two main anxieties about the teaching of Islam in an explicitly Christian context. First, if Islam is taught from a Christian perspective rather than in its own terms, there is the possibility that long-standing Christian biases against Islam may (perhaps unintentionally) creep into the teaching. Second, teachers may be less motivated to provide a full, accurate and balanced picture of Islam. This is why Muslims prefer Islam to be taught by Muslim teachers (Islamic Academy, 1985, p 6). Failing that, they prefer that reliable (preferably Muslim) sources of information should be used or contact made with practising Muslims. At the very least, teachers should have an accurate knowledge of Islam and the capacity to present it in a way in which a Muslim believer would perceive it. It remains an important principle, as Jackson (1997, p 134) points out, that 'voices from inside the traditions need to be taken very seriously'.

Many church schools currently admit a minority of Muslim pupils, and Muslim parents are often happy to send their children to such schools because they prefer them to be educated in an atmosphere of faith and respect for religion rather than one of scepticism and secularism; in any case, Islam does not deny fundamental truth to other religions, but simply asserts that their view of truth is incomplete. However, the anxiety remains among many Muslims that if Muslim children are exposed to Christian teaching and Christian values over an extended period, there may be a gradual drift away from their own faith (Halstead, 1992, p 47). Where Muslim children do attend church schools, therefore, it is important that their faith is respected (see IQRA Trust, 1991).

Learning about Islam

Of the three remaining approaches to the teaching of religious education currently adopted in schools (apart from confessionalism), the experiential approach (see, for example, Hammond, Hay, Moxon, Netto, Raban, Straugheir and Williams, 1990) is intended to introduce children to religion through personal and spiritual experience, and does not lend itself to teaching about specific faiths, least of all a faith such as Islam that is dependent on authority, self-discipline and submission. The approach based on religious artefacts (see, for example, Grimmitt, Grove, Hull and Spencer, 1991) is intended to capture children's interest in religion by providing them with opportunities to explore particular religious items in depth; but the process of engaging the children's attention through 'sensory perception' involving 'vivid and colourful' religious material (pp 8, 12) is not really in harmony with Islamic principles, since neither religious images, statues and icons nor hymn singing nor the burning of incense have any place in Islam. Such artefacts as are available, including prayer mats, Qur'an stands, prayer beads, Id greeting cards, and items of Middle Eastern clothing, are mainly cultural rather than religious artefacts, having no place in the Shari'a (Islamic law), though they may serve a very limited purpose in introducing children to some aspects of the way of life in Muslim countries.

That leaves the phenomenological approach. As you will know from an earlier module, this approach was popularised by Ninian Smart (1969, 1989) who analysed religion into six (and subsequently seven) dimensions that could be the focus of work in the classroom, and it is this approach which broadly underpins *The Westhill Project R.E. 5-16* (Read and Rudge, 1988-9).

Activity C5

Show how the seven dimensions of religion (ritual, mythological, doctrinal, ethical, social, experiential and material) can all be illustrated in Islamic faith and practice.

Comment on activity C5

You may have identified the following issues:

- *ritual*: the five pillars of Islam;
- *mythological* (that is, narrative): the hadith;
- *doctrinal*: belief in the oneness of God, the prophethood of Muhammad, the Qur'an as the word of God, and the day of judgement;
- *ethical*: the Shari'a;
- *social*: the umma (Islamic community), festivals, pilgrimage, communal activities at the mosque, family life;
- *experiential*: revelation; the emotional impact of listening to the Qur'an; the mystical experiences of Sufis;
- *material*: mosques, calligraphy.

Smart's seven dimensions can be utilised in either a thematic approach or a systematic approach to religious education. Thus children in primary schools may be given the theme of festivals for their religious education one term, and may learn about Id al-Fitr alongside Christmas, Divali, Hanukkah and Wesak. The aim is that over a period of years through the study of a variety of themes children will build up a reasonably comprehensive picture of religion, covering the different dimensions of religion at appropriate ages. Nevertheless, Muslims may have several anxieties about the thematic approach, apart from the frequent objection that children may confuse the different religions covered. First, though the approach may result in a 'reasonably comprehensive picture' of religion generally, it does not necessarily do justice to any particular faith or offer a coherent picture of the unity of that faith. Second, Islam may appear in a less favourable light than other religions to the uncommitted student; its festivals may be less fun than those of Hinduism, its prayer and fasting more rigid than those of Christianity, and its stories less appealing than those of Judaism. Third, studying the theme of sacred texts, for example, may lead pupils to the false assumption that the Qur'an occupies very much the same place for Muslims as the New Testament does for Christians.

Overall, many Muslims would prefer a systematic approach to the teaching of Islam (in which perhaps a whole term may be spent on the one religion), so that pupils may learn how the various elements of the religion fit together into a harmonious whole. However, it is recognised that pupils may not be ready to study some aspects of Islam until secondary school, and since that is rather late for children to receive their first introduction to Islam, the value of some thematic work in primary school is acknowledged. Some Muslims have suggested that the most useful work at the primary level is work which stresses those values and experiences which are common to all religions (Islamic Academy, 1985, p 5). A more general problem with the phenomenological approach from a Muslim perspective is that it is grounded ultimately not in religious values but in the liberal ones of critical openness, personal autonomy and freedom of personal choice (Halstead, 1992, p 43).

Resources for teaching Islam

Undoubtedly the most important resource for the teaching of Islam is the human one. Muslim parents or members of the local community may be invited to talk about their faith, and if there is a local mosque, the imam is often willing to act as a resource. Muslim pupils will also normally be willing to talk informally about their faith. Most mosques welcome non-Muslim visitors by prior arrangement, but note that although new mosques are currently opening in the UK at the rate of one a week, only a small percentage of these is purpose built, and the remainder may be converted warehouses, church halls or other suitable buildings. Children should be prepared carefully for the visit in advance: such preparation will include guidance about the removal of shoes, appropriate clothing and general respect for a place of worship, and also advice not to expect pews, altar, font, organ, hymn books, stained glass windows, statues, carvings or other artefacts that they may associate with a place of worship. The imam or another senior member of the mosque will normally be present to explain the significance of the washing facilities, the absence of furniture, the carpets on the floor, the *mihrab* (arch indicating the direction of Makka) and the *minbar* (pulpit).

Advice has already been given about the danger of over-reliance on the use of artefacts in the teaching of Islam, but a visual display incorporating prayer mats, pictures of mosques and the Ka'ba at Makka, examples of Islamic calligraphy and Islamic patterns and decorations, Qur'an stands, prayer beads (the 99 beads represent the 99 names of God), Id greeting cards, and items of Middle Eastern clothing may provide a helpful introduction to a project on Islam. Of course, the most important visual aid is the Qur'an itself, but care must be taken to treat it with respect at all times, for example by wrapping it in a special cloth, not placing anything on top of it, and displaying it as high as possible.

There is a dearth of high quality books for children on Islam, though the situation is gradually improving. Those produced by Muslim organisations have tended in the past not to be very attractively produced, whereas those written by non-Muslims, even when they avoid the grossest errors (such as providing illustrations depicting the Prophet Muhammad), have often been viewed with suspicion by Muslims because of minor errors of fact or emphasis.

Curriculum planning

The main principles to bear in mind when planning for the long or medium term include the following.

- You should follow the guidelines contained in the local Agreed Syllabus or the Diocesan Syllabus, as appropriate.
- Content should be linked to one or more of the general aims of teaching about Islam. It is helpful to bear in mind what contribution the chosen content might make to the pupils' spiritual, moral, social and cultural development.
- Content should be appropriate for the age and ability of the pupils. Other things being equal, it is advisable to start with the concrete with younger children, and move to the abstract as they get older; to start with the present day, and move to the past; to start with the local or national (for example, Islam in my city, or Islam in Britain), and move to the distant or international; to start with the familiar, and move to the less familiar or 'exotic' elements in Islam; to start by bringing Islam into thematic work, and move to systematic study of Islam later; to start with questions of fact, and move on later to questions of concept and questions of value. However, stories are a useful way of encouraging children's imaginative involvement with issues that are remote from their personal experience.
- Planning should take account of progression and continuity, both within and between the key stages. A current problem for religious education as highlighted in OfSTED reports is that work at Key Stage 3, after transfer to secondary school, does not always build on the good work done at Key Stage 2.
- Lessons should make use of a variety of approaches and resources, and offer a variety of tasks, appropriately differentiated. Activities may include reading, writing, discussing, listening, story-telling, model-making, drawing, constructing, recording, visiting, interviewing, and so on. Especially at KS1 and KS2, cross-curricular links should be borne in mind.

Key Stage 1

Learning at this stage will be developed most effectively through meeting with people and observing their behaviour, through listening to interesting stories, and through activities involving concrete objects. Where there are Muslim children in the class, teaching about Islam may be direct, but otherwise may be best incorporated as appropriate into more general themes such as families, sharing, journeys, buildings, clothing, celebrations, books and friends.

Key Stage 2

Thematic work will continue, with themes such as rites of passage, sounds, light, rules, communication, relationships, and patterns, shapes and spaces. More time may now be given to specifically Islamic sub-topics within the general themes, such as Muslim family life, going to the mosque, prayer, fasting during Ramadan, the Arabic language and the Qur'an. Stories such as the story of Bilal may lead on to a variety of work on the Call to Prayer as well as providing opportunities for discussion of a range of spiritual and moral issues (see Grimmitt, Grove, Hull and Spencer, 1991, pp 64, 68-9; Ashraf, 1988, pp 84-5). A more systematic approach to the teaching of Islam may be adopted in schools where Islam is part of the lived experience of some of the children. An extended project on the hajj (the pilgrimage to Makka) may involve cross-curricular elements and may, through the judicious use of imaginative writing and other approaches, help children to understand its spiritual and emotional significance for the believer (see Tames, 1982, pp 174-5).

Key Stage 3

The transition from KS2 to KS3 is important for a number of reasons. It is usually marked by a change of school, and so communication between the schools is important to ensure appropriate continuity and progression. Children will gradually become more familiar with abstract thinking, more open to influences outside the home and the school, and more willing to challenge orthodox opinion and the authority of teachers. Children may become bored more easily with things they perceive as irrelevant to their own lives, and may repeat anti-Muslim prejudice and stereotyping which they pick up from the media. Wise teachers will seek to win their pupils' confidence by encouraging them to adopt a critical approach to negative media images of Islam, to reflect on their own emotional responses to new or unfamiliar patterns of belief or behaviour, and to see the world through the eyes of others. There are three main approaches to the teaching of Islam at KS3. First, if it has not already been attempted, this may be the time to attempt a systematic study of Islam, bringing together all the key elements that have already been studied plus others that have not been covered so far into a coherent whole. Second, children's growing interest in moral issues may make this a good stage to introduce an Islamic perspective on personal morality and family values. Third, pupils may now be mature enough to see greater significance in Islamic symbols and rituals, and may be interested in specific issues such as life after death.

Key Stage 4

Religious education specialists will follow the chosen exam syllabus. Non-specialists will build on work started in KS3, studying, for example, Islamic perspectives on ethical issues such as the environment, the use of force or racial discrimination, perspectives on scientific issues such as the relationship between science and religion, and perspectives on cultural issues such as the impact of religion on art, architecture and literature.

Sixth form

Again, religious education specialists will follow the chosen examination syllabus. Here are some suggestions for topics which non-specialists may enjoy covering as part of a general studies course:

- rights, personal autonomy, law and the point of rules, with special reference to the Shari'a;
- religious experience and revelation, with special reference to Sufism;
- women in Islam;
- Islam and the modern world;
- Islamophobia.

Activity C6

Plan a unit of work on Islam or with a strong Islamic component for a chosen age group, to last for at least half a term. You will need to identify the Key Stage and the kind of school before you start planning.

Comment on activity C6

Your plans should include reference to a religious education syllabus and its overarching aims, and should contain a list of objectives, an overview of content, an outline of teaching strategies and planned activities, a list of resources, notes on differentiation and progression and some plans for assessment.

Assessment and evaluation

The first stage in evaluating the success of your teaching of Islam is to assess whether pupils' achievement matched the objectives you set for your lesson or your medium-term plans. To do this, you must first decide how to assess pupils' achievement, what assessment activities to use and whether to involve your pupils in self-assessment.

More generally, you need to check that the content and activities of the lesson or unit of work were appropriate to the age and level of the pupils, so that they were challenged without being out of their depth, and that the teaching strategies and presentation made the learning an enjoyable experience for the pupils.

You should reflect on the knowledge about Islam which you have passed on to the pupils. Have you managed to avoid superficiality, caricature and Christian or secular bias when talking about Islam (see Tames, 1982, p 148)? Do you think practising Muslims would be happy with your teaching?

You should also reflect on the extent to which you have helped children to learn from the study of Islam. Is there any evidence that your work on Islam has influenced their personal growth and moral development, their ability to empathise, their sensitivity and respect towards others, and their capacity to reflect on their own values and commitments?

Readers

For Judaism

Cohn-Sherbock, D. (1996), *A Concise Encyclopaedia of Judaism*, Oxford, Oneworld.

Sacks, J. (1993), *One People*, London, Lettman Library.

Werblowsky, R.J. and Wigoder, G. (1997), *The Oxford Dictionary of the Jewish Religion*, Oxford, Oxford University Press.

For Islam

Ashraf, S.A. (1988), *Islam: Teacher's Manual for the Westhill Project R.E. 5-16*, London, Mary Glasgow.

Erricker, C. (ed.) (1993), *Teaching World Religions: a teacher's handbook*, London, Heinemann.

Read, G. and Rudge, J. (eds) (1988-9), *The Westhill Project R.E. 5-16: Islam*, London, Mary Glasgow and Cheltenham, Stanley Thornes.

Tames, R. (1982), *Approaches to Islam*, London, John Murray.

Bibliography

For Judaism

Barnett, C. (1984), *A Jewish Family in Britain*, Exeter, Religious and Moral Education Press.

Bastide, D. (ed.) (1987), *Religious Education 5-12*, London, Falmer Press.

Bastide, D. (ed.) (1992), *Good Practice in Primary RE*, London, Falmer Press.

Byrne, A. and Malone, C. (1992), *Here I Am: a religious education programme for primary schools*, London, HarperCollins, (gives a Roman Catholic slant).

Cohen, A. (1975), *Everyman's Talmud*, New York, Shocken Press.

Cohn-Sherbok, D. (1997), *The Crucified Jew* (second edition), Grand Rapids, Michigan, Eerdmans.

Erricker C. (ed.) (1993), *Teaching World Religions*, Oxford, Heinemann.

Groome, T. (1991), *Sharing Faith: the Way of Shared Praxis*, San Francisco, Harper, (gives an American slant).

Jackson, R. and Starkings, R. (1990), *The Junior RE Handbook*, Cheltenham, Thornes.

Lazenby, D. (1993), *Eggshells and Thunderbolts: Religious Education and Christianity in the Classroom*, London, BBC Educational and Culham College Institute.

Lohan, R. and McClure, M. (1988), *Weaving the Web; a Modular Programme of Religious Education*, Glasgow, Collins.

Montefiore, C.H. and Lowe, H. (1974), *A Rabbinic Anthology*, New York, Shocken Press.

Pilkington, C.M. (1991) *Judaism: an approach for GCSE*, London, Hodder and Stoughton.

Read, G., Rudge, J. and Howarth, R.B. (1986) *How Do I Teach RE?*, London, Mary Glasgow Publications.

Smart, N. (1989), *The World's Religions*, Cambridge, Cambridge University Press.

Watson, B. (1993), *The Effective Teaching of RE*, London, Longman.

Wistrich, R.S. (1992), *Anti-Semitism*, London, Mandarin.

Wood, A. (1995), *Celebrate Jewish Festivals*, London, Heinemann.

For Islam

Ashraf, S.A. (1988), *Islam: teacher's manual for the Westhill Project R.E. 5-16*, London, Mary Glasgow.

Erricker, C. (ed.) (1993), *Teaching World Religions: a teacher's handbook*, London, Heinemann.

Grimmitt, M., Grove, J., Hull, J. and Spencer, L. (1991), *A Gift to the Child*, London, Simon and Schuster.

Halstead, J.M. (1992), Muslim perspectives on the teaching of Christianity in British schools, *British Journal of Religious Education*, 15, 43-54.

Hammond, J., Hay, D., Moxon, J., Netto, B., Raban, K., Straugheir, G. and Williams, C. (1990), *New Methods in RE Teaching: an experiential approach*, Harlow, Oliver and Boyd.

IQRA Trust (1991), *Meeting the Needs of Muslim Pupils: advice for teachers and LEAs*, London, IQRA Trust.

Islamic Academy (1985), *The Teaching of Islam in British Schools: an agreed statement*, Cambridge, Islamic Academy.

Jackson, R. (1997), *Religious Education: an interpretive approach*, London, Hodder and Stoughton.

Read, G. and Rudge, J. (eds) (1988-9), *The Westhill Project R.E. 5-16: Islam* (consists of four pupils' books Muslims 1-4, and a photopack), London, Mary Glasgow and Cheltenham, Stanley Thornes.

Runnymede Trust (1997), *Islamophobia: a challenge to us all*, London, Runnymede Trust.

Smart, N. (1969), *The Religious Experience of Mankind*, New York, Charles Scribner's Sons.

Smart, N. (1989), *The World's Religions*, Cambridge, Cambridge University Press.

Tames, R. (1982), *Approaches to Islam*, London, John Murray.

Watton, V.W. (1993), *Islam: a student's approach to world religions*, London, Hodder and Stoughton.

Teaching about Hinduism, Buddhism and Sikhism

Teaching about Hinduism, Buddhism and Sikhism

Unit A

Historical outlines

Denise Cush and Catherine Robinson

Bath Spa University College

Dr Wendy Dossett

Trinity College Carmarthen

and

Professor Brian Bocking

School of Oriental and African Studies

University of London

Contents

Introduction

The three units in this module are constructed differently from most of the other modules. In this unit we present three separate sections offering historical outlines of Hinduism, Buddhism and Sikhism. Each section is preceded by its own aims, but the recommended reading and the bibliography for all the sections are put at the end of the unit.

The second unit in the module uses the same method of placing the three religions in the order of Hinduism, Buddhism and Sikhism and deals with contemporary practices and current debates in the each religion. The third unit, again using the same method, presents ideas for teaching each religion in the classroom. The module therefore invites you to work through the three religions starting with this unit and with the oldest of the three religions, Hinduism, and then to see how each of these religious traditions has interacted with the others in its development, in its adjustment to the geo-political realities of the modern world, in the contemporary issues that occupy it and in its transfer to Britain. Of course, if you want to follow only one of the religions, then you can do so and all you have to do is to follow that particular thread through the three units. Yet, we think that you will be enriched by trying to work on a broad front because there are similarities as well as diversities between the religions and the challenges they present to modern readers.

One matter to be aware of, and it is mentioned at appropriate places, is the way the transliteration of words and names from non-Roman alphabets to the Roman alphabet with which we are familiar results in variant spellings and pronunciations. We have tried to help here by using suitable diacritical marks and by including a glossary.

A1 Hinduism

Aims

After working through part A1 of the unit you should be able to:

- engage with the issues surrounding the concept of Hinduism, and the challenges posed to western assumptions about religion;
- understand some of the major characteristics of the Hindu worldview in its rich diversity;
- appreciate the ways in which Hinduism has developed over millennia.

Overview

All three of the religions presented for study here appear to have originated in the Indian subcontinent. Hinduism has the most diffuse origins and is, in some respects, the hardest to define because it is part of the culture that carries it and which it shapes. Buddhism and Sikhism, by contrast, can be traced to the teachings of specific individuals who are regarded in some ways as Founders of these traditions. Buddhism has proved to be most adaptable to non-Indian cultures though Sikhs, compared with Hindus, historically have found it more acceptable to leave the sub-continent. All three traditions share certain presuppositions about the nature of the universe, and have significant concepts in common.

Introducing Hinduism

Wilfred Cantwell Smith famously observed 'the term "Hinduism" is, in my judgement, a particularly false conceptualisation, one that is conspicuously incompatible with any adequate understanding of the religious outlook of Hindus' (Smith, 1978, p 63). Even those scholars who do not accept Smith's argument tend to introduce their accounts with a discussion of the ways in which Hinduism diverges from what is represented as the norm for religions (typically that Hinduism has no founder, no one authoritative scripture or credal statement). Another common feature is a discussion of the derivation of the word 'Hindu' (generally that 'Hindu' is a mispronunciation of 'Sindhu', the Indo-Aryan word for river applied to the Indus, thus denoting the population of the area beyond the Indus rather than a specific religious group). However, it is necessary to recognise that Hinduism is a modern concept, 'the product of a socio-political process - a process of reification which has evolved during the last two centuries' (Frykenberg, 1991, p 33).

The process by which the modern concept of Hinduism has been constructed is now often analysed in terms of Orientalism defined by Edward Said as 'a western style for dominating, restructuring and having authority over the Orient' (Said, 1995, p 3). Imperialism, British rule over the sub-continent, shaped this process together with rationalism, a western intellectual movement emphasising the powers of human reason and encouraging the accumulation of 'facts' about religion, and romanticism, another western intellectual movement which rejected rationalism in favour of feeling and emotion. Both regarded the East as a source of spiritual renewal for the West. Yet members of the Indian élite were also active participants in this process, indeed, the editor of *The Collected Works of Swami Vivekananda* commented 'of the Swami's address before the Parliament of Religions (1893), it may be said that when he began to speak it was of "the religious ideas of the Hindus", but when he ended,

Hinduism had been created' (Vivekananda, 1986, p x). From an academic perspective, therefore, many scholars urge caution, Friedhelm Hardy explaining that 'although in popular writing the alleged content of "Hinduism" is rapidly developing a monolithic and stereotyped character, this is no more than a fairly arbitrary abstraction from a random set of facts' (Hardy, 1990, p 145).

Hindu worldview

Clearly, there are many related reasons why it is difficult to describe Hinduism or the Hindu worldview. Not only is it important to reflect regional, cultural and linguistic diversity and historical and contemporary developments but it is also important to consider the extent to which it is possible to do so while distinguishing between Hinduism and other 'Indian religions' such as Buddhism and Sikhism. This is why scholars frequently represent Hinduism not as *a* religion, rather as a family or federation of traditions. Notwithstanding, certain beliefs are widely shared by Hindus and are distinctive of, if not unique to, the Hindu worldview.

This world is to be understood in the context of vast aeons of time and regions of space. It is only one of many in a series as the universe undergoes cycles of creation, destruction and recreation, and within each cycle undergoes degeneration and decay from a time of virtue, longevity, prosperity and fertility to a time of moral weakness and physical decline, the *kali yuga*, the age in which we now live. The world is also one of many currently in existence within the Egg of Brahma which is at the centre of a still greater universe.

Living beings determine their own destinies by their actions (*karma*) and experience the consequences of their actions both in this lifetime and subsequent lifetimes as they transmigrate bound to the wheel of existence (*samsara*). Reincarnation can be in any of a multitude of forms, not just human, although a human birth is prized for its spiritual potential.

Human beings, in common with all living beings, have a permanent unchanging self (*atman*) or spirit (*purusha*), an essence which is successively re-embodied in the realm of *samsara* according to the balance of *karma* accrued. The self or spirit is not the body and, unlike the body which is born and dies, is birthless and deathless.

There are four goals or ends of human life (*purusharthas*):

- morality, righteousness, duty (*dharma*);
- wealth, power, material reward (*artha*);
- desire, aesthetics, pleasure (*kama*);
- salvation, release, liberation (*moksha*).

The last is regarded as the supreme goal or end. They all have their place in the proper conduct of human life although *dharma* and *moksa* are the most important.

Dharma is the eternal law of the universe, the order and harmony of society and polity, and morality governed by and in turn sustaining the cosmic balance. A man's duty is determined by his class (*varna*). Only a priest (*brahman*) can teach sacred knowledge (*Veda*). The special duty of a warrior (*kshatriya*) is to protect the people, that of a merchant (*vaishya*) to tend cattle, trade, lend money and cultivate land. These three classes are called the twice-born (*dvija*), below them are the serfs (*shudra*) whose only duty is to serve members of the other classes. A man's duty is also determined by his stage of life (*ashrama*) though only if he is one of the twice-born. These stages are student (*brahmacharya*), householder (*grihastha*), hermit *(vanaprastha)* and ascetic (*samnyasa*). *Varnashramadharma* is, however, an idealised scheme and as such its significance is ideological. It sets out the proper relationship of social groups and reconciles different lifestyles by arranging them in a sequence. A woman's duty (*stridharma*) is to be a loving and virtuous wife, venerating her husband as a God and consecrating her life to his service (*pativrata*). Again, it should be noted that this is an orthodox ideal and, while normative, has never been universal or uncontested.

Moksha can be described negatively: freed individuals no longer accumulates *karma* or transmigrates; instead, at the time of death, they are released from bondage to *samsara*. Positive descriptions of *moksha* differ greatly in line with the many different philosophical and theological understandings of Hindus. *Moksha* can be understood as ecstatic and joyful communion with a personal divinity or realisation of the identity of the self with an impersonal absolute or in any number of other ways.

Many Hindus live their lives as well as they can in the hope of securing a better reincarnation. Some Hindus, though, are concentrated on the achievement of *moksha* in this present life which they strive to do by following one or more of a multitude of paths. A popular scheme for categorising these paths is threefold:

- the way of knowledge (*jnana-yoga*), intuitive and immediate knowledge of ultimate reality;
- the way of action (*karma-yoga*), selfless and disinterested action;
- the way of devotion (*bhakti-yoga*), loving and faithful devotion to God.

Hindu views of the divine embrace both the one and the many as well as personal and impersonal views. A key feature is hierarchy whereby, for example, impersonal divinity may be seen as superior to personal divinities who, in turn, are superior to other divine and semi-divine beings, or, again, a specific personal divinity may be seen as superior to other personal divinities who are superior to other divine and semi-divine beings. Among the personal divinities, any of whom may be worshipped as the Supreme God or Goddess, are: Brahma and his consort, Sarasvati, the Goddess of learning; Vishnu and his consort, Shri-Lakshmi, the Goddess of fortune, Krishna and Rama, both of whom are listed as descent forms (*avataras*) of Vishnu when he incarnates to uphold righteousness, and their consorts, Radha and Sita; Shiva, his consort, Parvati, and their sons, Skandha, God of war, and Ganesha, the God of wisdom; and the independent Goddesses, Durga and Kali. Such divinities can be related and combined in different ways, for instance, the *trimurti* of Brahma, Vishnu and Shiva portrayed as the creator, preserver and destroyer of the universe respectively. Moreover, the concept of divinity has to be expanded to encompass village deities, local spirits, ancestors, enlightened seers, devoted saints, holy teachers (*gurus*) and heroic figures. There is thus a continuity, rather than a clear dividing line, between the human and the divine. Further definitions of these Hindu concepts can be found in Werner (1993) as well as other dictionaries and encyclopaedias.

Activity A1

Reflect upon the differences and similarities between 'Hinduism' and 'Christianity'.

Comment on activity A1

Amongst the issues that you should have considered are the notion of 'religion' itself and problem of the label 'Hinduism'. Major differences include cosmology, the number of lifetimes available, the makeup of the human being, the differentiated nature of moral duty within Hinduism, the supreme goal of life, the paths to it, and the concept of the divine. Nevertheless, some similarities may occur to you: the eternal soul, the importance of morality, some of the ways of understanding the supreme goal of life, the importance of love, and the more personal ways of conceiving God.

Hindu scriptures

The concept of scripture in Hinduism is not so clear cut as in those religions which have a single sacred book. There are innumerable texts which may be viewed as sacred literature. The conventional distinction is between *shruti* (revelation) and *smriti* (tradition).   In the former category is the Vedic literature, consisting of the four *Veda Samhitas* (collections of hymns): *Rig*, *Sama*, *Yajur*, *Atharva*; together with later literature associated with each of these four collections: the *Brahmanas*, *Aranyakas* and *Upanishads*.   In the latter category is the non-Vedic literature such as the *Puranas* (devotional theistic texts such as the *Bhagavata Purana* glorifying Krishna), *Dharmashastras* (texts expounding *dharma* such as the *Laws of Manu*) and Epics.   The Epics, the *Mahabharata* and the *Ramayana* are storehouses of theology and practical morality embedded in legendary narratives.   Probably the most popular Hindu scripture, the *Bhagavad-Gita* or Song of the Lord, is found within the *Mahabharata*.   However, it is frequently regarded as *shruti*, and indeed there is a third category of scripture, *agama*, regarded as revelation by sectarian adherents, which is alternative or supplementary to those scriptures accepted by the orthodox.   Thus different groups of Hindus recognise different texts as scriptures and rank them differently.   Moreover, the category of scripture includes much that would not be classified as such in Christianity, for example the auxiliary Vedic sciences such as grammar and astrology, statecraft and the proper conduct of courtesans.

For excerpts from Hindu scriptures see Embree (1972), O'Flaherty (1975) and Zaehner (1966).   A translation of *Bhagavad-Gita* is by Edgerton (1944).

The six orthodox *Darshanas*

Neither the term 'philosophy' nor 'theology' is an adequate translation of the word *darshana* (perspective or insight) which denotes six traditional schools of thought.   These are *Nyaya*, *Vaisheshika*, *Samkhya*, *Yoga*, *Mimamsa* and *Vedanta*.   Most influential have been *Samkhya-Yoga* and *Vedanta*.

Samkhya-Yoga combines the metaphysics of *Samkhya* with the practice of *Yoga*.   There are two ultimate principles, *Purusha* (spirit) and *Prakriti* (nature). Human beings confuse their true being as spirit with their psycho-physical form.   The goal of spiritual discipline, therefore, is to identify oneself as spirit as distinct from nature, the relationship between the two portrayed in terms of *purusha* as the audience for whom *prakriti* dances.   The performance is so captivating that the audience is caught up in it, even to the extent of forgetting its own identity.   Meditational techniques serve to detach the practitioner from the performance.   It is worth noting that *Samkhya* in its own right is non-theistic and that *Yoga*, though it includes a concept of God as a perfect spirit among many, does not attribute to God more than an exemplary role.

There are three sub-divisions of *Vedanta*, 'the end of the Vedas', that is, systematic expositions of the ideas contained in the *Upanishads*.   *Advaita* (non-dualism) postulates two levels of truth. At the level of ultimate truth there is only *Brahman*, the impersonal absolute which, if it is described, is characterised as being, consciousness and bliss. At this ultimate level there is an identity between *Brahman* and *Atman* (Self) but at the lower level of truth there appear to be many selves, all of whom have individual personalities. This apparent plurality of selves and the universe which they inhabit are ultimately illusory (*maya*) and to recognise this is to achieve liberation. Study and meditation, and often the monastic life, are employed to this end.

Vishishtadvaita (non-dualism with distinctions) also accepts that reality is one. However, *Brahman* is interpreted theistically as a personal God. *Brahman* alone has an independent reality. The world and the many selves are real, unlike in *Advaita*, but are completely dependent on *Brahman* for their existence. *Brahman* created the world deliberately and it serves the purposes of salvation by which selves who are in bondage may experience an ecstatic communion with God through his grace. Devotion and worship, as the appropriate responses to the divine, necessitate a certain distinction between the self and God.

This is developed further in *Dvaita* (dualism) which teaches that God, individual selves and the world exist permanently and separately while God has power over individual selves and the world which he shaped. Again, salvation is the gift of God but only to those whose devotion and purity of life enables them to enjoy an eternal relationship with God.

An excellent discussion of these schools of thought is provided by Hiriyanna (1958). A briefer treatment of the same subject by this author is Hiriyanna (1985). Primary material is excerpted in Embree (1972) and at length in Radhakrishnan and Moore (1957).

Historical development

As has already been discussed, it is very difficult to categorise such a complex phenomenon as Hinduism. A common scheme is to divide Hinduism according to allegiance to particular deities. Vaishnavism focuses on Vishnu and related deities, particularly Krishna who is often seen as superior to Vishnu. Shaivism concentrates on Shiva and related deities whereas Shaktism emphasises the Goddess in her own right in forms such as Durga and Kali. Nevertheless, many beliefs and practices do not fit into this scheme at all and many others cross the divides.

The origins of the phenomenon labelled Hinduism cannot be traced to a particular time and place and there are many contributing strands. Bearing this in mind, the following outline may be helpful.

?2500-?1700 BCE[1]: the Indus Valley civilisation

Hinduism is usually claimed to be at least 5000 years old. The reason for this is that there is archaeological evidence, discovered earlier this century, for a sophisticated, literate civilisation in the valley of the Indus river in what is now Pakistan, which exhibits features that can be related to later Hindu beliefs and practices. Unfortunately, the script has not yet been deciphered so, as with much interpretation of such material remains, there is an element of educated guessing which later evidence may prove to be wrong. The two main sites are at Harappa and Mohenjo-daro. Among the aspects which have been seen as suggestive of later Hinduism are the concern for cleanliness and purity, illustrated by an elaborate drainage system and large baths resembling modern temple 'tanks'. Some terracotta figurines are obviously female and have been seen as Goddesses. There are also ringstones which may prefigure the Hindu symbols of male and female (*lingam* and *yoni*). One of the most interesting seals depicts a horned God, sitting cross-legged and surrounded by animals, which suggests to some the Hindu God Shiva.

The Indus Valley culture seems to have ended around 1700 BCE. Many questions remain. Did the Aryans destroy this civilisation or did it collapse as a result of deforestation? Was this population subjugated to form the *Shudra* class or displaced to the south as the ancestors of the Dravidian speaking peoples? In addition this archaeological evidence, even if better understood, only refers to a small part of India. The complex origins of Hinduism are thus very imperfectly understood.

?1500-?500 BCE: the Vedic period

The first written evidence we have of the Hindu tradition is the scriptures known as the *Veda* (knowledge) which are dated c1000 BCE. These scriptures belong to a people who call themselves *Aryas*, nobles, in English, Aryans. They appear to have been a nomadic, cattle-herding, warrior people, who were thought to have come to India from central Asia and Eastern Europe from about 2000 BCE onwards. Their language, Sanskrit, is related to modern North Indian, and most other Indo-European, languages. The relationship between the Aryans and the indigenous population is very contentious for political reasons, such as seeming to deny that India has suffered from external oppression since time immemorial, or to assert that even Hinduism is derived from western sources.

The Vedic scriptures depict a pantheon of Gods (*devas*) and Goddesses (*devis*) who are related to natural forces such as the wind and storm. There is

---

[1] When studying non-Christian religions it is not appropriate to use the Christian form of dating - 'Before Christ' (BC) and 'Anno Domini' (AD). In the study of World Religions the conventional terms are CE (Common Era) = AD and BCE (Before the Common Era) = BC. The dates remain the same.

Dyaus Pitr, the sky father, Indra the storm God, perhaps the most powerful and best loved, Agni or fire, Varuna or sky, Surya or sun, Privithi or Earth, Mitra or sunlight. These Gods are still remembered, although overshadowed by later deities. Two of the Vedic Gods developed into deities popular today - Rudra, a prototype of Shiva, and Vishnu. The Vedic religion involved sacrifices, including animals, to the Gods in order to win their favour and obtain prosperity. Rituals included the use of an intoxicating plant called *soma,* and the Aryans also drank alcohol and ate meat. Their worldview seems to have been life-affirming, as they prayed for wealth, fertility, and many children. Life after death was viewed as going to the realm of the ancestors. Memorial rites, and many other sacraments, performed by Hindus nowadays evince a strong Vedic influence. The origin of the *varna* system is similarly evident in the scriptures of this period.

?800-?400 BCE: the Brahmanic and Upanishadic period

As the Vedic literature was transmitted in India, additions were made to the collections of hymns which reflect developments in religious thinking and practice. From the *Brahmanas* it appears that priestly ritual became more complex and that divine power began to be seen as intrinsic to the sacrificial ritual itself, so that correct performance of ritual, rather than the Gods, was the force behind the maintenance of the universe.

This obviously reinforced the status of the Brahmans and their position in the social hierarchy. Another impulse came from those who, possibly drawing on ancient indigenous traditions, renounced the world of material gain and dedicated their lives to meditation and philosophy. From such people came the texts known as the *Aranyakas* and *Upanishads* which explore questions of human and divine existence. The *Upanishads* introduced central concepts such as the *atman* within, rebirth, and ideas about God both theistic and monistic. From amongst such renouncers also developed the innovatory schools of thought such as Buddhism (c500) and Jainism which have much in common with Hinduism.

?300BCE-?900CE: classical Hinduism

From the third century BCE, with the emperor Ashoka, Buddhism became a major tradition in India. Ashoka gave Buddhism his vigorous patronage and furthered the expansion of the religion throughout India. Simultaneously Hinduism developed its classical form as a combination of aspects from the Brahmanical and ascetic traditions. Classics such as the *Bhagavad-Gita* (?400 BCE) reflect the complex combination of ideas. During this period, the complex system of castes or *jatis*, loosely related to the Vedic system of *varnas*, seems to have developed . Great philosophers such as Sankara (ninth century CE), the most famous exponent of *Advaita Vedanta*, elaborated their systems.

?800–?1400 CE: medieval period

From about the eighth century CE, a wave of devotional religion or *bhakti* influenced Hinduism. Medieval Hindu philosophers such as Ramanuja (twelfth century CE), founder of *Vishishtadvaita Vedanta*, and saints such as Mirabai stressed the love of a personal God. Theistic impulses may have been strengthened by the arrival of Islam in the subcontinent from 1000 CE onwards. This arrival also seems, by such means as the destruction of monastic centres, to have dealt the death blow to a Buddhism already in decline from about the ninth century.

c1500–c1800 CE: early modern period

Islam strengthened its hold on the northern part of India, with the reign of the Mughal empire. Sikhism developed from the fifteenth century, with some teachings reflecting Hindu ideas, and arguably never completely separating itself from the broad Hindu tradition. The *Sant* tradition of north India, from which Sikhism emerged, was an important devotional movement, with both Hindu and Muslim adherents.

c1800 CE: modern period

This saw the establishment of the British Raj in India, and also the emergence of movements of reform and revival as Hindus reinterpreted and restated their tradition, religiously, socially and politically. Hindus travelled throughout the Empire for work and many settled permanently overseas. Meanwhile, Hindu ideas were communicated to a British audience by scholarly and popular associations such as the Royal Asiatic and the Theosophical Societies as well as by Hindu apologists.

c1950 CE: contemporary

Particularly since the 1960s, Hindu ideas have become widely disseminated in the general population with the rise of the so-called Counterculture. Some British people have adopted a Hindu lifestyle, the most well-known being Hare Krishna devotees but also, for instance, followers of Sathya Sai Baba and practitioners of Iyengar Yoga. At the same time, Hindus have migrated to Britain, either directly from the sub-continent or indirectly via the ex-imperial possessions. In India, and to some extent also in the diaspora, different constructions of Hinduism are in evidence, ranging from universalism which preaches tolerance towards all religions as paths to the same goal, to *Hindutva* which asserts exclusive Hindu identity over other groups, especially Muslims.

The issue of historical development is particularly contentious in Hinduism. However, for useful information on the modern period which has been formative of present understandings of Hinduism, see Richards (1985).

Activity A2

Identify important aspects of the internal diversity of Hinduism, taking into account scriptures, schools of thought, and types of Hinduism as well as its historical development

Comment on activity A2

This is almost impossible to answer! You should have noticed that there is no agreement on the number or status of scriptures. There is an astonishing variety of views on topics such as the concept of God, the nature of reality, the human being, the goal of life and so on, articulated by different schools of thought. Hindus worship different deities, in a variety of ways. Moreover, with such a long and convoluted history, Hinduism has changed markedly over the centuries, without discarding earlier beliefs and practices.

For reasons that we have already established, what is now called 'Hinduism' contains within it a vast diversity of beliefs and practices and has, therefore, resources for an almost infinite adaptability to changing circumstances.

In the final unit of this module we will touch on western variants of Hinduism that illustrate its adaptability to the modern world and a new culture.

A2 Buddhism

Aims

After working through part A2 of this unit you should be able to:

- describe the life and teachings of the historical Buddha;
- understand some of the main features of Buddhist thought;
- describe the differences between Theravada and Mahayana Buddhism.

Overview

This unit provides you with a brief outline of the life and teachings of the historical Buddha[2], and a short account of the ways in which Buddhism changed and developed as it encountered different cultures during its spread through Asia.

Introducing Buddhism

The importance given to the life of the historical Buddha varies from school to school. Some schools pay very little attention to the traditional account of his life, and venerate instead other important Buddhist figures. However, some significant features of the traditional account of his life are offered here because of their explanatory power.

The events which took place during the first five centuries or so after the death of the Buddha are important in understanding how the Buddhist community survived and how Buddhism became a coherent religion which offered an alternative outlook in Hindu India. Buddhism did not, in fact, survive in India much beyond the thirteenth century, but by that time missionary activity and the simple movement of ideas along trade routes had ensured that Buddhism would survive, in a vast diversity of forms, in a variety of cultures.

An important distinction you should be able to make by the end of this unit, is between the two strikingly different forms or 'vehicles' of Buddhist teaching, namely the Theravada, 'Way of the Elders' and the Mahayana, 'Greater Vehicle'. Both forms are vigorous today, along with the tantric or Vajrayana tradition found predominantly in ex-patriot Tibetan communities.

Since the ground which must be covered in this unit is so vast, the information presented is inevitably selective rather than comprehensive. However, the material is specifically chosen to focus on crucial issues, both of teachings and philosophy, and of history, in the hope that your background reading will be informed by your study of this unit.

You might find it helpful to have read the unit on the historical development of Hinduism before attempting this unit since Hinduism provided the historical and religious context in which Buddhism arose.

Buddhism has been mediated through a number of languages. In this unit you will come across words from two languages: Pali (the language of

---

[2]The term 'the historical Buddha' refers to the man (often called Siddhartha, Shakyamuni or Gautama) who is presumed to have taught the main tenets of Buddhism in the sixth century BCE. The qualifying 'historical' is sometimes required in order to pinpoint exactly what is meant. In the wider Buddhist tradition the term 'Buddha' has all sorts of meanings and refers to beings other than the historical figure of Siddhartha.

Theravada Buddhism), and Sanskrit (the classical/religious language of India - and the language in which most of the Mahayana scriptures were originally compiled). The abbreviations P. and Skt will alert you to which language is being used. In most cases in this unit it is important to recognise each word in both languages.

Hindu background

John Snelling argues that one of the most fundamental features of the Indian religious outlook is the belief that there are many paths to the Ultimate (Snelling, 1987, p 13). Buddhism arose against a background of the many indigenous religions of India which have come to be referred to collectively as Hinduism. Whilst Buddhism is a religion characteristically tolerant of other paths, it changed, developed and often rejected Hindu notions.

It is therefore important to understand these notions with which, according to the traditional account, the Buddha grappled. It is also important to realise that these concepts received very different focus amongst the diverse groups that made up orthodox Hinduism.

First, Hindus in general believe in an eternal soul (*atman*) in all living things. For many Hindus, *atman* is equivalent to Brahman (God) and will ultimately return to Brahman. The Buddha claimed that this view was an obstacle since it encouraged attachment and ego-centrism. Buddhists find the doctrine of *anatman* or 'no-soul' more useful on the path to enlightenment.

Second, Hindus believe that one's position in life is the result of the fruition of *karma*, the class or caste system. Buddhists accept *karma*, but reject the idea that religious authority lies with an élite class. Saddhatissa (1985, p 22) notes that the Buddha accepted anyone who chose to follow him, regardless of their caste. However, vestiges of a class system remain in some of the countries in which Buddhism is practised.

Third, orthodox Hindus assign special significance to a body of scripture, *the Vedas*, which are seen as revealed. Indian religious groups who reject the authority of *the Vedas* are called unorthodox. Buddhism falls into this category.

Fourth, Buddhism does not address the question of whether there is a God. This is not seen as a useful pursuit since it results in suffering and does not lead to enlightenment. For this reason Buddhism is sometimes, erroneously, thought of as atheistic (and therefore not a religion). It is also not really correct to think of it as agnostic, since agnosticism implies a failure to come to a conclusion. The question is simply not addressed. However, in the Pali scriptures and in many Buddhist worldviews there is a category of beings which are deities, but these are, like humans, subject to impermanence and cannot lead the way to enlightenment. Many of the Buddha's audiences were made up of human beings and of Gods.

Historicity and significance of the Buddha

The huge corpus of Buddhist scriptures contains many stories concerning the life of the Buddha, many of which contradict each other, making it virtually impossible to form a coherent biography. Moreover, there is little historical proof outside the scriptures that the Buddha existed, so it may seem very dubious to begin a study of Buddhism with an examination of the life of its founder. In addition to these doubts it should also be pointed out that the historical Buddha is only a figure of significance in some schools of Buddhism. In other schools he is venerated along with other enlightened beings, who are seen as his equals, in others, little or no reference is made to him at all, and in still others it is not the historical personage who is important, rather that for which he stands.

However, in mitigation it should be pointed out that Buddhism as a body of teachings does not rely on historic certainty about the existence of the Buddha. Buddhism, unlike Christianity, is not a religion of *Heilsgeschichte* (salvation history). Without the historical Jesus, Christianity, it could be argued, would rest on somewhat sandy foundations. However, the Buddha does not have an equivalent role in Buddhism. He is often presented as simply a person who uncovered a path that had always been there. Whether it was he, or somebody else, or a whole group of people who gave the teachings is really unimportant.

Furthermore, Michael Pye has suggested that it seems reasonable to presume, given we do have evidence that something big did happen on the religious scene in India around the sixth century BCE, that one individual charismatic leader was the initiator (Pye, 1979, p 10).

From an educational point of view, the life of the Buddha is a useful place to start a study of Buddhism, though of course not the only one. We have to presume that almost all the scriptural accounts of the biography are devotional embellishments on facts that may well have been lost during the centuries that elapsed between the death of the Buddha and anything about him being committed to writing. However, those devotional embellishments tell us a huge amount about the way in which the Buddha was perceived by that early community. It might also be argued that it is much easier to understand the teachings when seen in the context of the search of a spiritually restless individual whom the scriptures tell us the man who became the Buddha was.

The account which follows focuses on some key points in the devotional biography of the Buddha which, as Davies Keown (1996, p 19) points out, is commemorated by Buddhists in ritual and pilgrimage.

From birth to enlightenment

Born in Lumbini in a region of northern India which is now Nepal, the boy who was to become the Buddha was the son of the head of a tribe called Shakya. Some scriptures name him Siddhartha, others Gautama (or Gotama), some both[3]. As the son of a warrior, Siddhartha shared his father's class status of Kshatriya and would have been expected to follow in his father's footsteps in every way.

Various auspicious occurrences attended his birth, including most importantly, a prophecy from an itinerant Hindu holy man that Siddhartha would become either a great warrior and leader like his father, or a great religious person. His father, keen that the former should come true, devised a plan for keeping Siddhartha from reflecting upon life in any way that would precipitate any religious enquiry into the meaning of life. Siddhartha remained a prisoner in paradise. He was unable to leave the confines of a large palatial estate, but he had his every want and need answered. He was perpetually surrounded by young and healthy people. He followed rigorous training and received the kind of education which would suit his future as the inheritor of his father's position. He married and had a child.

He became, however, restless and desired to encounter the world outside the palace, and at the age of twenty-nine, flouted his father's wishes and made journeys to the four gates of the estate. This event is known as the 'Four Passing Sights', and is arguably crucial in understanding the Buddhist outlook. At the first three gates he saw a sick man, an old man and a corpse in a funeral procession. These sights were a tremendous shock to the young man, since he had never experienced these aspects of life. He was unable to go back to his life of ease after seeing these sights, since the inevitability of sickness, old age and death happening to himself and his loved ones had the effect of tainting any pleasure, happiness or contentment, with the knowledge of impermanence. At the fourth gate he saw a sadhu, a Hindu renunciate. The holy man struck the distraught Siddhartha as surprisingly serene, since he was in the outside world and must have knowledge of the inevitability of impermanence. Siddhartha surmised that the sadhu must be in possession of some spiritual secret which allowed him peace in the midst of the corruption, decay and finitude that

---

[3] He is also devotionally called Shakyamuni, 'Sage of the Shakya Clan', and in the scriptures he is addressed as 'World-honoured One' or 'Bhagavat' (Lord).

defines human life, and left the palace, his wife and new baby, to follow the ancient Hindu path of renunciation. This renunciation of family life is identified by Peter Harvey (1990, p 18) as the symbolic precedent for the monastic life of Buddhists, monks and nuns.

For six years Siddhartha pursued the spiritual teachings of the Hindu tradition, and was taught by five great ascetics. The iconography which represents this period of his life shows the extremes to which he went in fasting and other ascetic practices in order to achieve the Hindu aim of overcoming the body to free the soul. In despair of finding the answers he sought, after six years of practice he gave up and ate some food, much to the chagrin of his teachers. He sat under a Banyan tree and began to meditate. During this period of meditation he achieved the religious experience which is known in Buddhism as enlightenment.

Activity A3

Briefly outline the ways in which the role of the Buddha in Buddhism differs from that of the role of Jesus in Christianity.

Comment on activity A3

The reason this task was set was to enable you to identify the status of the Buddha. You were asked to keep your response brief because, tackled seriously, the subject provides enough material for book length studies! There are, however, a number of crucial issues that you may have identified.

First, the Buddha is not deified in Buddhism. No tradition sees the historical Siddhartha as anything other than human. This obviously contrasts with the understanding of the person of Jesus in most Christian traditions. Many Buddhist traditions see the historical Buddha as an instance of the highest possible attainment, and venerate him as having 'gone beyond'[4], but his attainment is not a 'one-off', it is available to all. Jesus, however, understood as the Son of God, is unique.

Second, the historicity of the Buddha is not a crucial issue. Whether it was Siddhartha or someone else who uncovered the path is not important. In fact, if no-one uncovered the path it would simply be a tragedy for our age[5]; the

---

[4] For instance the Lotus Sutra of Mahayana Buddhism talks of the 'eternal Shakyamuni'; a being who has gone beyond birth and death (since birth and death are categories which belong to our enlightened realm and not to nirvana).

[5] Our age is only one age. The universe is, according to Buddhism, eternal (though ever-changing), and according to most traditions there have been other ages and other Buddhas.

path would still be there. The historicity, especially of the resurrection, of Jesus, would be considered by most Christians as fundamental to the religion.

Third, the historical Buddha is not a central figure in every Buddhist tradition. Many venerate other enlightened beings, and for others, the simple possibility of enlightenment, regardless of the individuals who may or may not have attained it, is important. In Christianity, in spite of the different Christological traditions, Jesus is always central.

Fourth, if you have been struck more by the similarity between the two figures you might have noted the similarity between the ethical teachings, the appearance of authority, the stress on compassion, and the ability to 'save' (to borrow a Christian term): the Buddha via the imparting of knowledge and the encouragement to practise, and Jesus through the request for faith and the promise of forgiveness.

The enlightenment

What happened at the climax of his period of meditation is seen by many as the founding event of Buddhism. A caveat is important here. According to Buddhists, the nature of enlightenment is beyond ordinary human categories and cannot satisfactorily or clearly be explained from within the confines of language, which is a human construct. Buddhists often say that there is little point *studying* the concepts as a separate and distinct activity from Buddhist *practice*. Enlightenment is an intuitive experience, which is not understandable or accessible through words, which belong to the unenlightened human realm. As Denise Cush (1993, p 18) puts it, it 'cannot be known by the unenlightened'. This presents the student, who has a commitment to objectivity, with a problem. Only enlightened people can understand enlightenment, and it cannot be satisfactorily explained to unenlightened people.

A possible solution to the problem lies in the fact that the Buddha ('the enlightened one' - Siddhartha's title after the enlightenment) *did* teach. He encouraged practices and used metaphors, allegories and other devices in order to bring his audience to the point where they could make the intuitive jump for themselves. For students of Buddhism, those practices, metaphors, allegories and so on provide material to study, and whilst that final intuitive leap is not the aim of the academic study of the religion, it is possible to reach a scholarly understanding of what that leap might entail.

As Robinson and Johnson (1982, pp 41-43) relate, the Buddha's first audience was the five ascetics, his erstwhile teachers. For them he formulated the teachings in a comparatively philosophical mode. He was later to use less philosophical and more allegorical techniques of teaching, according to the intellectual and spiritual capacities of any particular audience.

The first sermon, known devotionally as 'The First Turning of the Wheel of Dharma'[6], may be presumed to contain an account of the religious experience of enlightenment had by the Buddha under the Banyan tree[7]. The main theme of this sermon can be summarised in the Four Noble Truths and in the doctrine of Interdependent Origination.

The four noble truths

We shall analyse the four noble truths in turn. They state that:

- all life is (P.) *dukkha*/ (Skt) *duhkha*;
- the cause of (P.) *dukkha* is craving and grasping (P. *tanha* - literally 'thirst');
- craving and grasping may be overcome;
- the way to overcome craving and grasping is to follow the Noble Eightfold Path.

The first noble truth states that all life is *dukkha*. You will notice that the crucial term *dukkha* has been left untranslated. This is because there is no satisfactory translation for it. In your reading you will notice that it is commonly translated as 'suffering', and whilst this English term does capture a part of its meaning, to translate it simply in this way would be partial. Walpola Rahula (1978 [1959], p 16) points out that this common translation for *dukkha* is responsible for the view that English-speaking people sometimes take of Buddhism, that it is pessimistic. It could be argued that even in India, Buddhism would never have got off the ground if the Buddha's first truth, his description of reality, was that 'all life is suffering'. Any normal person would deny it. Perhaps much of life is suffering, but surely there are many pleasures and happinesses too. But the fact is that *dukkha* means much more than suffering. John Snelling (1987, p 52) elucidates:

> The Pali term *dukkha* is traditionally translated into English as 'suffering' but, though it certainly includes this concept, it possesses a wide spectrum of connotations besides. At one extreme it takes in the most dire form of spiritual and mental and physical pain: the agonies of cancer, for instance, and the anguish of someone who falls prey to total despair. It covers our everyday aches and pains, our petty dislikes and frustrations too; and it extends to very

---

[6] 'Dharma' meaning in this case 'teaching' or 'truth' as opposed to the Hindu use of the term to signify 'duty' or 'obligation'.

[7] Banyan is the type of tree (related to the fig) under which the Buddha meditated. The tree itself became a popular focus for devotion, for obvious reasons, and became known as the 'Bodhi Tree' ('bodhi' - enlightenment). A descendant of the original tree still grows in Bodh, Gaya (as the town is now called) and cuttings and even leaves from it adorn the shrines of Buddhist places of worship all over the world.

subtle feelings of malaise: that life is never quite right.... there is no such thing as *perfect*, unalloyed happiness or pleasure.   Even the most beautiful experience has a melancholy undertone simply because we know that it can't last. So *dukkha* touches everything that exists.

The second noble truth states that the cause of dukkha is clinging and grasping. It is helpful to see the truths in terms of the medical metaphor often utilised in Buddhism. The Buddha, in the first Truth, diagnoses the human condition. The second Truth identifies the all-important cause of our disease, and the last two show, first, that a cure is available, and second, the course of treatment required. 'Clinging and grasping' can easily be understood as the cause of much of our suffering and discomfort in life. Materialism, for instance, is often seen as the modern disease. Not having what we want is at best annoying or disappointing, at worst painful and tragic. The second Truth tells us that it is not lack, but our appetites which cause the problem. However, this truth is much more than just a homily against greed. We do not just cling to material things, we cling to people, believing they can make us happy, we cling to our beliefs believing they will bring us unfailing security and peace of mind, and most importantly we cling to ourselves - our worlds are 'me'-centred. All of these forms of clinging are naïve and cause us pain.

The third noble truth states that we can overcome clinging and grasping, and thereby defeat *dukkha*. Buddhism sees everything in the world to be in a causal relationship. *Dukkha* is dependent on clinging. Take clinging out of the equation, and *dukkha* disappears. The absence of *dukkha* is, of course, perfect spiritual freedom, or nirvana (P. *nibbana*)

The fourth noble truth describes the way in which one goes about overcoming grasping and attachment through the development of wisdom, morality and meditation. This development is conceived of as a path which has eight factors to be developed. The first two are concerned with *wisdom*, the last three are concerned with *meditation*, and the middle three are concerned with *morality*:

- right views;
- right thought;
- right speech;
- right action;
- right livelihood;
- right effort;
- right mindfulness;
- right concentration.

Interdependent origination

This doctrine describes reality as it is from the standpoint of enlightenment. Whilst the term 'interdependent origination' is the usual translation of (P.) *paticca samupada/* (Skt) *pratitya samutpada*, the concept is perhaps easier to understand as 'connectedness'. According to Buddhism, everything in the universe lies in a causal relationship with everything else. Therefore everything is fundamentally connected. Our experience of 'separateness' (the most persistent being the separateness of ourselves from everything else) is an illusion.

This doctrine underpins the no-self doctrine. If everything is radically connected then there can be no separate, differentiated self. It also underpins the Four Truths, which are obviously causally connected with each other, and the Eightfold Path which is efficacious in so far as the cultivation of wisdom, meditation and morality is causally linked to the cessation of ignorance, attachment and greed.

The sangha

The death of the Buddha is known as the *Mahaparinirvana*, 'the great and final nirvana'. According to traditional accounts, the physical cause of his death was food poisoning, a rather ignominious demise for a great religious hero perhaps, but the story serves to highlight the historical Buddha's humanity.

The teachings were preserved by the Buddha's followers through oral tradition, and the community, or *sangha*, met periodically in council to recite the teachings together in order to maintain consistency, to avoid the risk of the 'Chinese whispers' phenomenon which can attend oral tradition, and to discuss points of doctrine and the lifestyle requirements of monks and nuns. Eighteen slightly different schools of thought developed during this early period, only one of which survives today, the Theravada (literally - 'the Way of the Elders').

At the third council a schism in the *sangha* opened, due apparently to disagreement regarding claims which were being made for the capabilities of enlightened people (P. *arahat/* Skt *arhat*). This dispute paved the way for the development of the Mahayana or 'Greater vehicle', a new and distinctive form of Buddhism.

The Pali scriptures

Early in the first century CE, at the fourth council, which was held in Sri Lanka, the decision was made to end the oral tradition and to commit the teachings to writing. The language in which the teachings were etched on palm leaves was Pali, a Sinhalese language which was, of course, not the language that the Buddha would have spoken since he came from Magadha in Northern India. The leaves were collected into three baskets (P. *Tipitaka*/Skt *Tripitaka*):

- the Sutta pitaka, containing the teachings as remembered by the Buddha's disciples;
- the Vinaya pitaka, containing regulations for monks and nuns;
- the Abidhamma pitaka, containing commentaries on the teachings.

The Pali canon has been preserved, and is extant in its entirety today, and is exclusively referred to by the Theravada school. The Theravada inherits the doctrines of the conservative reformers involved in the aforementioned schism. Buddhist scriptures present the contemporary reader with a challenge, but an accessible translation of both Pali and Sanskrit texts by Edward Conze is still in print, *Buddhist Scriptures* (1959).

Rise of the Mahayana

The origins of the Mahayana (Greater Vehicle) are very much disputed by scholars (see, for example, Williams, 1989). The division in the *sangha* may well have provided the institutional origin of the movement, but this has to be seen in conjunction with the development of a tradition within the *sangha* of philosophical commentary on the teachings. Several important features of the Mahayana differentiate it from the Theravada.

First, in addition to the Pali canon, many other scriptures, mostly written in Sanskrit by Mahayanist philosophers (some identifiable, some not) are accepted. Much of the Sanskrit canon is no longer extant, and much of it is available to us through Chinese and Tibetan recensions.

Second, Mahayana Buddhism holds that the possibility of enlightenment is not necessarily restricted to those of monastic status. This belief arises from a philosophical argument propounded famously by the monk Nagarjuna (c150 BCE - c150 CE) who is sometimes thought of as the father of the Mahayana. Nagarjuna investigated the Buddha's doctrine of Interdependent Origination and concluded that if all phenomena are radically connected, then nirvana and samsara cannot be, from the standpoint of enlightenment, separate and distinct. They too must be interrelated or mutual. Thus nirvana is in a very important sense implicit in the here and now. It is not a far off goal, achievable only through lifetimes of effort and practice, it is here if we could but 'see' it. On this account, therefore, all beings are potentially enlightened, or have 'buddha-nature'.

Third, instead of celebrating the *arhat* as the pinnacle of spiritual achievement, Mahayanists celebrate the bodhisattva (lit. enlightenment being). Mahayanists argue that the process of becoming enlightened necessarily entails the penetration of connectedness. A bodhisattva perceives the non-differentiatedness of everything. This is insight or wisdom (Skt *prajna*). Beings who possess this sort of wisdom are necessarily compassionate, since they no longer experience their own separateness from the suffering (or more particularly, the *dukkha*) of others, and are therefore obliged to help them. Thus bodhisattvas, out of compassion (Skt *karuna*) defer their own attainment of full nirvana in order to re-engage with the world to assist others.

All sorts of beings are recognised as bodhisattvas, for example great teachers. The Mahayana tradition applies the epithet to Nagarjuna, and to the Buddha himself, who instead of remaining in a state of bliss under the bodhi tree re-engaged with the world for about forty-five years whilst he shared his wisdom. The Dalai Lama is considered by the Tibetan tradition to be a bodhisattva, and the huge variety of Mahayana Schools each consider different individuals to have bodhisattva status.

As well as historical human individuals, beings in realms other than this one, and beings from the infinite past are also considered to be bodhisattvas. These are often called celestial bodhisattvas, but this is misleading as it implies inappropriate realism. From the Mahayanist point of view existence and non-existence are both false views to which it is possible to become attached. These bodhisattvas function as archetypes in iconography for aspects of enlightenment. For example Manjusri represents Wisdom, his flaming sword cutting through ignorance and Avalokitesvara represents Compassion, his many heads showing his superior capacity to perceive suffering, and his many arms his superior capacity to assist others towards enlightenment.

Activity A4

Outline the significant ways in which the Mahayana differs from the Theravada.

Comment on activity A4

You may have discussed the following features.

- Theravada is predominantly a monastic movement; many Mahayana schools are lay orientated. In the Mahayana, enlightenment is available to all.
- Nirvana is a far off goal in Theravada, which may require lifetimes of effort and practice to achieve. In the Mahayana, nirvana is an equally difficult attainment, but it is potentially available in the here and now.

- The Mahayana attributes greatness to the bodhisattva, the Theravada to the *arahat*.
- The Mahayana tends to be more devotional than the Theravada. Bodhisattvas and buddhas are venerated.
- The term 'Mahayana' embraces an enormous diversity of schools. The Theravada is comparatively unified.
- Some Mahayana schools refer to the historical Buddha very little, if at all. In the Theravada he is central.

Spread of Buddhism

During the reign of the Indian Buddhist Emperor, Asoka (or Ashoka), (third century BCE) missionaries were sent to Sri Lanka and to Thailand, which are to this day Theravada countries as is Burma, although both Theravada and Mahayana have had periods of ascendancy here. Laos and Kampuchea both have Theravada histories but their respective Communist revolutions have made the future of Buddhism unsure. Indonesia has periodically come under the influence of both Theravada and Mahayana, though now it is of course more predominantly Islamic. That said, one of the most important Buddhist monuments, Borobodur, is situated in Java.

The Silk Road provided access north and Mahayana Buddhism entered China in the first century CE. From China it spread into Korea (fourth century CE), and entered Japan in the sixth century CE. Due perhaps to its isolation and the vigour of its indigenous religion, Bon, Tibet did not become Buddhist until the seventh century. Since 1959 Tibetan Buddhism has been practised largely outside of Tibet, owing to the Chinese occupation. Northern Vietnam belonged, until the tenth century, to China; so Vietnam inherited Chinese Mahayana, until its Communist revolution of 1975.

The spread of Buddhism to the West testifies to Buddhism's ability to adapt itself to the culture in which it finds itself. For a readable account, see Stephen Batchelor's (1994) *The Awakening of the West*. Britain had a key role to play in bringing Theravada Buddhism to the West because of its colonial connections with several Theravada countries. Tibetan Buddhism has held a particular fascination for westerners, perhaps because of the much publicised plight of the Tibetan monks, and their presence as exiles in many western countries. Zen, a form of Japanese Mahayana, has also achieved wide currency in the West.

A3 Sikhism

Aims

After working through part A3 of this unit you should have:

- gained an overview of the origins and development of Sikhism;
- acquired some understanding of the spiritual teachings of the Sikh gurus;
- begun to consider issues of Sikh history and identity.

Overview

This unit introduces you to the religious teachings of the Sikh gurus and offers a brief account of the origin and development of the Sikh faith up to the mid-twentieth century. The main topics covered are the religion of the first Sikh guru (Guru Nanak, d.1539) and his successors; the founding of the Sikh *Khalsa* at the beginning of the eighteenth century by the tenth Guru (Guru Gobind Singh, d.1708); and the emergence of the reforming *Singh Sabha* (Sikh Association) and related developments in the nineteenth and twentieth centuries. In the course of the unit, you will reflect on developing notions of Sikh orthodoxy and identity in preparation for unit 2 which deals with contemporary Sikhism, Sikh practice and Sikhism in Britain.

Introducing Sikhism

While working through this material you may need to look up unfamiliar words in the *Glossary of Sikh Terms* included at the end of this unit.

Sikhism is an Indian religion closely related to Hinduism. Originating in the Punjab ('five rivers') region of north India, it was inspired by the spiritual revelations and teaching activities of its first Guru, Nanak (1469-1539). Sikhs believe Nanak was divinely chosen by God to provide sincere devotees with the means of liberation from the round of rebirth. Nanak's small following of *sikhs* (disciples - pronounced 'six', not 'seeks') was drawn from a largely Hindu, but also Muslim, background. It grew over time into a significant religious movement led by a succession of revered gurus. Nanak and his successors taught that the formless One God is to be discovered 'within', through inward, devotional remembrance. The guidance of a Guru is essential. God is not found through the external religious rituals and ceremonies; these lead only to rebirth and further suffering. From a spiritual point of view distinctions of gender, caste and religious background are irrelevant.

Today, there are approximately sixteen million Sikhs in the world; perhaps fourteen million in the Punjab and the remaining two million in other parts of India and the rest of the world. The largest Sikh community outside India is in Britain; it includes many who came to the UK from East Africa. Sikhism encourages, as well as devotion to God, such values as honest living, commitment to family and service to the community. In general Sikhs have adapted well and prospered in new environments.

Studying Sikhism means understanding at least a few Punjabi terms such as *sikh, Guru, nam, khalsa, gurdwara*, since these represent significant ideas which cannot satisfactorily be translated into English. *Gurdwara*, for example, means a place where Sikhs reverence God through the form of the Guru. It is not a 'church', 'temple', 'mosque' or 'synagogue'.

'Sikhism' itself is a hybrid English word derived from '*sikh*' meaning follower or devotee. The Sikhs' own word for their religion is *gurmat* or 'Guru's teaching'. *Gurmat* points to the Guru, not the disciple, as the focus of the faith.

Activity A5

Basic concepts in the Guru's teaching (*gurmat*)

The following three clusters of Punjabi terms provide an outline of the Sikh Gurus' teaching on the world and our place in it. Look up the terms in each cluster in the *Glossary* and think about how they relate to each other, before moving on to the next cluster.

The first set of terms describes our *ordinary human condition*; how we acquired our human form in this world and what occurs when we do not take advantage of the opportunity afforded by a human birth to turn our mind Godwards:

- *haumai*;
- *jiva*;
- *karma*;
- *man*;
- *manmukh*;
- *samsara*.

The following terms describe the nature of God and *the state of liberation or salvation* to which a disciple of the Guru aspires:

- *Akal Purakh*;
- *bhakti*;
- *Gurmukh*;

- *moksha*;
- *nirankar*;
- *nirguna*.

Finally, these terms refer to the Guru's guiding grace and the disciple's effort; the *means by which* liberation is achieved:

- *amrit*;
- *Guru*;
- *gurbani*;
- *hukam*;
- *nam*;
- *nam simaran, nam japan*;
- *Shabad, shabda*.

Comment on activity A5

The *jiva* (soul, living being) is born into the world in a particular form as a result of *karma* (actions) of previous lifetimes. *Samsara* is the seemingly endless round of birth, death and rebirth in which we are trapped by *haumai* (egotism, self-obsession). Mistaking our temporary body and mind for something real and permanent, our mind (Punjabi: *man*) thinks only of 'I' and 'mine'; we are *manmukh* (rather than *gurmukh*: God-centred). By acting self-servingly, we are bound to be reborn, trapped in yet another form to fulfil our desires and receive our desserts.

Akal Purakh, 'The One Beyond Time', also described as *nirankar* (without form) and *nirguna* (without limiting qualities) is the only Reality; everything else is apparently real, not actually so. When merged with *Akal Purakh*, the *jiva* overcomes separation, duality and ego-centredness (*haumai*) and attains union with God in the permanent state described as *sach khand* (true realm). A *jiva* in this state is described as *Gurmukh* (God-focused - the opposite of *manmukh*), has lost all egotistical desires and has attained liberation (*moksha*) from the cycle of *samsara*.

The *Guru* is fundamental to this transformation; the formless Lord makes contact with his disciples through the *Guru*, so the *jiva* meets the *Guru* only by the Lord's inscrutable and all-pervading will (*hukam*). The *Guru* then guides the disciple to a life of meditation on God's 'name' (*nam simaran* or *nam japan*). *Nam* does not mean 'name' in the ordinary sense; it is a special term referring to the mystical expression of *Akal Purakh's* nature, also called '*shabad*' (word, logos) and *amrit* (nectar, ambrosia). *Nam simaran* can mean recitation of the scriptures (*bani, gurbani*), or repeating a name of God (such as '*wahiguru*'), or quiet meditation on the totality of God, or in general the avoidance of 'external' rituals in favour of inner attentiveness to *Akal Purakh*.

Who is the Guru?

The notion of 'Guru' is central in *gurmat* (Sikhism). It is worth spending some time on it, to avoid misunderstandings. The following passages concerning the Guru are taken from the Sikh holy scripture, the *Adi Granth*. Take time to appreciate the beauty and rhythm of the verses, even in English translation, as well as noting the ideas they contain. The following devotional verses have no special status; they are typical of the thousands of hymns or poems collected and arranged in the Adi Granth.

> The Guru's Word is the Sound-current of the nad; the Guru's Word is the Wisdom of the Vedas; the Guru's Word is all-pervading. The Guru is Shiva, the Guru is Vishnu and Brahma; the Guru is Parvati and Lakshmi. Even knowing God... God cannot be described in words. The Guru has given me this one understanding: there is only the One, the Giver of all souls. May I never forget Him! (AG p. 2)

> O humble servant of the Lord, O True Guru, O True Primal Being: I offer my humble prayer to You, O Guru. I am a mere insect, a worm. O True Guru, I seek Your Sanctuary. Please be merciful, and bless me with the Light of the Nam, the Name of the Lord. O my Best Friend, O Divine Guru, please enlighten me with the Name of the Lord. Through the Guru's Teachings, the Nam is my breath of life. The Kirtan of the Lord's Praise is my life's occupation. (AG p. 10)

> Through the Guru, the Lord shall dwell within your mind. Within the home of your own inner being, you shall obtain the Mansion of the Lord's Presence with intuitive ease. You shall not be consigned again to the wheel of reincarnation. (AG p. 14)

Although you may have found some of the language unfamiliar, the gist of the above passages is fairly clear. 'The Guru' is to all intents and purposes the same as, or closely identified with, the Lord, the 'True Guru' (*Satguru*). In the first extract, evidently addressed to an audience with a Hindu background, the Guru is identified with (and transcends) the highest Hindu divinities (Vishnu, Brahma, Shiva, Parvati and Lakshmi). At the same time the Guru is the messenger of the Lord, one who teaches *about* the Lord. The Guru is also one who bestows or communicates the Lord's 'name' (nam) which is the means by which the soul or *jiva* gains admittance to the mansion of the Lord, thereby escaping from the round of rebirth.

If you have already studied Hinduism, you will appreciate that Sikhism shares broadly the same view of life and ultimate goal as devotional Hinduism (and other 'yogic' traditions such as Buddhism and Jainism); namely escape from the round of rebirth and suffering. Only the means is different.

You will have noticed that the Guru is never referred to as 'he' or 'she' in the above passages. In English, the personal pronoun 'he' is generally used for the Guru, but this is misleading. The Guru is entirely beyond gender; indeed the Guru is formless; *nirguna*. The spiritual mystery at the heart of Sikhism is that the formless Lord, the 'true Guru' communicates with us and liberates us from rebirth through the Guru, who may take any form. *Akhal Purakh* may prescribe to act as the teacher and the messenger of God. Sikhs always revere God through the present form of the Guru. This is why pictures of Nanak and other past forms of the Guru are kept apart from the Guru of the *present* time, the Guru Granth Sahib.

The term 'Guru' means *both* the highest, formless Lord *and* whoever or whatever temporary form has been chosen to convey to us the message or liberating influence of that Lord. There is no adequate English translation for *Guru* in the Sikh tradition, so it will be left untranslated.

Gurmat (the Guru's teachings) in the Adi Granth

What follows is a typical passage from the Adi Granth which summarises the main aspects of the Gurus' teaching (AG p 124). Written by the third Guru, it is representative of the whole of the Adi Granth in both tone and content. The comments in the right hand column may help you to understand the meaning.

Within this cave [of the mind], there is an inexhaustible treasure.	To find God one must look within, first discovering the inner realms of the mind which contain an unsuspected treasure (God)...
Within it resides the Invisible and Infinite Lord.	and pass through the realms of mind to the formless Lord who is hidden at the core of things.
He Himself is hidden, and He Himself is revealed	The Lord is formless, yet for those able to see it, everything manifests the divine nature
Through the Word of the Guru's Shabad, ego and conceit are eliminated.	The effect of receiving the grace of nām or shabad (name or word) from the Guru is that the attractions of ego (haumai) and pride become insipid and disappear.
I am a sacrifice, my soul is a sacrifice, to those who enshrine the Ambrosial Nām, the Name of the Lord, within their minds. The taste of the Ambrosial Nām is very sweet! Through the Guru's Word, drink in this Nectar.	The divine Nām is ambrosial; like nectar. The writer (the Guru) says that he will give himself entirely to a person who has become gurmukh by imbibing the divine nectar. This refers to the mutual spiritual love of guru and disciple.

Subduing egotism, the hard door is opened. The priceless Nām is obtained by Guru's Grace.

When ego (haumai) is subdued (by nām simaran), an inner 'door', ordinarily closed, opens within the disciple and by the divine grace of the Guru the wonderful nectar of nām suffuses the mind.

Without the Shabad (Word), Nām is not obtained. By Guru's Grace, it is implanted within the mind.

Nām and shabad are interdependent (they represent the same thing seen from different perspectives). Nām is obtained solely by the grace of the Guru, not by human effort.

The Guru has applied the true ointment of spiritual wisdom to my eyes. Deep within me, the Divine Light has dawned, and the darkness of ignorance has been dispelled.

The Third Guru speaks here as a disciple who has himself realised God. His spiritual eyes have been opened, divine light suffuses his mind and ignorance (the sense of separateness from God which supports egoism) has departed.

My light has merged into the all-Light; my mind has surrendered, and I am blessed with Glory in the Court of the Lord.

The disciple realises that the illumination of his own soul is in fact a merging, or an opening-up of the individual soul to the divine light. The light of the individual soul is the light of God.

Those who look outside the body, searching for the Lord, will not receive the Nām; they shall instead be forced to suffer Pain.

'External' rituals, ceremonies, pilgrimages and purifications take even the sincere seeker after God in the wrong direction. Those who fail to 'look within' for God will not find liberation and will inevitably be reborn in this world to suffer the pain of embodied existence again.

The blind, self-willed manmukhs do not understand; but when they return back to their (real) home, then, as Gurmukhs, they find their real object.

Those who are ignorant of the inner way to God ignorantly insist that God is to be found through traditional religion, external rituals, reciting holy books etc., but a disciple who seeks and finds God within the mind realises that looking for God outside was a mistake all along.

By Guru's Grace, the True Lord is found. Within your mind within your body, see the Lord, and the filth of egotism will depart.

The formless Lord can be realised only through the Guru's grace; hence the need for a Guru. When the Lord is realised within, then egotism (haumai) dissolves and love, humility etc. take its place.

Joining the company of the holy, sing the Glorious Praises of the Lord forever, and be merged in the True Word (Shabad).

The state of disciples who have merged with God is indescribable, but it can be said that they join the blessed company of those who have already merged with God through the Word and who thus 'sing the glorious praises of the Lord forever'.

One who closes the nine gates and restrains the wandering mind, and enters through the Tenth Gate into himself, there hears the Unstruck Melody of the Shabad vibrating day and night.   Through the Guru's Teachings, the Shabad is heard.

The 'nine gates' is a traditional reference to the body. It means the external apertures (two eyes, two ears, two nostrils, mouth, and two 'lower apertures') through which sense-impressions enter the mind and the mind 'flows out' into the world. The 'tenth gate' is an inward aperture, revealed by the Guru as a gate or door leading into the 'cave' of the mind within (see verse 1). The disciple who enters this 'tenth gate' by following the instructions of the Guru comes into contact with the shabad or Nām.

Without the Shabad, there is only darkness within.   The real object is not found, and the cycle of rebirth does not end.

One who does not have the Guru's grace and guidance finds only darkness within the mind, if they go in at all. The reference is to forms of yogic practice which focus for example on the breath rather than on the Shabad (Word) or Nām (Name).

The key is in the hands of the True Guru; no one else can open this door (of the mind).

This verse emphasises the necessity of a Guru as spiritual guide; contrary to the view of certain ascetics and religious teachers, spiritual liberation cannot be obtained by human effort alone.

By perfect destiny is the Guru met.

One does not even come into contact with a Guru unless the Lord wills it. This refers to the idea of hukam or the inscrutable will of God which governs everything.

This wisdom is obtained by the Guru's grace...

See 16 above.

O Nanak, praise the Nām forever;

The third Guru, like the other Sikh Gurus, here refers to himself as 'Nanak'. The implication is that the external form of the human Guru has changed, but the Guru is the same.

As Gurmukh, enshrine it within your mind.

The Gurmukh is one who has so completely merged with the Lord, the Guru, that his or her words are the words of the Guru. This is the opposite condition to a manmukh whose mind is full of egotism and pride.

Development of the Sikh *Panth* (community)

Sikhs today regard Guru Nanak as the founder of the Sikh tradition and emphasise his uniqueness and originality. At the same time, most Sikhs would say that while *Gurmat* may be the only proper path to liberation for a born Sikh, people of other faiths do find their own way to God, for the formless Lord (*Akhal Purakh*) is not an exclusive possession of the Sikhs. The prominent inclusion in the Adi Granth of verses by many 'non-Sikh' spiritual teachers such as Kabir, Sheikh Farid and Namdev shows that the Sikh gurus did not regard their own teachings as particularly new or exclusive.

From the standpoint of the history of religions Nanak and his successors may be seen as spiritual teachers within what is loosely called 'the *Sant* tradition of north India'. The *Sant*s rejected institutionalised religion, external ritual and priestly hierarchies and saw liberation from rebirth as the result of interior meditation on the formless Lord through the help or spiritual grace of a Guru. Like Nanak, they saw caste and gender as irrelevant to spirituality and made no distinction between Hindu and Muslim disciples. In the Adi Granth the Gurus often criticise religious activities such as asceticism, pilgrimage, ritual and some types of yoga, not on the grounds that their practitioners have a wrong understanding of the goal of religion, but because the methods they are using simply do not work!

Kabir (1440-1518), a Muslim mystic and near-contemporary of Nanak makes the point strongly (these verses are in the Adi Granth, p 324):

> If Yoga (union with God) could be obtained by wandering around naked, then all the deer of the forest would be liberated. What does it matter whether someone goes naked, or wears a deer skin, if he does not remember the Lord within his soul? If spiritual perfection could be obtained by shaving the head, then why haven't sheep found liberation? If someone could save himself by celibacy, O Siblings of Destiny, why then haven't eunuchs obtained the state of supreme dignity? Says Kabir, listen, O men, O Siblings of Destiny: without the Lord's Name (nam), who has ever found salvation?

While Guru Nanak undoubtedly attracted a personal following, his disciples did not abandon their existing 'outward' identities (as Hindus or Muslims) or see themselves as constituting a separate Sikh 'religion'. There is nothing in Nanak's teaching to suggest that they should do so. Nanak was one among other Gurus teaching doctrines and practices consistent with the Sant tradition. It was Nanak's genius to impart these teachings in such a way that a following of devoted disciples was formed, and it is Nanak's teachings that have been handed down within the Sikh panth to the present day.

Nanak appointed a successor, Angad, to become Guru after his death. Angad in turn appointed the third Guru, Amar Das, and so on until the tenth Guru, Guru Gobind Singh.   The period of the human Gurus covered approximately 200 years and in that time the Sikh *panth* expanded, acquired a stronger separate identity, became dominated numerically by the *Jat* or farming caste, established a number of well-known centres including Amritsar and eventually attracted the attention, often hostile, of the Muslim rulers. The fifth Guru, Guru Arjan, was cruelly executed by the Mughal ruler Jahangir and tradition states that his son Guru Hargobind adopted what became the standard emblem of an increasingly militant Sikh panth: two swords representing *miri* (political or military might) and *piri* (spiritual power).   Contemporary Sikhs remember with anguish the suffering of the later Gurus under Muslim rule, and tradition also records that after the time of Hargobind the succession to the Guruship was hereditary and often contested.

Within the expanding Sikh community some of the responsibilities of the Guru had been devolved to *masands* or 'vicars' of the scattered Sikh panth. By the time of Guru Gobind Singh not only was the panth threatened by the Mughals but the powerful *masands* also represented a serious challenge to the Guru's authority. In 1699, the tenth Guru bypassed the *masands* and in a dramatic gesture established his own élite order of devoted sikhs (the *khalsa*, or 'pure') to protect the community from internal division and external oppression. The formation of the *khalsa* is seen as a turning point in Sikh religious history. The '5 Ks', the addition of 'Singh' and 'Kaur' to male and female names respectively and the ritual of *amrit pahul or amrit sanskar* (initiation to the *khalsa*) developed from this time. The Guru did not require all Sikhs to join the *khalsa* and they remain a minority. Guru Gobind Singh did not appoint a human successor, but advised his followers to seek spiritual guidance from the Adi Granth. Sikhs today regard this book as their Guru. It forms the focal point of any *gurdwara* and is referred to in personal terms as *Sri Guru Granth Sahib*.

During the eighteenth century a number of Sikh *misls* (independent armies) operated in the Punjab, tradition recording that they heroically defended the scattered elements of the *panth* against Muslim attacks. When the Muslim threat receded a self-governing Kingdom of the Punjab was established which lasted until annexation by the British in 1849. This fifty-year period is now seen by Sikhs as a 'golden age' in Sikh history. The ruler was Maharaja Ranjit Singh, whose relaxed approach to religious matters reflected the popular orthodoxy of the time. Harjot Oberoi (1994, p 420), in his revealing study of Punjabi religious communities in the pre-British period, states that:

> Asking an individual in mid-century Punjab if he was a Sikh, Hindu or Muslim was, at an epistemological level, quite absurd. The more relevant question would have been what sacred tradition he belonged to. The pluralist framework of the Sikh faith in the nineteenth century allowed its adherents to belong to any one of the following traditions: Udasi, Nirmala, Khalsa, Nanak-panthi, Ram Raia, Baba Gurditta, Baa Jawahir Singh, Guru Bagh Singh, Nihang, Kalu Panthi, Ram Dasi, Nirankari, Kuka and Sarvaria. Many of these Sikhs shaved their heads, some smoked tobacco, others were not particular about maintaining the five external symbols of the faith. In the absence of a centralised church and an attendant religious hierarchy, heterogeneity in religious beliefs, plurality of rituals, and diversity of lifestyles were freely acknowledged. A pilgrimage to the Golden Temple (at Amritsar) could be supplemented with similar expeditions to the Ganges at Hardwar or the shrine of a Muslim saint.... Contemporary vehicles of knowledge - myths, texts, narratives, folklore and plays produced by non-Sikh authors - were accorded a firm place within Sikh cosmology.

British rule saw the development of modern, centralising reform movements aimed at establishing Sikhism's identity, particularly in relation to Christianity and Hinduism. Most important of these was the Singh Sabha (Sikh Association) founded in Amritsar in 1873 by conservative *sanatan* or 'traditional' Sikhs, who shared the general view that Khalsa-style orthodoxy was only one element within orthodox Sikhism. They saw the Sikh panth as part of wider Hindu society and viewed *sahaj-dharis* (who do not adopt the outward symbols of *khalsa* or follow the Rahit code) as true Sikhs. However, under the influence of the Tat Khalsa ('True Khalsa') faction of the Singh Sabha, based in Lahore, the Singh Sabha soon began to promote a *khalsa*-style orthodoxy.

In the early twentieth century political campaigns were mounted by the Akali party for the restitution of gurdwaras which had become the hereditary property of independent, often Hindu-oriented, *mahant*s (proprietors). A central administrative body, the Shiromani Gurdwara Parbandhak Committee (SGPC) was formed in 1920 for the purpose of managing newly-acquired gurdwaras. The Sikh Gurdwaras Act of 1925 enabled the transfer of most gurdwaras in the Punjab from the *mahants* to the SGPC. The first legal definition of 'Sikh' was drafted for the 1925 Act and ran as follows:

> Sikh means a person who professes the Sikh religion or, in the case of a deceased person, who professed the Sikh religion or was known to be a Sikh during his lifetime. If any question arises as to whether any living person is or is not a Sikh he shall be deemed to be or to be not a Sikh according as he makes or refuses to make in such manner as the Provincial Government may prescribe the following declaration:

> I solemnly affirm that I am a Sikh, that I believe in the Guru Granth Sahib, that I believe in the Ten Gurus, and that I have no other religion.

The phrase 'have no other religion' is widely interpreted by *Khalsa* Sikhs to mean that a Sikh cannot also be a Hindu, though for many practical purposes, including marriage, the distinction between 'Hindu' and 'Sikh' remains relatively unimportant for many Punjabis. The trend towards *khalsa*-style orthodoxy is far more obvious in a definition of Sikh issued by the SGPC in 1950. It followed agreement on a standard version of the Rahit codes for Khalsa Sikhs, the *Sikh Rahit Maryādā*, and states:

> A Sikh is any person who believes in God (Akal Purakh); in the ten Gurus (Guru Nanak to Guru Gobind Singh); in Sri Guru Granth Sahib, other writings of the ten Gurus, and their teachings; in the Khalsa initiation ceremony instituted by the tenth Guru; and who does not believe in any other system of religious doctrine.

The 1947 Partition of India cut the Punjab in two, creating a sensitive border between India and the new Pakistan. Refugees swelled the proportion of Sikhs in Indian Punjab. Agitation for regional autonomy and ultimately a Sikh homeland ('Khalistan') eventually politicised Sikh communities worldwide. During the 1980s the Punjab was wracked with violence, culminating in the Indian army's attack in 1984 on the Sikhs' holiest shrine in Amritsar, the revenge assassination of Prime Minister Indira Gandhi and death and injury to many ordinary citizens during ensuing mob violence. Such events politicised Sikh communities worldwide and also stimulated debates among Sikhs about issues of identity and religiosity. Unrest and repression in Punjab (harrowingly documented from the Punjabi point of view in Pettigrew's study *The Sikhs of the Punjab)* coupled with the increasingly significant presence of Sikhs outside India are two factors which have drawn global attention to Sikhism, which has a much higher profile globally now than it had even twenty years ago.

Readers

For Hinduism

Brockington J.L. (1981), *The Sacred Thread: Hinduism in its continuity and diversity*, Edinburgh, Edinburgh University Press.

Flood G. (1996), *An Introduction to Hinduism*, Cambridge, Cambridge University Press.

Klostermaier K.K. (1994), *A Survey of Hinduism* (second edition), Albany, SUNY Press.

Knott, K. (1998), *Hinduism: a very short introduction*, Oxford, Oxford University Press.

Lipner, J. (1994), *Hindus: their religious beliefs and practices*, London, Routledge.

For Buddhism

Harvey, P. (1990), *An Introduction to Buddhism: teachings, history and practices*, Cambridge, Cambridge University Press.

Snelling, J. (1987), *The Buddhist Handbook: A complete guide to Buddhist teaching and practice*, London, Rider.

Cush, D. (1993), *Buddhism*, London, Hodder and Stoughton.

For Sikhism

McLeod, W.H. (1997), *Sikhism*, Harmondsworth, Penguin.

Singh, G. (1997), Sikhism, in *The Illustrated Encyclopedia of World Religions* Shaftesbury, Element.

Cole, W.O. (1994), *Sikhism* (Teach Yourself Series), London, Hodder and Stoughton.

Cole, W.O. and Sambhi, P.S. (1990), *A Popular Dictionary of Sikhism*, Richmond, Curzon.

Bibliography

For Hinduism

Edgerton, F. (trans) (1944), *Bhagavad-gita*, Cambridge, Massachusetts, Harvard University Press.

Embree, A.T. (ed.) (1972), *The Hindu Tradition*, New York, Random House.

Frykenberg, R.E. (1991), The emergence of modern 'Hinduism' as a concept and as an institution: a reappraisal with special reference to South India, in G.D. Sontheimer and H. Kulke (eds), *Hinduism Reconsidered*, New Delhi, Manohar.

Hardy, F. (1990), Hinduism, in U. King (ed.), *Turning Points in Religious Studies*, Edinburgh, T and T Clark.

Hiriyanna, M. (1958), *Outlines of Indian Philosophy* (fourth edition), London, George Allen and Unwin.

Hiriyanna, M. (1985), *The Essentials of Indian Philosophy*, London, George Allen and Unwin.

O'Flaherty, W.D. (ed.) (1975), *Hindu Myths*, Harmondsworth, Penguin.

Radhakrishnar, S. and Moore, C.A. (eds) (1957), *A Sourcebook in Indian Philosophy*, Princeton, Princeton University Press.

Richards, G. (ed.) (1985), *A Sourcebook of Modern Hinduism*, Richmond, Curzon.

Said, E.W. (1995), *Orientalism: western conceptions of the orient*, Harmondsworth, Penguin.

Smith, W.C. (1978), *The Meaning and End of Religion*, London, SPCK.

Vivekananda (1986), *The Collected Works of Swami Vivekananda*, volume 1, Calcutta, Advaita Ashrama.

Werner, K. (1993), *A Popular Dictionary of Hinduism*, Richmond, Curzon.

Zaehner, R.C. (1966), *Hindu Scriptures*, London, Dent.

For Buddhism

Batchelor, S. (1994), *The Awakening of the West*, London, Aquarian.

Conze, E. (1959), *Buddhist Scriptures*, Harmondsworth, Penguin.

Cush, D. (1993), *Buddhism*, London, Hodder and Stoughton.

Harvey, P. (1990), *Introduction to Buddhism*, Cambridge, Cambridge University Press.

Keown, D. (1996), *Buddhism: a very short introduction*, Oxford, Oxford University Press.

Pye, M. (1979), *The Buddha*, London, Duckworth.

Rahula, W. (1967), *What the Buddha Taught*, London, Gordon Fraser.

Robinson, R. and Johnson, W. (1982), *The Buddhist Religion: a historical introduction*, Belmont, Wadsworth.

Saddhatissa, H. (1985), *The Buddha's Way*, London, Allen and Unwin.

Snelling J. (1987), *The Buddhist Handbook: a complete guide to Buddhist teaching and practice*, London, Century.

Williams, P. (1989), *Mahayana Buddhism: the doctrinal foundations*, London, Routledge and Kegan Paul.

For Sikhism

Cole, W.O. and Singh, P.S. (1978), *The Sikhs: their religious beliefs and practices*, London, Routledge and Kegan Paul.

Cole, W.O. (1982), *The Guru in Sikhism*, London, Darton, Longman and Todd.

Cole, W.O. (1994), *Sikhism* (Teach Yourself Series), London, Hodder and Stoughton.

Cole, W.O. and Sambhi, P.S. (1990), *A Popular Dictionary of Sikhism*, London, Curzon.

Gold, D. (1987), *The Lord As Guru*, Oxford, Oxford University Press.

Grewal, J.S. (1990), *The Sikhs of the Punjab*, Cambridge, Cambridge University Press.

Juergensmeyer, M. and Barrier, N.G. (eds) (1979), *Sikh Studies: comparative perspectives on a changing tradition*, Berkeley, Berkeley Religious Studies Series.

Kohli, S.S. (1975), *Sikh Ethics*, New Delhi, Munshiram Manoharlal Publishers.

McLeod, W.H. (1976), *The Evolution of the Sikh Community*, Oxford, Clarendon Press.

McLeod, W.H. (1980), *Early Sikh Tradition: a study of the Janam-Sakhis*, Oxford, Clarendon Press.

McLeod, W.H. (1984), *Textual Sources for the Study of Sikhism*, Manchester, Manchester University Press.

McLeod, W.H. (1989), *Who is a Sikh? the problem of Sikh identity,* Oxford, Clarendon Press.

McLeod, W.H. (1997), *Sikhism*, Harmondsworth, Penguin.

Oberoi, H. (1994), *The Construction of Religious Boundaries: culture, identity and diversity in the Sikh tradition*, Oxford, Oxford University Press.

Pettigrew, J.M. (1995), *The Sikhs of the Punjab: unheard voices of state and guerilla violence*, London, Zed Books Ltd.

Robinson, C. (1996), Neither east nor west: some aspects of religion and ritual in the Indian army of the Raj, *Religion*, 26, 37-47.

Schomer, K. and W.H. McLeod, (eds) (1987), *The Sants: studies in a devotional traditon of India*, Delhi, Motilal Barnsasidass.

Shackle, C. (1986), *The Sikhs*, London, Minority Rights Group Ltd.

Singh, G. (tr.) (1978), *Sri Guru Granth Sahib* (four volumes), Chandigarh, World Sikh University Press.

Singh, G. (1995), *A History of the Sikh People*, New Delhi, Allied Publishers.

Singh, G. (1997), Sikhism, in *The Illustrated Encyclopedia of World Religions*, Shaftesbury, Element, pp 190-205.

Singh, K. (1977 (1963), *A History of the Sikhs (volume 1): 1469-1839*, Delhi, Oxford University Press.

Singh, K. (1977 (1966), *A History of the Sikhs (volume 2): 1839-1974*, Delhi, Oxford University Press.

Singh, Nikky-Guninder Kaur (1993), *The Feminine Principle in the Sikh Vision of the Transcendent*, Cambridge, Cambridge University Press.

Note: The *Guru Granth Sahib* (in Punjabi and English translations) plus other useful material is available on *Gurbani-CD*, a CD-ROM produced as a *sewa* (voluntary service) by Sikhs in the USA. Contact address: Sikh Missionary Center, PO BOX 62521, Phoenix, Arizona 85082, USA.

Glossary of Sikh terms

3HO	Healthy, Happy, Holy Organisation. See Sikh Dharma of the western Hemisphere.
5 Ks	See panj kakke.
Adi Granth	'Primal Collection'. See Guru Granth Sahib.
Akāl Purakh	The Being beyond time; the Lord.

Akālī Dal	Akali Party. The servants of the Being beyond Time. Sikh political party established in the struggle for restitution of gurdwaras. Continues as a Punjabi political party.
Akhaṇḍ pāṭh	An unbroken reading of the Guru Granth Sahib, taking two days or more, often conducted on occasions of birth, marriage death, or in connection with business or family affairs.
Amrit	Nectar. Ambrosia. A synonym and aspect of nam, shabad.
Amrit pāhul, Amrit Saṅskār	Amrit ceremony of initiation into the Khalsa.
Ardās	Formal Khalsa prayer repeated at the conclusion of most rituals. Translated in McLeod (1997) pp. 299-301.
Bāṇī	Word of the Guru = Gurbani.
Bhaktī	Devotion, love for God.
Bhātra	A religiously conservative peddler caste group who entered Sikhism probably in the nineteenth century. They tend to have separate gurdwaras, and as travellers were among the earliest Sikhs to become established in the UK.
Birādarī	Lineage, brotherhood, kin group.
Chauri	Fan made of peacock feathers or yak hair waved over the Guru Granth Sahib to denote its sovereign status.
Granth	'Collection' = Guru Granth Sahib.
Granthī	Reader of the Guru Granth Sahib, often the person in charge of a gurdwara.
Gurū	God, divine guide, spiritual preceptor, teacher, Lord.
Gurū Granth Sāhib	The Adi Granth as the Guru of the present time. The Adi Granth perceived as a personal Guru.
Gurbāṇī	The Guru's word. Can mean both verses from the scriptures and the primal shabad or nam.
Gurdwara, Gurduārā	Sikh temple. A place where the Guru resides.
Gurmat	The Guru's teaching. Sikhism.
Gurmukh	One who is so identified with the Guru that he becomes, or speaks with, the Guru's own voice. A true devotee. Opposite of *manmukh*.
Gurmukhī	The Punjabi script, so named for its connection with the Guru's teachings.
Gurpurb	Commemoration of the death of one of the human Gurus.
Haumai	Ego, self-ishness. Haumai keeps us attached to the world and destined for rebirth.
Hukam	Decree, will, command. God's ineluctable will, without the support of which liberation is impossible.
Hukam-nāmā	A decree; utterance by the Guru. A passage read at random at the close of a service and understood as the Guru's personal command.

Japjī	'Meditation' (= nam japan). The name of the first passage in the Adi Granth, including the Mūl Mantra. It is translated in McLeod *Sikhism* p 271ff. AG p 1ff.
Jaṭ	Punjabi farming caste, numerically dominant in the Sikh panth, probably since early in its development.
Jīva	Soul, living being; human being.
Kabīr	A teacher in the Sant tradition from a Muslim background who lived c1440-1518. There are 541 hymns by Kabir included in the Guru Granth Sahib.
Karāh-parshād	Food (usually a mixture of flour, sugar and ghee) blessed by the Guru, prepared in an iron dish and served to the sangat at Sikh sevices.
Karma	Action. In effect, a law of cause-and-effect, or payment and repayment, in which previous and present actions have present and future consequences.
Kesh-dhāri, kes-dhāri	Kes is uncut hair. A Kesh-dhari is a Sikh who retains uncut hair.
Khaṇḍe kī pāhul	Khalsa initiation ritual = Amrit pahul.
Khālsā	'Pure'. The order of Sikhs created by Guru Gobind Singh at the Baisakhi festival 1699.
Khatrī	Punjabi merchant caste represented in Sikhism.
Kīrtan	Singing, particularly of devotional hymns from the Adi Granth.
Mūl Mantra	'Root mantra'. The first words of the Adi Granth, summarising Gurmat. See unit 2 for translation.
Mahant	Gurdwara 'proprietors' in the eighteenth and nineteenth centuries. The 1925 Gurdwaras Act enabled transfer of control of the gurdwaras from the mahants.
Man	(Egotistical) Mind, which can be transformed into a God-permeated mind. See manmukh.
Manmukh	One devoted to the (selfish) mind and things of the world rather than God (see haumai).
Misl	Eighteenth century Sikh military bands.
Mokṣha	Liberation from rebirth, salvation, freedom, God-realisation.
Monā Sikh	Khalsa Sikhs or Sikhs from a Khalsa background who cut their hair.
Muktī	= Moksha, liberation.
Nād	Sound or vibration ('Hindu' term similar to nam).
Nām	'Name', divine vibration, essence, mystical manifestation of the Lord. Synonymous with shabad (word) and amrit (nectar). Bestowed by the Guru, it is the means to realise God through nam simaran.
Nām japan	= Nam simaran.

Nām simaraṇ	Any form of remembrance, recollection, or meditation upon the Nām, God's essence.
Nāmdev	A thirteenth century Sant from a tailoring background, sixty of whose hymns are included in the Adi Granth.
Nāmdhāri	A Khalsa-oriented, strictly vegetarian Sikh sect also known as Kukas, founded by Baba Balak Singh in the early nineteenth century and based in Ludhiana. Their belief is that Guru Gobind Singh did not die in 1708 but lived until 1812, appointing Balak Singh his successor. The second leader Satguru Ram Singh was deported to Burma after the British had executed 66 Namdharis by tying them to the mouths of cannons.
Niraṅkār	Formless, beyond form. An epithet of God, Akal Purakh, Waheguru.
Niraṅkāri	A nineteenth century Nanak-panthi movement (focused on Nanak's teachings rather than Guru Gobind Singh and the Khalsa) which has developed within Sikhism. The founder Baba Dayal (1783-1855) and the gurus who have succeeded him emphasis nam simaran of the formless (nirankar) lord.
Nirguṇa	'Beyond qualities'; unconditioned, ineffable.
Oabad	unstruck music emanating from the Lord. Also used for hymns, verses.
Pālki	The palanquin or dais on which the Guru Granth Sahib is placed and read.
Paṅgat	Status-free lines in the langar.
Pānj kakke, pānj kakar	The 5 Ks worn as 'outward symbols' by the Khalsa Sikhs. They are kes/kesh (uncut hair), kangha (wooden comb), kara (steel wristlet), kachh (breeches), kirpan (sword or dagger).
Pānj piāre	The five devoted ones. The first five Sikhs who offered to die for Guru Gobind Singh at the founding of the Khalsa. Subsequently five appointed leaders in Sikh ritual.
Panth	Literally path or spiritual system; used to denote the Sikh community.
Rāmgharhīā	Sikh artisan caste group mainly of carpenters (Tarkhans) who adopted the name Ramgharhia from a Tarkhan hero.
Rādhāsoāmī	Name of a contemporary nonsectarian movement with a line of human Gurus and large Sikh membership, based in the Punjab.
Rahit	Khalsa code of discipline. See Sikh Rahit Maryada.
Rahit nāmā	A recorded version of the code of discipline (rahit) for the Khalsa.
Ravidāsi	Follower of the outcaste cobbler or *chamar* Sant Ravidas (c. 1414-1526). Many chamars became Sikhs in the nineteenth century. They are emerging as a separate Sikh-style group, but focusing on Ravidas as their Guru.
Sach khaṇḍ	True realm or true home. A term for the realised state of oneness with God.

Sahaj	'Ease'. Synonym for liberation.
Sahaj-dhāri	Literally, one who attains sahaj. Commonly used to imply 'lax', non-observant of the Khalsa code.
Saṃsāra	The round of birth and death.
Sanātan	Eternal, ancient. General Hindu/Sikh term for spirituality that transcends man-made boundaries.
Saṅgat	The congregation, the Guru's community.
Sant	1. Type of spiritual teacher in the medieval Sant tradition. 2. A contemporary leader, usually charismatic and political or religious or both, within Sikhism, .
Sat Gurū	True Guru. God. The Lord. The Guru.
Sat Nām	'True Name' = Nam, God.
Shabad, shabda	'Word' (logos). Synonym of nam, essence of truth and reality.
Sheikh Farīd	1173-1263. Muslim pir (guru) in the Sant tradition. There are 134 hymns by Farid in the Adi Granth.
Shri Gurū Granth = Guru Granth Sahib.	
Siṅgh Sabhā	Sikh Association, founded in 1873. Two early factions were the Sanatan Sikhs and Tat Khalsa (q.v.).
Sikh	Learner, disciple. One who follows the instructions of a Guru.
Sikh Dharma of the Western Hemisphere	The official name of the movement referred to as '3HO'. Founded by Yogi Bhajan in 1971 it comprises American and other western members who practise kundalini yoga and observe Khalsa customs, separately from Punjabi Sikhs.
Sikh Rahit Maryada	The modern (1950) agreed version of the Rahit (q.v.) published by the SPGC.
Simaraṇ	Remembrance, recollection. See nam simaran.
SPGC	Shiromani Gurdwara Parbandhak Committee. Group formed to administer gurdwaras after the 1925 Gurdwaras Act. Now controls major gurdwaras in India.
Tat Khālsā	'True Khalsa' faction or movement. Prominent since the late nineteenth century (see Singh Sabha) for its insistence on the separate identity of Sikhs and emphasis on Khalsa orthodoxy.
Udāsīs	A community of ascetics which claims as its founder Siri Chand, one of Guru Nanak's sons.
Vāhigurū, Wāhigurū	'Praise to the Guru'. Widely used as the name of God in contemporary Sikhism.

Note on pronunciation and transliteration

Punjabi sounds do not correspond exactly to English, and romanised Punjabi is not pronounced as one might expect. As a *very* rough guide:

1. The 'th' sound is like 'th' in 'Courthouse', *not* 'th' in 'thin'.

2. Short 'a' is pronounced like (Southern) English 'u' as in 'run', *not* 'a' as in 'cat'.

3. Long 'ā' is pronounced 'aah'.

4. 'u' is pronounced as a short 'oo', *not* 'u' as in run.

5. The final vowel 'e' is pronounced 'ey'.

6. 'I' is pronounced as in 'it', *not* 'ee'.

Examples:

Ardās	Ur-daas
Adi Granth	Uddi Grunt-h
Amrit pāhul	Umrit paahool
Panth	punt-h
Pānj kakke	punj kukkey
Pānj piāre ṛ	paanj pyaarey
Sikh	Sick

Teaching about Hinduism, Buddhism and Sikhism

Unit B

Contemporary practice and current debates

Denise Cush and Catherine Robinson

Bath Spa University College

Dr Wendy Dossett

Trinity College Carmarthen

and

Professor Brian Bocking

School of Oriental and African Studies

University of London

Contents

Introduction

The three units in this module are constructed differently from most of the other modules. In this unit we present three separate sections offering contemporary practice and current debates relevant to Hinduism, Buddhism and Sikhism. Each section is preceded by its own aims, but the recommended reading and the bibliography for all the sections are put at the end of the unit.

B1 Hinduism

Aims

After working through part B1 of this unit you should be able to:

- understand contemporary forms of Hinduism, especially in Britain;
- appreciate Hindu ritual and social practices, together with aspects of iconography and mythology;
- engage with some contemporary debates within Hinduism about caste, women, ecology and attitudes to other faiths.

Overview

In this unit the focus is on Hindu, Buddhist and Sikh groups *in Britain* to prepare for teaching these religions in British classrooms. Inevitably some traditional religious practices, like pilgrimage, have been adapted for practical reasons and others have been impacted by modern secular life in Britain and other politico-cultural movements like feminism and environmental concern.

You will notice that technical terms, but not names, have been italicised in this unit. This is because they are transliterated from Sanskrit, the ancient sacred language of Hinduism. However, the system of transliteration used is only one of many, and is the simplest to use. Other systems rely on diacritical marks. In using other written sources, including dictionaries and indexes, you need to bear in mind that the spellings may be slightly different.

Hindus in Britain

There are probably about 800 million Hindus worldwide, the vast majority of whom live in India. Some estimates suggest that up to 400,000 Hindus may be resident in Britain, with Gujaratis constituting the largest regional group. Historically, there has been a special relationship between the Indian sub-continent and Hinduism. This has extended beyond the belief in the sacred geography of India as the holy motherland to the idea that it was not possible to be a Hindu except in India and the concomitant dread of 'crossing the Black Sea' and losing one's religious identity and social status. Even as late as the end of the nineteenth century, the young Gandhi had to undergo a purification ceremony to regain his caste on his return from Britain. Notwithstanding, Hindu cultural influence was diffused through Asia in ancient times, probably through migration which continues to be the primary mechanism by which Hinduism spreads. The notion of conversion, in the case of Hinduism, is at best extremely problematic because it is generally understood that in order to be a Hindu one must be born into a Hindu family.

The profile of the Hindu community in Britain is diverse with different migration histories (whether directly from India or indirectly from ex-colonies especially in East Africa), different castes, different language groups and different regional identities rather unevenly distributed across mainly urban inner-city areas of settlement. While most British Hindus would see themselves as belonging to a mainstream tradition, sometimes referred to as *sanatana dharma* (eternal religion), there are also Hindus with a particular allegiance to a distinct movement. Some of these movements have also gained western followers which complicates the issue of deciding who is a Hindu.

Among these movements are Swami Narayan, Sathya Sai Baba and ISKCON (International Society for Krishna Consciousness). The Swami Narayan movement traces its origins to an early nineteenth century figure who is believed to be an incarnation of God. Since the time of Lord Swaminarayan, there has been a lineage of four spiritual successors (*gurus*), devotion to whom is regarded as devotion to God. This movement remains largely Gujarati and has recently gained attention for building the first Hindu temple in Europe in accordance with ancient classical principles. Sathya Sai Baba attracts a large following of westerners and is chiefly memorable for his miraculous powers such as the manifestation of sacred ash and even jewels. Worshipped as Shiva, he is also respected by mainstream Hinduism and his image, easily recognisable by his Afro hairdo and bright orange robes, is found in many temples. Now (1999) aged 75, he is one of the most popular contemporary religious leaders. ISKCON, founded by A.C. Bhaktivedanta Swami Prabhupada in New York in 1966, was part of a mission to take the message of Chaitanya, a sixteenth century saint, to the West. Most devotees continue to be westerners who are committed to proselytising the teaching of devotion (*bhakti*) to Krishna as 'the Supreme Personality of Godhead'. They advocate the practice of chanting the names of God (*kirtana*) and their music and dancing on the streets of western cities has made them particularly prominent. Other important movements include the Brahma Kumaris, Iyengar Yoga, Rajneeshism and, more problematically, TM (Transcendental Meditation). For further information on Hinduism in Britain, see Bowen (1981), Burghart (1987), Jackson and Nesbitt (1993) and Knott (1986a); on Swami Narayan, see Williams (1984); on ISKCON, see Knott (1986b), and on Sathya Sai Baba, see Bowen (1988).

Temple

The temple (*mandir*) is seen as the dwelling-place of the divine. Its basic features are a main hall, a central shrine with an image, surmounted by a tower with a flag-pole, other halls and shrines with other images, surrounded by courtyards and gates. There are two main styles, North Indian and South Indian. Whereas in India a temple will be dedicated to one God, in Britain it is common to include shrines to Shaiva, Vaishnava and Shakta deities within one building. For example, the main shrine at the Bristol Hindu temple features Krishna and Radha, Shiva and Parvati and Rama, Sita and Lakshman while there are side shrines to Durga, Ganesha, Hanuman and the *trimurti* of Brahma, Vishnu and Shiva. In addition, there are often shrines to specific regional and caste foci of devotion as well as pictures of an array of saints, seers and respected figures, both Hindu and from other religious traditions. Thus, for instance, the Bristol temple has a shrine to Jalaram Bapu, a Gujarati holy man, and pictures of Gandhi, Jesus, Guru Nanak and Sai Baba. Most Hindu temples in Britain, unlike in India, are not purpose-built but adaptations of existing buildings, including churches and cinemas. Though their external appearance is unremarkable, internally they are ornate, highly decorated and brightly coloured. In India, Hindus make regular, if not frequent, visits to the temple to worship. In the diaspora the temple serves a minority community not just as a place of worship, but also as a cultural, educational and social centre. A useful introduction to the Hindu temple is Michell (1977).

Home shrines

Worship at the temple is not obligatory and, for most devout Hindus, daily worship centres on home shrines. Women often take a leading part in this activity and in Britain many temple communities started life as gatherings of family and friends meeting at a house with a particularly impressive shrine.

Worship, in the sense of devotional rituals directed towards personal divinities, is known as *puja*. Whether at home or in the temple, this may include offerings which involve all the senses: incense, water, flowers, perfumed and coloured pastes and powders etc. Food offered to the Gods is regarded as blessed and distributed to the devotees as *prashada*. Bells and cymbals are used to announce the presence of the worshipper and throughout the ceremony *Bhajans* (hymns) are sung and *mantras* (sacred formulae) are chanted. *Mandalas* (symbolic diagrams) are also a feature. *Arati*, often used as a synonym for *puja*, technically involves the offering of light, usually in the form of a ghee-filled lamp with five wicks, to deity images. Fuller (1992) includes a full discussion of many devotional rituals.

Images and iconography

A striking aspect of Hinduism is the multiplicity of images (*murti*). This has given rise to considerable misunderstanding and accusations of idolatry. There are two basic types of images, aniconic and iconic. The most famous aniconic image is the *linga*, the phallic form of Shiva. Especially revered are those images that are regarded as natural rather than created by artisans, for example *shalagrama* stones (ammonites) which are viewed as forms of Vishnu. Iconic images portray Gods and Goddesses in personal form in a variety of media in accordance with traditional rules. Such images require ritual consecration by which the divine takes up residence in the image. This is not idolatry in that the divine presence is not limited to the image but nevertheless the image mediates the divine reality to the worshipper. The Goddess Saraswati, for instance, is pictured as a beautiful woman dressed in white, riding upon a swan and holding in her four arms symbols of wisdom and culture (crystal beads, a book and a musical instrument). A characteristic of this iconography is that Gods and Goddesses have animal or mythological vehicles on which they ride, Ganesha, for example rides a rat or mouse. Among the most useful accounts are Eck (1985) and Kramrish (1965).

Mythology

The many Gods and Goddesses of Hinduism each have their own mythologies. Even if only the major all-India deities are considered, there is a vast range of stories expressed in a variety of forms, including song, dance and drama. These stories exist in distinct regional recensions and have developed over time. The major sources of these stories are the *Puranas* and Epics. Hindus look to these stories for insight into the divine, the relationship between the Gods and Goddesses and human beings.

One of the innumerable creation stories involves Vishnu who, between creations, sleeps resting on his snake upon the cosmic ocean with his wife Shri Lakshmi in attendance. As he wakes, from his navel emerges Brahma, the creator God, who in turn brings the universe into being. Vishnu's care for creation is emphasised in the stories of his *avataras* (descents or incarnations) when he assumes an earthly form in order to uphold righteousness. Traditionally, Hindus list ten *avataras*: the fish who saved the first people and their scriptures from the flood; the tortoise who helped recover the lost treasures of the Gods; the boar who rescued the earth; the man-lion who destroyed the demon, Hiranyakashipu; the dwarf who won back the earth for the Gods; Parashurama who killed the wicked *kshatriyas* (warriors) who had usurped the status of the priests; Rama who conquered Ravana, the demon king, who had imprisoned Sita, his wife; Krishna who defeated evil on many occasions; the Buddha who taught non-violence; and, in the future, Kalki who will re-establish order and harmony. The two most significant of these *avataras* are Rama and Krishna. Rama personifies the obedient son and faithful husband. He is also regarded as the ideal king and his rule is understood to be a time of peace and happiness when all his subjects conduct themselves in accordance with *dharma* (righteousness). Krishna is the mischievous baby, the playful adolescent, the charming lover and the wise counsellor, all of which are models for possible relationships with God.

In contrast to much Vaishnavite mythology, the stories of Shiva can be anarchic. Although he can also act to protect the world, he challenges the social conventions which Vishnu upholds. He unites in his person polar opposites being both creator and destroyer in his cosmic dance. As the great ascetic, he is lord of *yogis*, yet his union with Parvati is so passionate that it shakes the foundations of the world. For Shaivites, the superiority of Shiva over his rivals, Vishnu and Brahma, is demonstrated by the inability of the latter to discover a beginning or end to Shiva's *linga*.

The mythology of the Goddess, especially as Durga or Kali, has some similarities with both Vaishnavite and Shaivite myths in that she is the destroyer of evil but also a dangerous and uncontrolled character. Like Vishnu, she destroys the demons who threaten the cosmic order but, like Shiva with whom she is often associated, she has a wild and violent side. O'Flaherty (1975) contains a collection of Hindu myths. See also Zimmer (1972).

Festivals

Festivals are a major feature of Hindu religious life. They may be local or regional as well as national though, of course, the national festivals are celebrated in different ways according to local tradition. Among the most well-known are the following:

- Divali, the festival of lights (October/November) celebrates Shri Lakshmi,

Goddess of wealth and fortune, and the triumphant homecoming of Rama and Sita. Small lamps (*divas*) are lit, accounts are blessed, houses are decorated and cards and presents may be exchanged.

- Sarasvati Puja (January/February) is particularly important for schoolchildren because she is the patron Goddess of learning. School books and other resources are set before her shrine which may be specially constructed for the festival.
- Mahashivratri (January/February) is celebrated on the night of the full moon when devotees fast and sing praises of Shiva and his creative power. Milk or water is poured over the *linga*.
- Holi (February/March) is a spring festival with a carnival atmosphere, though this is more evident in India where there is a temporary relaxation in normal rules of behaviour between castes and genders. Bonfires are lit and coloured water is thrown at people in a general spirit of license. There are many stories associated with Holi, including Prahlada's devotion to Vishnu in spite of his demon ancestry and Krishna's play with the *gopis* (milkmaids).
- Raksha Bandhan (July/August) involves sisters tying *rakhis* (silken bracelets) around the wrists of their brothers in return for their brothers' protection. This is a very popular festival among children.
- Janamashtami/Krishna Jayanti (August/September) commemorates the birth of Krishna at midnight. The new-born baby is welcomed with music and singing and with offerings of butter and curds.
- Navaratri (September/October) is the 'Nine Nights' centred on worship of Durga and includes a stick-dance around a special six-sided shrine by girls or women in honour of the Goddess.

For further details on these and other festivals, see Jackson (1986).

Pilgrimage

Tirthayatra is often linked with the sacred geography of India. Pilgrims visit the four divine abodes at the cardinal points, as well as the subcontinent's rivers and mountains. The most holy of such places is Varanasi (Benares), situated on the bank of the Ganges. So sacred is this city that those who die within its precincts are believed to cross over from birth-and-death to release. Eck (1983) is an outstanding study of Varanasi as a pilgrimage centre. Morinis (1984) also offers an analysis of pilgrimage but with a focus on West Bengal.

Rites of passage

Samskaras (sacraments) mark each change of status and sanctify each stage of a person's life. There are nine sacraments connected with conception, pregnancy, childbirth and milestones in the child's early development such as weaning. These reflect the importance attached to having children, especially sons, and the fragility of early life. Initiation (*upanayana*) involves the investing of a young boy with the Sacred Thread which symbolises his entry into adult life of the religious community. Marriage (*vivaha*) is perhaps the most important sacrament of all. It is completed by the couple taking seven steps around the sacred fire, one for power, one for strength, one for wealth, one for fortune, one for descendants, one for good times and one for friendship. Funerals (*antyeshthi*) normally take the form of cremations with the resulting ashes being cast into rivers. Following this, and eventually annually, memorial rites (*shraddha*) are observed in which balls of rice are offered to the deceased and other ancestors. On British adaptations of Hindu rites of passage, see Killingley, Manski and Firth (1991).

Activity B1

Identify the most important aspects of a Hindu's religious life. In what ways would practice differ in the diaspora, especially Britain?

Comment on activity B1

You should have considered worship at home and in the temple, image worship, traditional stories, festivals, pilgrimage, rites of passage and membership of religious movements. Outside India, Hindus find themselves in a minority community. Temples are few and far between and tend to include a representative selection of deities and serve an additional socio-cultural function. An effort must be made to transmit traditional stories as they will no longer be absorbed from the surrounding culture and extended family. Festival observance has been somewhat constrained by the western calendar and milieu. Hindus are distanced from India and all its sacred sites so that opportunities for pilgrimage are limited. Efforts are being made to establish pilgrimage centres and routes in Britain. Rites of passage remain largely traditional with minor adaptations to British law.

Contemporary debates

Important issues of contemporary debate in Hinduism include caste, women, ecology and attitudes to other faiths.

Caste

This is a very complex and contentious issue. Caste can denote either the hierarchical principle in Indian society generally, in which case it refers to the *varnas* and to the *jatis,* or more narrowly, only to the latter. *Varnas* are the four classes of priests, warriors, merchants and serfs, whose origin and nature are set out in the most ancient Hindu scripture, the *Rig Veda.* There are thousands of *jatis,* which are endogamous groups, associated with particular trades or crafts, and practising commensality (eating together). These groups are ranked in terms of their relative ritual purity. The relationship between these two different systems is unclear, although it is commonplace for members of a *jati* to align their group with a particular *varna.*

The debate about caste centres on whether this arrangement is essential to the Hindu way of life. Traditionally, one became a Hindu by birth into a Hindu family and hence caste. However, a common reformist position is to reject the *jatis* but reinterpret the *varnas,* accepting that people have different aptitudes, but denying that this is hereditary. This approach was taken by Gandhi, who was especially concerned about the plight of the 'untouchables' or 'outcastes' (people who were regarded as particularly impure and accorded a lower status even than serfs). He condemned the way in which these people, whom he called 'Harijans' (children of God), were discriminated against by caste Hindus, for example preventing them from drawing water from the same well, and debarring them from access to temples. In contrast, B.R. Ambedkar, a contemporary of Gandhi, insisted that caste was fundamental to Hinduism, and on this basis, he rejected the religion itself. Committed to equality, and himself a member of one of the lowest social groups, he eventually became a Buddhist, viewing this as a more egalitarian indigenous tradition. As a result of the work of such campaigners, the constitution of independent India outlawed caste, and made special provision for the advancement of the lower social groups. These special provisions have on occasion aroused considerable resentment on the part of caste Hindus but, from the point of view of those groups intended to benefit from the measures, often seem tokenistic. Notwithstanding its worst excesses, caste as a kinship system or extended family has provided a sense of community, identity and a support mechanism for Hindus of every social status, and thus continues to be important in practice.

Dumont (1981) remains the classic discussion of caste though it has been criticised more recently. A thought-provoking approach to caste is taken by

Tully (1992) who examines how caste functions and why it still commands loyalty in contemporary India.

Women

There has been much discussion about the role and status of women. The traditional ideal is that of the *pativrata* (husband-vowed), a wife who is devoted to her husband. Her duty is defined as to worship her husband as a God and consecrate her life to his service. According to the lawbooks, this constitutes her only religious activity, her spiritual welfare solely dependent on her dedication to this task. Models of virtuous womanhood include Sita, faithful to Rama even under threat of death, and Savitri, who defied the God of death to win back her husband's soul. This means that women do not receive initiation, they are ineligible for Vedic study and cannot become priests. In addition, a number of practices have been condemned as injurious to women. Some of these practices such as *sati*, the immolation of a widow on her husband's funeral pyre, and child marriage together with the prohibition of widow remarriage have a justification by virtue of their inherence in tradition, whereas others such as female infanticide/foeticide and dowry death, the killing of a young bride whose family has supplied insufficient dowry, have no such legitimacy.

The position of women has been the subject of intense controversy and many Hindus have criticised the unequal treatment of women. In so doing, they have often drawn upon other aspects of the tradition which are interpreted as more favourable to women. These have included the *Bhakti* movement which rejects the spiritual significance of gender and reveres many women saints, for example Mirabai, and *Tantra* which respects all women as manifestations of the Goddess. Most frequently, commentators appeal to an idealised picture of ancient India reconstructed from the scriptures in which women are portrayed as the equals of men. Although some feminists would reject Hinduism as irredeemably misogynist, others argue that the tradition can be reinterpreted so that its true empowering message is revealed. The Goddess Kali, for instance, is cited as an alternative role model who is independent of male authority and an icon of power.

Leslie (1991) comprises a wide-ranging collection of essays concerning women and the Hindu tradition. Young (1987) gives a good historical overview which is brought up-to-date in Young (1994) with its focus on contemporary issues.

Ecology

Hindus, like other religious communities, have become aware of the environmental crisis comparatively recently. Many maintain that there are resources within the tradition which support an ecologically responsible approach, for example, the immanence of God in nature, the sacredness of plants and animals, notably the cow, the belief in non-violence (*ahimsa*), the tendency to vegetarianism, the possibility of reincarnation in animal form and, more generally, a philosophy of the oneness of all that is. Some Hindus assert that the adoption of Hindu values would ensure a sustainable future and, indeed, many claim ancient Indian civilisation should serve as the model for this. However, this construction of an ecologically sound Hinduism is predicated on a highly selective reading of the tradition and it can be argued that other aspects of the tradition militate against environmental concern. Notwithstanding, Hindus have made valuable practical contributions to the ecological cause, most famously in the Chipko (tree-hugging) movement opposing deforestation. See Cush and Robinson (1997) and Prime (1992) for very different perspectives.

Attitudes to other faiths

Many Hindus will express the view that all religions are just so many paths to the same goal. They are thus open to the idea that truth is to be found in every faith and are prepared to accept the validity of other religions. This universalism takes a variety of forms. Some will simply acknowledge the fundamental unity of religions. Others will recognise the differences between religions but uphold their equality. Another view is that different faiths are suitable for different cultures, whatever value is attached to these differences. A variant on this is to see different religions as suited to different stages of spiritual development through many lives. Some Hindus, implicitly or explicitly, suggest that Hinduism is superior to other religions precisely because it is prepared to admit that all religions have a positive part to play. In spite of this prevailing ideology of universalism, for many Hindus it is important to assert their identity over and above other groups. This is most evident in India where there is a perception, not shared by Muslims or Sikhs, that Hindus are threatened by both the secular state and powerful minority groups. These Hindus see the establishment of a truly Hindu state as the only viable means of safeguarding the integrity of the Hindu community. Thus attitudes to inter-faith dialogue differ greatly. If those Hindus most opposed to other communities are excluded, common attitudes range from a disinclination to participate since each religion is sufficient unto itself to an active interest in discovering the truths taught by other faiths. Apart from a few groups who seek converts, there is no missionary impulse in Hinduism, and experience of the proselytising zeal of Muslims and Christians has left Hindus with a deep suspicion of conversion which has influenced their approach to dialogue. Cush and Robinson (1995) have some views on this issue. Griffiths (1990) and Sharpe (1977) provide fascinating insights on Hindu-Christian relationships.

For a first-hand account of dialogue from a Christian point of view, though with relevance for understanding Hindu attitudes, see Klostermaier (1969).

Activity B2

Suggest what strategies contemporary Hindus might adopt in presenting their religion in a positive light to a western audience.

Comment on activity B2

You should have reflected on how Hindus reject criticisms of their religion and also emphasise aspects that will appeal to westerners. This involves a process of selective reinterpretation. For example, a Hindu might either stress the positive functions of caste or deny its importance to Hinduism. So far as women are concerned, a Hindu might point to feminine images of the divine and the putative position of women in ancient India. Ancient India may be adduced as evidence of Hinduism's ecological credentials as well as a variety of other evidence drawn from scripture, philosophy and practice. The portrayal of Hinduism in universalist terms is particularly attractive to westerners and is prominent in apologetic writing.

B2 Buddhism

Aims

After working through part B2 of the unit you should be able to:

- understand contemporary forms of Buddhism, especially in Britain;
- appreciate the diversity of Buddhism;
- engage with the contemporary debate within Buddhism about ecology.

Overview

You may find it helpful to have read through the section entitled 'Historical development of Buddhism' before embarking on this section.

This unit explores the issue of Buddhism's diversity and will introduce you to some of the features of contemporary Buddhism in Sri Lanka and Japan as case studies. Many other countries might have been chosen, and you are encouraged to research others if you have the opportunity. Arguably no one country can provide an ideal case study, since Buddhism varies so much even from region to region, but Sri Lanka has been chosen because it has a long Theravada history, and Japan because of the different schools of Mahayana Buddhism which are adhered to there. You will also study some of the features of Buddhism in the West and especially in Britain, and encounter one of the issues with which contemporary writers engage.

Since the ground which must be covered in this unit is so vast, the information presented is inevitably selective. However, the material used here is specifically chosen to focus on crucial issues in the hope that your background reading will be informed by your study of this unit.

In this unit technical terms, but not names, have been italicised. This is because they have been transliterated from languages which do not use the roman alphabet. There are a number of different ways of transliterating terms, and when using other written sources you need to be aware that you may come across different spellings.

Geographical spread of Buddhism

Buddhism began in India around two and a half millennia ago[1], but had by the thirteenth century CE all but died out in India. Before this occurrence, however, it spread, in different forms, over much of Asia. A number of countries can at the present time be called Buddhist: for example, Sri Lanka, Burma, Thailand, and the Himalayan kingdoms of Sikkim and Bhutan. Other countries have had long periods of Buddhist history, but are now predominantly Islamic or Christian: for example, Indonesia and Korea.

In other countries Buddhism has been more or less driven out fairly recently by communist revolution or invasion: for example China, Laos, Cambodia (Kampuchea), Vietnam, Mongolia, some parts of Russia, and Tibet. There is evidence however that Buddhism survives in these countries and is, in some areas, experiencing a renaissance. Tibetan Buddhism survives in exile, mainly in North India and Sikkim, but also in other parts of the world. A comparatively recent phenomenon has been the large scale spread of Buddhism to the West.

Unlike some other religions which originated in India, Buddhism is not restricted in any way to one ethnic group. Anyone can become a Buddhist regardless of nationality or class. This is undoubtedly one of the reasons it has spread more widely than Hinduism and Sikhism. These two religions only

---

[1] It is important to note here that Buddhists believe in an infinite universe, and many Buddhists believe that there have been other Buddhas in other times. Sakyamuni, or the historical Buddha, is the Buddha of our world and time.

travel, with a few exceptions, with Indian population movements. Converts are rare. The converse is true of Buddhism.

During the time of the Indian Buddhist Emperor, Ashoka, in the third century, Buddhist emissaries were sent to a number of Asian countries to found communities. Whilst Buddhism is rightly not normally thought of as a missionary religion, this early expansion did much to ensure a wide and varied demographic base for Buddhism in Asia. Other movements, along trade routes, spread Buddhism further afield. In some cases, such as in Japan, Buddhism was actively invited, and was perceived as being part and parcel of a superior culture in which the country wanted to participate.

The huge spread of Buddhism into different cultural settings meant that the doctrines and practices of Buddhism became highly diverse. This poses a problem for the student. It can be difficult to see how some forms of contemporary Buddhism relate to each other, and to the teachings of the historical Buddha, if indeed they do at all.

This problem arguably arises in part from a peculiarly western insistence on the importance of founders. The historical Buddha does not function in Buddhism in the same way that Jesus does in Christianity. The Buddha, according to tradition, uncovered a path to Enlightenment which had always been available and had, indeed, been uncovered by others in other aeons. The Pali canon provides the life and teachings of one enlightened being, there are others, and they may mediate ultimate truth to their audiences using techniques different from those employed by the historical Buddha. Thus, any idea that the historical Buddha's teachings provide a creed of Buddhism may not be conducive to understanding the reality of Buddhism in the world.

A Buddhist account often given for the diversity of the religion is that enlightened beings utilise whatever the situation provides them with to lead people out of ignorance. Thus, Buddhism does not aim to usurp culture, rather to work with it. Different people have different intellectual and spiritual capacities and need to have their *dukkha* (suffering resulting from attachment) addressed in different ways. Ultimate truth is not accessible directly except through experience. To those who have not experienced it, it must be mediated through metaphor, allegory, or what Buddhists would call 'conventional truths'. So, since cultures and individuals are different, Buddhism takes on different forms.

Spread of Buddhism to the West

As Stephen Batchelor (1994, p xii ff) describes in his *Awakening of the West* the first major western encounters with Buddhism were through missionaries, and through the various periods of European rule in Asia. Accounts of Buddhism given by missionaries and colonial bureaucrats vary in nature a great deal. Many viewed Buddhism as demonic, 'Godless' or, paradoxically, idolatrous. Others did not differentiate it from other indigenous religions. Some did attempt to study it seriously, but very often their motive in doing so was to be able to discredit it with authority. Information gleaned from these sources is therefore often rather suspect and tendentious. One Colonial bureaucrat however, T.W. Rhys Davids, who was a magistrate in Ceylon (now Sri Lanka), became sufficiently fascinated by the Pali canon that he established the Pali Text Society in 1881. The PTS still provides the most respected English translation of the canon.

More positive interest in Buddhism came from those interested in eastern spiritualities for their own sake. As Denise Cush (1993, pp 156 ff) reports, theosophists, occultists, spiritualists, aesthetes and orientalists of all kinds embraced the teachings of Buddhism with enthusiasm (along with many other eastern teachings). While outstanding and groundbreaking work was done by many scholars of this period, such as Friedrich Max Müller and Hermann Oldenberg, the work of many romanticised Buddhism as the spirituality for the age, combining the rational and the mystical. Others arguably distorted it by mixing its teachings with many others according to their own tastes.

Buddhism became very much part of popular culture in the 1950s and 60s. The Beat Poets (for instance Jack Kerouac) used Buddhist themes, and they in turn influenced the emerging popular music scene. Young people were attracted to the ideas of Buddhism and ultimately the religion became associated with a counter-culture, and even in some cases with mind-altering drugs.

Activity B3

Suggest some reasons why Buddhism is becoming increasingly popular in the West.

Comment on activity B3

This activity asks you to speculate about what it is about Buddhism which attracts westerners, and what is it about western society which has allowed Buddhism to take hold.

You might have argued that Buddhism's main appeal arises from its agnosticism. The answer to the question of whether there is a God is traditionally seen in Buddhism as not useful in the search for enlightenment.

An answer to the question of the meaning of life without reference to God cannot fail to be appealing to many in the secular latter half of this century.

You might also have argued that the emphasis on the individual and on experience might be what attracts westerners. Many would claim that the Christianity they have rejected was authoritarian, limiting and not relevant. Buddhism is seen in the West (though not altogether accurately) as a religion of the individual and experience, rather than a religion of revelation and faith. The Buddha always enjoined his followers to 'test the teachings' and not to believe anything they had not experienced. As suggested in some of the interviews with western Buddhists in Denise Cush's (1990) *Buddhists in Britain Today*, it is perhaps the image of Buddhism as a personal spiritual quest, in contradistinction to the 'giveness' of Christianity, which westerners find attractive.

In recent years, in association with the rise of psychotherapy and self-improvement programmes, perhaps especially in America, Buddhism has become popular as a religion of anti-materialism, anti-stress and spiritual development. Meditation and 'down-shifting' often go hand in hand.

You might have argued that the popularity of Buddhism in the West says less about Buddhism than it does about the spiritual vacuum created with the exodus from the churches. With the proliferation of information about religion and the popularity of travelling to exotic places, people have a vast array of religions and spiritualities from which to choose in the postmodern quest for identity and meaning.

Buddhism in Sri Lanka

According to tradition Buddhism was introduced to Sri Lanka in the third century BCE by Mahinda, the son of Ashoka, who was sent by his father to found a *sangha* on the island. Mahinda was accompanied by his sister Sanghamitta, who brought with her a cutting of the bodhi tree under which the Buddha became enlightened, and relics of the Buddha, to be installed in *stupas* or reliquaries often of huge size, and of distinctive shape, which have become a common feature of the Sri Lankan landscape.

Civil war and famine may have contributed to the decision to commit the Buddha's teachings to writing there. Up until that point, they had been preserved orally, but it may have been feared that in such unstable times, teachings could be lost. Thus, what has come to be known as the Pali canon was etched on palm leaves. Buddhism became the dominant religion on the island and the *sangha* were influential, advising, and sometimes even choosing rulers.

A schism in the *sangha* in the first century allowed Mahayana teachings to have a period of popularity, although the visit of the monk Buddhaghosa from India in the fifth century helped ensure that Mahayanist influence did not become strong. Tamil invasions and civil wars in the tenth and eleventh centuries wreaked havoc in the *sangha*, the order of nuns died out, and the ordination line for monks had to be reintroduced to Sri Lanka from Burma[2].

Once it had been re-established the *sangha* grew from strength to strength, though in the thirteenth century the island was divided again, many areas being ruled by Tamil kings who were Hindus. Invasions by the Portuguese and the Dutch in the sixteenth century, and the British in the nineteenth, brought Christianity to the island, though only Catholicism remains strong.

Whilst Hinduism, Christianity and to a lesser extent Islam, live side by side with Buddhism in Sri Lanka, Buddhism, as Gombrich (1989, p 138 ff) describes, remains the dominant religion, and is politically linked to Sinhalese national identity.

There is, as in all Theravadin countries, a sharp distinction between the religious lives of monks and that of lay-people. Monks are forbidden possessions, apart from a robe and bowl, and obey 227 moral precepts, including celibacy and keeping the *vassa*, or rainy season retreat. They are sustained by the lay community who offer food to the monastery. In return the monks teach. Whilst for the monks *nibbana* (Skt *nirvana*) is the religious goal, for lay people it is *punya*, or merit, which creates good *karma* and a better rebirth.

The life of lay people revolves around:

- 'taking refuge' by reciting the formula 'I take refuge in the Buddha, the *dhamma* (teachings) and the *sangha* (the community)';
- keeping the Five Precepts (to abstain from killing, stealing, indulging in sensual pleasure, false speech (lying, bearing false witness, being deliberately inflammatory etc.), using any substances which cloud the mind);
- observing festivals and making pilgrimages.

Sri Lankan Buddhists observe a number of festivals, the most important of which is Wesak, in May, which celebrates the birth, enlightenment and death of the Buddha. A festival distinctive to Sri Lanka is the Esala Perahera, in which a replica of the relic of the Buddha's tooth, kept in a temple in Kandy, is paraded around the city on the back of an elephant.

---

[2] One of the functions of a sangha is to ordain monks. Without a quorate sangha the ordination line is lost and an orthodox one must be imported from elsewhere.

Buddhism in Japan

The Japanese constitution of 1946, instigated by General MacArthur after the surrender of Japan, guarantees religious freedom and tax-free status for religious organisations. This has resulted in a new stability for Buddhism in Japan after a history of periods of ascendancy, decline and even suppression in favour of State Shinto.

The history of Buddhism in Japan is intimately connected with that of Shinto, the indigenous religion which venerates *kami* (deities). Certain rocks, trees, animals and mountains have *kami*, ancestors are considered to be *kami*, and in the past Emperors were considered to be kami. Shinto is a life-affirming, fertility celebrating religion of ritual purity. Most Japanese see birth, marriage and fertility as being the province of Shinto, and death as being the province of Buddhism. As Ian Reader (1991) argues throughout his *Religion in Contemporary Japan*, the distinction between the two religions is not sharp, thus posing a problem for scholars, especially western ones, who wish to impose an arguably false dichotomy on Japanese religiosity.

Buddhism in contemporary Japan falls into three broad schools: Zen, Jodo Shinshu and Nichiren Buddhism. All Japanese Buddhism is of the Mahayana stamp, but the differences between these schools constitute a microcosm of the diversity of Buddhism the world over. All three distinctively Japanese forms were founded during the Kamakura period (1185-1333) but trace their lineages through different transmissions. Zen is characterised by its staunchly Mahayanist belief that nirvana is implicit in the here and now, and may be captured in the often transitory experience of *satori*. *Satori* may be achieved through Zazen, sitting meditation, characteristic of the Soto Zen School, or through techniques designed to destroy categorical, dualistic reasoning such as the *koan* of the Rinzai Zen school. Jodo Shinshu is a form of Pure Land Buddhism, which venerates the Buddha Amida, who as a bodhisattva vowed to bring all beings to enlightenment after death in his Pure Land. Nichiren Buddhism venerates the Lotus Sutra, in which the nature of the Eternal Sakyamuni is revealed. Many forms of this are politically motivated, and there are a number of Nichiren related new religious movements.

One of the major features of Buddhism in Japan is its provision of funerals and memorial services. Death is an area of life which Shinto avoids since it is considered ritually polluting, so all Japanese bar a minority of Christians and members of new religious movements, have Buddhist funerals. Almost all Japanese households are registered with a Buddhist temple of one sort or another for the purpose of funerals and memorial services.

One of the main festivals is O-bon, in the summer, during which offerings are made to deceased ancestors.

Buddhism in Britain

The contemporary Buddhist scene in Britain is quite difficult to describe for a number of reasons. First, the huge diversity of Buddhism in the world is reflected, and perhaps exaggerated, in the Buddhism of Britain. There is no central organising authority in British Buddhism and, in the latter half of this century, the number of 'groups', of widely differing characteristics, has proliferated. A tricky question which arises in any study of British, or indeed western, Buddhism is 'Who is a Buddhist?' or to put it another way, 'What are the defining characteristics of a Buddhist?' We have already established that reference to the teachings of the historical Buddha is not always a useful criterion. Moreover, there are many people in Britain and the West who may use Buddhist meditation techniques, and yet see themselves as Christians, or consider themselves not religious at all. For others, Buddhist teachings may form a part of an eclectic worldview which includes other aspects of so-called eastern spirituality, or aspects of what might be termed 'New Ageism'. Some may study Buddhist scriptures or other secondary sources, and perhaps understand the world in Buddhist terms, and yet not practise.

Whilst it might be difficult to categorise individuals, there are a number of institutions in Britain which are explicitly Buddhist.

The British Buddhist Society was founded by Christmas Humphreys in 1924. The Society was initially Theravadin in outlook, since Theravada was the more familiar form in Britain, due to colonial contacts with Theravadin countries. Gradually, however, it came to develop a wider view of Buddhism, encompassing Zen and, later, Tibetan Buddhism. The Buddhist Society now is a non-sectarian organisation which has a large library and information service. It publishes the quarterly journal *The Middle Way* and runs meditation groups, seminar courses and retreats lead by practising Buddhists of many different traditions. Many of Britain's leading Buddhists live at the many monasteries and centres in Britain such as Chithurst in Hampshire and Amaravati in Hertfordshire, which are Theravadin and run according to the Thai tradition. Samye Ling is a Tibetan Kagyu Centre in Dumfriesshire, which has built a new retreat centre on Holy Island off the coast of Arran for meditation and interfaith activities. Throssell Hole Priory in Northumberland is a Soto Zen Monastery with more than a dozen resident monks.

Christmas Humphreys played a major role in the development of Buddhism in Britain. He was president of the British Buddhist Society for many years, and wrote many introductory books on Buddhism. He had a Theosophist background, as did many of the early transmitters of Buddhism to the West. The Theosophical Society, active at the turn of the century, was orientalist in character, and promoted the teachings of not only Buddhism, but other eastern spiritualities, spiritualism and the occult. Thus, Britain's relationship with

Buddhism has until perhaps quite recently been tainted with the romanticism of orientalism, which has arguably been hardly less damaging than the demonising of Buddhism by some Victorian missionaries.

Humphreys, of course, did not bring Buddhism to Britain single-handedly. It came with Buddhists from Buddhist countries, for example Sri Lanka and Burma. In more recent years, Japanese investing in British industries, especially in South Wales, have brought Japanese Buddhism, and Tibetans in exile in Britain have brought Tibetan Buddhism. Other writers, such as the prolific DT Suzuki, and Alan Watts, did much to establish Zen in Britain.

As well as the Buddhist Society, another important British institution is the Friends of the western Buddhist Order (FWBO) founded by an Englishman with the religious name of Sangharakshita. The FWBO combine elements from Theravada, Tibetan Buddhism and Zen, and see themselves as creating a Buddhism suitable for westerners. Members of the Order take a number of vows at ordination, but it is possible to belong to the order without taking these vows, as a 'friend'. A useful table showing the different schools of Buddhism in Britain in 1987 is to be found in Harvey (1990, p 312).

Other important Buddhist institutions include Angulimala, the Buddhist prison Chaplaincy organisation, which is run from the Forest Hermitage in Warwickshire, and the Buddhist School in Brighton, Sussex.

Activity B4

Given the enormous diversity of Buddhism, do you think it is possible to identify the 'essence' of Buddhism? Write a short response to this question.

Comment on activity B4

As you will have discovered during your reading there are an enormous number of introductory books on Buddhism, purporting to outline the basic beliefs of the religion. If your reading has been wide, and you have researched the huge diversity of beliefs and practices of Buddhism in different countries, you may have been left wondering what relation the Japanese 'salaryman' making offerings to ancestors he never knew at O-bon, the British accountant whose leisure time is spent playing squash and in Zen meditation, and the Burmese child catching fish from dried up rivers to release them in fresh water in order to acquire merit (Spiro, 1970 p 221) bear to one another. More importantly, you might have wondered what relation their lives bear to the Four Noble Truths, the Three Marks of Existence and the life of the historical Buddha, such as are found in the introductory books.

The problem of relating real life to abstract doctrinal formulations is one that concerns scholars of every religious tradition, but it is possible to argue that the problem is particularly acute in Buddhism.

You might want to argue that the Japanese, the Englishwoman and the Burmese are all deviant to a greater or lesser extent. To frame that sort of argument, of course, you would need to define 'normative' or 'orthodox' Buddhism. This has long been a preoccupation for scholars. Take for instance, simply the subtitle of Melford Spiro's seminal work; *Buddhism and Society: a great tradition and its Burmese vicissitudes*. The implication is that the Burmese do not practice the Great (or normative) tradition of Buddhism, but they practise their own mutation of it.

It might legitimately be asked, however, whether one could come to a meaningful definition of the essence of Buddhism if only a few (if any) contemporary Buddhists would recognise it. Ultimately any account of Buddhism which refers only to doctrines, or to the (many different) lives of the Buddha, must remain abstract.

Contemporary debates

Many, perhaps especially westerners, stereotype Buddhism as an escapist and monastic religion. The serene, meditating Buddha is seen as having gone beyond the cares of this world, and Buddhists are seen as struggling to extract themselves from the world, from human relationships, and from being bothered by pain or suffering, either their own or that of others.

This is a somewhat partial view. Many Buddhists are working, not only to counter an arguably false perception, but also to bring the teachings of Buddhism to bear on the pressing issues of our time, one of the most important of which is ecology.

The term 'Engaged Buddhism' was coined by the Vietnamese monk Thich Nhat Hanh in the 1950s, and refers to a particular view of the teachings which Engaged Buddhists, such as Batchelor and Brown (1992), argue reasserts what is fundamental to Buddhism, namely the idea of geo-political engagement.

The burgeoning literature on engaged Buddhism, and especially on Buddhism and ecology, explores the doctrines of connectedness (*pratitya samutpada*) and compassion (*metta, karuna*) and argues, with the Buddha, that the self is not a separate entity. Thus the Buddhist who has the wisdom, as the aphorism goes, to see the world in a grain of sand, cannot but be engaged with the world's concerns. Buddhism can appear somewhat anthropocentric, but Engaged Buddhists argue that anthropocentrism arises from a failure to appreciate the connectedness of the individual not only with other people, but also with animals, nature, the whole universe. Writers like Ken Jones argue that world transformation can take place if what he calls 'inner work' (1993, 165ff) is done by the individual to realise and deepen understanding of no-self, connectedness, and the karmic effects of greed.

An important movement in Engaged Buddhism was founded in the 50s in Sri Lanka. As Ken Jones (1989, pp 242-254) reports, Sarvodaya ('the awakening and welfare of all') initiated self help programmes in about a third of the country's poor villages. It had tremendous success in instituting eco-friendly agricultural activities, as well as reforming village administration so as to empower the marginalised, and to decentralise and democratise decision making. These reforms were based firmly in Buddhist doctrine, and emulate the project of the third century BCE Buddhist Emperor, Ashoka, to create a just and peaceful Buddhist society in which harm is not done to the environment.

Despite the huge successes of Engaged Buddhist philosophy in practice, it is important to point out that this fundamentally Buddhist attitude to nature does not feature greatly in government policies of Buddhist countries, many of which have poor records of care for the environment. It could be said that a paradox exists in Buddhism, just as it does in many other religions. Whilst Engaged Buddhists see social activism as core, others would interpret such passionate activity as a form of attachment to this world which distracts from the higher goal of enlightenment.

B3 Sikhism

Aims

After working through part B3 of the unit you should have:

- become acquainted with the elements of Sikh religious practice;
- engaged with issues in contemporary Sikhism;
- considered some developments in British Sikhism.

Overview

This unit covers major practices in Sikhism including congregational worship and other activities centred on the gurdwara, life-cycle rites, and other aspects of belonging to a Sikh community. The unit also addresses contemporary issues of authority, caste and identity in Sikhism and concludes with a brief survey of developments in British Sikhism.

The Gurdwara and the Guru Granth Sahib

Gurdwara means that place in which the Guru resides, and since the passing of the tenth Guru, Gobind Singh, the *Guru Granth Sahib* (*Adi Granth*) has been revered as the living form of the Guru. As well as the large communal *gurdwara* buildings found wherever a sizeable Sikh presence is established, many Sikh families have a *gurdwara* in their homes, typically an upper room reserved for a copy of the Adi *Granth*. In large Gurdwaras in India and elsewhere worship in the form of *kirtan* (singing verses from the scriptures in praise of the Sat Guru) goes on more or less unceasingly, but in Britain where the *sangat* (congregation) mostly can attend only on Sundays, full Gurdwara worship may be restricted to a few hours or certain days of the week.

All significant rites and ceremonies are performed in the presence of the Guru, which is placed on a raised dais or 'palanquin' (*palki*) in the centre or front of the Gurdwara and ritually uncovered and opened at the start of a service. While the Adi Granth is open it is always attended by a reader (*granthi)* who sits behind the Adi Granth, holding a *chauri* (the traditional equivalent of a fan) which symbolises that the Adi Granth is regarded as a sovereign. A member of the *sangat*, on entering the *Gurdwara* with head covered and shoes respectfully discarded at the door, approaches the Guru, makes an offering of money or food, bows low to the Guru with the forehead touching the floor and then greets the congregation in the usual Indian way with palms joined and sits down cross-legged on the floor (below the level of the Guru). Men and women customarily sit on separate sides of the central aisle, but this is not mandatory. Individuals of any religion, caste or nationality may enter a Gurdwara provided that they show respect to the Guru in their dress and behaviour and do not bring with them prohibited items such as tobacco or alcohol.

The main part of any Sikh service is *kirtan* or rhythmical, devotional singing in praise of the Sat Guru. This may continue for many hours while members of the *sangat* come and go. *Kirtan* is typically led by three musicians, male or female, and the congregation joins in as they wish. At certain times the *Adi granthi*, who may be trained in this skill but has no special 'priestly' status, will read passages from the *Granth* and there may also be a sermon of encouragement to devotion. At the beginning and/or end of a service a congregational prayer called *Ardas*, the Khalsa prayer, is spoken by a leader, each part punctuated by a salutation of Wahiguru! (Lord) from the sangat. The *Ardas* has a standard format; the first and second parts extol the ten gurus and the trials and achievements of the *panth*, while the third part is a petitionary prayer which is adapted to the circumstances of the local *sangat*. A portion of *karah prasad*, blessed food made of sugar, flour and ghee (clarified butter) is distributed to all present. Finally, a randomly chosen hymn from the Guru

Granth Sahib is read. This is known as the *hukam-nama* (command of the Guru for the sangat) and is regarded as the sacred gift of the Guru.

As well as the worship hall, a Gurdwara invariably includes a *langar* or free kitchen. In conformity with the early Gurus' rejection of caste distinctions in spiritual matters, food is served to anyone who attends. The meal is vegetarian in order to include everyone, though Sikhs are not prohibited from eating meat. Participants in the langar are seated regardless of status in long lines (pangat) to receive food. Sangat and pangat are two sides of the same coin; participating in the sangat implies an abandoning of worldly status. The character of the Guru's sangat is exemplified by everyone eating the same food together.

Whenever the Guru Granth Sahib is moved from place to place, it is carried above the head of its bearer. On ceremonial days such as the birth-anniversaries of the Sikh Gurus the scriptures are carried in a palanquin borne by four Sikhs preceded by another five, representing the *panj piare* (the five devoted disciples of Guru Gobind Singh) marching sword in hand. Other members of the *sangat* walk behind in a procession singing *kirtan*.

Life-cycle rites (*sanskara*)

There are four main life-cycle rites for Sikhs: naming ceremony, marriage, death and, where applicable, initiation into the Khalsa. Some Sikhs also celebrate the birth of a child and the occasion of a son's first tying the turban.

Naming ceremony

The mother accompanies her family to the Gurdwara as soon as she is able to travel after birth. During the ceremony the *Guru Granth Sahib* is opened at random, in a version of the *hukam-nama* ritual, and a name for the child is chosen beginning with the same letter as the first section on the left-hand page. The child's name is in this sense bestowed by the Guru. There is no distinction between male and female first names among Sikhs, but the name is supplemented by Singh (lion) for a boy and Kaur (usually translated 'princess') for a girl.

Marriage

The modern form of the Sikh marriage ceremony was established with the Anand Marriage Act of 1909. In conformity with *Tat Khalsa* thinking it was intended to underline the difference between Sikh and Hindu, though caste remains a major determinant in identifying a suitable partner and Sikh-Hindu marriages are not unusual among some sections of the Sikh community. The marriage ceremony takes place with the couple and their families present before the Guru Granth Sahib, the singing of *kirtan* and the recitation of *Ardas*. During the ceremony the bride is handed by her father a hem of the groom's clothing, to symbolise the transfer of her allegiance to her new family. Holding this hem, the bride follows the groom in a ritual circumambulation of the Guru Granth Sahib.

Death

In conformity with general Indian custom, the body is disposed of as quickly as possible, normally the same day, and by cremation. The body is not traditionally taken to a Gurdwara, though this has happened in some overseas countries including Britain. Ashes are supposed to be quickly dispersed. The 'Hindu' custom of taking the ashes to some specially holy place is officially discouraged, but many Sikhs like to deposit ashes in the river Sutlej near where Guru Hargobind died or, along with Hindus, in the Ganges at Hardwar. After the cremation a complete reading (*Akhand path*) of the Guru Granth Sahib may be performed on behalf of the deceased.

Initiation into the Khalsa

This ceremony (*Amrit sanskar* or *khande di pahul*), which is open to any suitable applicant who wishes to commit him or herself to the discipline of the Khalsa, is conducted by five initiated Khalsa Sikhs wearing the 5 Ks and representing the *panj piare*. Another sits with the Guru Granth Sahib and a seventh stands by the door for what is a private ceremony. During the lengthy ritual, the recitation of prescribed passages from the Guru Granth Sahib is accompanied by the stirring of *amrit* (here: sweetened water) with a sword. The candidate drinks five handfuls of amrit, which is also sprinkled on the eyes and hair, and receives God's 'name', the *Nam* of *Vahiguru* in the form of the *Mul Mantra*, the very first words of the Guru Granth Sahib, included in the early morning *Japji* recitation and which is a summary of Gurmat (AG p 1):

> There is one Supreme Being, the Eternal Reality, the Creator, without fear and devoid of enmity, immortal, never incarnated, self-existent, known by grace through the Guru.

The applicant also receives instruction in the *Rahit* and undertakes to avoid the four cardinal prohibited acts, namely (1) cutting of hair, (2) consuming *halal* meat, (3) sexual intercourse outside marriage and (4) using tobacco. Taking drugs, associating with reprobates, and so on, are also prohibited. The ceremony ends with the taking of a *hukam-nama*, the re-naming of any Sikh who does not already have a name from the Guru Granth Sahib and distribution of *karah prashad*.

Activity B5

Use whatever books and other resources on Sikhism are available to you to identify variations in belief, affiliation and practice within Sikhism, and suggest reasons for these variations. In light of your findings, how useful do you think it is to speak of 'official' and 'popular' forms of Sikhism?

Comment on activity B5

In observing that ...

> much of the conventional writing on Sikhism - especially by western scholars - focuses on divisions within the community and the disjunction between official beliefs and actual practice...

Gurharpal Singh (1997, p 200) identifies a general trend in modern scholarship on religion away from the 'world religions' approach - in which every faith is implicitly assumed to have its own discrete founder, scriptures, doctrines, ethics, community of believers and rituals - to a more 'anthropological' approach which is primarily concerned with what ordinary people actually believe and do, and which acknowledges that religious people, ideas and institutions are not divorced from changing historical and social circumstances. Such an approach is naturally cautious about claims by one section of a community to represent the whole community's 'orthodoxy'; the history of religions is to a large extent the history of competing claims of this kind!

Modern studies of Sikhism which look beyond the modern Khalsa's idealised version of Sikh history and Sikh practice have become a focus of controversy. Fundamental beliefs about Sikh history have recently been challenged by dispassionate academic research (in much the same way that the traditional Christianity's view of its own development was challenged by history, archaeology and comparative religion). This has occurred at a time when many Sikhs feel strongly that their very existence as a minority people is under threat. The Punjab is part of the sensitive Indian border with Pakistan, so most of the world's Sikhs reside in a region which the Indian government is particularly keen to control in the name of national security. The government also often appears to be promoting a 'Hindu' Indian identity which marginalises Sikhs, while from another quarter global secular materialism and exposure to alternative lifestyles threaten traditional Punjabi values and family structures.

Like other religious traditions, Sikhism belongs to the real world and involves people from different backgrounds with differing ideas and expectations. Even a brief acquaintance with Sikhs in India or overseas quickly dispels the notion that all (male) Sikhs have beards and wear turbans. How do we account for the discrepancy between what is presented as the 'ideal' and what we encounter as the reality? In the first unit of this module we encountered the 'Tat Khalsa' view that the Khalsa Sikh is the only orthodox Sikh. This idea gained momentum in the late nineteenth century and the 'Khalsa' Sikh voice is vigorous and influential in public debate about Sikhism today. Viewed from a Khalsa Sikh perspective, the differences between 'official beliefs and actual practice' in Sikhism appear as 'different levels of adherence to core beliefs and practices':

> Within Sikhism there are four main sub-identities, each distinguished by different levels of adherence to core beliefs and practices. The premier position is occupied by the *amrit-dhari* Khalsa (baptised Sikhs, 'Singhs') who are few in number but represent the orthodoxy. Those Singhs who are not baptised, but who wear the five symbolic 'Ks' (known as the *kesh-dhari* Khalsa) constitute the majority of Sikhs. Baptised and non-baptised Sikhs together account for nearly three-quarters of the Sikh population. The third category includes shaven Singhs (*mona* Sikhs) of baptised and non-baptised background who live in the Sikh diaspora. Finally there are non-Singhs (*Sahaj-dhari*s) who still follow pre-Khalsa pluralism and, in many cases, have assimilated practices from other religions. (Gurharpal Singh, p 202)

It is worth remembering that virtually all Sikhs are Sikh by birth and upbringing rather than by conversion, and it is a mistake to think of Sikhs as being an exceptionally religious people. Among those who are born Sikh may be found every kind and degree of religiosity including inward mysticism, politico-religious extremism, conventional adherence in 'progressive' and 'conservative' forms, apathy and outright rejection of religion. There are many devout Sikhs who do not regard the 'outward symbols' as the only sign of a true Sikh. Sikhs who cut their hair, shave and do not wear any of the '5 Ks', the so-called *sahaj-dharis*, do not necessarily see themselves as inferior to Khalsa or *kesh-dhari* Sikhs. Sectarian movements which attract Sikh adherents are significant too. The Nirankari movement, for example, generally accepted as a sectarian movement within Sikhism, is essentially *sahaj-dhari* in outlook, preaching inner *nam simaran* as taught by Nanak. It takes no interest in the Khalsa as such. The question of who is a 'true' or 'orthodox' Sikh is hotly contested and the issue is not resolved by a claim to orthodoxy on the part of one or other grouping among the world's 16 million Sikhs. To illustrate how a devoted Sikh's perspective might contrast with Khalsa orthodoxy, we can do no better than to cite this example from the village of Danda, near Hoshiarpur:

> The shrine to Banda Singh is maintained by an old Sikh devotee. Now a man in his nineties, he has tended the shrine since his youth. He has never married and perceives his service to the shrine as devotion to God and the Sikh Gurus. In his account of the origins of this long dedication to the shrine of Banda Singh, he claims that while passing the shrine as a young man, the *shakti* [spiritual power] of the shrine possessed him. His attitude towards the Khalsa was contemptuous. He accused them of reading the Guru Granth Sahib 'like parrots' and having no inner awareness of the truth revealed by Guru Nanak. (Greaves, 1996)

Describing a pilgrimage by Sikhs from Walsall in the East Midlands to the Punjab, Geaves is able to provide many other examples to show that contemporary Sikhs, both British and Punjabi, adhere today to a form of religiosity which seems closer to the pluralistic mid-nineteenth century Punjabi religion described by Harjot Oberoi (1994) than to the Khalsa ideal encountered in textbooks on Sikhism. Among 'alternative markers of Sikh identity' (that is, alternative to the textbook *amrit-dhari* ideal) are: (1) Sikhs who challenge the orthodox line of succession from the ten Sikh Gurus through to the Guru Granth Sahib, by allegiance to groups such as Namdhari, Nirankari and Radhasoami; (2) Sikh ascetics such as Udasis; (3) Sanatan Sikhs; (4) Sikhs who worship miracle saints and at village sacred sites; (5) Sikhs who believe in evil spirits, witchcraft, sorcery and magical healing; (6) Sikhs who draw on the Puranas (Hindu epics) more than on the Guru Granth Sahib; (7) Sikhs who do not perceive Sikh identity as a distinct religious tradition but as an ethnic identity (Geaves, 1996).

Influence of sants

Within contemporary Sikhism a number of influential spiritual (and sometimes political) leaders called 'sants' have emerged and in some cases attracted a significant following. Among the 'political' sants is Sant Jarnail Singh, killed during the Indian army's attack on the Golden temple in 1984, though his followers believe that he is alive and will reappear one day. Probably best-known of the 'spiritual' sants in Britain is Baba Puran Singh Karichowale, who inspired many errant Sikhs to return to the fold and who reformed Sikh practices in Britain from the 1970s onwards. Sants generally work to reinvigorate 'orthodox' Sikh practice focusing on the Guru Granth Sahib, while at the same time occupying a role somewhat analogous to a Guru in the eyes of their devotees. Space does not permit a discussion of individual sants here, but it is important in studying Sikhism to realise that the practice of receiving spiritual guidance from another human being is neither prevented nor discouraged within Sikhism. A Sikh in Britain and elsewhere can seek and find various ways of practising *nam simaran*, offering service (*sewa*), and conducting him or herself as a *gurmukh* in daily life within the broad context of 'Sikhism'. So long as a sant upholds the tenets of Sikhism and does not usurp the position of the Guru, he will be widely acknowledged and revered by Sikhs. People will come to get the darshan of a sant, whether or not they are committed followers. Where a sant rejects the Guruship of the Adi Granth, and is regarded instead as the Guru (for example in the Radhasoami movement, which has a large number of Sikh followers but attracts many Hindus and others as well) the sant and his movement are likely to be regarded as only partly Sikh, and by Khalsa Sikhs as not Sikh at all.

British Sikhism

To supplement this brief section you should read the two *DISKUS* articles by Sewa Singh Kalsi (Kalsi, 1994; 1995) who, as a Sikh in Leeds, has observed at first-hand many of the developments he describes. All the various aspects of Sikh history, teaching and practice mentioned so far have of course made some contribution to contemporary Sikh consciousness and practice in Britain, and are relevant to an understanding of British Sikhism.

Of the sixteen million or so Sikhs in the world today, about fourteen million live in The Punjab and the remaining two million elsewhere in India and the rest of the world. The largest Sikh community outside India is in Britain, with Canada close behind.

Sikhs started arriving in Britain in significant numbers in the 1950s. Initially single males, and predominantly members of the Jat caste from India, in the early days most removed their outward religious symbols (turban, hair and beard) in order to obtain jobs. Reflecting on his experience of going to a hairdresser, one pioneer Sikh migrant (Kalsi, 1994) said:

> All other Sikh migrants in our house had removed their turbans, hair and beards. I reluctantly agreed to go to the hair-dresser. For a couple of days I felt very depressed and felt as if I had lost a limb of my body. I remember that some Sikhs had saved their shorn hair neatly in their suit-cases. It was the most painful experience of coming to England.

Once a group of Sikhs settled in a particular area, building of a Gurdwara would begin, providing a project which united Sikhs from disparate backgrounds. An important further stimulus was the arrival of families of Sikhs from East Africa, following independence and Africanisation there. Many of the Ramgharia (carpenter) caste, educated in British colonial schools, already had substantial experience of living as 'diaspora' Sikhs outside India and their social aspirations on arrival in Britain reflected the high economic and social status they had achieved after emigrating from India to Africa generations earlier.

Within British Sikhism the role of caste is particularly evident. Separate gurdwaras have emerged run by Ramgharia, Ravidasi and Bhatra Sikhs, for example. As is well known, Guru Nanak rejected caste as an indication of spiritual status, stressing that nearness to God was based on one's quality of inner devotion, not degree of caste 'purity'. A Guru's disciples eating together in the langar or common kitchen (something which would not happen in ordinary social life) symbolised that in the presence of the Guru social distinctions were irrelevant. Nevertheless, the human Gurus themselves observed prevailing rules of caste in matters such as the marriage of their children, thus legitimating caste in social life. Sikhs, after all, are not required to live apart from ordinary society, which depends on caste for its structure. In particular, 'horizontal' caste relationships are essential for establishing kinship rules, defining who can marry whom.

Caste-based gurdwaras have in part emerged in response to disputes over how and by whom gurdwaras are run, in an essentially 'congregationalist' type of religion, where major decisions are made within the local *sangat* and a variety of political and decision-making strategies is employed ranging from democratic to autocratic. The politicisation of the overseas Sikh community in the 1980s at the time of the separatist Khalistan movement and the attack on the Golden temple accentuated continuing problems of authority and legitimacy in the management and operation of Sikh gurdwaras, problems which not unusually culminated in violence or lawsuits between opposing factions. Since these factions sometimes represented caste interests, the emergence of caste-based gurdwaras was one way to provide stability in the management of a gurdwara.

Kalsi offers the example of the 'Ramgharia Board' in Leeds, a members-only organisation which incorporates the Ramgharia Sikh Temple, Ramgharia Sikh Sports Club and Ramgharia Sikh Ladies' Circle. Membership is restricted to those of the Ramgharia caste (biradiri). Significantly, membership excludes non-Ramgharia Sikhs but includes the (non-Sikh) followers of Baba Vishvakarma, a Hindu God of craftsmen. A Ramgharia is defined as 'a Sikh Vishwakarma, both belonging to the same ancestral stock and having their remote origin on the Indian sub-continent', and marriages between Ramgharias and Vishvakarmas are a common occurrence. This is a clear indication that caste identity in this case outweighs 'religious' (that is, Sikh/Hindu) identity (Kalsi, 1994).

Analysis of matrimonial advertisements in a British Punjabi newspaper also indicates the importance of caste, and very often a preference for a clean-shaven (*sahaj-dhari*) groom. In an analysis of 33 such advertisements placed by Sikh parents for marriage partners for their sons and daughters, typically born in Britain, all indicated their caste identity (Jat, Ramgharia, Khatri etc.) and 17 of the 33 specified that their daughter was seeking a clean-shaven spouse or that their son was clean-shaven. Occupational status was a major consideration, for example (Kalsi, 1994):

> Jat Sikh parents seek suitable match for their daughter 26, 5 feet 2 inches. Born and educated in England. Graduated, works in Retail. Appreciates both cultures. Boy should be clean-shaven and professionally qualified.

Such advertisements, Kalsi suggests, indicate that the equation 'Sikh = Khalsa Sikh' does not hold sway among second-generation Sikhs growing up in Britain.

It would be wrong, however, to underestimate, either in India or in overseas Sikh communities including that in Britain, the significance of the normative

Khalsa view of Sikhism as a set of 'core' beliefs and standards to which all Sikhs should adhere. As was clearly intended by the tenth Guru, the Khalsa code of dress and behaviour makes Sikh identity visible. Like the quasi-military dress of the Salvation Army in Christianity, the external appearance of the *amrit-dhari* or *kesh-dhari* provides a powerful means by which Sikhs who wish to do so can publicly and uncompromisingly differentiate themselves from the secular society and from other visible religious or ethnic groups. It also offers a focus for self-respect and the respect of others. For many Sikhs the 'outward symbols' are exactly that: *symbols* of the demanding standard of inner devotion and outward conduct expected of the wearer, whose aim is never to disgrace the uniform of a 'saint-soldier'.

Readers

For Hinduism

Brockington, J.L. (1981), *The Sacred Thread: Hinduism in its continuity and diversity*, Edinburgh, Edinburgh University Press.

Flood, G. (1996), *An Introduction to Hinduism*, Cambridge, Cambridge University Press.

Klostermaier K.K. (1994), *A Survey of Hinduism* (second edition), Albany, SUNY Press.

Knott, K. (1998), *Hinduism: a very short introduction*, Oxford, Oxford University Press.

Lipner, J. (1994), Hindus: their religious beliefs and practices, London, Routledge.

For Buddhism

Batchelor, S. (1994), The Awakening of the West: the encounter of Buddhism and western culture, London, Aquarian.

Batchelor, M. and Brown, K. (eds) (1992), Buddhism and Ecology, London, Cassell.

Cush, D. (1993), Buddhism, London, Hodder and Stoughton.

For Sikhism

Cole, W.O. (1994), *Sikhism* (Teach Yourself Series), London, Hodder and Stoughton.

Cole, W.O. and Sambhi, P.S. (1990), *A Popular Dictionary of Sikhism*, Richmond, Curzon.

McLeod, W.H. (1997), *Sikhism*, Harmondsworth, Penguin.

Singh, G. (1997), Sikhism, in *The Illustrated Encyclopedia of World Religions*, Shaftesbury, Element.

English translations of the Adi Granth, pictures of Gurdwaras, introductions to Sikhism, downloadable sound files of Sikh prayers, and a daily *hukam-nama* ('Guru's order' from the Adi Granth) are among many other resources available on the Internet. Several Sikh-related sects also have web sites. A good starting-point is 'The Sikhism Homepage':

http://www.sikhs.org/topics.htm

You should also read in connection with this unit the following three articles published on-line in the internet Religious Studies journal *DISKUS*, available at:

http://www.uni-marburg.de/fb11/religionswissenschaft/journal/diskus

Geaves, R.A. (1996), Baba Balaknath: an exploration of religious identity, *Diskus* , 4 (1).

Kalsi, S.S. (1994), Sacred symbols in British Sikhism, *Diskus*, 2 (2).

Kalsi, S.S. (1995), Problems of defining authority in Sikhism, *Diskus*, 3 (2).

Bibliography

For Hinduism

Bowen, D. (ed) (1981), *Hinduism in England*, Bradford, Bradford College.

Bowen, D. (1988), *The Sathya Sai Baba Community in Bradford*, Leeds, Community Religions Project.

Burghardt, R. (ed) (1987), *Hinduism in Great Britain*, London, Tavistock.

Cush, D. and Robinson, C. (1995), The contemporary construction of Hindu identity: Hindu universalism and Hindu nationalism, *Diskus*, 2 (2).

Cush, D. and Robinson C. (1997), The sacred cow: Hinduism and ecology, *Journal of Beliefs and Values*, 18, 25-37.

Dumont, L. (1981), *Homo Hierarchicus: the caste system and its implications* (revised edition), Chicago, Chicago University Press.

Eck, D. (1983), *Banaras: city of light*, London, Routledge and Kegan Paul.

Eck, D. (1985), *Darsan: seeing the divine image in India*, Chambersburg, Anima.

Fuller, C.J. (1992), *The Camphor Flame: popular Hinduism and society in India*, Princeton, Princeton University Press.

Griffiths, P.J. (ed.) (1990), *Christianity Through Non-Christian Eyes*, New York, Orbis Books.

Jackson, R. (1986), Hindu Festivals, in A. Brown (ed.), *Festivals in World Religions*, London, Longman, pp 104-139.

Jackson, R. and Nesbitt, E. (1993), *Hindu Children in Britain*, Stoke-on-Trent, Trentham.

Killingley, D., Menski, W. and Firth, S. (1991), *Hindu Ritual and Society*, Newcastle, S.Y. Killingley.

Klostermaier, K. (1969), *Hindu and Christian in Urindaban*, London, SCM.

Knott, K. (1986a), *Hinduism in Leeds*, Leeds, Community Religions Project.

Knott, K. (1986b), *My Sweet Lord: the Hare Krishna Movement*, Wellingborough, Aquarian Press.

Kramrish, S. (1965), *The Art of India: traditions of Indian sculpture, painting and architecture*, London, Phaidon.

Leslie, J. (ed) (1991), *Roles and Rituals of Hindu Women*, London, Pinter.

Michell, G. (1977), *The Hindu Temple: an introduction to its meaning and forms*, London, Harper and Row.

Morinis, E.A. (1984), Pilgrimage in the Hindu tradition: a case study of west Bengal, Deli, Oxford University Press.

O'Flaherty, W.D. (trans) (1975), *Hindu Myths*, Harmondsworth, Penguin.

Prime, R. (1992), *Hinduism and Ecology: seeds of truth*, London, Cassell/WWF.

Sharpe, E. (1977), *Faith Meets Faith: some Christian attitudes to Hinduism in the nineteenth and twentieth centuries*, London, SCM.

Tully, M. (1992) *No Full Stops in India*, Harmondsworth, Penguin.

Williams, R.M. (1984), *The New Face of Hinduism, the Swaminarayan Religion*, Cambridge, Cambridge University Press.

Young, K.K. (1987), Hinduism, in A. Sharma (ed.), *Women in World Religions*, Albany, SUNY Press, pp 59-103.

Young, K.K. (1994), Hinduism, in A. Sharma (ed.), *Today's Woman in World Religions*, Albany, SUNY Press, pp 77-135.

Zimmer, H.R. (1972), *Myths and symbols in Indian Civilisation*, Princeton, Princeton University Press.

For Buddhism

Batchelor, M. and Brown, K. (eds) (1992), *Buddhism and Ecology*, London, Cassell.

Batchelor, S. (1994), *The Awakening of the West: the encounter of Buddhism and western culture*, London, Aquarian.

Cush, D. (1990), *Buddhists in Britain Today*, London, Hodder and Stoughton.

Cush, D. (1993), *Buddhism*, London, Hodder and Stoughton.

Gombrich, R. (1988), *Theravada Buddhism: a social history from ancient Benares to modern Colombo*, London, Routledge.

Harvey, P. (1990), *An Introduction to Buddhism: teachings, history and practices*, Cambridge, Cambridge University Press.

Jones, K. (1989), *The Social Face of Buddhism*, London, Wisdom.

Jones, K. (1993), *Beyond Optimism: a Buddhist political ecology*, Oxford, Jon Carpenter.

Reader, I. (1991), *Religion in Contemporary Japan*, London, Macmillan.

Snelling, J. (1987), *The Buddhist Handbook: a complete guide to Buddhist teaching and practice*, London, Rider.

Spiro, M. (1970), *Buddhism and Society: a great tradition and its Burmese vicissitudes*, Berkeley, University of California Press.

For Sikhism

Bains, T.S. and Johnston, H. (1995), *The Four Quarters of the Night: the life-journey of an emigrant Sikh*, Montreal and Kingston, McGill-Queen's University Press.

Barrier, N.G. and Dusenbery, V.A. (eds), (1989), *The Sikh Diaspora: migration and the experience beyond Punjab*, Delhi, Chanakya Publications.

Cole, W.O. (1982), *The Guru in Sikhism*, London, Darton, Longman and Todd.

Cole, W.O. (1994), *Teach Yourself Sikhism*, London, Hodder and Stoughton.

Cole, W.O. and Sambhi, P.S. (1978), *The Sikhs: their religious beliefs and practices*, London, Routledge and Kegan Paul.

Cole, W.O. and Sambhi, P.S. (1990), *A Popular Dictionary of Sikhism*, London, Curzon.

Geaves, R. (1996), Baba Balaknath: an exploration of religious identity, *Diskus*, 4 (2).

James, A.G. (1974), *Sikh Children in Britain*, Oxford, Oxford University Press.

Juergensmeyer, M. and Barrier, N.G. (eds) (1979), *Sikh Studies: comparative persepctives on a changing tradition*, Berkeley, Berkeley Religious Studies Series.

Kalsi, S.S. (1992), *The Evolution of a Sikh Community in Britain*, Leeds, Community Religions Project, University of Leeds.

Kalsi, S.S. (1994), Sacred symbols in British Sikhism, *Diskus*, 2 (2).

Kalsi, S.S. (1995), Problems of defining authority in Sikhism, *Diskus*, 3 (2).

Kohli, S.S. (1975), *Sikh Ethics*, New Delhi, Munshiram Manoharlal Publishers.

McLeod, W.H. (1980), *Early Sikh Tradition: a study of the Janam-Sakhis*, Oxford, Clarendon Press.

McLeod, W.H. (1984), *Textual Sources for the Study of Sikhism*, Manchester, Manchester University Press.

McLeod, W.H. (1989), *Who is a Sikh? the problem of Sikh identity*, Oxford, Clarendon Press.

McLeod, W.H. (1997), *Sikhism*, London, Penguin.

Oberoi, H. (1994), *The Construction of Religious Boundaries: culture, identity and diversity in the Sikh tradition*, Oxford, Oxford University Press.

302 Teaching about Hinduism, Buddhism and Sikhism

Pettigrew, J.M. (1995), *The Sikhs of the Punjab: unheard voices of state and guerilla violence*, London and New Jersey, Zed Books Ltd.

Schomer, K. and McLeod, W.H. (eds) (1987), *The Sants: studies in a devotional traditon of India*, Delhi, Motilal Barnsasidass.

Shackle, C. (1986), *The Sikhs*, London, Minority Rights Group Ltd.

Singh, G. (tr.) (1978), *Sri Guru Granth Sahib* (four volumes), Chandigarh, World Sikh University Press.

Singh, G. (1995), *A History of the Sikh People*, New Delhi, Allied Publishers.

Singh, G. (1997), Sikhism, in C. Richards (ed.), *The Illustrated Encyclopedia of World Religions*, Shaftesbury, Element, pp 190-205.

Singh, K. (1977), *A History of the Sikhs (volume 2): 1839-1974*, Delhi, Oxford University Press.

Singh, Nikky-Guninder Kaur (1993), *The Feminine Principle in the Sikh Vision of the Transcendent*, Cambridge, Cambridge University Press.

Note: The *Guru Granth Sahib* (in Punjabi and English translation) plus other useful material is available on *Gurbani-CD*, a CD-ROM produced as a *sewa* (voluntary service) by Sikhs in the USA. Contact address: Sikh Missionary Center, PO BOX 62521, Phoenix, Arizona 85082, USA.

Teaching about Hinduism, Buddhism and Sikhism

Unit C

Classroom teaching

Denise Cush and Catherine Robinson

Bath Spa University College

Dr Wendy Dossett

Trinity College Carmarthen

and

Professor Brian Bocking

School of Oriental and African Studies

University of London

Contents

Introduction

This unit is a bridge from the theoretical, historical and theological or philosophical ideas of the previous units into the classroom. This unit, like the previous two units, is divided into three sections dealing with Hinduism, Buddhism and Sikhism. It is designed so that it is possible to focus on only one of the religions and therefore to ignore the others. The teacher who wishes to present these religions at any point between Key Stage 1 and Key Stage 4 should be stimulated by the topics outlined here. As before, the bibliography for the whole of this unit is kept until the end where the teacher will also find a valuable list of classroom resources.

C1 Hinduism

Aims

After working through part C1 of this unit you should be able to:

- clarify your own reasons for teaching Hinduism and be prepared to justify this choice to colleagues, parents and governors;
- decide what aspects of Hinduism would be suitable for your particular school and syllabus, and at what stage these will be introduced;
- advise on a variety of resources to assist the teaching of Hinduism, having located and reviewed them;
- plan and execute a unit of work on Hinduism for at least one age group, using the full range of teaching and learning methods available;
- assess the learning outcomes of your unit of work and evaluate the success of your teaching.

Overview

This part of the unit provides a rationale for teaching Hinduism and then sets of topics suitable for different key stages and suggestions about how they might be taught.

Why teach about Hinduism?

There are many reasons why teachers may feel uncertain about teaching Hinduism. They may be anxious about the limits of their own knowledge and understanding and be apprehensive about misrepresenting the tradition. Hinduism is a complex religion and in many ways very different from the more familiar western religions. There may be no Hindu children in the school and, especially at primary level, some concern about confusing children with too many religions.

However, it is precisely because Hinduism represents a contrast with western faiths that it is so important to include it, even at primary level, in order to avoid establishing a model of religion drawn only from western faiths. If the children have no contact with Hindus in school, it is perhaps even more important that they are provided with the opportunity to appreciate the multi-cultural nature of the wider society, and avoid setting up misunderstandings and stereotypes. There are many aspects of Hinduism that lend themselves to reflective learning that will deepen the pupil's own spiritual development, as well as an understanding of Hindus. Among these are the concepts of God, ideas of life after death, non-violence, moral duty, concepts of time, space and reality and an inclusivist attitude to other faiths. Although there may be an argument for a certain priority being given to Christianity as the religion, if any, most likely to be encountered by the children in their lives outside school, attitudes are formed very early and, in any case, children are no more likely to be confused by the introduction of a variety of faiths than by different topics in other subjects. The key to effective learning is appropriate teaching.

A lack of previous academic study of Hinduism need not be a barrier if the teacher allows himself or herself the privilege of learning alongside the pupils. Links can be made with the nearest Hindu community to gain awareness of areas of sensitivity. There are now plenty of helpful resources such as those listed at the end of this unit.

Approaches to Hinduism

It is important to make clear to all concerned, and especially to reassure parents, that the approach is *non-confessional* that is, the aim is not to initiate pupils into the Hindu faith. Rather, the aim is to learn *about* Hinduism, in order to *understand* the Hindu view of life and the beliefs and practices of its adherents. This should not be merely cold factual information, however, but provide an insight into the experiences and feelings of the participants. An approach which attempts to be both impartial in description and empathetic in attitude is often referred to as *phenomenological*. Rather than engaging from the start with the truth claims of any tradition, these, together with any preconceived ideas, are put to one side in order to understand what the religion actually is. As this approach respects the self-understanding of the believers, it will also positively value the experience of Hindu children should there be any in the class. For discussion of the confessional and phenomenological approaches to religious education, see unit C of the module 'Philosophy of Religious Education' in *Religion in Education* (volume 1).

Religious Education in schools differs from the study of religions in that it is also concerned with the spiritual development of the pupil and with exploring the philosophical and moral issues raised by our shared human experience. In the words of the SCAA Model Syllabi, we are not only 'learning about', but also 'learning from', Hinduism. This means that at every stage of education the material from the tradition needs to be related to the experiences, interests and concerns of pupils in order for its relevance to be appreciated. Teachers often underestimate the ability of even the youngest pupils to engage with the philosophical questions posed by the study of religions. Pupils appreciate the opportunity in religious education to be able to express their own opinions on the 'Ultimate Questions' at the heart of human experience.

Effective religious education needs to use *creative* and *experiential* pedagogical methods. Much use can be made of the arts, including pictorial art, artefacts, drama, dance and music. Visits and visitors can provide direct contact with religious communities. In addition, many recent resources (videos, interactive CD-ROMs and the Internet) are valuable ways of involving pupils with the tradition. The term *experiential religious education* usually refers to the provision within the classroom of opportunities for pupils to explore their own emotional and spiritual responses in a direct way through such techniques as meditation, stilling exercises, silent reflection and guided fantasy. These techniques can be very useful in taking religious education beyond the merely informative and enabling pupils to engage with both the inner experiences of believers and their own personal beliefs and values. For further discussion of creative and experiential methods, see unit B of the module 'Method in Religious Education' and unit C of the module 'Philosophy of Religious Education', both of which are in *Religion in Education* (volume 1).

Continuity and progression

There has been much discussion about the appropriate age at which to introduce pupils to Hinduism. As stated above, it is important that pupils encounter Hinduism at least once during both primary and secondary phases of education (Baumfield *et al*, 1994). There is also debate about whether religious traditions are most effectively studied systematically, one religion at a time, or thematically, focusing on a dimension of religion across several traditions. There are advantages and disadvantages to both. For example, the systematic approach may be advocated as a means of studying the religion in its own terms but may be criticised for suggesting that religions exist independently of one another and the wider world. However, the thematic approach may be recommended as a means of highlighting the connections, both historical and contemporary, between religions but may be accused of distorting the traditions to fit preconceived categories.

Where, when and how Hinduism features in a given school scheme will depend upon the particular syllabus (LEA Agreed Syllabus, Diocesan Syllabus etc.) being followed and the individual circumstances of the school. As such syllabi suggest, different aspects of Hinduism seem appropriate for children at different Key Stages. Having said this, experience also shows that many topics can be addressed at any point as long as the ages and experience of the pupils are taken into account. The following list of possible topics, taken from the SCAA Model Syllabi, from Baumfield *et al* (1994) and from a variety of Agreed Syllabi, may prove helpful nevertheless.

Key Stage 1

- The Gods and Goddesses, especially Ganesha, Krishna, Rama, Lakshmi, Shiva.
- The Family, the extended family, brothers and sisters, Raksha Bandhan.
- Worship, home shrines, puja and arati.
- Festivals, for example, Divali, Krishna Janmashtami (Krishna's birthday).
- Respect for people and animals.
- Prashad (blessed food), vegetarianism, food for special occasions.
- Clothes, for instance, sari, Punjabi suit.
- Welcoming a new baby (life cycle rites).
- Greetings, Namaste.
- Stories from the scriptures, especially about Rama, Krishna and Ganesha.

Key Stage 2 (Years 3 and 4)

- The concept of God, forms and formlessness including Vishnu and his avatars (descent forms), Krishna, Rama, Hanuman, Lakshmi, Shiva, Ganesha, Kali, Durga, Sarasvati.
- The Temple, shrines, images, symbols, music, ceremonies especially arati.
- Festivals, for example, Holi, Divali, Raksha Bandhan.
- Family ceremonies including birth and marriage rites.
- Natural symbols, water, fire and light.
- Special people, the Hindu priest, gurus and swamis.

Key Stage 2 (Years 5 and 6)

- Creation stories.
- Pilgrimage, particularly to Varanasi.

- Signs and symbols, for instance, AUM (OM) and the swastika.
- Prayer and meditation, including Gayatri Mantra and Yoga.
- Festivals such as Navratri, Ramnavami, Dassehra.
- Time and timelessness, calendar and cosmology.
- Ancient Indian civilisation, Indus Valley/Harappa Culture (may link with history curriculum).
- Listening to Hindus talk about their life and faith.

Key Stage 3

- The concept(s) of God: Brahman, Brahman/atman, personal and impersonal.
- Iconography, recognising Hindu Gods and Goddesses.
- Concepts central to the Hindu worldview: samsara, atman, karma, dharma, moksha.
- Ways to moksha: karma, jnana and bhakti yoga.
- Cosmology: the cyclical view of time and a variety of creation stories.
- Sacred geography: rivers, mountains and places of pilgrimage.
- Morality: concept of dharma, four aims of life, four stages of life.
- Worship: puja at home and in the temple.
- The temple: architectural styles, functions in India and Britain.
- Festivals such as Navaratri, Shivratri, Ramnavami, Janmashtami.
- Faith in action, for example, Gandhi, gurus and saints.
- Rites of Passage: birth, initiation, marriage and death.
- Non-violence (ahimsa) and vegetarianism.
- Scripture, especially the Vedas, Puranas, Mahabharata (including Bhagavad-Gita) and Ramayana.

Key Stage 4

- The concept of God: polytheism, monism and theism and ways of reconciling all three.
- Hindu darshanas: advaita, vishishtadvaita, dvaita vedanta and samkhya-yoga.
- Cosmology and time: the four yugas and the nature of the present (kali) yuga.
- Yoga, meditation and mantras.
- Marriage and Hindu approaches to relationships, sexuality and family life.
- Death: funeral practices and beliefs.
- Suffering and evil.
- Varna and jati (caste) as controversial issues.
- Scriptures: Vedas, Upanishads, Epics and Puranas.
- Attitudes to other faiths and interfaith dialogue.
- Hinduism and modernity, Hinduism in diaspora.
- Hindu perspectives on moral and social issues, including medical ethics,

wealth and poverty, work and leisure, racism and prejudice, gender and sexism, crime and punishment, politics and government, drugs and alcohol, human rights, ecology and animal rights.

Depending on which aspects (if any) of Hinduism pupils have encountered previously, elements from the suggestions for earlier Key Stages may need to be incorporated into units of work for older pupils. In addition, although some topics suggest themselves as particularly suited to one age group, most topics can be adapted for any age group. It is important to liaise with the teachers and schools from which pupils come and to which they will be going, in order to avoid the situation where, for example they 'do' Divali four times, and never have the opportunity to explore the Hindu concepts of God. This can also be useful for sharing scarce resources.

Activity C1

Scrutinise the relevant Syllabus and existing school scheme for religious education (and in the primary school, if applicable, general topics) for the potential to teach Hinduism. How far is Hinduism already included? Where could it easily be included without too much disruption? Whether or not it is already there, where best would an in-depth systematic study of Hinduism fit?

Construct a rationale to present to a departmental or staff meeting for the teaching of Hinduism in general, and the aspects you have identified in particular, in your own school context.

If you are not currently employed in a school, either make contact with a local school in order to undertake this activity, or obtain an appropriate Agreed or Diocesan syllabus and construct your scheme and rationale for an imaginary school.

Comment on activity C1

This will depend very much on your individual circumstances. Some syllabi are more prescriptive than others and may already identify where Hinduism can be taught. Others have more general requirements that could be satisfied by a selection from a variety of religions. The latter case means more work but also more freedom. If you already have a whole-school scheme, you may need to argue for changes to include, or to increase the amount of, the teaching of Hinduism.

Your arguments for including Hinduism will include those in the introduction above, plus arguments specific to your school such as the presence of Hindu children or conversely the importance of multifaith religious education in an all-white rural school. Even such pragmatic considerations as the recent visit to India by a teacher or parent may help make the case.

Sample lessons for Key Stage 1

1. Gods and Goddesses can be introduced directly through artefacts. Young children often have less in the way of preconceived ideas than adults, and react positively and with understanding. One five year old explained to his teacher (who was having difficulty overcoming her conditioning about 'idols') 'Of course God has lots of heads, because he can see everywhere, can't he?' The book *A Gift to the Child* (Grimmitt, Grove, Hull and Spencer, 1991) suggests heightening the suspense by covering the image with a cloth and revealing it gradually. This resource has a useful chapter based on the God Ganesha, relating stories of Ganesha to children's own experience of anger and those to whom they are thankful, and contextualising the figure Ganesha within the life and worship of a little Hindu boy.

2. Just seeing the length and colours of a sari was in itself a kind of spiritual experience for a reception class. Although not really religion, this was the beginning of a positive attitude to other cultures, as well as an experience of the wonder of colour.

3. Krishna's birthday can be celebrated with a pretend shrine, using all the senses such as the smell of incense. Links can be made with children's own birthdays, and with their understanding of Christmas. There are lots of stories about Krishna suitable for this age group such as the story of his birth (see Cole and Lowndes, 1995), Krishna and the butter, Krishna eating dirt (see Palmer and Breuilly, 1994). Krishna the friend is explored in Hume and Sevier (1991). The elements of puja can be demonstrated, including the sharing of sweets.

4. Divali can be celebrated with the making of clay or plasticine diva lamps, Divali cards, rangoli patterns, making Indian sweets, setting up a shrine for Lakshmi and acting out the story of Rama and Sita. Masks can be made for the monkeys and the monsters in the story, or the play could be put on using shadow puppets.

5. A visit to the temple could emphasise the impact on the senses: the sight of colours and tinsel, the smell of incense, the taste of prashad, the feel of walking without shoes, the sound of bells, musical instruments and songs. Response to the experience can be made through a variety of creative arts back in the classroom, and perhaps presented later to the temple to say thank you.

Sample lessons for Key Stage 2 (Years 3 and 4)

1. Holi can be celebrated with roasted coconut and coloured streamers instead of water. The story of Prahlad can be told and dramatised (see Cole and Lowndes, 1995; Kadodwala, 1996). This is a story dealing with important issues such as when not to obey adults. Pupils can build a pretend bonfire and circumambulate it as Hindus would, making a positive wish for their own family, class and the world.

2. Raksha Bandhan gives an opportunity to celebrate our brothers and sisters (or for only children, cousins or friends). Rakhis and sweets can be made and exchanged with family and friends. Make a poster of all they ways we help and are helped by older or younger siblings and friends.

3. If Divali is celebrated in this age group, there is more scope for writing such as calligraphy in Indian languages, and making a storybook for the infants (there is a computer programme for BBC computers called 'Ramayana Tales', linked with the 'Watch' series, which can be an interesting way to do this).

4. Gods and Goddesses can be introduced by first getting children to draw their own personifications of good fortune, energy, love, strength, helpfulness, removing obstacles, beauty etc. They can then be compared with the Hindu equivalent. One boy's creation of 'Problem Pig', with many arms to solve different problems (including annoying teachers) proved an excellent preparation for Ganesha.

5. Visits to the temple can then focus on recognising the Gods and Goddesses, the shrines, images, symbols and ceremonies.

6. The power of natural symbols such as light, fire and water in Hinduism and other religions can be explored by means of silent reflection or a guided fantasy, such as watching a diva candle flame, imagining entering a fountain or stream that can change your life in some way.

Sample lessons for Key Stage 2 (Years 5 and 6)

1. Hindu creation stories can be analysed for implications about how we should treat animals and the planet (see Palmer and Bisset, 1993). Children can discuss what animal they might like to be reborn as, stressing that Hindus see animal rebirth as unfortunate. Poems could be written exploring the joys and distresses of animal life. Vegetarian menus could be planned.

2. Pilgrimage to the Ganges and elsewhere can be introduced by considering places special to the children, and a guided fantasy leading to an imaginary special place.

3. Meditation can be introduced by simple stilling and breathing exercises.

Feelings can be discussed. The purpose of prayer can be explored. Kadodwala (1996) includes an activity related to the Gayatri mantra, in which children compose their own ten word welcome to the new day, and display this on a rising sun.

4. Signs and symbols in everyday life can introduce Hindu symbols. The swastika is particularly good for revealing the multivalent nature of symbols, meaning quite different things to different people. Children can invent their own symbols, for example for particular emotions. The visit to the temple can concentrate on symbols and symbolic actions in worship.

5. Different calendars can be investigated, relating to the lunar and solar years. Cyclical and linear time can be explored by looking at events in the children's own lives that repeat and others that are once only. A calendar of Hindu festivals can be made, and groups research background information on each one. Children's imagination can be stimulated with the concepts of timelessness and the relativity of time, leading to creative writing.

6. Children can learn the stick dance and circle dance (danda ras and ras mandala) used to celebrate Navaratri.

Sample lessons for Key Stage 3

1. Pupils' existing knowledge of Hinduism can be diagnostically assessed by presenting pairs or small groups with pictures such as the Westhill Project's *Hindus Photopack*. Pupils can be asked to say what they think (or know) is going on in the picture, what questions they would like to ask about the picture, what they think people in the picture might be thinking.

2. Pupils can be introduced to the Gods and Goddesses by giving each child the name of a God or Goddess. They then have to find (as in party games) the other pupils with the same name. In these groups, using resources available in the classroom, they must find an image of their deity, a story about them and information as to who they are. They then introduce the deity to the class as if it were themselves. In the follow up visit to the temple, pupils enjoy recognising 'their' God, which mimics the concept of ishtadevata, one's chosen or favourite God, in Hinduism. Groups can present a story from the mythology of their God or Goddess in drama, mime, music, etc. Using artefacts or posters, pupils can, after silent reflection, make close observational drawings of their God or Goddess, perhaps with quiet music in the background, and add appropriate 'feeling' words to their picture. See Francis (1996) and O'Donnell (1992) for further ideas from the images of Ganesha and Shiva.

3. Pupils can make a timeline for their own lives, identifying significant events, both happy and sad. These can be shared with others, or kept private. These

can then be compared with the Hindu four stages of life and succession of samskaras.

4. A board game can be devised, 'the Hindu game of life', incorporating Hindu ideas about the four aims of life: karma: rebirth, the paths of jnana, karma and bhakti, winning by reaching moksha. Pupils can discuss their own beliefs about destiny: do we make our own, or is it fate or luck? Activities connected with this can be found in Francis (1996).

5. After studying the teachings of the Bhagavad-Gita, draw a large poster of Krishna, with six speech bubbles summarising his most important messages (see Kanitkar 1994).

6. After looking at the concept of dharma, duty, and the four stages of life, students list what they see as their own duties at this time of life. Discuss the idea of selfless action - without concern for result or reward - and write a story to illustrate this.

7. Using the pamphlet, *Teaching Hinduism 11-16 Christian Education Movement* (nd), explore the meaning of pilgrimage, focusing on the feelings of the pilgrim.

8. Yoga, meditation and mantra and undistracted attention are exemplified by activities in the Teacher's workbook to accompany Francis (1996).

Sample lessons for Key Stage 4

1. Investigate Hindu perspectives on a variety of moral and social issues. Two helpful books are Cole (1991) and Francis (1997). The CD-ROM *Aspects of Religion* contains useful material on the topics of crime and punishment, sex and marriage, medical ethics, war and peace, wealth and poverty, racism and sexism and the conservation of the environment.

2. Varna and caste can be investigated, stressing different perspectives such as that of Gandhi. Debate the advantages and disadvantages of caste, remembering that, for Hindus, there is more than one life (see Francis, 1997).

3. Collect newspaper items to illustrate the troubles of our time as a way into the concept of Kali yuga. Draw an abstract design to illustrate the feelings associated with the Kali yuga. For each of your stories attempt to explain how the suffering could be ameliorated by putting Hindu beliefs and values into practice.

4. Investigate the contribution of the Hindu darshanas to the concept of God and arguments for the existence of any form/formless divinity. Do Hindu ideas add to the existing western debates?

5. Hold an 'international summit' on environmental issues where students take the role of members of the religions you have studied putting forward their ideas on saving the planet. Have other students take the role of provocative journalists attempting to find awkward questions to ask the panel, based on aspects of the religion that might militate against environmental concern.

6. After studying Hindu temple architecture, and visiting at least one temple in Britain (and preferably also the Swaminarayan temple at Neasden), design a purpose built Hindu temple for today. It need not keep to traditional patterns, but needs to reflect the needs of Hindus in Britain.

Activity C2

Plan a unit of work on Hinduism that will last for at least half a term (minimum 6 sessions).

You need to specify the year group, the type of school (county primary, voluntary aided comprehensive and so on) and catchment area. This can be your own school or an imaginary one.

Explain how your unit satisfies the requirements of the appropriate syllabus and school scheme of work, including assessment arrangements, statutory or otherwise.

You might like to set out a summary of your unit of work in grid form, with headings such as activity, religious content, reference to syllabus, key questions, pupil learning: concepts, skills, attitudes, resources required, differentiation and means of assessment. Then give lesson plans in full.

In order to transcend the mere passing on of information, your unit of work should include at least one activity using each of the following: video, IT, posters/photographs, artefacts, an exercise in silent reflection or guided fantasy, drama or role-play, music and/or dance, creative art or craft work, a story from Hinduism, a visit or visitor and active learning.

How will you assess the planned learning outcomes and how will you evaluate the success of your teaching? If you have an opportunity to trial this unit of work, give an evaluation with ideas for future improvements.

Comment on activity C2

Make sure that all your suggested activities are suitable for the age and level of achievement of the pupils. Provide differentiated materials where necessary for those with special needs or levels of attainment in advance of the rest of the class. Check that all your activities would be acceptable to Hindus and do not give a misleading or one-sided picture of the tradition - have you suggested that Hinduism is all festivals and ceremonies, or all difficult concepts with little application to everyday life? Check that you have made links wherever possible with the interest and experiences of pupils, and given them an opportunity to reflect upon their own opinions and emotions.

If for examination work, make sure you have satisfied both the requirements of the GCSE syllabus AND the statutory Agreed/Diocesan Syllabus.

With regard to assessment: what counts as progress in learning in religious education? How will you be able to tell whether pupils have made progress? Remember that you are not merely testing factual recall, but also more subtle abilities such as understanding, creativity and personal sensitivity.

Resources

Key Stage 1

Cole, W.O. and Lowndes, J. (1995), *The Birth of Krishna and The Story of Prahlad*, Oxford, Heinemann.

Cooper, J. (1989), *Hindu Festivals*, Hove, Wayland.

Grimmitt, M., Grove, J., Hull, J. and Spencer, L. (1991), *A Gift to the Child*, Hemel Hempstead, Simon and Schuster.

Singh, R. and J. (1988), *The Amazing Adventures of Hanuman*, London, BBC.

Wood, J. (1988), *Our Culture: Hindu*, London, Franklin Watts.

Key Stage 1-2

Aggarwal, M. and Fairclough, C. (1984), *I am a Hindu*, London, Franklin Watts.

Bennett, O. (1987), *Holi: Hindu festival of spring*, London, Hamish Hamilton.

Deshpande, C. (1985), *Divali*, London, A and C Black.

Gavin, J. (1986), *Stories from the Hindu World*, London, MacDonald.

Jaffrey, M. (1987), *Seasons of Splendour*, Harmondsworth, Puffin.

Kadodwala, D. (1997), *Holi: the Hindu festival of colours*, London, Evans.

Kadodwala, D. and Gateshill, P. (1995), *Celebrate Hindu Festivals*, Oxford, Heinemann.

Kadodwala, D. 1996), *Hinduism*, London, Nelson.

Kanitkar, V.P. (1985), *Hinduism*, Hove, Wayland.

Kanitkar, V.P. (1986), *Hindu Stories*, Hove, Wayland.

Key Stage 2-3

Bahree, P. (1989), *The Hindu World*, London, MacDonald.

Bennett, O. (1986), *Diwali*, London, Macmillan.

Hirst, J. (1990), *Growing up in Hinduism*, London, Longman.

Jackson, R. (1989), *Religions Through Festivals: Hinduism*, London, Longman.

Kanitkar, V.P. (1994), *Hindu Scriptures*, Oxford, Heinemann.

Kerven, R. (1986), *Diwali*, London, Macmillan.

O'Donnell, K. (1992), *I Wonder...*, London, Hodder.

O'Donnell, K. (1993), *You're Dreaming!*, London, Hodder.

Oldfield, K. (1987), *Hindu Gods and Goddesses*, Derby, CEM.

Palmer, M. and Bisset, E. (1989/93), *Worlds of Difference* (second edition), Glasgow, Nelson.

Sutcliffe, S. and B. (1994), *Committed to Hinduism*, Norwich, RMEP.

Key Stage 3 - 4

Aylett, L. (1992), *Seeking Religion: the Hindu experience*, London, Hodder.

Francis, D. (1996), *Just a Thought*, London, Hodder.

Jackson, R. and Nesbitt, E. (1990), *Listening to Hindus*, London, Unwin Hyman.

Penney, S. (1988), *Hinduism*, London, Heinemann.

Wayne, E., *et al* (1996), *Hindus*, Oxford, Heinemann.

Key Stage 4

Cole, W.O. (1991), *Moral Issues in Six Religions*, Oxford, Heinemann.

Francis, D. (1997), *The Road to Somewhere*, London, Hodder.

Kanitkar, V.P. (1989), *Hinduism*, Cheltenham, Stanley Thornes.

Mercier, S.C. (1991), *Hinduism*, London, Longman.

Voiels, V. (1997), *Hinduism: a new approach*, London, Hodder.

C2 Buddhism

Aims

After working through part C2 of this unit you should be able to:

- clarify your own reasons for teaching Buddhism and be prepared to justify this choice to colleagues, parents and governors;

- decide what aspects of Buddhism would be suitable for your particular school and syllabus, and at what stage these will be introduced;

- advise on a variety of resources to assist the teaching of Buddhism, having located and reviewed them;

- plan and execute a unit of work on Buddhism for at least one age group, using the full range of teaching and learning methods available;

- assess the learning outcomes of your unit of work and evaluate the success of your teaching.

Overview

This part of the unit outlines reasons for teaching about Buddhism and then sets out suitable topics for each Key Stage.

This part of the unit uses the spellings of terms as recommended in the SCAA Model Syllabi for Religious Education (1994), but you will find a variety of spellings of the same term in the textbooks you use. This is because of the use of different systems of transliteration.

Why teach about Buddhism?

Buddhism is often the last religion any teacher may wish to tackle. There are a number of reasons for this. Teachers may feel that they know little about the subject, or that their training enables them to tackle the monotheistic faiths and perhaps Hinduism, but not Buddhism. They may think that Buddhism does not lend itself well to classroom presentation because of its comparative lack of festivals, rites of passage, and apparent lack of iconography beyond images of the Buddha. Its corpus of scriptures is hugely complex and difficult to summarise and so, arguably, are its teachings.

Some teachers may have reservations about it because of its agnosticism regarding an omnipotent God. This reservation has a number of features. Some may feel that because of this, confusion could so easily arise in the minds of children about the nature of worship when they encounter the religion. They may also feel that because Buddhism is not a human response to God, it has little to offer to spiritual and moral development. In short, some feel that introducing Buddhism could undermine work done with children in other areas of the religious education/studies curriculum.

Some may argue that children are not likely to meet Buddhists, so learning about the religion should have a low priority on the already packed timetable. Others may feel that Buddhism is simply too difficult, both for themselves and for the children. All of these reservations are understandable, but we should question their legitimacy.

Teachers now have a wealth of multimedia resources available to them for teaching about Buddhism at all Key Stages. A glance at the bibliography for this unit will confirm this. It is a rare teacher who arrives in the classroom with all the background knowledge assimilated, with all the community contacts made, with all the artefacts to hand, to enable him or her to teach all six religions that may be required. Teachers are well used to learning alongside their pupils.

Whilst it is often felt that Buddhism does not have the richness of, say, Hinduism, in terms of clear, distinct festivals, rites of passage, and so on, this feeling is not really based on fact. Admittedly, the diversity of Buddhist practices may cause initial confusion, but in reality this diversity is a virtue. It provides a vast range of material upon which to draw. Just to illustrate this, it is worth mentioning the numerous festivals celebrated in different countries: Obon and Hanamatsuri in Japan, the Festival of the Tooth in Sri Lanka, Wesak in Theravadin countries, and so on. It is also worth mentioning the richness of Tibetan iconography and ritual, the abundance of Zen poetry and art, the lives of young Theravadin monks, the lifestyles and priorities of Theravadin lay-people, and of course the compelling and educationally rich biographies of the Buddha and other enlightened beings. Easy to manage scriptures can be found in the *Dhammapada* and in the *Jataka* literature.

The claim that children are not likely to meet Buddhists is a bogus one on two counts. Buddhism is one of the fastest growing religions in Britain, not so much due to immigration, but rather, because of the wide appeal Buddhism has in the post-Christian West. Therefore children *might* meet Buddhists, and those that do not will almost certainly encounter the ideas of Buddhism in some form or other in our own culture. Second, if the only legitimate reason for learning about world religions is to equip potential neighbours to understand each others' beliefs, then the agenda of religious education is much more limited than those working in the field believe it to be. Crucial concerns for most educators include spiritual and moral development, educating citizens of the global (not just the British) community, fostering an ability to face 'ultimate questions', and encouraging the development of tolerance, understanding, critical faculties and empathy.

The charge that an encounter with Buddhism might undermine other work done in religious education is one that needs looking at carefully. Teachers who do teach about Buddhism often argue that Buddhism throws light on other religions, because it provides a contrast to them. For example, a British Buddhist was asked by a child why she kept the precepts, when there was no God 'looking'. The Buddhist concluded from this question that the child had not even begun to understand the notion of keeping commandments in Christianity and other religions, let alone in Buddhism. She argued that the introduction of the Buddhist perspective into the child's religious education, whilst educational in itself, would also help her understand the notion in other religions. Many teachers would argue that introducing Buddhism can help children really reflect on ultimate questions outside of the usual model of humanity relating to an omnipotent God. Since Buddhism (at least as it is presented in most agreed syllabi) starts from experience as opposed to from a creed or set of beliefs, it is actually well suited to spiritual and moral development.

Approaches to Buddhism

Any approach to Buddhism in a county or religious school will be non-confessional, except in the very rare case of an independent Buddhist school (of which there is currently only one in Britain). This is not to say, however, that only facts will be learned. Both of the SCAA Model Syllabi set attainment targets for each Key Stage which ask pupils to both 'learn about' and 'learn from' religions. Meeting these targets requires a diversity of skills, from critical analysis to empathy and self-reflection. 'Learning from' a religion which may not be one's own should not be understood as a confessional activity. Rather, religious stories, rituals and so on should be used as stimuli for children's own reflection on ultimate questions, morality, feelings, relationships and other aspects of human experience. In this way, religious education in schools can contribute to the spiritual and moral development of pupils.

Presentations of Buddhism, both in text books and in the classroom, often suffer from one of two problems: either the religion is trivialised or it is romanticised. A teacher who fails to reflect what Buddhism is for Buddhists, is distorting the subject matter and therefore being less than honest with pupils. Unfamiliar practices often do seem rather odd, to teachers as well as to pupils, and it is all too easy to slip into presenting them as 'these strange activities about which we have to learn', without really attempting to bring the meaning of the practice home to pupils.

Romanticising religious beliefs and practices can be just as damaging to pupils understanding. For example, it is widely assumed that Buddhism is a monastic, ascetic, anti-materialistic religion. The attempt to present the monastic tradition of Buddhism as normative makes the religion seem very exotic and interesting, and such a presentation might certainly engage the interest and enthusiasm of a class. This understanding of Buddhism is, however, both partial and romantic, and therefore not very accurate or helpful.

As well as avoiding the pitfalls of either trivialising or romanticising Buddhism, teachers also need to take account of continuity and progression. Different Agreed and Diocesan Syllabi take different approaches to the way in which religions are introduced. They may be introduced individually and systematically at different Key Stages or, as is more common, they may be introduced thematically, where the same aspect of a number of religions would be studied together, such as 'holy books', 'ultimate questions', 'leaders' and so on. Both strategies have much to be said for them, but equally both have their limitations. Examination syllabi, of course, almost always take the systematic approach. Whatever the style of the syllabus, teachers have to make difficult decisions about what to introduce and when. These decisions will depend on the age and ability of the children, what the children have studied before, resources available, and possibly the religious profile of the school or class.

To meditate or not to meditate?

One of the key practices in many (though not all) forms of Buddhism is meditation. Obviously meditation as a practice will feature as part of the content of any syllabus on Buddhism, but many Buddhists and many teachers would argue that in order to really understand Buddhism, children must have first hand experience of meditation. This is a highly controversial area.

Arguments often offered in favour of using mediation in the classroom include the following:

- many Buddhists would argue that understanding comes only with practice; you cannot describe what meditation is, since it is at heart a personal experience;
- children enjoy the novelty of trying to meditate, and therefore enjoy the lesson;
- actual experience grounds religious concepts; a visit to a place of worship does so much to help focus work done on a religion, because it is a real experience, not just abstract words and pictures, and the same is true of the experience of meditation;
- it is spiritually good for children to spend quiet time looking inward.

Arguments often offered against using mediation in the classroom include the following:

- using meditation in the classroom sails perilously close to a confessional approach; one would not, after all, ask children to pray in the classroom, at least not in the context of religious education;
- only a Buddhist can really lead anyone in meditation;
- sitting quietly, closing eyes etc. can be difficult for some children and can even be a bit disturbing or frightening.

Different teachers will have different opinions on this issue. Many would argue that real Buddhist meditation can only take place within a tradition, so only a teacher who happened to be a Buddhist could undertake this. However, such an exercise could easily, and possibly quite rightly, be interpreted as involving a compromise of the spiritual autonomy of the children, and would therefore be unacceptable. However, this is not to say that stilling exercises or guided visualisations are not highly effective teaching strategies and ones that can be used with impunity so long as the children are fully aware of the nature of what they are doing, and that those who are uncomfortable are accommodated. In stilling exercises it is possible for children to get hints of what meditation might be like.

Activity C3

What characteristics would you say a robust approach to Buddhism at all Key Stages would have?

Comment on activity C3

Here are some suggestions. A robust approach might:

- develop knowledge, understanding and critical evaluation;
- encourage empathy;
- strike a balance between 'learning about' and 'learning from';
- contribute to spiritual and moral development;
- take account of continuity and progression;
- take account of differing abilities in the classroom;
- use creative and experiential teaching techniques: see unit B of the module 'Method in Religious Education' and unit C of the module 'Philosophy of Religious Education', both of which are in *Religion in Education* (volume 1);
- take a wide, serious, empathetic yet unromantic view of Buddhism;
- use Buddhism to help children understand other religions;
- use Buddhist understandings of reality when looking at 'ultimate questions';
- understand the complexity and diversity of Buddhist beliefs and the ways in which these relate to the individual and to society in Buddhist countries: Denise Cush's (1990) *Buddhists in Britain Today* contains useful interviews with British Buddhists;
- make use of visiting speakers, either Buddhists or people who have visited Buddhist countries: you can find the address of your local Buddhist group in the *UK Buddhist Directory*, published by the Buddhist Society;
- make use of trips - there are some beautiful temples in Britain, such as the Thai Temple (the Buddhapadipa) in Wimbledon; and a trip to the shrine room of a local group might be just as rewarding;
- make use of artefacts, to bring the daily lives of Buddhists home to children;
- make use of cross-curricular links, perhaps especially with Geography,

History, Science, Music and Art; contributing to general studies programmes and to personal and social development.

Continuity and progression

Different aspects of Buddhism and different approaches to teaching and learning are appropriate at different Key Stages. What follows are two suggestions for topic areas for each Key Stage gleaned from a variety of textbooks and syllabi. These suggestions should counter the claim introduced at the beginning that Buddhism does not provide enough of the right kind of material for classroom work, but they are brief suggestions only.

Key Stage 1

- The Life of the Buddha, especially giving up all his possessions and his luxurious lifestyle in order to search for the truth: this could encourage reflection on how possessions can be distracting and the desire for them become all consuming. How easy is it for a rich man to give up all he owns? Children could reflect on their own favourite things and whether they would be able to give them up. Teachers' resources include Carrithers (1983), Cush (1993), Davey-Latham (1995) and Snelling (1987).
- Jataka Tales: these are traditionally seen as the previous lives of the Buddha, but are ideal for young children since they are moral tales often involving animal characters. The Clear Vision Trust's pack *The Monkey King* (1997) is a superb video and worksheet resource for this sort of work. The Clear Vision Trust has also produced material for Key Stage 2 (1994) and Key Stage 3 (1996).

Key Stage 2

- Children in this age group may be responsive to stilling exercises. Guided visualisation of the four passing sights or of Siddhartha's despair after six years of austerities leading to his opting for the 'middle way' may be exceedingly fruitful.
- Denise Cush in a chapter on teaching Buddhism in *Teaching World Religions* (Erricker, 1993) describes a *metta* (loving-kindness) 'meditation' in which the child first visualises a warm glow of kindness. First you direct this feeling towards yourself, hoping for health and happiness for yourself. Then you direct it towards a 'neutral' person, wishing for the same things for that person, and then to someone with whom you do not get on. Finally you imagine the warm feeling extending to all people everywhere and repeat the wish 'may all beings be happy'.

Key Stage 3

- Buddhist morality: the precepts, the vinaya, the eightfold path, connectedness, the bodhisattva. Children could investigate the nature of rules: why they are useful, why we try to keep them, fear of punishment and so on. Teachers might refer to Rahula (1959) or Robinson and Johnson (1982).

- Children could investigate the nature of suffering and its relationship with desire. Research could be undertaken into news reports of examples of suffering, using papers, the Internet and CD ROMS. Collections could be made of advertisements designed to increase desire for things. The *Dhammapada*, translated by Mascaro (1973), would be a good scripture to use in conjunction with this kind of work. Children could explore the concept of the bodhisattva. Who works to combat suffering in our world today?

Key Stage 4

- Experience suggests that pupils at this Key Stage favour an issues based, as opposed to a content-based, approach. Buddhism has much to say about environmental issues, about war and violence, about alcohol and drugs and about the nature of human life. Buddhism and Science might be an interesting topic to tackle, as might the nature of personal identity in Buddhism (No-self, rebirth, connectedness, and so on). Teachers might refer to Harvey (1990) and Keown (1996).

- Exploration of Tibetan iconography might be a compelling activity at this Key Stage. Advanced understanding requires sensitivity to symbol and metaphor, and most will enjoy studying the stories about and characteristics of the different bodhisattvas and historical figures, and of mandalas, mudras and mantras. *Buddhism: A New Approach* (1996) leads the pupil through this symbolism, asking questions at every stage.

Activity C4

Plan a unit of work on Buddhism that will last for at least half a term (minimum 6 sessions). Write up your unit, including all the relevant contextual information. To do so you will need to take the following factors into account:

- the age group of the children;
- the type of school: country primary, comprehensive, voluntary aided, and its catchment area;
- the requirements of the relevant Agreed Syllabus, Diocesan Syllabus or examination syllabus;
- the assessment arrangements for your unit;

- aims and objectives of the unit;
- differentiation;
- the resources that you will require: try to use a diversity of different types;
- the teaching strategies you will use;
- whether visitors or trips might be appropriate;

You may use your own school, or you may create an imaginary one. If you are in a position to trial your unit, evaluate your efforts and suggest future improvements.

Comment on activity C4

Have you taken all the factors into consideration? Is your unit suitable for the age and ability of the pupils? Did you provide differentiated materials for children with difficulties and for higher achievers? Does your material romanticise or trivialise any aspect of Buddhism? Do you think the parents of a Buddhist child in your class would be satisfied with your treatment of their religion? Has there been an opportunity for children to learn from as well as to learn about the religion? How effective do you think your assessment strategy is? What sort of things were you testing for? How will you know whether pupils have understood and have benefited from your unit of work? Does your unit contribute to spiritual and moral development in any way? Does it have anything to offer to the development of cross-curricular links?

Resources

Key Stage 1-2

Clear Vision Trust (1994), *Buddhism for Key Stage Two* (video set, teacher's handbook, worksheets), Manchester, The Clear Vision Trust.

Clear Vision Trust (1997), *The Monkey King and Other Tales* (video set, teacher's handbook, worksheets), Manchester, The Clear Vision Trust.

Ganeri, A. (1996), *Beliefs and Cultures: Buddhist*, London, Franklin Watts.

Samarasekara, D.U. (1986), *I am a Buddhist*, London, Franklin Watts.

Snelling, J. (1985), *Buddhist Festivals*, Hove, Wayland.

Snelling, J. (1986), *Buddhist Stories*, Hove, Wayland.

Snelling, J. (1987), *The Life of the Buddha*, Hove, Wayland.

St Pierre, M. and Casey, M. (1996), *My Buddhist Life*, Hove, Wayland.

Thorley, S. (1997), *Buddhism in Words and Pictures*, Norwich, RMEP.

The Jataka Tales Series (at least 19 different stories translated so far), Dharma Publishing.

Key Stage 3

Bancroft, A. (1984), *Festivals of the Buddha*, London, RMEP.

Bancroft, A. (1984, 1992), *The Buddhist World*, Hemel Hempstead, Simon and Schuster.

Clear Vision Trust (1996), *Living Buddhism: Buddhism for Key Stage Three*, Manchester, The Clear Vision Trust.

Connolly, P. and H. (1989), *Religions through Festivals: Buddhism*, London, Longman.

Naylor, D. and Smith, A. (1987), *The Buddha: a journey*, London, Macmillan.

Penney, S. (1989), *Buddhism*, Discovering Religion Series, London, Heinemann.

Sutcliffe, S. and Sutcliffe, B. (1995), *Committed to Buddhism*, Norwich, RMEP.

Thorley, S. (1997), *Buddhism in Words and Pictures*, Norwich, RMEP (Key Stages 2 and 3).

GCSE, Key Stage 4 and Short Course

Cole, W.O. (1991), *Moral Issues in Six Religions*, Oxford, Heinemann.

Connolly, P. and H. (1992), *Buddhism*, Cheltenham, Stanley Thornes.

Clarke, S. and Thompson, M. (1996), *Buddhism: a new approach*, London, Hodder and Stoughton.

Morgan, P. (1984), *Buddhism in the Twentieth Century*, Amersham, London, Hulton Educational Publishers.

Weatherley, L. (1992), *Buddhism*, Themes in Religion Series, Harlow, Longman.

C3 Sikhism

Aims

After working through part C3 of this unit you should be able to:

- clarify your own reasons for teaching Sikhism and be prepared to justify this choice to colleagues, parents and governors;
- decide which aspects of Sikhism would be suitable for your particular school and syllabus, and at what stage these will be introduced;
- advise on a variety of resources to assist the teaching of Sikhism, having located and reviewed them;
- plan and execute at least one unit of work on Sikhism for at least one age group, using the full range of teaching and learning methods available;

- assess the learning outcomes of your unit of work and evaluate the success of your teaching.

Overview

This part of the unit outlines reasons for teaching about Sikhism and then sets out suitable topics for each Key Stage.

Why teach about Sikhism?

Sikhism is not the most common of non-Christian religions to find being taught in schools. There are several reasons for this. First, numerically Sikhs are small compared with the major world religions like Islam and Christianity - under 20 million as opposed to over 1000 million. Sikhism is relatively young, with a history of five centuries rather than millennia. It has been debated whether Sikhism really qualifies as a 'world religion' as the majority of adherents (c 14 million) live in the Punjab. In other European countries that teach 'world religions', such as Norway, Sikhism is not normally included in the curriculum, and teachers are often not aware of Sikhs as a distinct group. However, it is particularly important to teach about Sikhism in Britain as the Sikhs in the UK represent the largest Sikh community outside the Indian subcontinent. The history of British colonialism and its aftermath explains the connection. Many Sikhs served in the British Indian armies in the First and Second World wars. The disruptions of the partition of India in the 1940s, the need for labour in Britain from commonwealth countries in the 1950s and 60s, the expulsion of East African Asians in the 1970s and the trouble in India in the 1980s all served to bring Sikhs to the UK. In the 1990s there are small numbers of Sikhs in most countries, so it can now be classed as a 'world religion'.

Although few in number, the Sikhs that choose to wear turbans are highly visible in the wider community, and even quite small children will be aware of their existence. It is important from an early age to explore why people might wear distinctive clothing, and that such diversity is something to be celebrated rather than mocked or feared.

Sikhism is an interesting faith to study, as in some ways it breaks down the usual categories of 'eastern' and 'western' traditions, having some elements in common with Islam as well as its close relationship with 'Hinduism'. The blurred edges between 'Sikhism' and 'Hinduism' lead to a healthy questioning of the validity of such labels.

There are many aspects of Sikhism that lend themselves to reflective learning that will deepen the pupil's own spiritual development, as well as an understanding of Sikhs. Among these are the concept of God in Sikhism (including God's lack of gender), selflessness and service to others, equality of race, caste, gender and religion, the importance of religious freedom and tolerance, the spiritual value of music, pride in identity and courage to stand up for one's beliefs, concepts of life after death, a critique of materialism and an explanation of the current state of the world.

Approaches to Sikhism

It is important to make clear, and especially to reassure parents, that the approach is *non-confessional*, that is, the aim is not to initiate pupils into the Sikh faith. Rather, the aim is to learn *about* Sikhism, in order to *understand* the Sikh view of life and the beliefs and practices of Sikhs. This should not be merely cold factual information, however, but provide an insight into the experiences and feelings of the people being studied. An approach that attempts to be both impartial in description and empathetic in attitude is often referred to as *phenomenological*. Rather than engaging from the start with the truth claims of any tradition, these, together with any preconceived ideas, are put to one side in order to understand what the religion actually is. As this approach respects the self-understanding of the believers, it will also positively value the experience of Sikh children should there be any in the class. For further discussion of the confessional and phenomenological approaches to religious education, see unit C of the module 'Philosophy of Religious Education' in *Religion in Education: volume 1*, pp 255-288.

Religious Education in schools differs from the study of religions in that it is also concerned with the spiritual development of the pupil and with exploring the philosophical and moral issues raised by our shared human experience. In the words of the SCAA Model Syllabi we are not only 'learning about', but also 'learning from', Sikhism. This means that at every stage of education the material from the tradition needs to be related to the experiences, interests and concerns of pupils in order for its relevance to be appreciated. Teachers often underestimate the ability of even the youngest pupils to engage with the philosophical questions posed by the study of religions. Pupils appreciate the opportunity in religious education to be able to express their own opinions on the 'ultimate questions' at the heart of human experience.

Effective religious education needs to use creative and experiential pedagogical methods. Much use can be made of the arts, including pictorial art, artefacts, drama, dance and music. In the case of Sikhism, drama has to be used with care, as it is not thought appropriate by many Sikhs for anyone to act the part of the Gurus.   Visits and visitors can provide direct contact with religious communities.   In addition, many recent resources (videos, interactive CD-ROMs and the Internet) are valuable ways of involving pupils with the tradition.   The term *experiential religious education* usually refers to the provision within the classroom of opportunities for pupils to explore their own emotional and spiritual responses in a direct way through such techniques as meditation, stilling exercises, silent reflection and guided fantasy.   These techniques can be very useful in taking religious education beyond the merely informative and enabling pupils to engage with both the inner experiences of believers and their own personal beliefs and values.   For further discussion of creative and experiential methods, see unit B of the module 'Method in Religious Education' and unit C of the module 'Philosophy of Religious Education' both of which are in *Religion in Education: volume 1.*

It is important to convey to pupils the diversity of Sikhism.   As with other traditions, it is impossible to state that 'all Sikhs' believe this or practise that. 'Sikhism' is really just a convenient shorthand and in some ways a recent 'invention'.   What we are really looking at are the beliefs and values of people, who have their own individual or group interpretations and ideas.

Continuity and progression

There is much debate about the appropriate age to introduce children to faiths other than their own.   Some argue that children should start with what is close to home, the traditions of their family or the country in which they live, which in Britain 'are in the main Christian' (Education Reform Act 1988).   It is said that introducing too many traditions too soon will 'confuse' children.   On the other hand, attitudes are formed very early, so children need to be introduced to the pluralism of beliefs from an early age otherwise they are in danger of forming the notion that Christianity is normative and that any other perspectives are deviant.   People (including infants and their families) do differ in their beliefs and values, and this does not need to be seen as a problem.

There is also debate about whether religious traditions are most effectively studied systematically, one religion at a time, or thematically, focusing on a dimension of religion across several traditions.   There are advantages and disadvantages to both.   For example, the systematic approach may be advocated as a means of studying the religion in its own terms but may be criticised for suggesting that religions exist independently of one another and the wider world.   However, the thematic approach may be recommended as a means of highlighting the connections, both historical and contemporary, between religions but may be accused of distorting the traditions to fit preconceived categories. Obviously, a balance of both approaches has much to commend it.

Where, when and how Sikhism features in a given school syllabus will depend upon the particular syllabus (LEA Agreed Syllabus, Diocesan Syllabus, etc.) being followed and the individual circumstances of the school. Some syllabi leave it up to schools to choose which religions to study at each stage. Increasingly, syllabi produced since 1994 when SCAA brought out the 'Model Syllabi' are becoming more prescriptive in order to ensure that pupils have met all six major world faiths before leaving school. Where this is the case, it is rare that Sikhism is specifically recommended for primary level (for example, Devon recommends Judaism and Hinduism, Somerset recommends Judaism, Hinduism and Islam). On the other hand, few of these syllabi limit study to the featured religions, and there is much to be said for encountering all six religions at least once in the primary years and again at secondary (see Baumfield *et al*, 1994). As such syllabi suggest, different aspects of Sikhism seem appropriate for children at different Key Stages. Having said this, experience also shows that many topics can be addressed at any point as long as the ages and experience of the pupils are taken into account. The following list of possible topics, taken from the SCAA Model Syllabi, The Third Perspective and a variety of Agreed Syllabi, may prove helpful nevertheless.

Key Stage 1

- The ceremony for naming babies.
- The meaning of the names 'Singh' and 'Kaur'.
- The concept of God and importance of always remembering God.
- Greetings - Sat Sri Akal.
- Guru Nanak as a special person for Sikhs.
- Guru Nanak's birthday (October/November).
- Sewa and the importance of helping others.
- The turban, the 5 Ks and traditional women's and children's clothes in topic on clothes/materials.
- Suitable stories from the Sikh tradition (see Bibliography).
- The significance of sharing food in the Gurdwara.

Key Stage 2 (Years 3 and 4)

- The Sikh Gurus as examples of leaders, pictures of the Gurus.
- The festivals of Baisakhi and Divali.
- The story of Guru Hargobind and his cloak.
- The Sikh wedding ceremony.
- The Gurdwara as a place of worship.
- Worship in the Gurdwara and at home, repetition of the 'name' of God.

- Symbols: the nisan sahib, the khandha, ik onkar, the 5 Ks.
- The 5 Ks as a uniform with a meaning.
- The sharing of karah parshad and the langar (food).
- The variety of Sikh music: devotional music in the Gurdwara, contemporary bhangra.

Key Stage 2 (Years 5 and 6)

- The Sri Guru Granth Sahib as a sacred book.
- Calligraphy using Gurmukhi script.
- Sikh identity: the Khalsa and the amrit ceremony.
- The concept of God in the Mul Mantra: God as immanent in all creation and beyond time.
- Special places such as the Golden Temple at Amritsar.
- Stories of courage from the lives of the Gurus.
- Codes for living - Sikh moral precepts.
- The importance of work.
- The concept of reincarnation and ultimate union with God.
- The oneness of the human race.
- Gender equality in Sikhism.
- Stories attacking materialism such as Guru Nanak and the Rich Man (see Palmer and Breuilly, 1994).

Key Stage 3

- The concept of God: formless (nirguna) and timeless, creator of all.
- Concepts central to the Sikh worldview such as samsara, karma, jiva, bhakti, haumai, manmukh, gurmukh, moksha, guru, hukam.
- The ten Sikh Gurus and their teachings. The Gurus as exemplars.
- Commitment to justice: courage, war and peace.
- The Guru Granth Sahib as revelation (gurbani), the significance of non-Sikh contributors, the Dasam Granth.
- Worship in the home and Gurdwara.
- The 5 Ks and the moral precepts of khalsa Sikhs.
- Gurdwaras: architectural style and some famous gurdwaras; pilgrimage.
- Rites of passage: birth, marriage, initiation, death.
- Festivals: Gurpurbs and melas.
- Different movements in Sikhism such as followers of a particular sant.

Key Stage 4

- Material as KS3 if not already covered.
- The concept of God as transcendent and immanent, titles for God.
- The concept of Guru.

- Evil, suffering and death in the world: kal yug.
- Beliefs about life after death.
- History of Sikhism in India and in diaspora.
- The Sikh communities in Britain.
- Varieties of Sikhism and associated groups such as Ravidasis, Valmikis.
- The Gurdwara - organisation.
- Sikh perspectives on personal moral issues such as relationships, sexuality, marriage and the family, medical ethics, drugs and alcohol.
- Sikh perspectives on contemporary issues such as racism, gender, wealth and poverty, work and leisure, crime and punishment, war and peace, ecology and animal rights.
- Sikh perspectives on interfaith dialogue and particular relationships with Islam and Hinduism.
- The Khalistan question.

Depending on which aspects (if any) of Sikhism pupils have encountered previously, elements from the suggestions for earlier Key Stages may need to be incorporated into units of work for older pupils. In addition, although some topics suggest themselves as particularly suited to one age group, most topics can be adapted for any age group. It is important to liaise with the teachers and schools from which pupils come and to which they will be going, in order to avoid the situation where, for example they 'do' the 5 Ks four times, and never have the opportunity to explore the concepts of God and Guru. This can also be useful for sharing scarce resources.

Activity C5

Scrutinise the relevant syllabus and existing school scheme for religious education (and in the primary school, if applicable, general topics) for the potential to teach Sikhism. How far is Sikhism already included? Where could aspects of Sikhism easily be included without too much disruption? Whether or not it is already there, where best would an in-depth systematic study of Sikhism fit?

Construct a rationale to present to a departmental or staff meeting for the teaching of Sikhism in general, and the aspects you have identified in particular, in your own school context.

If you are not currently employed in a school, either make contact with a local school in order to undertake this activity, or obtain an appropriate Agreed or Diocesan syllabus and construct your scheme and rationale for an imaginary school.

Comment on activity C5

This will depend very much on your individual circumstances. Some syllabi are more prescriptive than others and may already identify where Sikhism can be taught. Others have more general requirements that could be satisfied by a selection from a variety of religions. The latter case means more work but also more freedom. If you already have a whole-school scheme, you may need to argue for changes to include, or to increase the amount of, the teaching of Sikhism.

Your arguments for including Sikhism will include those in the introduction above, plus arguments specific to your school such as the presence of Sikh children or conversely the importance of multifaith religious education in an all-white rural school. Even such pragmatic considerations as the recent visit to India by a teacher or parent or your newly acquired knowledge of and enthusiasm for Sikhism may help make the case.

Sample lessons for Key Stage 1

1. Guru Nanak as person special to Sikhs can be introduced through his picture. What sort of a person does he look like? Why do we have pictures of people who are special to us? Do you have such pictures in your home? Draw a picture of someone special to you and/or Guru Nanak. There are several versions of stories about Guru Nanak suitable for this age group (see Grimmitt *et al* 1991; Cole and Lowndes, 1995; Palmer and Breuilly, 1994). Grimmitt (1991) gives a guided fantasy of a journey through a magic river to a special place, to help give children some insight into Nanak's religious experience. This also contributes to the child's own spiritual development, whether or not they can make the connection with Nanak.

2. Guru Nanak's birthday would fit with an autumn term topic of birthdays, leading up to Christmas. The story of Guru Nanak's birth can be found in Palmer and Breuilly (1992, 1994). Compare Sikh celebrations of his birthday with your own birthday celebrations - Sikhs eat together, remember his teaching, sing his songs.. Why do we celebrate birthdays?

3. The Sikh naming ceremony can be compared with other ceremonies known to the children to welcome babies into the world or to their parent's faith community. These can be role played by small groups of children. Sikh children obtain their names by a random opening of the Guru Granth Sahib - they are given a name starting with the same letter as the first word on the randomly opened page. Look at the meaning of some common Sikh names (see Palmer and Breuilly, 1992) and the significance of the names Singh (Lion) and Kaur (princess) given to Sikhs. Do your own names mean anything? Who

chose them and why? Make decorated name cards for your desks or lockers (for youngest children provide templates of their names for them to decorate). If you could change your name, what would you like to be called?

4. The concept of sewa or service of others can be illustrated from Sikh stories such as Nanak and the holy men, Bhai Kananya (see Singh, 1993; Palmer and Breuilly, 1994). Who do we rely on for help? Who might need our help and how can we help them? What can we do to help the poorest people?

5. An appreciation for the diversity of cultural customs can be learned early by examining a variety of clothing, including a Sikh turban and traditional women's and children's clothes. Children will enjoy seeing just how long a turban length is, and seeing one put on, either in real life or on a video, is an unforgettable experience. The colours and textures of women's clothes ('punjabi suit' and shawl or chuni) are attractive to children. What are our own favourite clothes? Do we have special clothes for special occasions?

6. A visit to a Gurdwara could emphasise the impact on the senses - the bright sparkly decoration, the colours, the incense, the music, the taste of karah parshad, the feel of walking without shoes and having to cover your head. A variety of creative arts activities could lead on from the experience.

7. The experience of sharing karah parshad and food in the langar could lead to a discussion of what the sharing of food means. When do we share food? How do you feel when someone shares their sweets with you or when you share your things with them?

Sample lessons for Key Stage 2 (Years 3 and 4)

1. The festival of Baisakhi (April 13) can be celebrated by learning the story of Guru Gobind and the start of the Khalsa (found in Arora, 1987). A drama based on the events can be organised. It is traditional for people to represent the 'panj piare' by dressing up in golden yellow, but it is not appropriate to play the Guru. After learning about the renewal of the Nisan Sahib, children could make their own mini Sikh flags and/or design a flag for their class. Look at how Baisakhi is celebrated in Britain and in the Punjab, where it is also a harvest festival.

2. The Sikh uniform of the 5 Ks can be looked at in relation to other uniforms. What is the meaning to Sikhs of the 5 Ks and why are they important? (links with Baisakhi) The 5 Ks and other Sikh symbols can be explored through a collection of actual artefacts. The CEM/REAP package 'Touch and Learn: Sikhism' is excellent for this. There are 20 cards which follow a pattern of direct encounter with the object and initial guesses, background information on the object and questions relating the object to the children's own experience,

for example Sikhs might wear a miniature kangha, kirpan and khanda round their necks - have you seen other symbols like this? What could you wear round your neck to express what was important to you? If you cannot get hold of this pack, you can make up your own cards following this idea. Having looked at the symbolism of the khandha, you can design your own symbolic badge, or one for the class or school. It is very important to stress that not all Sikhs wear the 5 Ks.

3. The Sikh Gurus as leaders. Discuss the qualities of good leaders, research the lives of the ten Sikh Gurus and their leadership qualities. Discuss the similarities and differences between the Gurus, both in their pictures and their life stories. Which do you admire most?

4. Sikh music, both devotional and contemporary popular music, can be shared with children. This is done in Grimmitt (1991) through the experience of a Sikh boy, Sabjit, who plays music in the gurdwara. What are our favourite songs/tunes? Can we make our own music using Indian drums and cymbals?

5. Most people are more familiar with the Hindu than the Sikh Divali. The same sweets and clay lamps can be made, but the story is that of Guru Hargobind and his cloak (see Richards, 1996). This leads to a discussion of freedom of religion as a human right, and whether everyone who joins in a celebration believes the same thing (think of Christmas). Divali cards based on a Sikh theme make a change. Who else has been imprisoned for their beliefs?

6. *Eggshells and thunderbolts* (see video list) contains a sequence of children simulating a Sikh wedding.

Sample lessons for Key Stage 2 (Years 5 and 6)

1. In the context of other sacred books, children can explore the particular centrality of the Guru Granth Sahib as the Guru for the present age. The ways in which it is honoured (platform, canopy, romallas, chauri, bed, decorations) can be researched. Ideally visit a Gurdwara to see the place of the Guru Granth, or failing that use a video. Make a chauri. Make a special class book including favourite poems, good ideas, prayers if appropriate and decide where/how to keep it to show that it is special. Copy some Gurmukhi calligraphy. Write out and decorate the Mul Mantra.

2. Make and share karah parshad (most children's books on Sikhism give the recipe).

3. Look at the Sikh code of conduct (as in Richards, 1996). Compare it with other such codes. Make up a code of conduct for your classroom. Would classroom rules in a Sikh school be different?

4. Make a 3D picture of the Golden Temple. Engage in a guided fantasy of visiting a special place of your own (see Grimmitt, 1991).

5. Learn Sikh games: Kabadi and Guli Danda in relation to the festival of Hola Mohalla. What has sport and physical fitness to do with religion?

Sample lessons for Key Stage 3

1. Sikh artefacts: a secondary version of Key Stage 2 Years 3 and 4 activity 2 involves giving different artefacts to small groups of students to guess what they might be and then research them from a selection of textbooks. This is more meaningful if before or after this activity pupils explore objects that are special to themselves and why. Another idea is to place a selection of religious and non-religious items in the room and ask pupils to choose one that means something to them personally or fascinates them. Pupils only have to share personal feelings if they want to.

2. Courage (taken from Francis, 1997a; 1997b): look at the lives of the Sikh Gurus focusing on their courageous actions. Make a list of the different sorts of courage exhibited. Imagine arriving at the scene shortly after one of these events. What sort of questions would you ask of bystanders, and what sort of answers might they give you? Think of situations that might arise in the lives of young people of your own age requiring courage. What are the possible reactions, and which exhibit real courage?

3. Discuss examples of inequality and fairness in our society. How does the sharing of karah parshad and langar demonstrate Sikh commitment to equality? What else do Sikhs do to work towards eliminating inequalities? What could schools do to demonstrate their commitment to equality?

4. After a visit to a local Gurdwara, often a building converted from other uses, and after looking at pictures or videos of famous Indian gurdwaras, design a purpose built modern Gurdwara, explaining the significance of every feature. This could be a group activity creating a blueprint or model.

5. Discuss the advantages and disadvantages of distinctive clothes such as school uniforms and football strips, and relate to the concept of the 5 Ks. Look more deeply at the symbolic meaning of the 5 Ks. Francis (1996a, 1996b) has a guided fantasy about the Sikh concept of the Kal Yug - the 'Dark Night of Falsehood'. This could lead to an abstract design symbolising evil, with one or more of the 5 Ks used to combat this evil.

6. Write a postcard home about a Sikh festival as celebrated in India.

7. Design the ideal community (its rules, meeting place, rites of passage etc.) and relate to the concept of the Khalsa (see Mercier, 1993).

8. Having studied the values of Sikhism, make a list of rules for a school run on Sikh principles.

Sample lessons for Key Stage 4

1. Look at the lives of the Gurus from the perspective of political prisoners and the work of Amnesty International.

2. Write a letter from a Sikh father to an unemployed son, bearing in mind Sikh views on the importance of work, the life of Guru Nanak, and other Sikh values.

3. Research the relationship of the Sikh community with Britain, for example the contribution of Sikh soldiers to the two world wars.

4. Explore the complexity of the Sikh concept of Guru. Who or what plays any analogous role in non-Sikh lives or your own?

5. Research Sikh perspectives on moral, social, environmental and philosophical issues. Cole (1991), Francis (1997a, 1997b) and the CD-ROM *Aspects of Religion* will be very helpful for this. Use your research to present a Sikh view in a debate, a poster, a radio or TV broadcast. Note that there may not be one 'Sikh view' on these issues. Explain why Sikh principles may lead to different courses of action, both sincere.

6. Collect newspaper articles illustrating the problems of the contemporary world. Relate this to Guru Nanak's concept of the 'Dark Night of Falsehood' (Kal Yug) as an explanation. What do Sikhs think can be done to put things right?

7. Using the Goodwill Art Service pack of 30 postcards, pupils in pairs can research aspects of Sikh belief and practice. Step 1 is to guess what the picture might be, make a list of questions to ask about the picture, discuss the possible feelings of any people in the picture. Step 2 is to research answers to the questions using the information sheets and available textbooks. This could be used either as an introductory or a revision exercise, and could lead to presentations or display.

Activity C6

Plan a unit of work on Sikhism that will last for at least half a term (minimum 6 sessions). You need to specify the year group, the type of school (county primary, voluntary aided comprehensive and so on) and catchment area. This can be your own school or an imaginary one. Explain how your unit satisfies the requirements of the appropriate syllabus and school scheme of work, including assessment arrangements, statutory or otherwise. You might like to set out a summary of your unit of work in grid form, with headings such as activity, religious content, reference to syllabus, key questions, pupil learning: concepts, skills, attitudes, resources required, differentiation and means of assessment. Then give lesson plans in full.

In order to transcend the mere passing on of information, your unit of work should include at least one activity using each of the following: video, IT, posters/photographs, artefacts, an exercise in silent reflection or guided fantasy, drama or role-play, music and/or dance, creative art or craft work, a story from Sikhism, a visit or visitor and active learning.

How will you assess the planned learning outcomes and how will you evaluate the success of your teaching? If you have an opportunity to trial this unit of work, give an evaluation with ideas for future improvements.

Comment on activity C6

Make sure that all your suggested activities are suitable for the age and level of achievement of the pupils. Provide differentiated materials where necessary for those with special needs or levels of attainment in advance of the rest of the class. Check that all your activities would be acceptable to Sikhs and do not give a misleading or one-sided picture of the tradition, for example have you suggested that all Sikhs are Khalsa, or support the campaign for Khalistan? Check that you have made links wherever possible with the interests and experiences of pupils, and given them an opportunity to reflect upon their own opinions and emotions.

For examination work, make sure you have satisfied both the requirements of the GCSE Syllabus *and* the statutory Agreed/Diocesan Syllabus.

Resources

Key Stage 1/2

Aggarwal, M. (1984), *I am a Sikh*, London, Franklin Watts.
Arora, R. (1987), *Guru Nanak and the Sikh Gurus*, Hove, Wayland.
Arora, R. (1986), *Religions of the World: Sikhism*, Hove, Wayland.
Babraa, D.K. (1989), *Religions through Festivals: Sikhism* (KS 2/3), London, Longman.
Bennett, O. (1985), *A Sikh Wedding*, London, Hamish Hamilton.
Bennett, O. (1990), *Our New Home*, London, Hamish Hamilton.

CEM (1992), *Touch and Learn Sikhism*, Derby, CEM.

Clutterbuck, A. (1990), *Growing up in Sikhism*, (KS 2/3) Harlow, London, Longman.

Cole, W.O. and Lowndes J. (1995), *Guru Nanak*, (KS 1) Oxford, Heinemann.

Cole, W.O. and Sambhi, P.S. (1986), *Baisakhi*, Norwich, RMEP.

Davidson, M. (1982), *Guru Nanak's Birthday*, Norwich, RMEP.

Harrison, S. (1986), *Amardip and Rema: two Sikh children visit India*, London, Macmillan.

Richards, C. (1996), *Sikhism*, London, Nelson.

Singh, D. (1992), *The Sikh World*, Hemel Hempstead, Simon and Schuster.

Singh, R. (1987), *Stories from the Sikh World*, London, MacDonald.

Wood, J. (1988), *Our culture: Sikh*, (KS 1) London, Franklin Watts.

Mainly for Key Stage 3/4

Bennett, O. (1990), *Listening to Sikhs*, (KS 3) London, Unwin Hyman.

Clutterbuck, A. (1990), *Growing up in Sikhism*, (KS 2/3), Harlow, London, Longman.

Cole, W.O. (1991), *Moral Issues in Six Religions*, Oxford, Heinemann.

Emmett, P. (1994), *The Sikh Experience*, (KS3) London, Hodder and Stoughton.

Francis, D. (1996a), *Just a Thought*, London, Hodder and Stoughton.

Francis, D. (1997a), *The Road to Somewhere*, London, Hodder and Stoughton.

Penney, S. (1988), *Sikhism*, Oxford, Heinemann.

Sambhi, P.S. (1994), *The Guru Granth Sahib*, Oxford, Heinemann.

Thorley, S. (1993), *Sikhism in words and pictures*, (KS 2/3), Norwich, RMEP.

For GCSE

Draycott, P. (1996), *Sikhism, a new approach*, London, Hodder and Stoughton.

Sambhi, P.S. (1989), *Sikhism*, Cheltenham, Stanley Thornes.

Readers

For Hinduism

It is difficult to recommend one single book on the teaching of Hinduism. Both Jackson (1990) and Palmer and Breuilly (1992 or 1993) have brief outlines of the tradition for teachers. Another introduction is provided by Kanitkar and Cole (1995). Killingley (1984) and Jackson and Killingley (1988) are more substantial introductions for teachers, with ideas for introducing the religion to pupils.

For Buddhism

Use of material will depend on the age and ability of the children being taught. However, good introductions for teachers are Cush (1990) and Harvey (1990). For recommendations for teaching Buddhism (and other religions) to children try Erricker (1993).

For Sikhism

There is no definitive tome on the teaching of Sikhism in schools. One volume introductions to the tradition often recommended to teachers include:

Cole, W.O. (1994), *Teach Yourself Sikhism*, London, Hodder and Stoughton.

Cole, W.O. and Sambhi, P.S. (1989), *The Sikhs: their religious beliefs and practices*, London, Routledge.

Cole, W.O. and Sambhi, P.S. (1990), *A Popular Dictionary of Sikhism*, Richmond, Curzon Press.

McLeod, W.H. (1997), *Sikhism*, Harmondsworth, Penguin.

Bibliography

For Hinduism

Baumfield, V., *et al* (1994), *The Third Perspective*, Exeter, Exeter University.

Christian Education Movement (nd), *Teaching RE: Hinduism 11- 16*, Derby, CEM.

Copley, T. *et al* (1991), *Forms of Assessment in RE*, Exeter, Exeter University Press.

Cole, W.O. (1991), *Moral Issues in Six Religions*, Oxford, Heinemann.

Cole, W.O. and Lowndes, J. (1995), *Sunshine Religious Stories: Teacher's Guide*, Oxford, Heinemann.

Francis, D. (1996a), *Just a Thought*, London, Hodder.

Francis, D. (1997a), *The Road to Somewhere*, London, Hodder.

Hume, B. and Sevier, A. (1991), *Starting with me*, London, Belair Publications.

Jackson, R. (1990), *The Junior RE Handbook*, Cheltenham, Stanley Thornes.

Jackson, R. and Killingley, D. (1988), *Approaches to Hinduism*, London, John Murray.

Kadodwala, D. (1996), *Hinduism*, London, Nelson.

Kanitkar, V.P. (1994), *Hindu Scriptures*, Oxford, Heinemann.

Kanitkar, V.P. and Cole, W.O. (1995), *Teach Yourself Hinduism*, London, Hodder and Stoughton.

Killingley, D. (ed) (1984), *A Handbook of Hinduism for Teachers*, Newcastle, Grevatt and Grevatt.

O'Donnell, K. (1992), *I Wonder...*, London, Hodder.

Palmer, M. and Bisset, E. (1993), *Worlds of Difference* (new edition), London, Nelson.

Palmer, S. and Breuilly, E. (1992), *R.E.A.L. Infant Teachers Handbook*, London, Collins.

Palmer, S. and Breuilly, E. (1993), *R.E.A.L. Junior Teachers Handbook*, London, Collins.

Palmer, S. and Breuilly, E. (1994), *A Tapestry of Tales*, London, Collins.

For Buddhism

Buddhist Society, *The UK Buddhist Directory* (a regularly updated list of the various monasteries and centres of Buddhism in the UK - available from the Buddhist Society).

Carrithers, M. (1983), *The Buddha*, Oxford, Oxford University Press.

Clear Vision Trust (1994), *Buddhism for Key Stage 2*, Manchester, Clear Vision Trust.

Clear Vision Trust (1996), *Living Buddhism (Buddhism for Key Stage 3)*, Manchester, Clear Vision Trust.

Clear Vision Trust (1997), *Monkey King (Buddhism for Key Stage 3)*, Manchester, Clear Vision Trust.

Cush, D. (1990), *Buddhists in Britain Today*, London, Hodder and Stoughton.

Cush, D. (1993), *Buddhism*, London, Hodder and Stoughton.

Dovey-Latham, H. (1995), *Teaching About World Faiths: curriculum support for teachers*, Wickford, Essex Development and Advisory Service.

Erricker, C. (ed.) (1993), *Teaching World Religions: a teachers handbook produced by the SHAP working party on world religions in education*, London, Heinemann.

Harvey, P. (1990), *Introduction to Buddhism: teaching, history and practices*, Cambridge, Cambridge University Press.

Keown, D. (1996), *Buddhism: a very short introduction*, Oxford, Oxford University Press.

Mascaro, J. (1973), *The Dhammapada*, Harmondsworth, Penguin.

Rahula, W. (1967), *What the Buddha Taught*, London, Gordon Fraser.

Robinson, R., and Johnson, W. (1982), *The Buddhist Religion: a historical introduction*, Belmont, Wadsworth.

SCAA (1994), *Religious Education: model syllabus, model 1 living faiths today*, London, SCAA.

SCAA (1994), *Religious Education: model syllabus, model 2 questions and teachings*, London, SCAA.

Snelling, J. (1987), *The Buddhist Handbook: a complete guide to Buddhist teaching and practice*, London, Century.

For Sikhism

Baumfield, V., *et al* (1994), *The Third Perspective*, Exeter, Exeter University

CEM (1991), *Sikhism, a pictorial guide*, Derby, CEM.

Cole, W.O. (1994), *Teach Yourself Sikhism*, London, Hodder and Stoughton.

Cole, W.O. and Sambhi, P.S. (1989), *The Sikhs: their religious beliefs and practices*, London, Routledge.

Cole, W.O. and Sambhi, P.S. (1990), *A Popular Dictionary of Sikhism*, Richmond, Curzon.

Cole, W.O. and Lowndes J. (1995), *Sunshine Religious Stories: teacher's guide*, Oxford, Heinemann.

Francis, D. (1996b), *Just a Thought Workbook*, London, Hodder and Stoughton.

Francis, D. (1997b), *The Road to Somewhere Workbook*, London, Hodder and Stoughton.

Grimmitt, M., Grove, J., Hull, J. and Spencer, L. (1991), *A Gift to the Child*, Hemel Hempstead, Simon and Schuster.

McLeod,W.H. (1997), *Sikhism*, Harmondsworth, Penguin.

Mercier, C. (1993), An ideal community: a secondary classroom project introducing Sikhism, in C. Erricker (ed.) *Teaching World Religions: a teacher's handbook*, London, Heinemann.

Palmer, S. and Breuilly, E. (1992), *R.E.A.L. Infant Teacher's Handbook*, London, Collins

Palmer, S. and Breuilly, E. (1993), *R.E.A.L. Junior Teacher's Handbook*, London, Collins.

Palmer, S. and Breuilly, E. (1994), *A Tapestry of Tales*, London, Collins.

Singh, G. (1997), Sikhism, in C. Richards (ed.), *The Illustrated Encyclopaedia of World Religions*, Shaftesbury, Element.

Singh, K. (1993), Truthful living and the unity of life: Sikhism in the primary classroom, in C. Erricker (ed.), *Teaching World Religions: a teacher's handbook*, London, Heinemann.

Research Methodology

Research Methodology

Unit A

Research in religious education and church school studies: part one

Professor Leslie J. Francis

University of Wales

Bangor

Contents

Introduction

Aims

After working through this unit you should be able to:

- understand how empirical research has been applied to the fields of religious education and church school studies;
- assess the strengths and limitations of different research traditions;
- critically apply the fruits of research to educational practice.

Overview

Units A and B of this module provide a broad overview of the developments of empirical research traditions in religious education and church school studies from the early 1960s until the present day. Cross-references are made to other units and modules in which some of these traditions are explored in greater depth or with further application. The emphasis in the present unit is on helping the reader to engage with the research methods employed and to test out the strengths and limitations of these methods. Since this unit is concerned with assessing empirical methods more use is made of experience and activities than is general in other units within the series.

The module places empirical research in religious education into an historical framework. Three main periods are identified. The first period, embracing the 1960s, sees a renewed interest in empirical research and is characterised by seven important, but diverse, studies. The second period, embracing the 1970s and 1980s, is characterised as the age of measurement. The third period, beginning in the 1990s, is characterised as the return to qualitative studies. The first two periods are covered in unit A. The third period is covered in unit B.

A1 New era

A new impetus for research in religious education emerged in Britain during the early 1960s, heralded by seven key figures: Harold Loukes, Violet Madge, Ronald Goldman, Kenneth Hyde, Edwin Cox, R.J. Rees and Colin Alves, each of whom published a major study between 1961 and 1967. Each of these authors seems to have worked independently and established a precedent which others followed. The idea of doing research in religious education has to some extent, therefore, been shaped by these early pioneers. We propose to examine each in turn and to invite you to engage with the individual studies.

This new impetus for research in the early 1960s was driven by some very practical concerns. Twenty years after the 1944 Education Act had so firmly embedded religious education within the school curriculum, significant shifts in the social, political, educational, moral, religious and theological climates were raising questions about the appropriateness and effectiveness of this statutory provision (Mathews, 1966).

Harold Loukes

Harold Loukes was reader in education at the University of Oxford when he published his study *Teenage Religion* (1961). The research underpinning this book was conducted in two stages. In stage one Loukes arranged for six schools to tape-record discussions held by 14 year olds in the presence of a class teacher or researcher during ordinary lessons on religious topics. In this way he attempted to catch the authentic and spontaneous voices of young people frankly expressing their own convictions, confusions and struggles.

Recognising that the method employed in stage one may only have captured the views of the more vocal members of the class, stage two was intended to bring out the voices of the other pupils as well. For stage two Loukes selected a number of typical quotations drawn from the recorded discussions. These typical quotations were then submitted to 502 pupils within a further eight schools for their written comments.

On the basis of these data Loukes concluded that in their responses to religious education, 14 year olds were confused rather than hostile, and that they were ambivalent rather than rejecting. As he listened to the voices of these young people, Loukes heard them say that they found the subject matter of religious education interesting and important, but that they found the manner and method of teaching totally boring.

A decade or so later Harold Loukes applied the same basic approach of tape-recording classroom discussions to a separate but related area of the curriculum. The fruits of this project were published in his book *Teenage Morality* (1973).

Between these two studies, Loukes (1965) also employed a more quantitative approach in his *New Ground in Christian Education*. In this study he set out to identify schools in which religious education was thought to be successful, by writing to Local Education Authorities, training colleges and university departments. In this way some 500 schools were nominated. A questionnaire sent to these schools to profile their religious education curriculum elicited a 50% response rate. Then these schools were asked to let some of their pupils complete a questionnaire.

Activity A1

Try to replicate the first method used by Harold Loukes in *Teenage Religion and Values*. Tape-record one classroom discussion on a religious topic. If this is not possible, think through what might have happened. Focus on the following questions.

- What determines who speaks?
- What influence does the teacher or researcher have on what is said?
- Do you hear what the pupils really think or what they want others to believe they think?
- How do you analyse and document what you have heard?
- Would another 'researcher' have heard the same things?
- How objective is the exercise?

Comment on activity A1

You may have come to recognise how important it is to listen to pupils and to give close attention not only to their views, but also to the manner in which and the language through which these views are expressed. At the same time you may have begun to doubt how much this important and valuable part of the educational *process* can really be described as educational *research*. Perhaps you may feel that the whole exercise is too subjective and too selective. But how else could such a broad sweep of information be collected about young people's views?

Activity A2

Try to replicate the second method used by Harold Loukes in *Teenage Religion and Values*. Select something which you have heard young people say about religion, then invite a class of pupils to write their own reactions to and comments about what you have heard. Focus on the following questions.

- How can the pupils be motivated to write?
- Should the pupils be assured of anonymity and confidentiality?
- How much does the exercise become a test of writing skills and vocabulary?
- How much are the pupils trying to please you or to shock you?

- How much are the pupils influencing what each other is writing?
- How honest and frank are the pupils being?
- How do you analyse and document what they have written?
- Would another 'researcher' come to the same conclusion?

Comment on activity A2

You may have come to recognise the value of collecting direct feedback on the subject of religious education by inviting the pupils to write their responses. At the same time you may have begun to doubt how much this important and valuable part of the education *process* can really be described as educational *research*. Perhaps the real problem is to do with the wide range of views expressed and the difficulty of finding a theoretical framework within which to locate those views. And how do we know that a different group of pupils would not have said something quite different? How do we know that a different researcher would not have chosen to highlight different emphases in the pupils' responses?

Violet Madge

Violet Madge was senior tutor at Rolle College of Education when she published her study *Children in Search of Meaning* (1965). The research underpinning this book was less systematic and less disciplined than Loukes' study among teenagers. As a consequence, however, it is even richer in illustrative material. Madge gathered her material in a variety of ways, including observations involving 200 children. She explains her method in the following words.

> Whenever opportunities occurred during my year's secondment, personal observations were made of children engaged in spontaneous activities, but I have also drawn on previous observations made over a period of years. In addition, I have included some observations contributed by parents and teachers, as well as recollections of childhood by adults.

At the beginning of the 1970s Violet Madge published a second book, *Introducing Young Children to Jesus* (1971). In this book Madge examined children's statements about Jesus and on the basis of these statements developed implications for curriculum design.

Activity A3

Try to replicate the method used by Violet Madge in *Children in Search of Meaning*. For a week keep a careful note of your observations of young people in their search for meaning. Note, too, recollections which come to your mind from previous experiences, observations contributed by parents and teachers, and recollections of childhood by adults. At the end of the week organise your material and assess its usefulness.

Comment on activity A3

By the end of the week you were probably amazed at the quantity and diversity of the material you had collected. The problem now remains as to how to sort out what is more valuable in that material and what is less valuable. How conscious have you been of the implicit criteria you have applied when selecting what to record? What implicit theories and models have you applied?

Ronald Goldman

Ronald Goldman was lecturer in educational psychology at the University of Reading when he published his study *Religious Thinking from Childhood to Adolescence* (1964). The research underpinning this book was grounded in a recognised research methodology and a recognised theoretical framework. The framework was provided by Piagetian developmental psychology. The methodology was provided by the clinical interview. What Goldman set out to do was to apply a method and a theory which had already proved useful in other curriculum areas to the field of religious education.

In essence Piaget's research is concerned with the development of cognitive processes, with the way in which the ability to think undergoes qualitative changes during childhood and adolescence. The module on Spiritual and Moral Development in *Religion in Education: volume 2*, pp 137-198, provides much more detail about Piagetian developmental psychology. The theory distinguishes between three developmental stages in thinking which are characterised as pre-operational thinking, concrete operational thinking and formal operational thinking.

The clinical interview technique meant that Goldman interviewed children in depth one at a time following a structured sequence of questions. The interview allowed Goldman to probe the answers given and to test the children's understanding and grasp of what they said.

The conversation in the interviews was driven by two main devices. First, the pupils were asked to listen to three tape-recorded bible stories: Moses and the burning bush, the Israelites crossing the Red Sea and the temptations of Jesus in the wilderness. After each story they were asked probing questions about their understanding of the narratives. For a full appreciation of this part of the research, it is necessary to look at one of the three bible passages used and to examine the questions employed to probe the passage. Here is the way in which Goldman presented the story of the burning bush, not by using a recognised translation of the account in the bible, but by creating his own paraphrase.

> A man called Moses was one day looking after a flock of sheep in a rather lonely place, close to a mountain.
>
> Suddenly an angel appeared to Moses in a flame of fire, out of the middle of a bush. The curious thing was that the fire was burning away, but the bush itself wasn't burnt.
>
> Moses said to himself: 'I must go and look at it closer, to see why the bush isn't burned.' Now when God saw Moses come nearer to the bush, God called out from the middle of the bush, 'Moses! Moses!' And Moses, not knowing who it was calling, said, 'Here I am.'
>
> And God said: 'Come no closer and take off your shoes. You are standing on holy ground.' Then God spoke again and said, 'I am your father's God, and the God of great men like Abraham and Isaac and Jacob.'
>
> Then Moses hid his face, for he was afraid to look at God.

Here are five of the eight questions which Goldman asked about this passage to probe the children's 'religious thinking' about the story. Only answers to the three questions marked with an asterisk were interpreted to assess Piagetian stages of thinking.

> It says at the end of the story that Moses hid his face because he was afraid to look at God.
>
> - Why do you think Moses was afraid to look at God? Any other reason(s)?*
>
> - Should he have been afraid to look at God? Yes/No/d.k. Why?/Why not?
>
> - Would you have been afraid? Yes/No/d.k. Why?/Why not?
>
> Supposing Moses had got over his fear and looked at God.
>
> - What do you think he would have seen?
>
> - What sort of man, face, expression, light, fire, angel?
>
> Why do you think the ground upon which Moses stood was holy?*
>
> - Is God everywhere? Yes/No/d.k/unsure. Then is everywhere holy, or just special places?
>
> - Is this ground holy? Yes/No/d.k./unsure. Why? Why not?

How would you explain the bush burning, and yet not being burnt?

- How do you think such a thing could happen?*

If Moses had been deaf, do you think he would have heard God calling him?

- Why/Why not?

- If there had been other people near, would they have heard God calling Moses?

- Why/Why not?

Second, the pupils were asked to look at three pictures, one at a time, and to answer questions about the pictures. The pictures were used as a 'projective device'. Each picture presented a child of the same sex and age as the child being interviewed. The child being interviewed was then asked questions about the child in the picture. The assumption is that when answering for the child in the picture, the interviewee is answering about himself or herself. The three pictures showed a family going to church, a boy or a girl at prayer, and a boy or a girl looking at a mutilated bible.

Again for a full appreciation of this part of the research, it is necessary to examine the questions employed to probe the picture. Here are some of the questions Goldman posed about the picture showing a boy or a girl praying.

To whom is the boy/girl praying?

What does the boy/girl pray about?

- For *himself*? What does he pray for himself?

- For *others*? What does he pray for others?

- Are there any favourite prayers he says each time he prays?

Why do you think the boy/girl prays?

Is God/Jesus/Spirit ... there in the room with the boy/girl?

If He is, how does the boy/girl know He is there?

- Can he hear God's voice?

- Can he see God in any way?

- Can he feel God in any way?

Does what the boy/girl ask for in prayer ever come true?

- How does he know they do come true?

- Do some of his prayers not come true? Yes/No/d.k/unsure.

- Why do you think some don't come true?

Employing this amount of material in a clinical interview is time consuming. As a consequence Ronald Goldman based his findings on a sample of 200 pupils, ten boys and ten girls within each year group between the ages of six and 17, treating 15, 16 and 17 year olds as one age group.

Using the statistical technique of scalogram analysis, Goldman interpreted the findings of these interviews as evidence for the view that religious thinking develops through an invariant sequence of stages during childhood and adolescence in line with the Piagetian model. This analysis was based on the pupils' answers to just five of the many questions asked in the interviews. On the basis of this analysis Goldman concluded that before the onset of formal operational thinking, occurring from the age of 13 or 14 upwards, religious thinking was seriously restricted.

To understand Goldman's conclusion it is important to be clear about his definition of 'religious thinking'. For Goldman religious thinking means the capability to think logically about religion. The problem Goldman faced in applying this definition was to distinguish between the *processes* of religious thinking (with which Piagetian psychology is mainly concerned) and the *content* of religious thinking (with which theology is mainly concerned). Re-reading Goldman's study, it seems that he valued a liberal theological position more highly than a conservative theological position.

The year after publishing *Religious Thinking from Childhood to Adolescence* (1964) Ronald Goldman published a second book *Readiness for Religion* (1965), which proposed a fresh approach to religious education, based not on scripture but on life themes. This approach was consistent with the findings from his research but could not be logically derived from the research. *Readiness for Religion* was influential in changing the face of religious education in county schools, beginning with the new West Riding Agreed Syllabus (West Riding, 1966).

Goldman's research method stimulated a number of other researchers to build on his pioneering work, applying the same theoretical framework to specific aspects of religious development, including Bull (1969), Brisco (1969), Kingam (1969), Miles (1971), Greer (1972b), Whitehouse (1972), Richmond (1972), Fagerlind (1974) and Morley (1975). For example, Bull (1969) followed the path from religion to morality in his study of *Moral Judgement from Childhood to Adolescence*. Whitehouse (1972) selected the biblical narrative of Zacchaeus, to avoid the emphasis on miraculous events which was present in the three stories used by Goldman, and interviewed 20 first year and 20 fourth year junior pupils from two closely matched county and Roman Catholic schools. Related studies used the clinical interview technique to explore the child's ideas of eucharistic presence (Jaspard, 1971), the priest's occupations (Dumoulin, 1971), themes of resurrection and hell (Darcy and Beniskos, 1971), and the concept of God (Nye and Carlson, 1984).

Activity A4

Make a tape-recording of the narrative of the burning bush in the form in which Goldman used the story. Arrange to conduct clinical interviews with a few young people of different ages, using Goldman's questions. In conducting these interviews it is important to observe the strictest guidelines on child protection and safety and may be wise to obtain parental permission. Reflect on the following issues:

- What are the practical and ethical issues involved in conducting clinical interviews among children and young people?
- How comfortable did the children feel?
- How much does the interviewer influence what the children say?
- How easy is it to disentangle the process of thinking from the content of thinking?
- How much did the *form* in which the story was presented influence the answers to the questions?

Comment on activity A4

You may have become aware how difficult it is to conduct an interview without influencing the way in which the child responds to the questions. You may have noticed how some children will keep talking in order to command and prolong your attention. You may have felt that some children would be overawed by being questioned in this way.

Once you started to use Goldman's narrative you may have noticed how Goldman made subtle changes to the way in which the narrative is recounted in the bible. Did these changes heighten the feeling of the supernatural in the story? Once you started to use Goldman's questions you may have felt that they missed some of the core theological and religious potential within the story. If you wanted to research religious thinking during childhood and adolescence, what questions would you wish to ask?

Responding to Goldman

Goldman's research was not only the most influential study of the 1960s, it was also the most controversial. The debate about Goldman's research included studies by Howkins (1966), Hyde (1968, 1984), Godin (1968), Cox (1968), Langdon (1969), Attfield (1974), Murphy (1977), Roy (1979), Greer (1980b), McGrady (1982), Maas (1985), Gobbel and Gobbel (1986), Petrovich (1988) and Slee (1986a, 1986b, 1990). These studies have criticised Goldman for over-reliance on the Piagetian framework or for misuse of this framework; for distorting the biblical material used to stimulate the interviews or for failing to select a proper range of biblical material; for confusing analysis of stages of thinking with styles of theological preference or for giving unfair preference to a liberal theological perspective; for misunderstanding or misapplying statistical techniques to qualitative data; for failing to demonstrate a sound link between his research findings and curriculum recommendations.

For example, Slee (1986b) examined the two methods of data analysis which formed the basis of Goldman's developmental theory of religious thinking: content analysis and scalogram analysis. She concluded that both methods were subject to grave limitations and weaknesses and cannot substantiate Goldman's theory of religious thinking development. Francis (1979a) suggested that more careful consideration be given to the meaning of the phrase 'the development of religious thinking'. He argued that current use of this phrase disguises three very different notions which he distinguishes as *thinking about religion, thinking religiously* and *thinking in religious language*. Each of these different constructs requires a different research method. Goldman's research, he argued, was concerned solely with thinking about religion and should not be generalised as if it also embraced the other two notions.

A number of empirical studies, working within a range of research traditions, have suggested that primary school children are capable of a much richer and more developed understanding of religious ideas and concepts than those with which Goldman credited them, including Van Bunnen (1965), Gates (1976) and Murphy (1979). Streib (1994) gives attention to the continuing place of magical feeling and thinking in adolescence and adulthood.

Kenneth Hyde

Kenneth Hyde was senior lecturer in divinity at Furzedown College of Education when he published his study *Religious Learning in Adolescence* (1965). The research reported in this book brought quantitative methods to religious education. Hyde developed four pencil and paper tests, concerned with image of God, religious concepts, religious knowledge and attitude towards religion. The attitude towards religion measure contained six sub-scales, measuring attitude towards God, bible, religion, institutional church, and churchgoing. In this way Hyde brought to research in religious education the theories and techniques of social psychology developed for attitude measurement. The point of attitude measurement is that the information reported produces an overall attitude score rather than the percentage responses to individual questions. This issue is discussed in greater detail in unit C of the present module.

From the responses of over 3500 pupils to these tests, Hyde concluded that, while religious attitudes consistently fell over the 11-16 age range, and while girls consistently showed more favourable attitudes than boys, pupils who attended church once a month or more were much less likely to experience erosion of positive attitudes with age, and such erosion as did occur was greatly retarded. Linking his findings together, Hyde concluded that 'religious learning depends significantly on religious attitudes, and attitudes are closely connected with churchgoing'.

Kenneth Hyde's work did not result in significant changes in religious education, but it did influence the future trend of research in that field. In particular Hyde's instruments were subsequently employed by several other researchers, including Miles (1971), Richmond (1972) and Mark (1979). Insufficient researchers, however, used Hyde's instruments for them to become properly established in the field.

Activity A5

Kenneth Hyde's attempt to 'measure' change in religious attitudes between the ages of 11 and 16 rested on his ability to devise questions which worked equally well among 11 and 16 year olds. Draw up a set of questions of your own to do this job. Then discuss these questions with some 11 year olds and some 16 year olds. Listen carefully to their comments on your questions and begin to draw up a list of points to be kept in mind when writing questions to span different ages.

Comment on activity A5

You have probably begun to find that the questions which work best are simple, short and direct, but also avoid patronising the older pupils. How well do simple questions or statements like the following work? 'Do you believe in God?' 'I think religious education is boring.' Having tried out your questions on young people you have probably also come to appreciate how important it is to 'field-test' questions before writing them into questionnaires to be administered to thousands of pupils!

Edwin Cox

Edwin Cox was lecturer in education at the University of Birmingham when he published his study *Sixth Form Religion* (1967). This research also employed quantitative methods, although in a less sophisticated way than Hyde. Edwin Cox's questionnaire set out to gauge opinions rather than to scale attitudes. This distinction is discussed in greater detail in unit B of the present module.

This project, sponsored by the Christian Education Movement, was concerned to discover what the élite group of young people in the second year of the grammar school sixth form thought about the following issues: existence of God, Jesus, life after death, bible, church, religious education, personal religious behaviour and a series of moral behaviours. In total 96 grammar schools contributed up to 25 pupils each, making a total sample of 2276 completed questionnaires.

In his analysis, Cox presented the percentage of pupils holding positive and negative opinions on the various topics and gave extracts from the pupils' more extended responses to open-ended questions to demonstrate how they had come to their conclusions. According to Cox, these findings confirmed the general approval of religious education by pupils, although their answers also indicated a desire for reform. The rich source of quantitative data provided by Cox's study could answer many more focused questions than were containable within his book *Sixth Form Religion*. Two subsequent papers explored the relationship between co-education and religious belief (Wright and Cox, 1967a) and between moral judgement and religious belief (Wright and Cox, 1967b).

The questionnaire which Edwin Cox designed for *Sixth Form Religion* helped to shape a future trend in research in religious education. Two sets of studies are of particular significance.

First, Cox's original data were collected in 1963. Perhaps for the first time he had provided a detailed and accurate map of sixth form opinion on religious matters. Having provided such a map it would be possible to monitor how things were changing over time. Thus, in collaboration with Derek Wright, Edwin Cox's original study was replicated seven years later in 1970. The results were reported in two papers concerned with changes in attitude towards religious education and the bible (Wright and Cox, 1971a) and changes in moral belief (Wright and Cox, 1971b). Both analyses demonstrated that traditional values were changing among sixth-formers. For example, while in 1963 77.3% of the girls and 57.5% of the boys agreed with the statutory provision of religious education, by 1970 the proportions had fallen to 45.6% of the girls and 28.5% of the boys. Such comparisons can, of course, only be made if *precisely* the same questions are addressed to samples constituted in the same way at different points in time. Having mapped the changes between 1963 and 1970 it is perhaps to be regretted that Edwin Cox did not repeat the study again.

Second, Edwin Cox's questionnaire was adapted by John Greer in Northern Ireland. During 1968 Greer administered the questionnaire among second year sixth form pupils attending county and Protestant voluntary schools. The results were reported in his book *A Questioning Generation* (1972a). This enabled a comparison to be made between England and Northern Ireland. Of even greater significance, however, was Greer's determination to replicate his study at ten-yearly intervals, in 1978 and 1988 (Greer, 1980a, 1989). This provides a unique study of change over a 20 year period. In Northern Ireland pupil support for religious education was increasing, not declining over this period. The proportion of boys in favour of statutory religious education rose from 47.1% in 1968 to 54.6% in 1988. The population of girls in favour rose from 63.0% in 1968 to 69.8% in 1988.

The important findings were generated from quite simple but clearly structured multiple choice questions as illustrated by the following example.

> Place a tick against the ONE sentence that MOST NEARLY expresses your own feeling:
>
> 1. There is definitely no life after death.
>
> 2. The soul survives death and is reincarnated in another existence.
>
> 3. After death those who have faith in God through Jesus will enjoy eternal life in heaven and those who do not have faith will go to hell.
>
> 4. Heaven is being with God and hell is separation from God.
>
> 5. After death men are rewarded for the quality of living in this life.

Activity A6

Examine the example questions taken from Edwin Cox and John Greer and write further questions in the same style to reflect your particular interests in young people's religious views. Now try out your questionnaire on a group of young people. When they have filled in your questionnaire ask them to write their comments on how they see your questions or arrange a group discussion on the theme. Then tabulate the findings.

Comment on activity A6

You have probably discovered how difficult it is to write simple clear questions which leave no room for ambiguity or misunderstanding. But once such questions have been developed young people are able to express their opinions clearly and easily.

R.J. Rees

R.J. Rees was researcher at the University College of North Wales, Bangor, when he published his study *Background and Belief* (1967). This research provides a very different perspective on assessing views on religious education. It is, in a sense, a retrospective study. Rees sent questionnaires to 583 third year students at Oxford, Cambridge and Bangor to assess their experience of religious education in the sixth form, alongside a survey of their current religious beliefs and practices. Of the 583 questionnaires sent out, 433 were returned.

The analysis is a simple presentation of statistics enlivened by illuminating quotations from the respondents' answers to open-ended questions. Rees found, for example, that 23% of the students who had attended boarding school and 21% of the students who had attended day school were 'generally bored or resentful of time wasting' in sixth-form religious education, while 49% of boarding school and 48% of day school students had 'enjoyed lessons and particularly valued them for the discussion they included'.

Colin Alves

Colin Alves was lecturer in divinity at King Alfred's College Winchester when he published his study *Religion in the Secondary School* (1968). Undertaken on behalf of the Education Department of the British Council of Churches, this was a project of considerable ambition. The first aim of the project was to discover where religious education was meeting with success and to identify the factors underlying such success. Loukes' list of about 300 schools characterised by successful religious education was complemented by a random list of schools. Altogether 637 schools were invited to participate and 539 accepted the invitation. In 1965 20,000 questionnaires were despatched for completion by the highest ability stream of their fourth formers. Only 13 of the schools failed to return the completed questionnaires. The pupils' questionnaires were scored to rank order the schools, stratified into 12 groups according to three criteria: mixed, boys and girls, large and small, grammar and modern. For the next stage of the project the seven or eight top and bottom scoring schools were identified within each of the 12 categories, and questionnaires were sent to the head teacher and religious education staff. For the third stage of the project a further batch of questionnaires was completed within the top scoring schools by the pupils who had spent longest in those schools (sixth formers in grammar schools and fifth formers in modern schools).

Alves' questionnaire contained a test of pupils' knowledge of the New Testament, pupils' insight into the meaning of New Testament quotations, belief and attitude items about Jesus, the bible and the church rated on a five point Likert scale, items relating to moral choices and questions about personal religious identity and practice.

These data were employed in a number of imaginative ways to explore the correlates of positive pupil responses to religious education. Had the project been conducted a decade later with the advantages of computer-generated multi-variate analyses so much more could have been learnt from the database. One of the main conclusions to which Alves drew attention concerned the importance of geography in shaping responses to religious education. Alves concluded that 'generally speaking the nearer one gets to London the less favourable the attitude to Christianity becomes'. Alves also reported a more positive attitude towards religious education in girls' single sex schools than in boys' single sex schools or mixed schools. Alves' questionnaire has not been taken up by other researchers.

A2 Age of measurement

Some of the pioneering studies of the 1960s had begun to demonstrate the power of quantitative studies in generating insights into religious education and religious development. Hyde, Cox, Rees and Alves had all employed questionnaires which could lead to some kind of quantitative data. Apart from Hyde, however, they had not drawn significantly on the theories and techniques of the developing branch of social psychology known as psychometrics. Greater attention is given to the understanding of psychometrics in unit B of this module.

In essence psychometrics is concerned with the more *precise* measurement of psychological characteristics. There has, for example, been a long history of measurement in the fields of intelligence testing and personality assessment. The 1970s saw the development of a clearer concern to apply psychometric theories and techniques to the areas of religious education and religious development. This movement has continued to the present day.

This section illustrates the application of psychometric approaches to religious education and religious development by concentrating on four main areas. The first area builds on Ronald Goldman's work to measure religious thinking. In the early 1970s John Peatling developed a test known as *Thinking about the Bible*. In the 1990s D. Linnet Smith pioneered an improved measure of religious thinking. The second area builds on a major field in social psychology to measure attitude toward religion. In the early 1970s Leslie

Francis developed a test known as the *Francis scale of attitude toward Christianity* which has subsequently been employed in more than a hundred studies.   The third area concerns religious language comprehension and is illustrated by a test developed by E.B. Turner.   The fourth area builds on James Fowler's theory of faith development and is illustrated by a test developed by Michael Barnes, Dennis Doyle and Byron Johnson.

Thinking about the Bible

Goldman's research raised a number of questions about the correlates of the development of religious thinking, concerning issues like the comparative influence of home background and school curriculum on promoting or inhibiting the development from one stage to the next.   The problem with Goldman's method of the clinical interview is that, since each interview takes so long, it becomes very costly to build up a database of sufficient size to enable the statistical modelling of potential influences.   Peatling (1973, 1974, 1977) proposed an imaginative solution to this problem by developing a criterion referenced multiple choice pencil and paper test, known as *Thinking about the Bible* (*TAB*). This instrument was designed to generate scores on six scales of religious thinking.   Peatling employed the same version of the same three bible stories as Goldman: Moses and the burning bush, Crossing the Red Sea, and the Temptations of Jesus.   After listening to a tape recording of each story, the pupils were presented with a series of four multiple choice questions.   Each question was followed by four possible answers.   The pupils were asked to choose the answer they liked most (to be marked M) and the answer they liked least (to be marked L).

The four possible answers to each question were selected as being representative of four levels of religious thinking, styled as *very concrete, concrete, abstract* and *very abstract*.   These four levels of thinking were arranged in random order.   When scoring the instrument, six scores were produced for each pupil.   In addition to the very concrete, concrete, abstract and very abstract scores, the very concrete and concrete scores were combined to produce a *total concrete* score, while the very abstract and abstract scores were combined to produce a *total abstract* score.

Here are some examples of Peatling's questions posed after listening to the story about the burning bush.

> If Moses had been deaf, do you think he would have heard God calling him?

- God could have restored his hearing, as Jesus did when he healed the deaf.

- Maybe when God calls everyone can hear, even if they are deaf.

- Perhaps this story is about Moses' trying to find some meaning while on the mountain, and he called his discovery 'God'.

- Yes: God was very close to Moses.

Why do you think Moses was afraid to look at God?

- Being confronted with a power that supposedly made man, rules the world, and governs men would frighten anyone.

- God made Moses afraid to look at him.

- Moses felt unworthy; he was a sheep herder, and not a great man, like Abraham.

- Perhaps Moses realised he was not perfect and, thus, a sinner like all men. So when he thought God called him, he was afraid.

Peatling's original study, based on 1994 pupils in the USA, suggested that abstract religious thinking was not attained until later than Goldman's estimate of 14 years two months. Peatling (1976) discussed a similar approach to the assessment of moral judgement.

Activity A7

Examine the example items presented above from Peatling's test *Thinking about the Bible*. Identify which items are designed to score on concrete religious thinking and which items are designed to score on abstract religious thinking. To what extent do you recognise these items as concerned with the *process* of religious thinking, or to what extent do you consider that they also deal with the *content* of religious thinking? How easy would it be for a mature conservative Christian to score as an abstract thinker on Peatling's questionnaire?

Comment on activity A7

You probably found it relatively easy to distinguish between concrete and abstract answers. You may have been puzzled by the distinctions between very concrete and concrete or between abstract and very abstract. You will also have noticed how the answers differ both in terms of length and in terms of theological complexity.

Responding to Peatling

Peatling's *Thinking About the Bible* measure has been reapplied in the USA by Peatling and Laabs (1975), Peatling, Laabs and Newton (1975) and Hoge and Petrillo (1978), in Finland by Tamminen (1976, 1991), in Northern Ireland by Greer (1981a, 1982a), in Eire by McGrady (1990, 1994a, 1994b) and in England, Northern Ireland and Eire by Kay (1981e).

Peatling's measure, *Thinking About the Bible* has been significantly criticised from both conceptual and psychometric perspectives. For example, Greer (1983a) argued that item selection within the forced choice format might be influenced not only by preferences for stages of thinking but also by variability in readability and in theological perspective. He also maintained that, while the test appears to give a useful measure of the level of religious thinking in which *groups* are operating, it does not seem to be a valid indicator of the level of religious thinking revealed by the interview of *individual* pupils. McGrady (1983) argued that the six scales proposed by the instrument to measure underlying developmental constructs both misrepresent Goldman's categories, and quantify the results of the measurement in a manner inconsistent with Piagetian stage theory.

Assessing religious thinking

After reviewing the problems associated with Peatling's attempt to measure religious thinking D. Linnet Smith (1998) proposed a different solution. Her aim was to return to Goldman's original questions used in the clinical interviews and to the examples he produced to illustrate the different stages of thinking. In selecting these examples she was careful to distinguish between theological content and operational level.

Smith's pencil and paper test concentrated on just one biblical narrative, the story of the burning bush. Unlike Goldman she did not write her own interpretation of this story but employed the version presented in the *Good News Bible*. A tape recording of this version of the story was played to the pupils before they were asked to complete the questionnaire.

The questionnaire employed six main questions, derived from Goldman's original study, but rephrased slightly for two reasons. First, the adapted questions were more suitable for a pencil-and-paper test; second, they tried to avoid the assumption that the events described really happened. The questions were as follows.

- The storyteller says that the bush was burning and yet not burnt. Why was this?

- The storyteller says that Moses was told to take off his shoes because he was standing on holy ground. Why was this?
- In the story it says that Moses was afraid to look at God. Why was this?
- Here are some attempts to describe what Moses would have seen if he had got over his fear.
- Here are some answers to the question 'If Moses had been deaf would he have been able to hear God talking to him?'
- These are some answers to the question 'Do you think this sort of experience happens to people today?'

Following each of these questions Smith displayed a range of possible answers. Some of these answers were selected from among those reported by Goldman to represent three levels of thinking (intuitive, concrete and abstract). Other answers were added to allow the pupils the opportunity to reject the story completely or to respond in a conservative but theologically informed way. The pupils were required to register their response to each answer on a three point scale: agree, not certain, and disagree.

After extensive field-testing and careful statistical procedures of item analysis, Smith identified six distinct scales from the pattern of responses the pupils gave to these questions. She then selected the answers which worked most consistently to identify the six distinct scales and reduced each scale to an economical but reliable length. The six scales she defined as measuring:

- intuitive level of thinking (12 items);
- concrete level of thinking (12 items);
- abstract level of thinking (12 items);
- positive thinking (12 items);
- rejection (7 items);
- theological thinking (5 items).

All but the five item scale reached highly satisfactory levels of internal consistency, with alpha coefficients in excess of 0.8.

The scale of *rejection* draws together responses which clearly show that the pupil totally rejects the story. The scale of *theological thinking* draws together responses which represent conservative but theologically informed thinking. The scale of *positive thinking* draws together responses which reflected a positive approach at the abstract level of thinking with the conservative but theologically informed approach to the question. The three scales of *intuitive*, *concrete* and *abstract* thinking demonstrated that a number of the responses identified by Goldman as representing specific stages of thinking cohered in the expected manner. At the same time, other responses identified by Goldman clearly did not function in the way which he predicted.

Having developed these four scales, Smith set out to test their construct validity. In other words, does the test perform as Goldman's theory would predict? According to Goldman's theory the mean score for intuitive thinking should decrease with age, while the mean score for abstract thinking should increase with age. Comparing the responses of pupils over years 7, 8, 9 and 10 Smith found no evidence for either of these claims. Then she compared the mean scores against the frequency of attendance at worship. Here she found a strong relationship between attendance at church and the means for Goldman's so-called different levels or stages of religious thinking. This suggests that, while the test is not measuring different *stages* of thinking related to age, the test is measuring different *styles* of thinking, which are themselves related to personal religious practice.

From her analyses D. Linnet Smith drew the following four main conclusions. First, she concluded that the examples of answers given by children which Goldman claims as representing different stages of cognitive development do not cohere together as well as might have been expected. Reliability analysis of the original sets of answers produced surprisingly low alpha coefficients. In other words, sophisticated statistical analyses did not support Goldman's impressions about the data he collected

Second, however, she concluded that, once refined, Goldman's items can form coherent subgroups which can be used to assess aspects of pupils' thinking about the bible story. In other words, although Goldman's method of identifying responses may not have been all that accurate, his idea was worth pursuing further.

Third, while the subgroups of items can be shown to have content validity, they do not appear to have construct validity. In other words, the subgroups of items clearly describe the forms of thinking Goldman posited, but these forms of thinking do not perform in the way he anticipated. Since the scales do not distinguish between different age groups of pupils they are unlikely to be measuring different *stages* of thinking.

Fourth, while the scales do not show significant correlations with age, they do show significant correlations with church attendance. In other words the instrument appears to be measuring a type or *style* of thinking which is related to a religious component of the pupils' lives rather than to their age and stage of cognitive development.

Here is an example from Smith's questionnaire. In response to the question 'The storyteller says that the bush was burning and yet not burnt. Why was this?' the following answers were offered for the pupils to rate on the three point scale of agree, not certain, and disagree. The answers are not, however, presented in the order in which they occur in Smith's questionnaire.

- The flames could have been God, flames that didn't burn (1).
- Moses was lying when he said that the bush looked as though it was burning (2).
- It could have been a brilliant light with no heat like a light bulb (3).
- God made it not burn; he can do anything (4).
- It might have been imitation flames like bits of red paper on the bush (5).
- It was a flame of goodness, not a burning flame that God put there (6).
- God who created the laws of chemistry could make the bush burn and yet not burn away (7).
- The fire could have been above the bush then the bush would not burn (8).

Activity A8

Examine the examples given from Smith's questionnaire and try to identify which items belong to each of the six scales of:

- intuitive level of thinking;
- concrete level of thinking;
- abstract level of thinking;
- positive thinking;
- rejection;
- theological thinking.

Be aware that positive thinking reuses items already assigned to other scales.

Invite children and adults to listen to the *Good News Bible* version of the story from Exodus 3.1-6 and to record their responses to these eight answers. What do you learn from their replies?

Comment on activity A8

You have probably identified the following grouping of items: intuitive (5, 8), concrete (1, 4), abstract (6, 3), rejection (2), theological thinking (7) and positive thinking (6, 7). Smith (1998) in *Journal of Beliefs and Values* tells you how to obtain the full questionnaire if you want to pursue this instrument further.

Measuring attitudes

During the mid-1970s Francis (1976) advanced a somewhat different critique of Goldman's research. He drew attention to the way in which the link between Goldman's programmes of research and curriculum development hinged on a series of untested assumptions regarding the relationships between pupil attitudes and stages of thinking and between pupil attitudes and curriculum content. This critique led to a new initiative concerned with promoting a series of interrelated studies into the development of attitudes towards Christianity during childhood and adolescence.

This new initiative built on the long established tradition in social psychology concerned with 'attitude scaling'. The idea behind attitude scaling is that deep-seated and relatively stable underlying attitudes are reflected in the less stable opinions which people express. It is the mathematically established pattern between opinions which indicate the directionality and intensity of underlying attitudes.

After reviewing previous research in the area, Francis (1979b) recognised that, while a series of studies had explored aspects of pupil attitudes towards religion in recent years (Garrity, 1960; Jones, 1962; Johnson, 1966; Alatopoulos, 1968; Esawi, 1968; Taylor, 1970; Turner, 1970; Povall, 1971; Lewis, 1974; Westbury, 1975; Russell, 1978), the problem in integrating and synthesising the findings from these studies resulted from the diversity of measuring instruments used. As a consequence, in a paper entitled 'Measurement reapplied', Francis (1978a) invited other researchers to collaborate with him in using the same measuring instrument, the Francis scale of attitude toward Christianity described by Francis (1978b).

This 24-item scale was developed after systematically testing the five different approaches to attitude scaling proposed by Thurstone (1928), Likert (1932), Guttman (1944), Edwards (1957) and Osgood, Suci and Tannenbaum (1957) among different age groups. The Likert method of scaling emerged as the most reliable and robust over the school age population. The items are concerned with the pupils' affective responses to God, Jesus, bible, prayer, church and religion in school, assessed on a five point scale, ranging from *agree strongly*, through *not certain*, to *disagree strongly*. Considerable evidence is now available on the reliability and validity of this instrument during childhood and adolescence (Francis, 1988) and on the influence of different test conditions (Francis, 1979c, 1981). The scale has been modified for use among adults by Francis and Stubbs (1987) and Francis (1992a). Short forms of the instrument have been developed for use among young people (Francis, Greer and Gibson, 1991; Francis 1992b) and among adults (Francis, 1993a). The scale has also been subjected to significant scrutiny and criticism, for example by Greer (1982, 1983b) and Levitt (1995). The scale is not recommended for use among young people under the age of 8 years.

Francis developed his scale of attitude toward Christianity by assembling a pool of 110 items, collected from earlier scales, children's writing and interviews with children. To be included in this pool items had to meet two criteria. They had to be concerned with God, Jesus, bible, prayer, church or religion in school. They had to reflect the affective or evaluative dimension which characterises attitudes. Tests of item analysis were then employed in order to select the 24 items which consistently cohered to form a unidimensional scale. The 24 items eventually selected for the scale are presented below. The items followed by an asterisk are reverse scored.

- I find it boring to listen to the bible*
- I know that Jesus helps me
- Saying my prayers helps me a lot
- The church is very important to me
- I think going to church is a waste of my time*
- I want to love Jesus
- I think church services are boring*
- I think people who pray are stupid*
- God helps me to lead a better life
- I like to learn about God very much
- God means a lot to me
- I believe that God helps people
- Prayer helps me a lot
- I know that Jesus is very close to me
- I think praying is a good thing
- I think the bible is out of date*
- I believe that God listens to prayers
- Jesus doesn't mean anything to me*
- God is very real to me
- I think saying prayers does no good*
- The idea of God means much to me
- I believe that Jesus still helps people
- I know that God helps me
- I find it hard to believe in God*

In the published version of this scale each item is followed by the pattern of letters: AS A NC D DS which are defined as *agree strongly, agree, not certain, disagree* and *disagree strongly*. Respondents are asked to circle one letter against each item. The scale is scored by counting AS as 5 and DS as 1, except in the case of the asterisked items where the scoring is reversed.

Activity A9

Copy the Francis scale of attitude toward Christianity into a questionnaire and invite at least two classes of pupils to complete the questionnaire. Try to find classes of different age groups. Now calculate the scale score for each pupil.

Compare the average scores for boys and for girls. Compare the average scores of different age groups.

Comment on activity A9

You are likely to have found that older pupils record a lower average score than younger pupils and that girls record a higher average score than boys.

Locating attitudes

The Francis scale of attitude toward Christianity has now been employed in upwards of 100 published studies which integrate to provide a cumulative picture of the personal, social and contextual factors relating to attitudes toward Christianity during childhood and adolescence. These studies fall into seven main groups (Francis, 1993b).

First, a series of descriptive studies has charted how attitudes toward Christianity change as children grow up, how attitudes differ between boys and girls, and how the situation varies between different cultures. Examples of such studies are provided in England (Francis, 1989a), Scotland (Gibson, 1989b), Northern Ireland (Francis and Greer, 1990a), Kenya (Fulljames and Francis, 1987b) and Nigeria (Francis and McCarron, 1989). Other studies have extended the jigsaw into Catholic schools in England (Francis, 1987b), Scotland (Gibson and Francis, 1989) and Northern Ireland (Greer and Francis, 1991).

Second, a series of studies has been conducted throughout the same schools at four yearly intervals since 1974. Such replication allows careful monitoring of how the young person's response to Christianity is changing over time (Francis, 1989b, 1989c, 1992c).

Third, several studies have concentrated on identifying the character and influence of denominational schools, at primary (Francis, 1984, 1986a, 1987a) and secondary level (Francis and Carter, 1980; Francis, 1986b; Long, 1989; Francis and Greer, 1990b). Boyle (1984) explored the relative influence of Catholic middle and secondary schools among 12 year olds.

Fourth, a group of studies has focused specifically on the influence of home and parents. Gibson, Francis and Pearson (1990) and Francis, Pearson and Lankshear (1990) isolated the role of social class. Francis and Gibson (1993a) isolated the relative influence of mothers and fathers on sons and daughters at two different stages in development. Kay (1981a) explored the relationship between parental marital happiness and their children's attitudes toward religion. Francis, Gibson and Lankshear (1991) charted the influence of Sunday school attendance.

A fifth set of studies has modelled the influence of personality on individual differences in religious development, including the function of neuroticism (Francis, Pearson, Carter and Kay, 1981a; Francis, Pearson and Kay, 1983a; Francis and Pearson, 1991), extraversion (Francis, Pearson, Carter and Kay, 1981b; Francis, Pearson and Kay, 1983b; Francis and Pearson, 1985a) and psychoticism (Kay, 1981b; Francis and Pearson, 1985b; Francis, 1992d). Francis, Pearson and Kay (1983c, 1988) and Pearson and Francis (1989) explored the relationship between religiosity and lie scale scores or truthfulness. Francis and Pearson (1987) charted the role of religion in the development of empathy during adolescence. Pearson, Francis and Lightbown (1986) modelled the relationship between religion and impulsivity and venturesomeness during adolescence. Other studies in this tradition are exampled by Francis, Pearson and Stubbs (1985), Francis and Pearson (1988), Francis, Lankshear and Pearson (1989) and Francis and Montgomery (1992).

A sixth set of studies has explored the relationship between attitudes toward Christianity and attitudes toward science, giving particular attention to the ideas of scientism and creationism (Fulljames and Francis, 1987a, 1988; Francis, Gibson and Fulljames, 1990; Fulljames, Gibson and Francis, 1991; Francis, Fulljames and Gibson, 1992; Fulljames, 1996).

Other studies have employed the attitude scale to explore issues like the religious significance of denominational identity (Francis, 1990; Francis and Greer, 1999), the impact of popular religious television (Francis and Gibson, 1992), the influence of pop culture (Francis and Gibson, 1993b), the contribution of conversion experiences (Kay, 1981c) or religious experiences (Greer and Francis, 1992; Francis and Greer, 1993), the relationship between religion and prejudice (Greer, 1985), the impact of teaching world religions on adolescent attitude toward Christianity (Kay, 1981d), and the relationship between religion and just world beliefs (Crozier and Joseph, 1997), schizotypal traits (Diduca and Joseph, 1997), altruism (Eckert and Lester, 1997), intelligence (Francis, 1998), psychological wellbeing (Francis, Jones and Wilcox, 1997), happiness (Robbins and Francis, 1996; Francis and Lester, 1997), gender orientation (Francis and Wilcox, 1996, 1998), social desirability (Gillings and Joseph, 1996), self-esteem (Jones and Francis, 1996), personality type (Jones and Francis, 1999), the transition to formal operational thinking (Kay, Francis and Gibson, 1996), obsessionality (Lewis, 1996) and life satisfaction (Lewis, 1998).

Religious language comprehension

Turner (1978) set out to develop a standardised test of religious language comprehension. He argues that vocabulary gives a good estimate of capacity for conceptual thought. Although the complexity of the relationship between language and thought is very evident in relation to religious ideas, Turner suggests that a carefully constructed test of religious language may be a suitable means of assessing the understanding of religious concepts.

Drawing on the wider field of research concerned with language and formation, Turner argues that it is by means of words that many abstract concepts are developed which can be utilised in the absence of exemplars. This is important in respect of religious concepts which often have no physical referents at all and must be explicated in terms of distinctive words and phrases.

According to Turner, one of the best ways of assessing the understanding of religious ideas would be a carefully constructed test using biblical words. While it would not be legitimate to equate biblical language with religious concepts, it would be reasonable to suggest that a good knowledge of biblical language is evidence that religious concepts are well developed.

Turner began by identifying a pool of 130 words which had 'acquired specific biblical-theological meaning' from two bible dictionaries. Each word was presented to the pupils on an individual card in individual interviews, and they were asked for explanations. Some words were presented without specifying a context. The word 'parable' came into this category. Other words were presented in the context of verses cited from the *Revised Standard Version* of the bible. The word 'bread' came into this category, since the biblical context was necessary to make the metaphorical significance of the word clear. Following the model used in some tests of mental ability, Turner adopted a dichotomous scoring system for the answers: *right* or *wrong*.

In order to be able to grade the words in terms of difficulty, Turner specified criteria by which a correct answer could be judged. For example, 'bread' was defined by many pupils as 'something you eat', while others said, 'He gives us our food and all.' Some answers indicated an understanding of Christ as the sustainer of both physical and spiritual life and noted a relevance to the eucharist. Turner's criteria accepted the 'insightful' answers as correct and gave no credit for literalism.

Methods of item analysis were used to identify the best forty items for the test. Twenty items were selected from the 'quotations' list and twenty items were selected from the 'words' list. Here are five examples from each of the two lists:

- resurrection;
- prophet;
- confession;
- baptise;
- parable;
- lamp (Thy word is a *lamp* to my feet and a light to my path);
- bread (The Jews then murmured at him, because he said, 'I am the *bread* which came down from heaven');
- adoption (God sent forth his Son, so that we might receive *adoption* as sons);
- fear (Now therefore *fear* the Lord and serve him in sincerity and in faithfulness);
- height (He looked down from his holy *height*, from heaven the Lord looked at the earth).

Activity A10

Examine the examples given from Turner's test of religious language and develop your own list alongside these examples. Write these words and quotations on individual cards. Try out Turner's list and your list among some young people and among some adults. Tape record the answers. How easy is it to decide whether the answers are 'correct' or 'incorrect'. Invite colleagues to listen to the recorded answers, provided you have permission to do this from the people you interviewed. See how closely your judgements about the answers agree with their judgements.

Comment on activity A10

You may have found Turner's method a helpful way of distinguishing between pupils who have a good grasp of religious language and pupils who do not. A large number of words is necessary to make sure that what is being tested is the wider field of *religious language* and not merely whether the pupils recognise a small number of words used in a religious context. It is easier to be clear about the definition of some words than about the definition of other words. The extent to which different assessors reach the same judgement about whether or not a given definition should be counted as correct provides an indication of how reliable the test is in practice.

Turner's standardised test of religious language comprehension has also been used in studies by Turner (1980) and by Jamison (1989).

Assessing faith stages

Just as Goldman attempted to identify stages in religious thinking by means of the structured clinical interview, so James Fowler (1981) attempted to identify stages in faith development by means of structured interviews. A fuller discussion of Fowler's theory of faith development is provided in *Religion in Education: volume 2* pp 148-168.

Fowler's view of faith development attempts to synthesise seven aspects which he defines as *form of logic, perspective taking, form of moral judgement, social awareness, relation to authority, form of world-coherence* and *symbolic function*. On the basis of the detailed coding and scoring of faith development interviews, Fowler defined six stages and a pre-stage. He defined the stages as follows: stage zero, *primal faith*; stage one, *intuitive-projective faith*; stage two, *mythic-literal faith*; stage three, *synthetic-conventional faith*; stage four, *individuative-reflective faith*; stage five, *conjunctive faith*; stage six, *universalising faith*. By the time *Stages of Faith* was published in 1981, 359 interviews had been conducted.

Fowler's faith development interviewing technique has been used by a number of other researchers, like Leavey and Hetherton (1988). The underlying theory has been used to influence the churches' approaches to Christian education (Astley, 1991), pastoral counselling (Droege, 1984), ministry among the mentally retarded (Schurter, 1987), work with older adults (Shulik, 1988), campus ministry (Chamberlain, 1979) and pastoral care (Fowler, 1987).

In view of its wide application, Fowler's theory has been subject to theological and psychological scrutiny. Some theologians would argue that what Fowler means by faith is not what their religious tradition means by faith. Some psychologists would argue that Fowler's method of research fails to establish empirically that the seven aspects of faith cohere into a meaningful structure, that there are in fact six distinct forms or styles of faith (or seven including primal faith), or that these styles of faith necessarily unfold in a stage sequence. Further helpful commentary on faith development theory is provided in collections of essays edited by Dykstra and Parks (1986), Astley and Francis (1992) and Fowler, Nipkow and Schweitzer (1992).

Just as Peatling (1973, 1974, 1977) tried to translate Goldman's theory into a pencil-and-paper test, so Barnes, Doyle and Johnson (1989) attempted to develop a paper-and-pencil test to assess Fowler's model of faith stages. They produced a simple instrument inviting respondents to make a forced-choice selection among nine sets of paired statements. The test was designed to distinguish between the faith stages most likely to be represented among the population on which their study was based. This population comprised two groups: 275 members of the College Theology Society (a largely Catholic group of college teachers of theology and religious studies) and 304 members of a Catholic parish in Dayton, Ohio.

In developing this scale Barnes, Doyle and Johnson took the view that statements devised to reflect different aspects of the same stage of faith development ought to be selected by the same respondents a high percentage of the time. They also recognised that their cross-sectional survey was not able to test Fowler's claim that these different forms of faith are really 'stages' appearing sequentially in the life of an individual, as that would properly require a longitudinal study. Consequently they prefer to speak in terms of faith 'styles' rather than in terms of faith 'stages'.

Their instrument concentrated on measuring stages two through five, with the main emphasis on stages three through five as the style most typical of adults, according to Fowler's own work. There were nine faith-style items in all, each a set of paired statements. The respondents were asked to choose between the two statements of each pair by using a Likert-type scale: A a ? b B. Those who chose 'A' or 'a' were scored as agreeing with the first statement, and those who chose 'b' or 'B' were scored as agreeing with the second statement. In each case the respondents were given a choice between statements designed to represent different styles of faith.

The statements were devised to represent three aspects of each style, as a way of testing for the internal coherence of each style. The style two person was characterised as finding relatively little coherent logic to larger sequences of life's events, as equalling power with authority, and as seeing interpersonal relations as a series of deals made between people. The style three person was characterised as displaying concern for loyalty to a leader, as showing concern for conformity to group standards, and as preferring a fairly literal storytelling way of understanding doctrines. The style four person was characterised as adopting a universalist outlook concerned to relate all aspects of reality together, as valuing an overall coherence of beliefs in a fairly logical way, and as displaying a sense of adherence to objectively valid norms rather than just to their own group standards. The style five person was characterised as appreciating the tentativeness of all standards, as displaying openness and flexibility of belief and tolerance of differences, and as valuing general human wellbeing over all other standards.

On the grounds that, according to Fowler's findings, few adults would consistently choose style two statements, Barnes, Doyle and Johnson included only three style two items, just to identify and control for those who would select responses for other styles at random when no style two option was given. There were five statements each for style three, style four, and style five. Faith style groups were formed of those respondents who had chosen any given category of answer at least four times out of the five possible (or two times out of three for faith style two).

Here are some examples of the questions developed by Barnes, Doyle and Johnson.

1. A Those who do what God wants are given special rewards.
    B God grants comfort and strength to those who are loyal and faithful.
2. A A good way to relate to God is to do what God wants, so that God will help you in return.
    B It is best to think of God as utterly and freely giving.
3. A Following Christ with loving devotion is more important than having a thorough and correct understanding of true doctrine.
    B It is important to reflect on one's beliefs to make them reasonable and logically coherent.
4. A God's revealed truth is meant for all people everywhere.
    B No set of religious beliefs is the whole and final truth for everyone.

Activity A11

Examine the examples given from Barnes, Doyle and Johnson's list of faith style items. Within these eight statements they would claim to have two items representing each of the four faith styles. Drawing on their definitions of the characterisation of the four styles identify the statements representative of each style. Using the same definitions develop statements of your own. Pair these statements in the same way as in the original scale and test them out among a sample of people. Do people tend to select statements which show a consistent preference for the same range of faith styles? How do people feel about being presented with forced-choice comparisons in this way?

Comment on activity A11

According to the test constructors faith style two is represented by statements 1A and 2A, faith style three by statements 1B and 3A, faith style four by statements 3B and 4A, and faith style five by statements 2B and 4B.

Readers

Francis, L.J., Kay, W.K. and Campbell, W.S. (eds) (1996), *Research in Religious Education*, Leominster, Gracewing.

Bibliography

Alatopoulos, C.S. (1968), A study of relationship between religious knowledge and certain social and moral attitudes among school leavers, Unpublished M.Phil. dissertation, University of London.

Alves, C. (1968), *Religion and the Secondary School*, London, SCM.

Astley, J. (ed.) (1991), *How Faith Grows: faith development and Christian Education*, London, National Society and Church House Publishing.

Astley, J. and Francis, L.J. (eds) (1992), *Christian Perspectives on Faith Development: a reader*, Leominster, Fowler Wright and Grand Rapids, Michigan, Eerdmans.

Attfield, D. (1974), A fresh look at Goldman: the research needed today, *Learning for Living*, 14, 44-49.

Barnes, M., Doyle, D. and Johnson, B. (1989), The formulation of a Fowler scale: an empirical assessment among Catholics, *Review of Religious Research*, 30, 412-420.

Boyle, J.J. (1984), Catholic children's attitudes towards Christianity, Unpublished M.Sc. dissertation, University of Bradford.

Brisco, H. (1969), A study of some aspects of the special contribution of Church of England aided primary schools to children's development, Unpublished M.Ed. dissertation, University of Liverpool.

Bull, N.J. (1969), *Moral Judgement from Childhood to Adolescence*, London, Routledge and Kegan Paul.

Chamberlain, G.L. (1979), Faith development and campus ministry, *Religious Education*, 74, 314-324.

Cox, E. (1967), *Sixth Form Religion*, London, SCM.

Cox, E. (1968), Honest to Goldman: an assessment, *Religious Education*, 63, 424-428.

Crozier, S. and Joseph, S. (1997), Religiosity and sphere-specific just world beliefs in 16- to 18-year olds, *Journal of Social Psychology*, 137, 510-513.

Darcy, F. and Beniskos, J.M. (1971), Some people say: the themes of resurrection and hell as perceived by 6 to 8 year old children receiving religious instruction, *Lumen Vitae*, 26, 449-460.

Diduca, D. and Joseph, S. (1997), Schizotypal traits and dimensions of religiosity, *British Journal of Clinical Psychology*, 36, 635-638.

Droege, T.A. (1984), Pastoral counselling and faith development, *Journal of Psychology and Christianity*, 3, 4, 37-47.

Dumoulin, A. (1971), The priest's occupations as perceived by 6-12 year old children, *Lumen Vitae*, 26, 316-332.

Dykstra, C. and Parks, S. (eds) (1986), *Faith Development and Fowler*, Birmingham, Alabama, Religious Education Press.

Eckert, R.M. and Lester, D. (1997), Altruism and religiosity, *Psychological Reports*, 81, 562.

Edwards, A.L. (1957), *Techniques of Attitude Scale Construction*, New York, Appleton-Century-Crofts.

Esawi, A.R.M. (1968), Ethico-religious attitudes and emotional adjustment in children aged 11-18 years, Unpublished Ph.D. dissertation, University of Nottingham.

Fagerlind, T. (1974), Research on religious education in the Swedish school system, *Character Potential*, 7, 38-47.

Fowler, J.W. (1981), *Stages of Faith: the psychology of human development and the quest for meaning*, San Francisco, Harper and Row.

Fowler, J.W. (1987), *Faith Development and Pastoral Care*, Philadelphia, Fortress Press.

Fowler, J.W., Nipkow, K.E. and Schweitzer, F. (1992), *Stages of Faith and Religious Development*, London, SCM.

Francis, L.J. (1976), An enquiry into the concept 'readiness for religion', Unpublished Ph.D. dissertation, University of Cambridge.

Francis, L.J. (1978a), Measurement reapplied: research into the child's attitude towards religion, *British Journal of Religious Education*, 1, 45-51.

Francis, L.J. (1978b), Attitude and longitude: a study in measurement, *Character Potential*, 8, 119-130.

Francis, L.J. (1979a), Research and the development of religious thinking, *Educational Studies*, 5, 109-115.

Francis, L.J. (1979b), The child's attitude towards religion: a review of research, *Educational Research*, 21, 103-108.

Francis, L.J. (1979c), The priest as test administrator in attitude research, *Journal for the Scientific Study of Religion*, 18, 78-81.

Francis, L.J. (1981), Anonymity and attitude scores among ten and eleven year old children, *Journal of Experimental Education*, 49, 74-76.

Francis, L.J. (1984), Roman Catholic schools and pupil attitudes in England, *Lumen Vitae*, 39, 99-108.

Francis, L.J. (1986a), Denominational schools and pupil attitude towards Christianity, *British Educational Research Journal*, 12, 145-152.

Francis, L.J. (1986b), Roman Catholic secondary schools: falling rolls and pupil attitudes, *Educational Studies*, 12, 119-127.

Francis, L.J. (1987a), *Religion in the Primary School: partnership between church and state?* London, Collins Liturgical Publications.

Francis, L.J. (1987b), Measuring attitudes towards Christianity among 12- to 18-year-old pupils in Catholic schools, *Educational Research*, 29, 230-233.

Francis, L.J. (1988), The development of a scale of attitude towards Christianity among 8-16 year olds, *Collected Original Resources in Education*, 12, fiche 1, A04.

Francis, L.J. (1989a), Measuring attitude towards Christianity during childhood and adolescence, *Personality and Individual Differences*, 10, 695-698.

Francis, L.J. (1989b), Drift from the churches: secondary school pupils' attitudes toward Christianity, *British Journal of Religious Education*, 11, 76-86.

Francis, L.J. (1989c), Monitoring changing attitudes towards Christianity among secondary school pupils between 1974 and 1986, *British Journal of Educational Psychology*, 59, 86-91.

Francis, L.J. (1990), The religious significance of denominational identity among eleven year old children in England, *Journal of Christian Education*, 97, 23-28.

Francis, L.J. (1992a), Reliability and validity of the Francis scale of attitude towards Christianity (adult), *Panorama*, 4, 1, 17-19.

Francis, L.J. (1992b), Reliability and validity of a short measure of attitude towards Christianity among nine to eleven year old pupils in England, *Collected Original Resources in Education*, 16, 1, fiche 3, A02.

Francis, L.J. (1992c), Monitoring attitudes toward Christianity: the 1990 study, *British Journal of Religious Education*, 14, 178-182.

Francis, L.J. (1992d), Is psychoticism really a dimension of personality fundamental to religiosity? *Personality and Individual Differences*, 13, 645-652.

Francis, L.J. (1993a), Reliability and validity of a short scale of attitude towards Christianity among adults, *Psychological Reports*, 72, 615-618.

Francis, L.J. (1993b), Attitudes towards Christianity during childhood and adolescence: assembling the jigsaw, *The Journal of Beliefs and Values*, 14, 2, 4-6.

Francis, L.J. (1998), The relationship between intelligence and religiosity among 15 to 16 year olds, *Mental Health, Religion and Culture*, 1, 185-196.

Francis, L.J. and Carter, M. (1980), Church aided secondary schools, religious education as an examination subject and pupil attitudes towards religion, *British Journal of Educational Psychology*, 50, 297-300.

Francis, L.J., Fulljames, P. and Gibson, H.M. (1992), Does creationism commend the gospel? a developmental study among 11-17 year olds, *Religious Education*, 87, 19-27.

Francis, L.J. and Gibson, H.M. (1992), Popular religious television and adolescent attitudes towards Christianity, in J. Astley and D.V. Day (eds), *The Contours of Christian Education*, pp 369-381, Great Wakering, McCrimmons.

Francis, L.J. and Gibson, H.M. (1993a), Parental influence and adolescent religiosity: a study of church attendance and attitude toward Christianity among adolescents 11 to 12 and 15 to 16 years old, *International Journal for the Psychology of Religion*, 3, 241-253.

Francis, L.J. and Gibson, H.M. (1993b), Television, pop culture and the drift from Christianity during adolescence, *British Journal of Religious Education*, 15, 31-37.

Francis, L.J., Gibson, H.M. and Fulljames, P. (1990), Attitude towards Christianity, creationism, scientism and interest in science among 11-15 year olds, *British Journal of Religious Education*, 13, 4-17.

Francis, L.J., Gibson, H.M. and Lankshear, D.W. (1991), The influence of Protestant Sunday Schools on attitude towards Christianity among 11-15 year olds in Scotland, *British Journal of Religious Education*, 14, 35-42.

Francis, L.J. and Greer, J.E. (1990a), Measuring attitudes towards Christianity among pupils in Protestant secondary schools in Northern Ireland, *Personality and Individual Differences*, 11, 853-856.

Francis, L.J. and Greer, J.E. (1990b), Catholic schools and adolescent religiosity in Northern Ireland: shaping moral values, *Irish Journal of Education*, 24, 2, 40-47.

Francis, L.J. and Greer, J.E. (1993), The contribution of religious experience to Christian development: a study among fourth, fifth and sixth year pupils in Northern Ireland, *British Journal of Religious Education*, 15, 38-43.

Francis, L.J. and Greer, J.E. (1999), Attitude toward Christianity among secondary pupils in Northern Ireland: persistence of denominational differences? *British Journal of Religious Education*, 21, 175-180.

Francis, L.J., Greer, J.E. and Gibson, H.M. (1991), Reliability and validity of a short measure of attitude towards Christianity among secondary school pupils in England, Scotland and Northern Ireland, *Collected Original Resources in Education*, 15, 3, fiche 2, G09.

Francis, L.J., Jones, S.H. and Wilcox, C. (1997), Religiosity and dimensions of psychological well-being among 16-19 year olds, *Journal of Christian Education*, 40, 1, 15-20.

Francis, L.J., Lankshear, D.W. and Pearson, P.R. (1989), The relationship between religiosity and the short form JEPQ (JEPQ-S) indices of E, N, L and P among eleven year olds, *Personality and Individual Differences*, 10, 763-769.

Francis, L.J. and Lester, D. (1997), Religion, personality and happiness, *Journal of Contemporary Religion*, 12, 81-86.

Francis, L.J. and McCarron, M.M. (1989), Measurement of attitudes towards Christianity among Nigerian secondary school students, *Journal of Social Psychology*, 129, 569-571.

Francis, L.J. and Montgomery, A. (1992), Personality and attitudes towards Christianity among eleven to sixteen year old girls in a single sex Catholic school, *British Journal of Religious Education*, 14, 114-119.

Francis, L.J. and Pearson, P.R. (1985a), Extraversion and religiosity, *Journal of Social Psychology*, 125, 269-270.

Francis, L.J. and Pearson, P.R. (1985b), Psychoticism and religiosity among 15 year olds, *Personality and Individual Differences*, 6, 397-398.

Francis, L.J. and Pearson, P.R. (1987), Empathic development during adolescence: religiosity the missing link? *Personality and Individual Differences*, 8, 145-148.

Francis, L.J. and Pearson, P.R. (1988), Religiosity and the short-scale EPQ-R indices of E, N and L, compared with the JEPI, JEPQ and EPQ, *Personality and Individual Differences*, 9, 653-657.

Francis, L.J. and Pearson, P.R. (1991), Religiosity, gender and the two faces of neuroticism, *Irish Journal of Psychology*, 12, 60-68.

Francis, L.J., Pearson, P.R., Carter, M. and Kay, W.K. (1981a), The relationship between neuroticism and religiosity among English 15- and 16-year olds, *Journal of Social Psychology*, 114, 99-102.

Francis, L.J., Pearson, P.R., Carter, M. and Kay, W.K. (1981b), Are introverts more religious? *British Journal of Social Psychology*, 20, 101-104.

Francis, L.J., Pearson, P.R. and Kay, W.K. (1983a), Neuroticism and religiosity among English school children, *Journal of Social Psychology*, 121, 149-150.

Francis, L.J., Pearson, P.R. and Kay, W.K. (1983b), Are introverts still more religious? *Personality and Individual Differences*, 4, 211-212.

Francis, L.J., Pearson, P.R. and Kay, W.K. (1983c), Are religious children bigger liars? *Psychological Reports*, 52, 551-554.

Francis, L.J., Pearson, P.R. and Kay, W.K. (1988), Religiosity and lie scores: a question of interpretation, *Social Behaviour and Personality*, 16, 91-95.

Francis, L.J., Pearson, P.R. and Lankshear, D.W. (1990), The relationship between social class and attitude towards Christianity among ten and eleven year old children, *Personality and Individual Differences*, 11, 1019-1027.

Francis, L.J., Pearson, P.R. and Stubbs, M.T. (1985), Personality and religion among low ability children in residential special schools, *British Journal of Mental Subnormality*, 31, 41-45.

Francis, L.J. and Stubbs, M.T. (1987), Measuring attitudes towards Christianity: from childhood into adulthood, *Personality and Individual Differences*, 8, 741-743.

Francis, L.J. and Wilcox, C. (1996), Religion and gender orientation, *Personality and Individual Differences*, 20, 119-121.

Francis, L.J. and Wilcox, C. (1998), Religiosity and femininity: do women really hold a more positive attitude toward Christianity? *Journal for the Scientific Study of Religion*, 37, 462-469.

Fulljames, P. (1996), Science, creation and Christianity: a further look, in L.J. Francis, W.K. Kay and W.S. Campbell (eds), *Research in Religious Education*, pp 257-266, Leominster, Gracewing.

Fulljames, P. and Francis, L.J. (1987a), Creationism and student attitudes towards science and Christianity, *Journal of Christian Education*, 90, 51-55.

Fulljames, P. and Francis, L.J. (1987b), The measurement of attitudes toward Christianity among Kenyan secondary school students, *Journal of Social Psychology*, 127, 407-409.

Fulljames, P. and Francis, L.J. (1988), The influence of creationism and scientism on attitudes towards Christianity among Kenyan secondary school students, *Educational Studies*, 14, 77-96.

Fulljames, P., Gibson, H.M. and Francis, L.J. (1991), Creationism, scientism, Christianity and science: a study in adolescent attitudes, *British Educational Research Journal*, 17, 171-190.

Garrity, F.D. (1960), A study of the attitude of some secondary modern school pupils towards religious education, Unpublished M.Ed. dissertation, University of Manchester.

Gates, B.E. (1976), Religion and the developing world of children and young people, Unpublished Ph.D. dissertation, University of Lancaster.

Gibson, H.M. (1989a), Attitudes to religion and science among school children aged 11 to 16 years in a Scottish city, *Journal of Empirical Theology*, 2, 5-26.

Gibson, H.M. (1989b), Measuring attitudes towards Christianity among 11-16 year old pupils in non-denominational schools in Scotland, *Educational Research*, 31, 221-227.

Gibson, H.M. and Francis, L.J. (1989), Measuring attitudes towards Christianity among 11- to 16- year old pupils in Catholic schools in Scotland, *Educational Research*, 31, 65-69.

Gibson, H.M., Francis, L.J. and Pearson, P.R. (1990), The relationship between social class and attitude towards Christianity among fourteen- and fifteen-year-old adolescents, *Personality and Individual Differences*, 11, 631-635.

Gillings, V. and Joseph, S. (1996), Religiosity and social desirability: impression management and self-deceptive positivity, *Personality and Individual Differences*, 21, 1047-1050.

Gobbel, R. and Gobbel, G. (1986), *The Bible: a child's playground*, London, SCM.

Godin, A. (1968), Genetic development of the symbolic function: meaning and limits of the works of Goldman, *Religious Education*, 63, 439-445.

Goldman, R.J. (1964), *Religious Thinking from Childhood to Adolescence*, London, Routledge and Kegan Paul.

Goldman, R.J. (1965), *Readiness for Religion*, London, Routledge and Kegan Paul.

Greer, J.E. (1972a), *A Questioning Generation*, Belfast, Church of Ireland Board of Education.

Greer, J.E. (1972b), The child's understanding of creation, *Educational Review*, 24, 94-110.

Greer, J.E. (1980a), The persistence of religion: a study of adolescents in Northern Ireland, *Character Potential*, 9, 3, 139-149.

Greer, J.E. (1980b), Stages in the development of religious thinking, *British Journal of Religious Education*, 3, 24-28.

Greer, J.E. (1981a), Religious attitudes and thinking in Belfast pupils, *Educational Research*, 23, 177-189.

Greer, J.E. (1981b), Religious experience and religious education, *Search*, 4, 1, 23-34.

Greer, J.E. (1982), A comparison of two attitude to religion scales, *Educational Research*, 24, 226-227.

Greer, J.E. (1983a), A critical study of 'Thinking about the Bible', *British Journal of Religious Education*, 5, 113-125.

Greer, J.E. (1983b), Attitude to religion reconsidered, *British Journal of Educational Studies*, 31, 18-28.

Greer, J.E. (1985), Viewing 'the other side' in Northern Ireland: openness and attitude to religion among Catholic and Protestant Adolescents, *Journal for the Scientific Study of Religion*, 24, 275-292.

Greer, J.E. (1989), The persistence of religion in Northern Ireland: a study of sixth form religion, 1968-1988, *Collected Original Resources in Education*, 13, 2, fiche 20, G9.

Greer, J.E. and Francis, L.J. (1991), Measuring attitudes towards Christianity among pupils in Catholic secondary schools in Northern Ireland, *Educational Research*, 33, 70-73.

Greer, J.E. and Francis, L.J. (1992), Religious experience and attitude toward Christianity among secondary school children in Northern Ireland, *Journal of Social Psychology*, 132, 277-279.

Guttman, L. (1944), A basis for scaling qualitative data, *American Sociological Review*, 9, 139-150.

Hoge, D.R. and Petrillo, G.H. (1978), Development of religious thinking in adolescence: a test of Goldman's theories, *Journal for the Scientific Study of Religion*, 17, 139-154.

Howkins, K.G. (1966), *Religious Thinking and Religious Education*, London, Tydale Press.

Hyde, K.E. (1965), *Religious Learning in Adolescence*, University of Birmingham Institute of Education, Monograph No. 7, London, Oliver and Boyd.

Hyde, K.E. (1968), A critique of Goldman's research, *Religious Education*, 63, 429-435.

Hyde, K.E. (1984), Twenty years after Goldman's research, *British Journal of Religious Education*, 7, 5-7.

Jamison, H.E. (1989), Religious understanding in children aged seven to eleven, Unpublished Ph.D. dissertation, The Queens University of Belfast.

Jaspard, J.M. (1971), The 6-12 year old child's representation of the eucharistic presence, *Lumen Vitae*, 26, 237-262.

Johnson, W.P.C. (1966), The religious attitudes of secondary modern county school pupils, Unpublished M.Ed. dissertation, University of Manchester.

Jones, J.A. (1962), An investigation into the response of boys and girls to scripture as a school subject in certain co-education grammar schools in industrial South Wales, Unpublished M.A. dissertation, University of Wales (Swansea).

Jones, S.H. and Francis, L.J. (1996), Religiosity and self-esteem during childhood and adolescence, in L.J. Francis, W.K. Kay and W.S. Campbell (eds), *Research in Religious Education*, pp 189-205, Leominster, Gracewing.

Jones, S.H. and Francis, L.J. (1999), Personality type and attitude toward Christianity among student churchgoers, *Journal of Beliefs and Values*, 20, 105-109.

Kay, W.K. (1981a), Marital happiness and children's attitudes to religion, *British Journal of Religious Education*, 3, 102-105.

Kay, W.K. (1981b), Psychoticism and attitude to religion, *Personality and Individual Differences*, 2, 249-252.

Kay, W.K. (1981c), Conversion among 11-15 year olds, *Spectrum*, 13, 2, 26-33.

Kay, W.K. (1981d), Syllabuses and attitudes to Christianity, *Irish Catechist*, 5, 2, 16-21.

Kay, W.K. (1981e), Religious thinking, attitudes and personality amongst secondary pupils in England and Ireland, Unpublished Ph.D. dissertation, University of Reading.

Kay, W.K., Francis, L.J. and Gibson, H.M. (1996), Attitude toward Christianity and the transition to formal operational thinking, *British Journal of Religious Education*, 19, 45-55.

Kingan, B.A. (1969), The study of some factors hindering religious education of a group of primary school children, Unpublished M.Ed. dissertation, University of Liverpool.

Langdon, A.A. (1969), A critical examination of Dr Goldman's research study on religious thinking from childhood to adolescence, *Journal of Christian Education*, 12, 1, 37-63.

Leavey, C. and Hetherton, M. (1988), *Catholic Beliefs and Practices*, Melbourne, Australia, Collins Dove.

Levitt, M. (1995), 'The church is very important to me.' A consideration of the relevance of Francis' attitude towards Christianity scale to the aims of Church of England aided schools, *British Journal of Religious Education*, 17, 100-107.

Lewis, C.A. (1996), Religiosity and obsessionality, in L.J. Francis, W.K. Kay and W.S. Campbell (eds), *Research in Religious Education*, pp 219-227, Leominster, Gracewing.

Lewis, C.A. (1998), Towards a clarification of the association between religiosity and life satisfaction, *Journal of Beliefs and Values*, 19, 119-122.

Lewis, J.M. (1974), An examination of the attitudes of pupils towards the content and method of teaching religious education in certain co-educational comprehensive schools in Wales, Unpublished M.Ed. dissertation, University of Wales (Swansea).

Likert, R. (1932), A technique for the measurement of attitudes, *Archives of Psychology*, 140, 1-55.

Long, J.F. (1989), A study of Catholic secondary schools in the Archdiocese of Armagh with special reference to RE, Unpublished D.Phil. dissertation, University of Ulster.

Loukes, H. (1961), *Teenage Religion*, London, SCM.

Loukes, H. (1965), *New Ground in Christian Education*, London, SCM.

Loukes, H. (1973), *Teenage Morality*, London, SCM.

Maas, R.M. (1985), Biblical catechesis and religious development: the Goldman project twenty years later, *Living Light*, 22, 124-144.

McGrady, A.G. (1982), Goldman: a Piagetian based critique, *The Irish Catechist*, 6, 19-29.

McGrady, A.G. (1983), Teaching the bible: research from a Piagetian perspective, *British Journal of Religious Education*, 5, 126-133.

McGrady, A.G. (1990), The development of religious thinking: a comparison of metaphoric and operational paradigms, Unpublished Ph.D. dissertation, University of Birmingham.

McGrady, A.G. (1994a), Metaphorical and operational aspects of religious thinking: research with Irish Catholic pupils (part 1), *British Journal of Religious Education*, 16, 148-163.

McGrady, A.G. (1994b), Metaphorical and operational aspects of religious thinking: research with Irish Catholic pupils (part 2), *British Journal of Religious Education*, 17, 56-62.

Madge, V. (1965), *Children in Search of Meaning*, London, SCM.

Madge, V. (1971), *Introducing Young Children to Jesus*, London, SCM.

Mark, T.J. (1979), A study of cognitive and affective elements in the religious development of adolescents, Unpublished Ph.D. dissertation, University of Leeds.

Mathews, H.F. (1966), *Revolution in Religious Education*, Oxford, Religious Education Press.

Miles, G.B. (1971), The study of logical thinking and moral judgements in GCE bible knowledge candidates, Unpublished M.Ed. dissertation, University of Leeds.

Morley, H.C. (1975), Religious concepts of slow learners: an application of the findings of Ronald Goldman, *Learning for Living*, 14, 107-110.

Murphy, R.J.L. (1977), The development of religious thinking in children in three easy stages? *Learning for Living*, 17, 16-19.

Murphy, R.J.L. (1979), An investigation into some aspects of the development of religious thinking in children aged between 6 and 11 years, Unpublished Ph.D. dissertation, University of St Andrews.

Nye, W.C. and Carlson, J.S. (1984), The development of the concept of God in children, *Journal of Genetic Psychology*, 145, 137-142.

Osgood, C.E., Suci, G.J. and Tannenbaum, P.H. (1957), *The Measurement of Meaning*, Urbana, University of Illinois Press.

Pearson, P.R. and Francis, L.J. (1989), The dual nature of the Eysenckian lie scales: are religious adolescents more truthful? *Personality and Individual Differences*, 10, 1041-1048.

Pearson, P.R., Francis, L.J. and Lightbown, T.J. (1986), Impulsivity and religiosity, *Personality and Individual Differences*, 7, 89-94.

Peatling, J.H. (1973), The incidence of concrete and abstract religious thinking in the interpretation of three bible stories by pupils enrolled in grades four through twelve in selected schools in the Episcopal Church in the United States of America, Unpublished Ph.D. dissertation, University of New York.

Peatling, J.H. (1974), Cognitive development in pupils in grades four through twelve: the incidence of concrete and abstract religious thinking, *Character Potential*, 7, 1, 52-61.

Peatling, J.H. (1976), A sense of justice: moral judgment in children, adolescents and adults, *Character Potential*, 8, 1, 25-34.

Peatling, J.H. (1977), On beyond Goldman: religious thinking and the 1970s, *Learning for Living*, 16, 99-108.

Peatling, J.H. and Laabs, C.W. (1975), Cognitive development of pupils in grades four through twelve: a comparative study of Lutheran and Episcopalian children and youth, *Character Potential*, 7, 107-117.

Peatling, J.H., Laabs, C.W. and Newton, T.B. (1975), Cognitive development: a three sample comparison of means on the Peatling scale of religious thinking, *Character Potential*, 7, 159-162.

Petrovich, O. (1988), Re-review: Ronald Goldman's Religious Thinking from Childhood to Adolescence, *Modern Churchman*, 30, 2, 44-49.

Povall, C.H. (1971), Some factors affecting pupils' attitudes to religious education, Unpublished M.Ed. dissertation, University of Manchester.

Rees, R.J. (1967), *Background and Belief*, London, SCM.

Richmond, R.C. (1972), Maturity of religious judgements and differences of religious attitudes between ages of 13 and 16 years, *Educational Review*, 24, 225-236.

Robbins, M. and Francis, L.J. (1996), Are religious people happier? a study among undergraduates, in L.J. Francis, W.K. Kay and W.S. Campbell (eds), *Research in Religious Education*, pp 207-217, Leominster, Gracewing.

Roy, P.R. (1979), Applications of Piaget's theory of cognitive development to religious thinking, with special reference to the work of Dr R.G. Goldman, Unpublished M.Ed. dissertation, University of Liverpool.

Russell, A. (1978), The attitude of primary school children to religious education, Unpublished M.Phil. dissertation, University of Nottingham.

Schurter, D.D. (1987), Fowler's faith stages as a guide for ministry to the mentally retarded, *Journal of Pastoral Care*, 41, 234-240.

Shulik, R.N. (1988), Faith development in older adults, *Educational Gerontology*, 14, 291-301.

Slee, N.M. (1986a), Goldman yet again: an overview and critique of his contribution to research, *British Journal of Religious Education*, 8, 84-93.

Slee, N.M. (1986b), A note on Goldman's methods of data analysis with special reference to scalogram analysis, *British Journal of Religious Education*, 8, 168-175.

Slee, N.M. (1990), Getting away from Goldman: changing perspectives on the development of religious thinking, *Modern Churchman*, 32, 1, 1-9.

Smith, D.L. (1998), That burning bush again: the psychometric assessment of stages in religious thinking, *Journal of Beliefs and Values*, 19, 71-82.

Streib, H. (1994), Magical feeling and thinking in childhood and adolescence: a developmental perspective, *British Journal of Religious Education*, 16, 70-81.

Tamminen, K. (1977), What questions of life do Finnish school children reflect on? *Learning for Living*, 16, 148-155.

Tamminen, K. (1991), *Religious Development in Childhood and Youth: an empirical study*, Helsinki, Suomalainen Tiedeakatemia.

Taylor, H.P. (1970), A comparative study of the religious attitudes, beliefs and practices of sixth formers in Anglican, state and Roman Catholic schools and an assessment of religious opinion upon them asserted by home and school, Unpublished M.Phil. dissertation, University of London.

Thurstone, L.L. (1928), Attitudes can be measured, *American Journal of Sociology*, 33, 529-554.

Turner, E.B. (1970), Religious understanding and religious attitudes in male urban adolescents, Unpublished Ph.D. dissertation, The Queen's University of Belfast.

Turner, E.B. (1978), Towards a standardised test of religious language comprehension, *British Journal of Religious Education*, 1, 14-21.

Turner, E.B. (1980), Intellectual ability and the comprehension of religious language, *Irish Journal of Psychology*, 4, 182-190.

Van Bunnen, C. (1965), The burning bush: the symbolic implications of a bible story among children from 5-12 years, in A. Godin (ed.), *From Religious Experience to a Religious Attitude*, pp 171-182, Chicago, Loyola University Press.

West Riding (1966), *Suggestions for Religious Education: West Riding agreed syllabus*, Wakefield, County Council of the West Riding of Yorkshire.

Westbury, J.I. (1975), Religious beliefs and attitudes of pupils in east London comprehensive school: factors influencing the pupils and implications for religious education, Unpublished M.Ed. dissertation, University of Leicester.

Whitehouse, E. (1972), Children's reactions to the Zacchaeus story, *Learning for Living*, 11, 4, 19-24.

Wright, D. and Cox, E. (1967a), Religious belief and co-education in a sample of sixth form boys and girls, *British Journal of Social and Clinical Psychology*, 6, 23-31.

Wright, D. and Cox, E. (1967b), A study of the relationship between moral judgement and religious belief in a sample of English adolescents, *Journal of Social Psychology*, 72, 135-144.

Wright, D. and Cox, E. (1971a), Changes in attitudes towards religious education and the bible among sixth form boys and girls, *British Journal of Educational Psychology*, 41, 328-331.

Wright, D. and Cox, E. (1971b), Changes in moral belief among sixth form boys and girls over a seven year period in relation to religious belief, age and sex differences, *British Journal of Social and Clinical Psychology*, 10, 332-341.

Research Methodology

Unit B

Research in religious education and church school studies: part two

Professor Leslie J. Francis

University of Wales

Bangor

Contents

Introduction

Aims

After working through this unit you should be able to:

- understand how empirical research has been applied to the fields of religious education and church school studies;
- assess the strengths and limitations of different research traditions;
- critically apply the fruits of research to educational practice.

Overview

Units A and B of this module provide a broad overview of the developments of empirical research traditions in religious education and church school studies from the early 1960s until the present day. Cross-references are made to other units and modules in which some of these traditions are explored in greater depth or with further application. The emphasis in the present unit is on helping the reader to engage with the research methods employed and to test out the strengths and limitations of these methods. Since this unit is concerned with assessing empirical methods, more use is made of experience and activities than is general in other units within the series.

The model places empirical research in religious education into an historical framework. Three main periods are identified. The first period, embracing the 1960s, sees a renewed interest in empirical research and is characterised by seven important, but diverse, studies. The second period, embracing the 1970s and 1980s, is characterised as the age of measurement. The third period, beginning in the 1990s, is characterised as the return to qualitative studies. The first two periods were covered in unit A. The third period is covered in unit B. Unit B concludes by illustrating how some specific topics have been studied.

B1 Return to qualitative studies

The emphasis on quantitative studies during the 1970s and 1980s was greeted by some as establishing a proper scientific and empirical basis for knowledge in religious education. Others, however, saw the approach as too restrictive and of limited value in terms of the insights applicable to practice. Possibly as a reaction against the quantitative approach of the 1970s and 1980s, during the 1990s a new interest emerged in qualitative studies.

This section illustrates the renewed interest in qualitative studies by drawing attention to three major contributions, the Children and Worldviews Project at Chichester, the Children's Spirituality Project at Nottingham and the Religious Education and Community Project at Warwick.

Children and Worldviews Project

The Children and Worldviews Project was set up in 1993 as a collaborative venture, funded by three colleges of higher education: Chichester Institute, King Alfred's College Winchester and La Sainte Union College Southampton. Full details of the project are provided in *The Education of the Whole Child* by Erricker, Erricker, Ota, Sullivan and Fletcher (1997).

The Children and Worldviews Project was established to examine the ways in which children think, learn and view the world in which they live. The project set out to listen to children in settings where they feel at ease, whether this be a classroom, a playground or, in one instance, a rubbish dump. The project approached listening to children through the use of story, poetry and the discussion of themes. The children themselves set the agenda. At each stage the project team discussed with teachers what children were saying.

Erricker, Erricker, Ota, Sullivan and Fletcher (1997, p 23) describe their approach to research in the following terms:

> Most research is conducted in the context of a defined body of knowledge which, educationally, will relate to a specific curriculum area. This research was unable to fit into that context. It is research into children's thinking, but not to identify stages which their thinking has reached according to predetermined criteria relating to rationality, intelligence or moral maturity. We rejected such schematised approaches on the basis that we were not concerned with children's ability to think according to prescribed expectations. We were concerned to know how well they were able to construct explanations of events and strategies for dealing with issues that arose in their personal lives.

This approach was developed from three clear principles:

- the lack of a clear hypothesis which they were trying to confirm or disprove;
- the complexity of the research situation;
- the impossibility of an objective stance by the researcher.

The implications of each of these principles, as the project interpreted them, will be discussed in turn.

First, the project team tried to enter the field of research with no definite ideas of what was being sought or what would be found. They had identified an area of interest, namely what children felt was important in their lives, what coloured the way they looked at the world, and what affected the way they learned. They believed that they had to listen to children and identify the important things to follow-up in what they said.

Second, the project team argued that the infinite variation within children and within the contexts in which they live is far too complex to be reduced to quantitative measures. They argued that the qualitative research framework was properly child-centred, allowing the children space and time in which to express themselves freely and without the hindrances of adults presuming to give them the appropriate tools and language.

Third, the project team acknowledged the subjectivity of the researchers, allowing them to bring their intuition and personal involvement to the research situation. All members of the team kept research logs, in which they recorded how they felt anticipating going into schools to talk with children or teachers, how they felt while carrying out the research, and their feelings afterwards.

Children were selected for interview in consultation with the headteacher. Children were generally interviewed in small groups with four or five emerging as the best size group.

Drawing on this research method, Erricker, Erricker, Ota, Sullivan and Fletcher (1997) illustrate the findings of their research by exploring six topics:

- children's experience of conflict and loss;
- children's religious and scientific thinking;
- the identity of 'Asian' children;
- taking children's stories to other children;
- children and parental separation;
- religious identity and children's worldviews.

In the chapter on of children's experience of conflict and loss, Clive Erricker draws on the results of paired interviews with three girls and three boys. The children were first interviewed at the age of seven and again at the age of nine. Here is the conversation involving two children (V and J) after they had listened to Brian Patten's poem 'Looking for Dad'.

Q Where do you think Dad has gone?

J Up in heaven.

Q J, tell me what happens when you go up to heaven.

J You see God and that.

V I think that in heaven you can ride a white pony and have marshmallows. Before my nan died she told me lots of things because she knew she was going to die and she told me about all the things she was going to do and she said she was going to send me a postcard. Before she went she gave me a piece of paper and stuck a photograph on it. I've still got it.

She said she would be happy and she wanted me to be happy when she died. On that day she got a picture of her and all the family, stuck it on a postcard and wrote on the back 'I'll see you in your heart'. Now she's always with me. Now I talk to her all the time. I talk to her when I'm lonely. When I've argued with my friends I go and sit on the wall and think about her and talk to her. When I get fed up I sit there and talk to her about my friends. She tells me that she's riding on things. She says she's having a really nice time. She says she's going to ring me up. She says things in my head, she rings up my brain and talks to me. When she went up in heaven she took one of her special secrets. She took it with her and she can just ring me up, it's clever. This special secret makes her able to do that.

I keep on wanting to tell people things but they don't understand. I know everyone's in heaven who has died. Grandma tells me. She works in a cleaners. She washes all the clouds in heaven. She's got lots and lots of friends in heaven. She hopes we'll stay alive a long time but she wants me to go up there to see her. I'd like to go and see her but if you go up there you've got to stay there. You can't go unless you've died. Heaven is high, high in the sky, it's higher than space.

I've never worried about these things. I just keep it in my heart. It's not a problem. It makes me quite sad they (people) don't believe. But when God talks to them they will know. We are very, very lucky that just some people care in this world. Like me and my friends and everybody in this school, I hope, we care, we keep this planet going. I think heaven is part of this planet.

My nan was burnt when she died, cremated. I think that's better than worms coming into your coffin.

In his analysis of this dialogue, Clive Erricker makes the following points.

- She was prepared to make such a personal statement in the presence of other children, not just her own friends.
- She makes it with conviction. She is committed to an interpretation of her grandmother's death that is more than a fanciful idea.
- The metaphorical language she uses is necessary to an interpretation and communication of her experience.
- Through this explanation she clearly gains empowerment.
- The explanation necessitates further reflection on metaphysical ideas related to her grandmother's continued existence. Thus, God, the world and the sustaining power of love become important.
- Childlike and rather Disneyesque imagery becomes used for and functions to provide a vehicle for a more profound personal purpose: to locate the possibility of her continued relationship with her grandmother beyond death.
- It points to the significance of a particular traumatic experience in generating and utilising a child's reflective capabilities in a way that would not have focused them otherwise.
- Her explanation does not depend on a use of any overtly religious or Christian doctrine to substantiate her views, suggesting that a nurturing in

explicitly Christian ideas has not been necessary to the creation of her own explanation.

Activity B1

Reflect on the preceding discussion between Q, J and V. What does this tell you about children's worldviews? Now examine Clive Erricker's analysis of this interview. How well justified are his observations? What other observations would you like to make on that interview? What do you consider to be the strengths and weaknesses of the research methodology.

Comment on activity B1

It is, of course, difficult to assess a research tradition from one brief example. Proper judgement needs to be grounded in an appreciation of a wide range of data emerging from the Children and Worldviews Project. In addition to the material presented in *The Education of the Whole Child* by Erricker, Erricker, Ota, Sullivan and Fletcher (1997), other findings from the Children and Worldviews Project have been published elsewhere. Erricker and Erricker (1995) draw on the research to identify the ways in which children's story telling can be understood, addressed and valued by taking into account its ontological significance. Erricker and Erricker (1996) drew on the research to illustrate children's spirituality. Ota (1997) draws on the research to discuss the experience of Muslim and Sikh children coping with different value systems. Ota, Erricker and Erricker (1997) draw on the research to profile the 'secrets' of the playground. Erricker (1998) draws on the research to examine the effect of death, loss and conflict on children's worldviews.

Children's Spirituality Project

The Children's Spirituality Project grew out of the concerns of the Religious Experience Research Centre (Alister Hardy Centre) at Westminster College Oxford and was shaped by the research perspectives of David Hay within the University of Nottingham. David Hay came to this project with a well established interest in religious experience broadly conceived as reflected in his books *Exploring Inner Space* (1982) or *Religious Experience Today: studying the facts* (1990a). Full details of the project are provided in *The Spirit of the Child* by Hay with Nye (1998). Other introductions to the background to their project are provided in essays by Nye (1996), Hay, Nye and Murphy (1996) and Nye and Hay (1996).

The Children's Spirituality Project grew out of the opportunities and challenges posed by the 1988 Education Reform Act which required teachers to attend to the spiritual dimension of education. Hay and Nye argue that much of the traditional vocabulary of spirituality is not available to children belonging to a secular culture. This in turn leads to two key problems.

- What conceptual boundaries can be set to the term 'spirituality'?
- How can we identify categories of children's experience which belong to this realm?

In addressing the first question, Hay and Nye quote with approval the following extract from Karl Rahner's (1974, p 160) *Theological Investigations* which invites us to imagine a world in which all religious institutions have disappeared and the word 'God' no longer exists.

> And even if this term were ever to be forgotten, even then in the decisive moments of our lives we should still be constantly encompassed by this nameless mystery of our existence... even supposing that those realities which we call religions... were totally to disappear... the transcendentality inherent in human life is such that (we) would still reach out towards that mystery which lies outside (our) control.

Accordingly Hay and Nye conceive of an innate spiritual capacity in childhood, but recognise that this may focus in particular ways and take different and changing forms as children's other capacities develop.

In addressing the second question, Hay and Nye propose a set of three interrelated themes or categories of spiritual sensitivity, which they define as:

- awareness sensing;
- mystery sensing;
- value sensing.

The first category, awareness sensing, associated with spirituality typically refers to a reflexive or meta-cognitive process, that of being attentive towards one's attention or being aware of a particular sensation or awareness. Four sub-categories of awareness sensing are defined as: here and now, tuning, flow, and focusing.

The second category, mystery sensing, associated with spirituality typically refers to experience that is in principle incomprehensible and indicative of the transcendent. Two sub-categories of mystery sensing are defined as: wonder and awe, and imagination.

The third category, value sensing, emphasises the role played by emotion in spirituality. Three sub-categories of value sensing are delight and despair, ultimate goodness, and meaning.

From the outset David Hay and Rebecca Nye argue that researchers working in this tradition are unlikely to be able to retain a detached attitude towards the object of their research. According to Hay and Nye (1998, pp 79-80):

> During the three years when we were researching children's spirituality, Rebecca Nye and I were not neutral observers located at some Archimedean point outside the universe, detached from all personal concern with spiritual or religious issues. At weekends Rebecca was running the children's Sunday School in St Philip's Cathedral in Birmingham. During the same period I had become attracted to the Spiritual Exercises of St Ignatius Loyola and spent just over a year undertaking the exercise in daily life.

In the course of their project a total of 38 children had conversations with Rebecca, 18 of whom were aged between six and seven and 20 between 10 and 11. Of the 38 children 28 were classified as having no religious affiliation, four were Church of England, four were Muslim and two were Roman Catholic. The children were recruited from one school in Nottingham and one school in Birmingham. Nye had up to three meetings with each of the children, and each tape-recorded conversation lasted about half an hour. The children were interviewed on a one-to-one basis.

The conversation with each child began with a very loosely structured, light chat about the child's interests and life story. The transition from general issues towards spirituality was typically (but not always) initiated by inviting the children to talk about one of a set of photographs. The following images were included:

- a girl gazing into a fire;
- a boy looking out of his bedroom window at the stars;
- a girl looking tearfully at her dead pet gerbil in its cage;
- a boy standing by himself in a playground, ignored and perhaps unhappy;
- a boy standing on a wet pavement, having dropped some food on the ground, looking up with his hands spread out;
- scenes of waves whipped up in stormy weather.

During the major part of the discussion there was no overt mention of religion or religious experience unless the subject was brought up spontaneously by the child. However, toward the end of the sequence of meetings, if religion had not emerged spontaneously as a subject it was introduced, usually by asking about school assembly. Finally, if it seemed appropriate, direct reference to religion or spiritual awareness might be mentioned and the children might be asked whether they recognised this area in their own experience.

The tape-recorded conversations with these 38 children generated over a thousand typed pages of transcript. Nye read and re-read these transcripts in order to generate an interpretative framework. She decided to approach these data in two ways.

The first approach resembled that of case studies. Nye interrogated the transcripts of individual children in order to identify each child's individual spirituality. Here she spoke in terms of a kind of personal 'signature' for each child. Nye introduced the spiritual signature of a girl named Ruth (Hay and Nye, 1998, p 85) by drawing attention to the way in which she imagined heaven:

> A mist of perfume, with gold walls, and a rainbow stretched over God's throne... but a transparent mist, like a... I can't explain it. Like a smell. A real cloud of smell, a lovely smell... like the smell that you get when you wake up on a dull winter morning, and then when you go to sleep, and you wake up, the birds are chirping, and the last drops of snow are melting away, and the treetops, shimmering in the breeze, and it's a spring morning... (Then she added:) I suppose it's not a season at all, not really, because (it's) just a day in delight, every day.

Interpreting this passage, Nye comments as follows:

> Ruth's imaginative response, drawing on nature, her senses and an appreciation of the mysterious transformations that occur in life, pervaded many of her comments in other 'non-religious' contexts. This could be traced to the opening remarks in her first interview. When offered the choice to draw 'anything at all' while we chatted, she replied: 'I like nature... (Why?)... just because I like it. I don't know. And it's so beautiful to be in the world.'

Reflecting on the 'signature phenomenon', Nye draws the following conclusion (Hay and Nye, 1998, p 99).

> The practical implication is that one needs to enquire carefully about and attend to each child's personal style if one is to 'hear' their spirituality at all. At a theoretical level this implies that we cannot neatly distinguish the spiritual aspects from the psychological features of a child's life.

The second approach tried to identify patterns or conclusions which were common across the individual children. In this connection Nye identified two different kinds of conversation which were of particular relevance:

- dialogue that employed religious ideas and language;
- non-religious dialogue that implicitly conveyed that the child was engaged in something more than the casual or mundane.

As an example of 'religious dialogue' Nye draws on conversations with six year old John (Hay and Nye, 1998, pp 101-102). John came from a family who were sympathetic to Christian belief but who attended church no more than twice a year. Having listened to John's religious beliefs, Nye asked him how he came to hold his beliefs. In his response John described a religious experience (Hay and Nye, 1998, p 102).

> I worked about it and I received... one day... I was with my mum and I begged her... um... for me to go to um... some church. And we did it and... I prayed... and after that praying... I knew that good was on my side. And I heard him in

my mind say this: 'I am with you. Every step you go. The Lord is with you. May sins be forgiven.'

Later John described his encounter with the Holy Spirit in the following terms:

> Well once I went um... in the night and I saw this bishopy kind of alien. I said, 'Who are you?' And he said, 'I am the Holy Spirit.' I did think he was the Holy Spirit.

As an example of 'implicitly spiritual discourse' Nye draws on a conversation with ten year old Harriet. Towards the end of the conversation Harriet generated a flood of unanswerable questions, culminating in wondering about the origin of the universe and human life. Finally, Harriet suggested that, faced with such mystery yet yearning for meaning, 'Perhaps we've got to, like, ask the clouds. The clouds have been there millions and millions of years.' Nye then asked Harriet if she felt there was some organising principle behind it all. Harriet replied (Hay and Nye, 1998, p 109):

> Well there must be somewhere, somehow - or else, how would it keep reproducing? Like it (?) made a flower, a dandelion. Where did the wind come from to blow all the petals off to make them fall on the floor to make more?... (*in a whisper*) It's puzzling.

Nye concluded from this analysis that there is a continuum of children's spirituality. At one end are those who perceive spiritual matters in terms of questions or principles. Then there are those who go on to make unconscious or conscious associations with the traditional language of religion. At the other end of the continuum are those who have experienced their spirituality directly and personally in the form of religious insights.

Activity B2

Reflect on the two examples given above from Rebecca Nye's conversations with John and Harriet as examples of 'religious dialogue' and of 'implicitly religious discourse'. What do you consider can be learnt from these conversations about children's spirituality? What are the main strengths and weaknesses of the method of research advanced by David Hay and Rebecca Nye? Try replicating their study by holding a similar conversation with a child.

Comment on activity B2

This method of research clearly promotes a great deal of respect for the individual child. The two key problems which need addressing remain 'What counts as spirituality and why?' and 'Would the child have said the same, or even similar things to another interviewer?'

Religious Education and Community Project

The Religious Education and Community Project is part of the work of the Warwick Religions and Education Research Unit, under the directorship of Robert Jackson and in collaboration with Judith Everington and Eleanor Nesbitt. This project employed ethnographic research to underpin curriculum development in religious education. Helpful introductions to both the research and the curriculum development is provided by Jackson (1996a) in an essay entitled 'Ethnographic research and curriculum development' and by Jackson (1997) in his book *Religious Education: an interpretive approach*. Jackson's argument is that religious education should present religions as they are perceived and lived by their adherents, rather than as reified belief systems. Ethnographic research, he argued, provides the method for uncovering how it is that adherents perceive and live their faith.

The Religious Education and Community Project integrated a series of studies conducted throughout the 1980s and 1990s among children from different religious communities in Britain. The projects focused on children in the 8-13 age range, using participant observation, informal and semi-structured interviews, documentary analysis and photography.

The studies concentrated on individual children mainly in the context of their families and religious membership groups, although some attention was also given to religious education in day schools.

Robert Jackson and Eleanor Nesbitt initiated this research tradition in 1984, in a study exploring formal religious nurture among Hindu children in different parts of England. This was followed by a second much larger study of Hindu children in Coventry and by a third study, among children from two Punjabi caste-based movements with an ambiguous identity as either Hindu or Sikh.

The Coventry study began with participant observation in a variety of Hindu events, followed by semi-structured interviews with children between the ages of 8 and 13, and the detailed case studies of twelve children over an 18 month period. The findings from this study are reported by Jackson and Nesbitt (1993) in their book *Hindu Children in Britain*. Here they report the research thematically, using quotations from children on topics such as the children's self-perception, food and fasts, prayer and worship, and formal religious teaching. The style of this research can be illustrated by their description of Anita (Jackson, 1997, pp 66-67).

At school Anita wore the same style of school uniform as any other girl in her class. Her spoken English showed no signs of being her second language. Her favourite school subjects were the sciences and she participated enthusiastically in school sports. She was at ease with her peer group and she had high academic aspirations.

At home among her family, Anita mainly spoke Gujarati. Like the rest of her family Anita was a devotee of Sathya Sai Baba and talked with considerable knowledge, understanding and feeling about his teaching, his miracles and his values. She described in detail a visit to Sathya Sai Baba's headquarters at Puttaparthi in South India in order to have his *darshan* ('sight') and to receive his blessing. Like most of our interviewees, Anita regarded herself as a 'foreigner' and distinguished herself from 'the India people' while in India, but described herself as 'Indian' when in Britain. She felt no inner conflict in making these situationally different identifications.

In the evenings, Anita and her family sang *bhajans* (devotional songs) before the shrine to Sathya Sai Baba, situated at one end of the living room. On at least one evening per week they were joined by other families, with Anita - dressed in the white clothes worn by Sathya Sai Baba's devotees - often leading the worship, playing *tabla* and harmonium, and performing the arti ceremony. She attended *Bal Vikas* ('child development') classes run by Sai devotees, and once a year attended a youth camp. In the classes she learned 'silent sitting', a meditation technique, and explored the movement's central values of truth (*satya*), righteous conduct (*dharma*), peace (*shanti*), love (*prem*) and non-violence (*ahimsa*). She also received instruction on food, health and hygiene, especially the importance of a vegetarian diet and the principle of *jutha*, her *guru* emphasising that when serving food the spoon must never touch people's plates.

Activity B3

How well do you feel you know Anita from the preceding extract from *Hindu Children in Britain* by Jackson and Nesbitt (1993)? What do you regard as essential description in this text, and what do you regard as interpretation and commentary? What are the main strengths and weaknesses of the method of research advanced by Robert Jackson and Eleanor Nesbitt? Try replicating their study by observing a religious group in your own area.

Comment on activity B3

Ethnographic research can provide rich insights into the self-understanding of adherents to religious groups. Two key problems with the method concern its time-consuming nature and the inevitable subjectivity involved in determining what is observed and how it is interpreted.

Extending the focus

Following their initial pioneering work among Hindu children, Robert Jackson and his associates conducted similar research among other faith groups. For example, in 1990 they initiated a three year study of research among 8-13 year old Christian and Sikh children in Coventry and Jewish and Muslim children in parts of Birmingham. Analysing the findings from this study among Christian children, Jackson and Nesbitt (1992) found that the children's understanding and expression of their Christian tradition was very similar to that of their parents and church leaders. However, particularly in the case of families from ethnic minorities, children experienced a less homogenous body of belief and practice than their parents, for example, because of differences in ethos between home and church (in the Punjabi case) or in Catholic practice in the home and in the voluntary aided church school (in the Ukrainian case). Minorities, such as the Ukrainians and Greek Cypriots, whose scriptures and liturgical material were in an archaic form of their mother tongue, promoted formal language teaching, whereas for the Punjabis, whose families had been converted by British missionaries, mother tongue maintenance was a less important issue.

All the case-study children said that they believed in the existence of God, some picturing God in a human form, with others understanding God to be 'spirit', regarded as powerful, incorporeal and formless. While belief in God, Jesus and the authority of the bible was common to all groups, belief in the Holy Spirit was more varied. Most children did not refer to the Holy Spirit unprompted, and the most explicit references came from three Jamaican Pentecostals who mentioned speaking and singing in tongues as evidence of 'being filled'. One girl belonging to a 'New church' spoke of 'gifts of the Spirit', especially speaking with tongues, done more at home than at church. One Greek Orthodox parent affirmed that it is the Holy Spirit who is active in the church now (for example, in mystically changing bread and wine into the body and blood of Christ).

Belief in saints and angels more or less conformed to sub-traditional demarcation, with the Roman and Ukrainian Catholics mentioning their existence and the Orthodox reporting their present activity. Belief in the devil, while not general, united children from the Orthodox and Pentecostal, Charismatic and Evangelical congregations. With regard to the after-life, some children held different ideas concurrently, rejecting or adopting beliefs as their own in the light of personal experience (such as the death of a grandparent) or the teaching of their parents and churches. On life after death, perhaps more than any other subject, children revealed the way in which they sifted different beliefs and arrived at individual conclusions (Nesbitt, 1993).

Other findings from the Religious Education and Community Project are presented in a series of articles and chapters. For example, Jackson (1989, 1996b) focuses on aspects of Hinduism; Nesbitt (1990) examines the Valmiki community in Coventry; Nesbitt (1992) focuses on issues raised by ethnographic studies of children's participation in worship; Nesbitt (1993) examines children's views on life after death; Nesbitt (1995) examines the cultural history and cultural choices of Punjabis in Britain; Nesbitt (1997a, 1997b) focuses on aspects of the experience of young Sikhs; Nesbitt (1998a) explores the self-understanding of young British Hindus as 'British', 'Asian' and 'Hindu'; Nesbitt (1998b) explores the relationship between young Hindus' and Sikhs' experiences of their faith tradition outside school with its presentation in school; Nesbitt and Jackson (1992) compare the perceptions held by Hindu and Christian children of each other's religion; Nesbitt and Jackson (1993) explore cultural transmission in a Diaspora Sikh community; Nesbitt and Jackson (1995) concentrates on Sikh children's use of 'God'; Woodward (1992) focuses on Jewish children.

B2 Research topics

A second way to construct a map of research methods in religious education and church school studies is through identifying some specific topics of interest and by illustrating how these topics have been researched. This section identifies nine topics: locating religious education within the context of pupils' wider appreciation of school and the curriculum, understanding the development of religious language during childhood and adolescence, appreciating the nature and correlates of religious experience, tracing the roots of pupils' images of God, understanding the development of prayer during childhood and adolescence, complementarity in religious thinking, research into school worship, the character and effectiveness of Catholic schools, and the character and effectiveness of Anglican schools.

Locating religious education

There has been a long history of research concerned with locating pupils' attitudes towards religious education alongside their attitudes towards other areas of the curriculum, going back to an early study by Lewis (1913). Studies enabling this comparison undertaken since 1960 include Garrity (1960), Williams and Finch (1968), Povall (1971), Greer and Brown (1973), Ormerod (1975), Keys and Ormerod (1976), Harvey (1984) and Francis (1987b).

A relatively unambiguous picture emerges from these disparate studies, locating religious education among the lowest positions, at the least favourable end of the attitudinal continuum. For example, Williams and Finch (1968) reported that religious education was assigned the thirteenth rank position by boys and the eleventh rank position by girls with regard to usefulness, and the thirteenth rank position by both boys and girls with regard to interest. Their study embraced fourteen school subjects. Harvey (1984) reported that religious education was assigned, among 18 school subjects, sixteenth place by boys and seventeenth place by girls. Francis (1987b) found that religious education jostled with music lessons to occupy the place of the least preferred school subject in each year from the third year of the junior school to the fourth year of the secondary school.

Another set of studies has explored the range of factors which may influence pupils' responses to religious education. A number of studies have found that girls take a more positive view of religious education than boys. Archer and Macrae (1991) took this issue of sex differences one step further and asked 60 children, between 11 and 12 years of age, to rate 17 school subjects on a seven point semantic differential scale from masculine to feminine. They found that religious education was rated in third place towards the feminine end of the continuum, closely followed by home economics and typing. A number of studies have also reported a less positive view of religious education among older pupils in comparison with younger pupils. For example, McQuillan (1990) invited 1,724 pupils to respond to the question 'How much do you learn about religion at school?' on a three point scale: *a lot, something* and *nothing*. She found that the response *a lot* declined from 50% in year seven to 27% in year eleven. A third important predictor of a more positive response to religious education has been found to be religious affiliation. This was shown to be the case, for example, by Lewis (1974) in a study conducted among 320 fourth year secondary pupils in 13 coeducational comprehensive schools in South Wales.

During the 1960s, 1970s and 1980s several studies reported on adults' attitudes towards religious education, including a national probability sample (Goldman, 1965) and surveys of parents (May, 1967; May and Johnston, 1967; Greer, 1970). Other studies explored the attitudes of teachers, including May (1968), Kay (1973), Bedwell (1977) and Burgess (1975, 1980), and the provision made within schools, including local studies in Lancashire (Benfield, 1975), Lincolnshire (Bailey, 1979) and Gloucestershire (Francis, 1987a).

Orchard (1991, 1994) has analysed HMI reports on religious education between 1985 and 1991. In the first study Orchard tested the proposition that the problems of religious education in schools were largely due to the multi-faith content of lessons, and concluded that the weakness of religious education lay much more in the lack of time and skilled teaching. In the second study Orchard concluded that the 1988 Education Reform Act had done little to reverse the poor standing of the subject. In spite of reassurances from government that religious education enjoyed parity with other subjects in the basic curriculum, schools have failed to allocate time and resources for its delivery.

Understanding religious language

One particularly significant response to Goldman's research was a renewed interest in religious language. In a paper entitled 'A new approach to the study of the development of religious thinking in children', Murphy (1978) argued that researchers in the area of religious education should draw on the experimental techniques at present associated with 'the study of children's language and word meaning development'. He supported his case by discussing two techniques employed to investigate the meanings which certain religious words hold for children in research by Deconchy (1965, 1968) and Murphy (1979).

Murphy's ideas are developed further by Francis (1979) who built on traditions in the philosophy of religious language (Ramsey, 1957; Van Buren, 1972) to argue that research regarding the development of religious language needs to undertake a systematic investigation of two things: the way in which religious discourse uses language in an odd fashion to convey a special experience, and existing research regarding the child's ability to use language in ways which point beyond the constraints of the literal meaning of the individual words themselves. In a secular context examples of research into using language in special ways include studies of similes (Malgady, 1977), metaphors (Billow, 1975, 1981), verbal humour (Brodzinsky, 1975), jokes (Brodzinsky, 1977), riddles (Fowles and Glanz, 1977) and proverbs (Honeck, Sowry and Voegtle, 1978). In a religious context some studies have begun to explore the child's response to religious allegory (Greenacre, 1971), parables (Ainsworth, 1961; Gregory, 1966; Debot-Sevrin, 1968; Beechick, 1974; Murphy, 1977) and metaphor (McGrady, 1990, 1994a, 1994b).

For example, Murphy (1977) explored the understanding of 200 pupils, drawn from four schools, between the ages of seven and 11, making 40 for each year group. Although the project was concerned with six parables (the two houses, the rich fool, the good Samaritan, the sower, the Pharisee and the tax collector, and the lost sheep), each child was read just four of the parables. Although the research method was based on the semi-structured interview, some pupils were given a multiple choice questionnaire instead. Three levels of understanding were applied. At the first level the child can only repeat facts or elements of the parable, and shows no more than a literal application of the parable. At the second level the child can make an application in a simple way, that shows a movement in the direction of understanding the allegorical meaning of the parable. At the third level the child shows an understanding of the allegorical meaning of the parable.

McGrady (1990, 1994a, 1994b) explored the metaphorical and operational aspects of religious thinking among a sample of 117 Irish Catholic pupils. In this study McGrady proposed a paradigm of six capabilities relating to the metaphorical component of religious thinking, which he defined as recognition, comprehension, production, elaboration, interrelation and validation. Fifty-eight of the pupils completed semi-clinical interviews based on McGrady's *Metaphor and Model Test of Religious Thinking*, consisting of seven sections. Section one required subjects to complete and explain four common religious metaphors drawn from biblical and liturgical sources. Section two required recognition and comprehension of four probably unfamiliar religious metaphors. Section three required recognition, comprehension and interrelation of two parabolic statements of Jesus. Section four examined parental metaphors of the divine, inviting subjects to explore images of God as a father and as a woman feeding her child. Section five discussed the subject's personal metaphors of the divine and required subjects to interrelate these with other metaphors presented during the interview. Section six explored three important religious questions, namely the meaning of life, the meaning of suffering, and belief in an afterlife, and required subjects to select metaphors from among those discussed previously and to elaborate on them in terms of their usefulness in approaching the three questions. Section seven invited the subjects to consider why metaphors are used as part of religious discourse.

For the other 59 pupils the interviews were based on Goldman's use of the story of the temptations of Jesus. McGrady's findings contradicted Goldman's view that the use of biblical material should be restricted before the onset of formal operations by demonstrating that pupils were able to think metaphorically before the onset of formal operations. McGrady argues that rather than enhancing readiness for the examination of biblical material, formal operations may actually inhibit the pupils' appreciation by limiting the realm of that which is perceived as truthful. On these grounds McGrady concluded that, rather than waiting for the emergence of formal operations before introducing young people to biblical material, it may be necessary to strengthen their metaphorical capabilities to withstand the reductionist aspects of early formal operations.

Religious experience

Although studies of religious experience conducted among adults often draw attention to remembered events during childhood and adolescence (Robinson, 1977a, 1977b, 1978), comparatively little attention has been given to researching religious experience among school pupils. Five notable exceptions are provided by Elkind and Elkind (1962), Paffard (1973), Miles (1983), Robinson and Jackson (1987) and a set of studies by Greer (1981, 1982), Greer and Francis (1992) and Francis and Greer (1993).

Elkind and Elkind (1962) found that a high percentage of a group of 144 high school pupils in the USA had 'recurrent' and 'acute' experiences in which they had felt close to God. In England, Paffard (1973) produced evidence of the common occurrence of 'transcendental experiences' among 400 sixth form pupils and undergraduates. Miles (1983) undertook a detailed study among 137 sixth form students to test three hypotheses: that transcendental experience forms an element in the experience of adolescents; that teaching can improve students' understanding of transcendental experience; and that understanding improves students' attitudes towards transcendental experience. Comparisons were made between a group of 82 students who followed a taught programme about transcendental experience and a control group of 55 students. Attitudes were assessed by semantic differential tests, while levels of understanding were assessed by Piagetian type interviews. Robinson and Jackson (1987) conducted a questionnaire survey among 6,576 pupils from the age of 16 upwards. Factor analysis identified ten potential scales within the questionnaire, including measures of numinous experience and mystical experience. The survey also presented the pupils with two model passages presenting accounts of religious experiences. These two model passages were then followed by questions probing the pupils' own understanding and experiences.

Greer (1981) reported on a survey conducted among 1,872 upper sixth form pupils at controlled (Protestant) voluntary schools in Northern Ireland in 1978. The data demonstrated that 38% of the boys and 51% of the girls replied 'yes' to the question, 'Have you ever had an experience of God, for example, his presence or his help or anything else?' Over a quarter of the pupils described this experience and Greer classified their descriptions under nine headings, namely, guidance and help, examinations, depression and sickness, death, answered prayer, God's presence, conversion experiences, good experiences and miscellaneous. Greer (1982) reported on the findings of including the same question in a survey conducted in 1981 among 940 Roman Catholic and 1,193 Protestant pupils between the ages of 12 and 17 in Northern Ireland. The answer 'yes' was given to this question by 31% of the Protestant boys, 39% of the Protestant girls, 35% of the Roman Catholic boys and 64% of the Roman

Catholic girls. Greer and Francis (1992) and Francis and Greer (1993) employed two different samples to explore the contribution of religious experience to the development of positive religious attitudes among secondary school pupils in Northern Ireland. They concluded that the acknowledgement and naming of personal religious experience was associated with the formation of more positive attitudes towards Christianity.

Hay (1988, 1990b) discussed the bearing of empirical studies of religious experience on education.

Images of God

A significant strand in the empirical psychology of religion has been concerned with the relationship between parental images and representations of God (Vergote and Tamayo, 1981). Differences in research methods used, populations examined, and concepts employed by these studies, however, led to four different and conflicting views. First, the pioneering study by Nelson and Jones (1957) drew attention to a strong relation between the concept of God and the mother image for both male and female subjects. A second group of studies by Strunk (1959), Godin and Hallez (1965) and Deconchy (1968) indicated that the relation between God and mother (or the feminine image) was pre-eminent in men, whereas in women the relation between God and father (or the masculine image) predominated. Third, Vergote, Tamayo, Pasquali, Bonami, Pattyn and Custers (1969) found that, in their American samples, both males and females emphasised the paternal image of God rather than the maternal image and that this tendency was even stronger in males than females. The paternal image of God was also emphasised by both boys and girls within the two Asian communities reported by Vergote and Aubert (1973). Fourth, Vergote, Bonami, Custers and Pattyn (1967) found that, in their French-speaking Belgian sample, both males and females emphasised the parental image of God corresponding to their own sex.

A very different research tradition concerned with images of God was pioneered by Harms (1944) who asked children to imagine God or 'the highest being they thought to exist' and then to draw or paint what they imagined. From his analysis of these drawings Harms discerned three stages of development, described as fairy tale, realistic and individualistic. This tradition has been carried on by Pitts (1976, 1977, 1979). Heller (1986) also employed drawings, alongside letters to God, doll play and interviews.

A third research tradition is used by Hilliard (1959) who asked 608 pupils in four secondary schools to write on the topic 'My idea of God'. They were given no prompting or assistance 'in the hope that what they wrote would be a spontaneous expression of their own ideas'. More recently, Oger (1970) and Ludwig, Weber and Iben (1974) invited children to write letters to God and analysed their content.

A fourth research tradition in this area is illustrated by Claerhout and Declercq (1970) who employed a photo-test to explore adolescents' images of Jesus among 1,200 pupils attending Catholic schools. Forty photos were used. The pupils were asked to identify the images they would be inclined to prefer and the images they would be inclined to reject, and then to justify their choices.

Prayer

Research concerned with prayer during childhood and adolescence falls into three main strands. The first strand, grounded in developmental psychology, has attempted to discover stages in the development of the concept of prayer. For example, Long, Elkind and Spilka (1967) identified three stages in their sample of 160 boys and girls between the ages of five and 12. In the first stage, between the ages of five and seven, children had a global conception of prayer in the sense that their comprehension of the term was both vague and fragmentary. In the second stage, between the ages of seven and nine, children had a concrete differentiated conception of prayer and recognised that it involved verbal activity. At this stage, however, prayer was still an external activity, a routine form, rather than personal and internal. In the third stage, between the ages of nine and 12, children had an abstract conception of prayer in the sense that it was regarded as an internal activity deriving from personal conviction and belief. Other studies in this tradition include Elkind, Spilka and Long (1968), May (1977, 1979), Worten and Dollinger (1986), Rosenberg (1990) and Scarlett and Perriello (1991).

A second strand of research has concentrated on mapping changing patterns of belief in the causal efficacy of prayer during childhood and adolescence. For example, Brown (1966) explored the responses of 398 boys and 703 girls between the ages of 12 and 17 to seven situations: success in a football match, safety during battle, avoidance of detection of theft, repayment of a debt, fine weather for a church fête, escape from a shark and recovery of a sick grandmother. In relation to each situation he addressed two questions: Is it right to pray in this situation? and Are the prayers likely to have any effect? The data demonstrated a consistent age-related trend away from belief in the causal efficacy of petitionary prayer. Other studies in this tradition include Godin and van Roey (1959), Thouless and Brown (1964), Brown (1968) and Tamminen (1991).

A third strand of research, grounded in social psychology, has attempted to discover the social and contextual influences on individual differences in the practice of prayer during childhood and adolescence. For example, Francis and Brown (1990) examined the influence of home, church and denominational identity on an attitudinal predisposition to pray and the practice of prayer among 4,948 11 year old children in England. Francis and Brown (1991) replicated this study among 711 16 year olds. They demonstrate that among 16 year olds the influence of church is stronger and the influence of parents is weaker than among eleven year olds. Another study in this tradition, by Janssen, de Hart and den Draak (1989, 1990), demonstrated significant differences in praying practices according to religious affiliation among s 16 and 17 year old Dutch high school pupils.

Complementarity in religious thinking

The conflict between science and religion has been noted by a number of studies concerned with adolescent religiosity, including Poole (1983), Gibson (1989), Reich (1991) and Fulljames, Gibson and Francis (1991). A valuable theoretical framework for understanding this conflict is provided by Reich (1989) who argues that:

> It is the maturity of children's thinking which influences the way they see the relationship between science and religion. We must therefore study the stages of cognitive development to see how the crisis in the views of the world develops. The crucial factor is whether alternative structures of interpretation can be understood as complementing each other, and we shall suggest that it is the achievement of this 'complementarity' which enables young people to pass through critical stages of their development. Complementarity enables people to co-ordinate 'conflicting' statements and to arrive at synoptic points of view.

According to Reich's theoretical schema, the development of complementarity, if fully formulated, would consist of five consecutive levels of thinking. When confronted by two alternative theories, at the first level of thinking it is characteristic that either one or the other theory is declared correct. At the second level of thinking there is some examination of the possibility that both theories are correct. At the third level of thinking both theories are regarded as necessary for a satisfactory description or explanation. Reich regards this third level as the appearance of genuine complementarity in thinking. At the fourth level of thinking both theories are immediately understood as complementary, and the mutuality of their relationship is discussed. At the fifth level the problem is considered afresh starting from basic principles and a sophisticated synopsis of logically possible explanations and relationships is presented.

An empirical study by Oser and Reich (1987) concluded that about two-thirds of the decisions made by six to ten year olds were at level one, while about 80% of the decisions made by the 20- to 25-year olds in their sample were at level four.

School worship

In spite of its central place in school life in England and Wales, the daily act of collective worship has received little research in its own right, although a number of surveys concerned with the broader issue of religious education include some reference to school worship. For example, Greer (1972) found that 93% of parents agreed with the school day beginning with an act of collective worship. Among sixth form pupils, however, the proportion fell to 62% among girls and 40% among boys. A recent survey of religion and values among more than 13,000 13- to 15-year olds in England and Wales found that only 6% of this age group agreed with the view that schools should hold a religious assembly every day. Even among those pupils who attended church every week, the proportion increased to no higher than 17% (Francis and Kay, 1995).

Brimer (1972) set out to explore the practices and attitudes of primary school head teachers and their fourth year junior pupils in the city of Birmingham. He found that, while 61% of head teachers rated assemblies as very important, this view was shared by only 27% of their pupils. Pritchard (1974) undertook case studies of worship in Church of England primary schools.

A major study into school worship and assemblies was initiated within the University of Southampton in the early 1980s. The report of the pilot survey by Souper and Kay (1982) described the situation in Hampshire on the basis on an 83% response rate from a total survey of the secondary schools and a 72% response rate from a survey of one in four of the primary schools. The analysis considered issues like who conducts the assemblies, where assemblies are held, how assemblies relate to the religious education syllabus and the general curriculum, the use of prayer and singing, drama and audio-visual aids, withdrawal from assemblies and pressure for change.

Souper and Kay (1983) followed this pilot study with a survey in independent schools. No report emerged, however, from their parallel major study in state maintained schools.

Catholic schools

Research in religious education is also concerned with the wider issues of the religious distinctiveness and effectiveness of denominational schools, Here the international nature of the Catholic church has generated a wide international literature.   Key studies are provided as follows: in the USA by Neuwien (1966), Greeley and Rossi (1966), Greeley, McCready and McCourt (1976), Greeley (1982), Lesko (1988), Marsh and Grayson (1990), Francis and Egan (1990), Marsh (1991) and Bryk, Lee and Holland (1993); in Australia by Leavey (1972), Flynn (1975, 1985), Fahy (1976, 1978, 1980, 1992), De Vaus (1981) and Francis and Egan (1987); and in Canada by McLaren (1986).

Research into the distinctiveness and effectiveness of Catholic schools in the UK has its roots in studies by Brothers (1964), Spencer (1968), Hornsby-Smith and Petit (1975) and Hornsby-Smith (1978). More recent studies on Catholic schools in the UK have employed three main techniques.   Participant observation was employed by Burgess (1983, 1987) to make a detailed case study of one Catholic comprehensive school in England and by Murray (1985) to compare a Catholic school and a Protestant school in Northern Ireland. Dent (1988) used unstructured interviews to profile five different Catholic schools. Francis and colleagues employed psychometric techniques to assess the influence of Catholic schools on the pupils. For example, in a comparative study of ten and 11 year old pupils attending County, Anglican and Catholic primary schools in 1974, 1978 and 1982, Francis (1986a) concluded that Catholic schools contribute to the development of positive religious attitudes among pupils of this age, after controlling for the influence of home and church. A similar conclusion is suggested by Francis (1987a) among 11 year old pupils. In a study of 2,895 pupils attending five Catholic secondary schools Francis (1986b) drew attention to the way in which these schools had a less positive influence on pupils from non-Catholic backgrounds, even when they were practising members of other denominations. Egan and Francis (1986) and Egan (1988) went one step further in their study of the fifth year pupils attending 15 of the 16 Catholic secondary schools in Wales and highlighted the different influence of these schools on non-Catholic, lapsed Catholic and practising Catholic pupils. In a study in Scotland, Rhymer (1983) and Rhymer and Francis (1985) drew attention to the equal influence of separate Catholic schools and separate Catholic religious education provision within non-denominational schools, in comparison with Catholic pupils who attended non-denominational schools in which separate religious education provision was not available.

Other recent research perspectives on Catholic schools in Britain are provided by Hanlon (1989) on provisions for religious education, Arthur (1992, 1993, 1994a, 1994b), including studies of parental involvement, policy perceptions of head teachers and governors, admissions policies and curriculum, by Morris (1994) on the academic performance of Catholic schools, and by Tritter (1992) on the effect of religious schools on their students' moral values.

Anglican schools

There is considerably less research on the distinctiveness and effectiveness of Anglican schools than on Catholic schools. Francis (1986c) explored the attitudes of teachers in Anglican primary schools and found that the younger teachers were less sympathetic to the church school system than older teachers. Kay, Piper and Gay (1988) and Francis and Stone (1995) reported on the attitudes of governors of Anglican schools. Francis (1987a) compared the provision for religious education in Anglican and county primary schools. He found that the church schools adopted a more church-related approach to religious education. In two studies into the impact of Anglican primary schools on the pupils' attitudes towards religion, Francis (1986a) found that Church of England voluntary aided schools exerted a negative influence compared with county schools, and Francis (1987a) found that Church of England voluntary controlled schools exerted a negative influence compared with county schools. In two studies exploring the impact of Anglican secondary schools on pupil attitudes, Francis and Brown (1991) identified a negative influence on attitude towards prayer, while Francis and Jewell (1992) found no influence, either positive or negative, on attitude towards the church. In two studies exploring the impact of Anglican primary schools on local church life, Francis and Lankshear (1990, 1991) identified a significant positive influence in both rural and urban settings. O'Keeffe (1986) explored the role of church schools in a multi-cultural, multi-racial context. She drew on information from 103 Church of England and county schools of both primary and secondary level in Greater London, the North-West and the West Midlands, including interviews with 102 headteachers, 67 religious education teachers and 139 parents whose children were attending church schools. Two other studies provide profiles of Anglican primary and secondary schools in the diocese of London (Gay, Kay, Newdick and Perry, 1991a, 1991b).

In a study concerned with multi-cultural education, Ball and Troyna (1987) concluded that both Anglican and Catholic schools have lagged behind county schools in promoting multi-cultural education. Cox and Skinner (1990) reported on an early stage of a curriculum development project based in five church aided primary schools in a north Warwickshire town. It set out to uncover the attitudes of the teachers to multi-faith religious education and to assess the impact of in-service training. The authors concluded that the teachers had welcomed a multi-faith approach to religious education, and they had found the change to this approach less difficult than they had expected. Higgins (1989) analysed the ways in which the syllabuses of religious education developed for use in Church of England voluntary aided schools. He was concerned with how the syllabuses treated the role of women in the context of the current social and ecclesiastical debate. He found the syllabuses uninformed by these contemporary perspectives.

Activity B4

Select one of the research topics discussed in this section and consider the following four questions.

- What has most surprised you in the research discussed?
- What more do you need to know in order to assess this research?
- What implications can you identify for educational practice in school, church or family?
- What further research would be helpful in this area?

Comment on activity B4

You may well have come to the view that good educational research raises new questions as well as answers old questions. It is for this reason that good research reports often conclude by identifying an agenda for further work.

Readers

Helpful further material can be found in L.J. Francis, W.K. Kay and W.S. Campbell (eds), *Research in Religious Education*, Leominster, Gracewing, and K.E. Hyde (1990), *Religion in Childhood and Adolescence: a comprehensive review of the research*, Birmingham, Alabama, Religious Education Press.

Bibliography

Ainsworth, O. (1961), A study of some aspects of the growth of religious understanding of children aged between 5 and 11 years, Unpublished Dip.Ed. dissertation, University of Manchester.

Archer, J. and Macrae, M. (1991), Gender-perceptions of school subjects among 10-11 year olds, *British Journal of Educational Psychology*, 61, 99-103.

Arthur, J. (1992), The Catholic school and its curriculum, *British Journal of Religious Education*, 14, 157-168.

Arthur, J. (1993), Policy perceptions of headteachers and governors in Catholic schooling, *Educational Studies*, 19, 275-287.

Arthur, J. (1994a), Parental involvement in Catholic schools: a case of increasing conflict, *British Journal of Educational Studies*, 42, 174-190.

Arthur, J. (1994b), Admissions to Catholic schools: principles and practice, *British Journal of Religious Education*, 17, 35-45.

Bailey, J.R. (1979), Religious education in Lincolnshire secondary schools, *British Journal of Religious Education*, 1, 89-94.

Ball, W. and Troyna, B. (1987), Resistance, rights and rituals: denominational schools and multicultural education, *Journal of Educational Policy*, 2, 15-25.

Bedwell, A.E. (1977), Aims of religious education teachers in Hereford and Worcester, *Learning for Living*, 17, 66-74.

Beechick, R.A. (1974), Children's understanding of parables: a developmental study, Unpublished D.Ed. dissertation, Arizona State University.

Benfield, G. (1975), Religious education in secondary schools: a close look at one area, *Learning for Living*, 14, 173-178.

Billow, R.M. (1975), A cognitive developmental study of metaphor comprehension, *Developmental Psychology*, 11, 415-423.

Billow, R.M. (1981), Observing spontaneous metaphor in children, *Journal of Experimental Child Psychology*, 31, 430-445.

Brimer, J. (1972), School worship with juniors, *Learning for Living*, 11, 5, 6-12.

Brodzinsky, D. (1975), The role of conceptual tempo and stimulus characteristics in children's humour development, *Developmental Psychology*, 11, 843-850.

Brodzinsky, D. (1977), Children's comprehension and appreciation of verbal jokes in relation to conceptual tempo, *Child Development*, 48, 960-967.

Brothers, J. (1964), Church and School: a study of the impact of education on religion, Liverpool, University of Liverpool Press.

Brown, L.B. (1966), Ego-centric thought in petitionary prayer: a cross-cultural study, *Journal of Social Psychology*, 68, 197-210.

Brown, L.B. (1968), Some attitudes underlying petitionary prayer, in A. Godin (ed.), *From Cry to Word: contributions towards a psychology of prayer*, pp 65-84, Brussels, Lumen Vitae Press.

Bryk, A.S., Lee, V.E. and Holland, P.B. (1993), *Catholic Schools and the Common Good*, Cambridge, Massachusetts, Harvard University Press.

Burgess, B.G. (1975), A study of the attitudes of primary school teachers in Essex and Walsall to religious education and worship, Unpublished M.Phil. dissertation, University of London, Institute of Education.

Burgess, B.G. (1980), A further study of opinions of Essex primary teachers about religious education and school assembly in the context of contemporary controversy, Unpublished Ph.D. dissertation, University of London, Institute of Education.

Burgess, R.G. (1983), *Experiencing Comprehensive Education: a study of Bishop McGregor School*, London, Methuen.

Burgess, R.G. (1987), Studying and restudying Bishop McGregor School, in G. Walford (ed.), *Doing Sociology of Education*, pp 67-94, Barcombe, Falmer Press.

Claerhout, J. and Declercq, M. (1970), Christ in the mind of the adolescent: photo-test and enquiry in Catholic education, *Lumen Vitae*, 25, 243-264.

Cox, E. and Skinner, M. (1990), Multi-faith religious education in church primary schools, *British Journal of Religious Education*, 12, 102-109.

Debot-Sevrin, M.R. (1968), An attempt in experimental teaching: the assimilation of a parable by normal and maladjusted children of the 6-7 age group, in A. Godin (ed.), *From Cry to Word*, pp 135-158, Brussels, Lumen Vitae Press.

Deconchy, J.P. (1965), The idea of God: its emergence between 7 and 16 years, in A. Godin (ed.), *From Religious Experience to a Religious Attitude*, pp 97-108, Chicago, Loyola University Press.

Deconchy, J.P. (1968), God and the parental images, in A. Godin (ed.), *From Cry to Word*, pp 85-94, Brussels, Lumen Vitae Press.

Dent, R. (1988), *Faith of Our Fathers: Roman Catholic schools in a multifaith society*, Coventry, City of Coventry Education Department.

De Vaus, D.A. (1981), The impact of Catholic schools on the religious orientation of boys and girls, *Journal of Christian Education*, 71, 44-51.

Egan, J. (1988), *Opting Out: Catholic schools today*, Leominster, Fowler Wright.

Egan, J. and Francis, L.J. (1986), School ethos in Wales: the impact of non-practising Catholic and non-Catholic pupils on Catholic secondary schools, *Lumen Vitae*, 41, 159-173.

Elkind, D. and Elkind, S. (1962), Varieties of religious experience in young adolescents, *Journal for the Scientific Study of Religion*, 2, 102-112.

Elkind, D., Spilka, B. and Long, D. (1968), The child's conception of prayer, in A. Godin (ed.), *From Cry to Word*, pp 51-64, Brussels, Lumen Vitae Press.

Erricker, C. (1998), Journeys through the heart: the effect of death, loss and conflict on children's worldviews, *Journal of Beliefs and Values*, 19, 107-118.

Erricker, C. and Erricker, J. (1996), Where angels fear to tread: discovering children's spirituality, in R. Best (ed.), *Education, Spirituality and the Whole Child*, pp 184-195, London, Cassell.

Erricker, C., Erricker, J., Ota, C., Sullivan, D. and Fletcher, M. (1997), *The Education of the Whole Child*, London, Cassell.

Erricker, J. and Erricker, C. (1995), Children speaking their minds, *Panorama*, 7 (1), 96-109.

Fahy, P.S. (1976), School and home perceptions of Australian adolescent males attending Catholic schools, *Our Apostolate*, 24, 167-188.

Fahy, P.S. (1978), Religious beliefs of 15,900 youths: attending Australian Catholic schools, years 12, 10, 8, 1975-1977, *Word in Life*, 26, 66-72.

Fahy, P.S. (1980), The religious effectiveness of some Australian Catholic high schools, *Word in Life*, 28, 86-98.

Fahy, P.S. (1992), *Faith in Catholic Classrooms*, Homebush, New South Wales, St Paul Publications.

Flynn, M.F. (1975), *Some Catholic Schools in Action*, Sydney, Catholic Education Office.

Flynn, M.F. (1985), *The Effectiveness of Catholic Schools*, Homebush, New South Wales, Saint Paul Publications.

Fowles, B. and Glanz, M.E. (1977), Competence and talent in verbal riddle comprehension, *Journal of Child Language*, 4, 433-452.

Francis, L.J. (1979), Research and the development of religious thinking, *Educational Studies*, 5, 109-115.

Francis, L.J. (1986a), Denominational schools and pupil attitude towards Christianity, *British Educational Research Journal*, 12, 145-152.

Francis, L.J. (1986b), Roman Catholic secondary schools: falling rolls and pupil attitudes, *Educational Studies*, 12, 119-127.

Francis, L.J. (1986c), *Partnership in Rural Education: church schools and teacher attitudes*, London, Collins Liturgical Publications.

Francis, L.J. (1987a), *Religion in the Primary School: partnership between church and state?* London, Collins Liturgical Publications.

Francis, L.J. (1987b), The decline in attitude towards religion among 8-15 year olds, *Educational Studies*, 13, 125-134.

Francis, L.J. and Brown, L.B. (1990), The predisposition to pray: a study of the social influence on the predisposition to pray among eleven year old children in England, *Journal of Empirical Theology*, 3, 2, 23-34.

Francis, L.J. and Brown, L.B. (1991), The influence of home, church and school on prayer among sixteen year old adolescents in England, *Review of Religious Research*, 33, 112-122.

Francis, L.J. and Egan, J. (1987), Catholic schools and the communication of faith: an empirical inquiry, *Catholic School Studies*, 60, 2, 27-34.

Francis, L.J. and Egan, J. (1990), The Catholic school as 'faith community': an empirical enquiry, *Religious Education*, 85, 588-603.

Francis, L.J. and Greer, J.E. (1993), The contribution of religious experience to Christian development: a study among fourth, fifth and sixth year pupils in Northern Ireland, *British Journal of Religious Education*, 15, 38-43.

Francis, L.J. and Jewell, A. (1992), Shaping adolescent attitude towards the church: comparison between Church of England and county secondary schools, *Evaluation and Research in Education*, 6, 13-21.

Francis, L.J. and Kay, W.K. (1995), *Teenage Religion and Values*, Leominster, Gracewing.

Francis, L.J. and Lankshear, D.W. (1990), The impact of church schools on village church life, *Educational Studies*, 16, 117-129.

Francis, L.J. and Lankshear, D.W. (1991), The impact of church schools on urban church life, *School Effectiveness and School Improvement*, 2, 324-335.

Francis, L.J. and Stone, E.A. (1995), School governors and the religious ethos of C of E voluntary aided primary schools, *Educational Management and Administration*, 23, 176-187.

Fulljames, P., Gibson, H.M. and Francis, L.J. (1991), Creationism, scientism, Christianity and science: a study in adolescent attitudes, *British Educational Research Journal*, 17, 171-190.

Garrity, F.D. (1960), A study of the attitude of some secondary modern school pupils towards religious education, Unpublished M.Ed. dissertation, University of Manchester.

Gay, J., Kay, B., Newdick, H. and Perry, G. (1991a), *A Role for the Future: Anglican primary schools in the London diocese*, Abingdon, Culham College Institute.

Gay, J., Kay, B., Newdick, H. and Perry, G. (1991b), *Schools and Church: Anglican secondary schools in the London diocese*, Abingdon, Culham College Institute.

Gibson, H.M. (1989), Attitudes to religion and science among school children aged 11 to 16 years in a Scottish city, *Journal of Empirical Theology*, 2, 5-26.

Godin, A. and Hallez, M. (1965), Parental images and divine paternity, in A. Godin (ed.), *From Religious Experience to a Religious Attitude*, pp 65-96, Chicago, Loyola University Press.

Godin, A. and van Roey, B. (1959), Imminent justice and divine protection, *Lumen Vitae*, 14, 129-148.

Goldman, R.J. (1965), Do we want our children taught about God? *New Society*, 5, 139, 8-10.

Greeley, A.M. (1982), *Catholic High Schools and Minority Students*, New Brunswick, Transaction Books.

Greeley, A.M., McCready, W.C. and McCourt, K. (1976), *Catholic Schools in a Declining Church*, Kansas City, Sheed and Ward.

Greeley, A.M. and Rossi, P.H. (1966), *The Education of Catholic Americans*, Chicago, Aldine Publishing Company.

Greenacre, I. (1971), The response of young people to religious allegory, Unpublished Dip.Ed. dissertation, University of Birmingham.

Greer, J.E. (1970), The attitudes of parents and pupils to religion in school, *Irish Journal of Education*, 4, 39-46.

Greer, J.E. (1972), *A Questioning Generation*, Belfast, Church of Ireland Board of Education.

Greer, J.E. (1981), Religious experience and religious education, *Search*, 4, 1, 23-34.

Greer, J.E. (1982), The religious experience of Northern Irish pupils, *The Irish Catechist*, 6, 2, 49-58.

Greer, J.E. and Brown, G.A. (1973), The effects of new approaches to religious education in the primary school, *Journal of Curriculum Studies*, 5, 73-78.

Greer, J.E. and Francis, L.J. (1992), Religious experience and attitude toward Christianity among secondary school children in Northern Ireland, *Journal of Social Psychology*, 132, 277-279.

Gregory, H.M. (1966), Parables in the secondary school, Unpublished Diploma in Religious Education dissertation, University of Nottingham.

Hanlon, K. (1989), A survey on religious education in Roman Catholic secondary schools in England and Wales, *British Journal of Religious Education*, 11, 154-162.

Harms, E. (1944), The development of religious experience in children, *American Journal of Sociology*, 50, 112-122.

Harvey, T.J. (1984), Gender differences in subject preference and perception of subject importance among third year secondary school pupils in single-sex and mixed comprehensive schools, *Educational Studies*, 10, 243-253.

Hay, D. (1982), *Exploring Inner Space*, Harmondsworth, Penguin.

Hay, D. (1988), The bearing of empirical studies of religious experience on education, Unpublished Ph.D. dissertation, University of Nottingham.

Hay, D. (1990a), *Religious Experience Today: studying the facts*, London, Mowbray.

Hay, D. (1990b), The bearing of empirical studies of religious experience on education, *Research Papers in Education*, 5, 1, 3-28.

Hay, D. and Nye, R. (1998), *The Spirit of the Child*, London, Fount.

Hay, D., Nye, R. and Murphy, R. (1996), Thinking about childhood spirituality: review of research and current directions, in L.J. Francis, W.K. Kay and W.S. Campbell, *Research in Religious Education*, pp 47-71, Leominster, Gracewing.

Heller, D. (1986), *The Children's God*, Chicago, University of Chicago Press.

Higgins, J.L. (1989), Gender and Church of England diocesan syllabuses of religious education, *British Journal of Religious Education*, 1, 58-62.

Hilliard, F.H. (1959), Ideas of God among secondary school children, *Religion in Education*, 27, 1, 14-19.

Honeck, R.P., Sowry, B.M. and Voegtle, K. (1978), Proverbial understanding in a pictorial context, *Child Development*, 49, 327-331.

Hornsby-Smith, M.P. (1978), *Catholic Education: the unobtrusive partner*, London, Sheed and Ward.

Hornsby-Smith, M.P. and Petit, M. (1975), Social, moral and religious attitudes of secondary school students, *Journal of Moral Education*, 4, 261-272.

Jackson, R. (1989), Hinduism: from ethnographic research to curriculum development in religious education, *Panorama*, 1 (2), 59-77.

Jackson, R. (1996a), Ethnographic research and curriculum development, in L.J. Francis, W.K. Kay and W.S. Campbell (eds), *Research in Religious Education*, pp 145-162, Leominster, Gracewing.

Jackson, R. (1996b), The construction of 'Hinduism' and its impact on religious education in England and Wales, *Panorama*, 8 (2), 86-104.

Jackson, R. (1997), *Religious Education: an interpretive approach*, London, Hodder and Stoughton.

Jackson, R. and Nesbitt, E.M. (1992), The diversity of experience in the religious upbringing of children from Christian families in Britain, *British Journal of Religious Education*, 15, 19-28.

Jackson, R. and Nesbitt, E.M. (1993), *Hindu Children in Britain*, Stoke on Trent, Trentham.

Janssen, J., de Hart, J. and den Draak, C. (1989), Praying practices, *Journal of Empirical Theology*, 2, 2, 28-39.

Janssen, J., de Hart, J. and den Draak, C. (1990), A content analysis of the praying practices of Dutch youth, *Journal for the Scientific Study of Religion*, 29, 99-107.

Kay, B.W., Piper, H.S. and Gay, J.D. (1988), *Managing the Church Schools: a study of the governing bodies of Church of England aided primary schools in the Oxford diocese*, Abingdon, Culham College Institute Occasional Paper 10.

Kay, W. (1973), Some changes in primary school teachers' attitudes to religious and moral education, *Journal of Moral Education*, 3, 407-411.

Keys, W. and Ormerod, M.B. (1976), Some factors affecting pupils' preferences, *The Durham Research Review*, 7, 1109-1115.

Leavey, C. (1972), The transmission of religious moral values in nine Catholic girls schools, *Twentieth Century*, 27, 167-184.

Lesko, N. (1988), *Symbolizing Society: stories, rites and structure in a Catholic high school*, London, Falmer Press.

Lewis, E.O. (1913), Popular and unpopular school subjects, *Journal of Experimental Pedagogy*, 2, 89-98.

Lewis, J.M. (1974), An examination of the attitudes of pupils towards the content and method of teaching religious education in certain co-educational comprehensive schools in Wales, Unpublished M.Ed. dissertation, University of Wales (Swansea).

Long, D., Elkind, D. and Spilka, B. (1967), The child's concept of prayer, *Journal for the Scientific Study of Religion*, 6, 101-109.

Ludwig, D.J., Weber, T. and Iben, D. (1974), Letters to God: a study of children's religious concepts, *Journal of Psychology and Theology*, 2, 31-35.

McGrady, A.G. (1990), The development of religious thinking: a comparison of metaphoric and operational paradigms, Unpublished Ph.D. dissertation, University of Birmingham.

McGrady, A.G. (1994a), Metaphorical and operational aspects of religious thinking: research with Irish Catholic pupils (part 1), *British Journal of Religious Education*, 16, 148-163.

McGrady, A.G. (1994b), Metaphorical and operational aspects of religious thinking: research with Irish Catholic pupils (part 2), *British Journal of Religious Education*, 17, 56-62.

McLaren, P. (1986), *Schooling as a Ritual Performance*, London, Routledge and Kegan Paul.

McQuillan, M. (1990), An analysis of religious education provision, in one town, for children aged seven to sixteen years, Unpublished M.Phil. dissertation, University of Manchester.

Malgady, R.G. (1977), Children's interpretation and appreciation similes, *Child Development*, 48, 1734-1738.

Marsh, H.W. (1991), Public, Catholic single-sex, and Catholic coeducational high schools: their effects on achievement, affect and behaviour, *American Journal of Education*, 99, 320-356.

Marsh, H.W. and Grayson, D. (1990), Public/Catholic differences in the High School and Beyond data: a multigroup structural equation modelling approach to testing mean differences, *Journal of Educational Studies*, 15, 199-236.

May, P.R. (1967), Why parents want religion in school, *Learning for Living*, 6, 4, 14-18.

May, P.R. (1968), Why teachers want religion in school, *Learning for Living*, 8, 1, 13-17.

May, P.R. (1977), Religious judgements in children and adolescents: a research report, *Learning for Living*, 16, 115-122.

May, P.R. (1979), Religious thinking in children and adolescents, *Durham and Newcastle Research Review*, 8, 24, 15-28.

May, P.R. and Johnston, D.R. (1967), Parental attitudes to RE in state schools, *Durham Research Review*, 18, 127-138.

Miles, G.B. (1983), A critical and experimental study of adolescents' attitudes to and understanding of transcendental experience, Unpublished Ph.D. dissertation, University of Leeds.

Morris, A.B. (1994), The academic performance of Catholic schools, *School Organisation*, 14, 81-89.

Murphy, R.J.L. (1977), Does children's understanding of parables develop in stages? *Learning for Living*, 16, 168-172.

Murphy, R.J.L. (1978), A new approach to the study of the development of religious thinking in children, *Educational Studies*, 4, 19-22.

Murphy, R.J.L. (1979), An investigation into some aspects of the development of religious thinking in children aged between 6 and 11 years, Unpublished Ph.D. dissertation, University of St Andrews.

Murray, D. (1985), *Worlds Apart: segregated schools in Northern Ireland*, Belfast, Appletree Press.

Nelson, M.O. and Jones, E.M. (1957), An application of the Q-technique to the study of religious concepts, *Psychological Reports*, 3, 293-297.

Nesbitt, E.M. (1990), Religion and identity: the Valmiki community in Coventry, *New Community*, 16, 261-274.

Nesbitt, E.M. (1992), Photographing worship: issues raised by ethnographic study of children's participation in acts of worship, *Visual Anthropology*, 5, 285-306.

Nesbitt, E.M. (1993), Children and the world to come: the views of children aged eight to fourteen on life after death, *Religion Today*, 8 (3), 10-13.

Nesbitt, E.M. (1995), Punjabis in Britain: cultural history and cultural choices, *South Asia Research*, 15, 221-240.

Nesbitt, E.M. (1997a), Splashed with goodness: the many meanings of *Amrit* for young British Sikhs, *Journal of Contemporary Religion*, 12, 17-33.

Nesbitt, E.M. (1997b), Sikhs and proper Sikhs: young British Sikhs' perceptions of their identity, in P. Singh and N.G. Barrier (eds), *Sikh Identity: continuity and change*, Delhi, Manohar.

Nesbitt, E.M. (1998a), British, Asian and Hindu: identity, self-narration and the ethnographic interview, *Journal of Beliefs and Values*, 19, 189-200.

Nesbitt, E.M. (1998b), Bridging the gap between young people's experience of their religious traditions at home and school: the contribution of ethnographic research, *British Journal of Religious Education*, 20, 102-114.

Nesbitt, E.M. and Jackson, R. (1992), Christian and Hindu children: their perceptions of each others' religious traditions, *Journal of Empirical Theology*, 5 (2), 39-62.

Nesbitt, E.M. and Jackson, R. (1993), Aspects of cultural transmission in a Diaspora Sikh community, *Journal of Sikh Studies*, 18, 52-66.

Nesbitt, E.M. and Jackson, R. (1995), Sikh children's use of 'God': ethnographic fieldwork and religious education, *British Journal of Religious Education*, 17, 108-120.

Neuwien, R.A. (ed.) (1966), *Catholic Schools in Action*, Notre Dame, Indiana, University of Notre Dame Press.

Nye, R. (1996), Childhood spirituality and contemporary developmental psychology, in R. Best (ed.), *Education, Spirituality and the Whole Child*, pp 108-120, London, Cassell.

Nye, R. and Hay, D. (1996), Identifying children's spirituality: how do you start without a starting point? *British Journal of Religious Education*, 18, 144-154.

Oger, J.H.M. (1970), Letters to God, *Lumen Vitae*, 25, 93-115.

O'Keeffe, B. (1986), *Faith, Culture and the Dual System: a comparative study of church and county schools*, Barcombe, Falmer Press.

Orchard, S. (1991), What was wrong with religious education? an analysis of HMI reports 1985-1988, *British Journal of Religious Education*, 14, 15-21.

Orchard, S. (1994), A further analysis of HMI reports 1989-1991, *British Journal of Religious Education*, 16, 21-27.

Ormerod, M.B. (1975), Subject preference and choice in co-educational and single sex secondary schools, *British Journal of Educational Psychology*, 45, 257-267.

Oser, F. and Reich, K.H. (1987), The challenge of competing explanations: the development of thinking in terms of complementarity, *Human Development*, 30, 178-186.

Ota, C. (1997), Learning to juggle: the experience of Muslim and Sikh children coping with different value systems, *Journal of Beliefs and Values*, 18, 227-234.

Ota, C., Erricker, C. and Erricker, J. (1997), The secrets of the playground, *Pastoral Care in Education*, 15 (4), 19-24.

Paffard, M. (1973), *Inglorious Wordsworth*, London, Hodder and Stoughton.

Pitts, V.P. (1976), Drawing the invisible: children's conceptualisation of God, *Character Potential*, 8, 1, 12-24.

Pitts, V.P. (1977), Drawing pictures of God, *Learning for Living*, 16, 123-129.

Pitts, V.P. (1979), *Children's Pictures of God*, Schenectady, New York, Character Research Press.

Poole, M.W. (1983), An investigation into aspects of the interplay between science and religion at sixth form level, Unpublished M.Phil. dissertation, University of London, King's College.

Povall, C.H. (1971), Some factors affecting pupils' attitudes to religious education, Unpublished M.Ed. dissertation, University of Manchester.

Pritchard, C.B. (1974), Worship in the primary school: case studies in Church of England schools, Unpublished M.Ed. dissertation, University of Liverpool.

Rahner, K. (1974), *Theological Investigations 11*, London, Darton, Longman and Todd.

Ramsey, I.T. (1957), *Religious Language*, London, SCM.

Reich, H. (1989), Between religion and science: complementarity in the religious thinking of young people, *British Journal of Religious Education*, 11, 62-69.

Reich, H. (1991), Beliefs of German and Swiss children and young people about science and religion, *British Journal of Religious Education*, 13, 65-73.

Rhymer, J. (1983), Religious attitudes of Roman Catholic secondary school pupils in Strathclyde region, Unpublished Ph.D. dissertation, University of Edinburgh.

Rhymer, J. and Francis, L.J. (1985), Roman Catholic secondary schools in Scotland and pupil attitude towards religion, *Lumen Vitae*, 40, 103-110.

Robinson, E. (1977a), *The Original Vision*, Oxford, Religious Experience Research Unit.

Robinson, E. (1977b), *This Time-Bound Ladder*, Oxford, Religious Experience Research Unit.

Robinson, E. (1978), *Living the Questions*, Oxford, Religious Experience Research Unit.

Robinson, E. and Jackson, M. (1987), *Religion and Values at 16+*, Oxford, Alister Hardy Research Centre and CEM.

Rosenberg, R. (1990), The development of the concept of prayer in Jewish-Israeli children and adolescents, *Studies in Jewish Education*, 5, 91-129.

Scarlett, W.G. and Perriello, L. (1991), The development of prayer in adolescence, *New Directions for Child Development*, 52, 63-76.

Souper, P.C. and Kay, W.K. (1982), *The School Assembly in Hampshire*, Southampton, University Department of Education.

Souper, P.C. and Kay, W.K. (1983), *Worship in the Independent School*, Southampton, University of Southampton Department of Education.

Spencer, A.E.C.W. (1968), An evaluation of Roman Catholic educational policy in England and Wales 1900-1960, in P. Jeff (ed.), *Religious Education: drift or decision?* pp 165-221, London, Darton, Longman and Todd.

Strunk, O. (1959), Perceived relationship between parental and deity concepts, *Psychological Newsletter*, 10, 222-226.

Tamminen, K. (1991), *Religious Development in Childhood and Youth: an empirical study*, Helsinki, Suomalainen Tiedeakatemia.

Thouless, R.H. and Brown, L.B. (1964), Petitionary prayer: belief in its appropriateness and causal efficacy among adolescent girls, *Lumen Vitae*, 19, 297-310.

Tritter, J. (1992), An educated change in moral values: some effects of religious and state schools on their students, *Oxford Review of Education*, 18, 29-43.

Van Buren, P. (1972), *The Edges of Language*, London, SCM.

Vergote, A. and Aubert, C. (1973), Parental images and representations of God, *Social Compass*, 19, 431-444.

Vergote, A. Bonami, M., Custers, A. and Pattyn, M. (1967), Le symbole paternel et sa signification religieuse, *Review de Psychologie et des Sciences de l'Education*, 2, 191-213.

Vergote, A. and Tamayo, A. (1981), *The Parental Figure and the Representation of God*, The Hague, Mouton.

Vergote, A., Tamayo, A., Pasquali, L., Bonami, M., Pattyn, M-R. and Custers, A. (1969), Concept of God and parental images, *Journal for the Scientific Study of Religion*, 8, 79-87.

Williams, R.M. and Finch, S. (1968), *Young School Leavers*, London, HMSO.

Woodward, P. (1992), Jewish children under the camera: an ethnographic study of Jewish children in Britain, *Visual Anthropology*, 5, 307-330.

Worten, S.A. and Dollinger, S.J. (1986), Mothers' intrinsic religious motivation, disciplinary preferences, and children's conceptions of prayer, *Psychological Reports*, 58, 218.

Research Methodology

Unit C

Empirical and statistical considerations

Dr William K. Kay

Centre for Theology and Education

Trinity College

Carmarthen

Contents

Introduction

Aims

After working through this unit you should be able to:

- understand key statistical terms;
- calculate several common statistics;
- assess the appropriate statistics for typical research problems;
- understand the basic functions of SPSS software.

Overview

This unit gives you an opportunity to get to grips with statistical concepts and methods. After introducing you to key terms it takes you through a step-by-step process that will enable you to calculate certain well known statistics for yourself. We take the view that, as you make these calculations, you are more likely to appreciate just what the statistics involved are and mean.

Following this the unit introduces you to the best known statistical software on the market (SPSS). This part of the unit is intended to build up your confidence about using the software yourself and so add a quantitative component to your own research. This part of the unit deals with computing means, t-tests, chi square, correlation, oneway analysis of variance, two way analysis of variance, multiple regression, reliability and factor analysis.

We are aware that some students have a fear not only of mathematics but also of computers and statistics. This unit is intended to dissipate this fear and to help you engage in the practicalities of quantitative research.

C1 Key concepts

Population and sample

Research frequently makes use of the notion of a *population*. Population, in this context, refers to a complete set of people, values or events that can be held together under a common definition. We might talk of the population of terrier dogs in Manchester, the population of values held by 14 year old teenagers in Britain or the population of OfSTED inspections in 1996. In each case the population refers to a fixed number of entities that is, in principle, knowable. A *sample* is a collection from a population and the idea of a sample is simply to enable a general description of the population by treating the characteristics of the sample as an accurate measure of the characteristics of the population.

There are two questions that arise here. First, how should the sample be constituted? Second, what size of sample should be collected? With regard to the type of sample, the most usual kind is a *probability* sample or *random* sample that is based upon the collection of data from the population by chance mechanisms. For example, if you wish to take a 10% random sample from one hundred schools, you might simply number the schools between 1 and 100 and choose ten numbers at random, perhaps from a random numbers table or a computer programme designed to generate random numbers, and approach the schools thus identified. Alternatively, if the schools were arranged alphabetically, you might choose every tenth name. The crucial point to observe about this kind of sample is that each member of the population has an equal chance of being included.

A slightly different kind of procedure can be followed if particular known characteristics of the population need to be reflected in the sample. For example, suppose in your group of hundred schools there are ten single-sex schools for girls only. If you follow the random procedures suggested above, the girls schools might slip through your net and fail to be represented. So you might adopt the *quota* procedure instead. You would divide the population into the 90 boys schools and the ten girls schools and then select nine schools at random from the boys group and one school at random from the girls group. In this way you would still end up with a sample of ten schools but you would be confident that it would reflect the basic categories of the population from which it was drawn. Quota samples are particularly useful where the researcher knows that the categories within the population will need to be compared with each other during analysis. By using a quota sample you know that you will select representatives of the different categories. In this respect, a quota sample functions like a very big random sample but is cheaper to collect.

In practice samples cannot always be selected using random procedures and, for this reason, *convenience* or *opportunity* samples are used on the assumption that the subjects within them provide a reasonable representation of the whole population. For example, the teacher planning to write a textbook for use nationally might try out some ideas on a class he or she teaches every Wednesday morning. The Wednesday morning class is a convenience sample but, in the circumstances, may be just as good as a full-scale random sample.

How big should a sample be? This is a much more difficult question to answer and, in general, the answer is, when a random sample is being generated, 'the bigger the better'. Again, in practice, it is likely that considerations of cost, time and availability will affect the researcher's eventual decision. From the statistical point of view, however, the researcher must take note of the likely course of analysis. If, as suggested above, analysis depends upon the comparison of subgroups within the sample, then it is important to obtain a large enough sample to allow the subgroups to grow to a reasonable size. For instance, once you wish to compare older boys in a sample with older girls you have already divided the sample into quarters (into half by dividing by gender and then into half again dividing by age[1]). If multiple regression (see C4) is used then, as a rule of thumb, a minimum of 30 cases per independent variable are normally desirable (Kerlinger, 1973, p 282).

A more sophisticated method of deciding on sample size can make use of known statistical properties (see next section) derived from previous studies or from pilot studies upon the population. Basically, the concept here is that larger samples will have to be drawn from populations that show greater variability. If you think about this, it is obvious enough. If you are sampling the height of the population within a city where Americans and Japanese both live, you would need to draw a bigger sample than would be the case if only Japanese or only Americans lived in the city. Americans tend to be taller than Japanese and the danger of a small sample is that you miss out extremities within the range and so do not reflect the population as it really is. If the population is very homogeneous, however, then a small sample will tend to pick up all the features in which you are interested.

The main problem generated by small sample sizes is that we may have no idea of the variability within the population - indeed this may be why we carry out a survey in the first place! If we *do* have an idea of variability (presumably from previous studies) then the formula for calculating sample size ($n = sd^2/SE^2$ where n=sample size, sd=standard deviation and SE=standard error) may be helpful. Specific programmes to help in the calculation of desirable sample size have been developed (Peers, 1996). The SPSS software package designed to do this is called Sample Power.

Response rate

The response rate to a survey is the number of completed and returned questionnaires as a percentage of those that were sent out (assuming that only one questionnaire was sent to each member of the population). If you send out 250 questionnaires and receive 125 back, your response rate is 50%. Clearly, a less than perfect response rate reduces the effective sample size and for this reason many researchers prefer to assess how big a sample they need and then multiply up when distributing a questionnaire, in order to make an allowance

---

[1] I am assuming age is split in two: younger pupils and older pupils.

for failures to respond. If you need a sample of 250, then you may need to send out 500 questionnaires on the assumption that only half will be returned. If the response rate is better than you anticipated, nothing is lost except a small amount of money.

Levels of measurement

Anything that can be classified and varies is called a variable. It is usual to divide variables into the following types. *Nominal* variables are simply names. Variables like religious affiliation or gender are nominal. *Ordinal* variables are classifications that can be arranged in order though the difference between the points in the range is not equal. Attendance at church may be weekly, monthly, occasionally or never and there is no presumption that the distance between 'weekly' and 'monthly' is the same as 'occasionally' and 'never'. All that can be said is that these four classifications are arranged in a non-arbitrary order of descending frequency[2]. *Interval* level variables are similar, but here the classifications have a similar distance between the different points. A pupil may be classified as being absent from school on one, two, three or four occasions during the term. Likert-type items where respondents are asked whether they agree strongly, agree, are not certain, disagree or disagree strongly may also be taken as interval level variables. It is reasonable to assume that the distance between 'agree' and 'agree strongly', for instance, is the same distance as between 'disagree' and 'disagree strongly'.

The most useful kind of scale in educational research is generally the *interval* scale, which is based on the presumption that the points within the scale fall upon a continuum so, for instance, that the distance between a score of 10 and a score of 20 is the same as the distance between a score of 50 and a score of 60. Finally, a *ratio* scale can be produced which has the same properties as the interval scale but also a meaningful zero. A weight of 0 kg means that no part of the quantity being measured is present. For example, weight is generally assessed by a ratio scale. Thus, a weight of 0 kg means that no part of the quantity being measured is present. By way of contrast, temperature is assessed by an interval scale. Thus, a temperature of 0° C does not mean that there is no temperature, simply that it is at the freezing point designated by this particular unit of measurement.

---

[2] Nominal and ordinal level scales often produce distributions that are not normal (that is, they do not form the familiar bell curve).

Validity

Questions may be asked about the validity of variables. Several kinds of validity may be distinguished. *Content validity* refers to the adequacy of the content of items. There is no point in trying to construct a scale measuring attitude towards fox hunting by asking questions only about horses and hounds. The content of the items, the actual meaning of the words used in the items, should correspond with the range of meaning found in the concept that is being addressed. Thus, a scale about fox hunting ought to contain items referring to every aspect of the subject. To aid this process it is usual to ask several informed professionals, while still in the early stages of scale construction, to review the adequacy of item content so as to avoid idiosyncratic and subjective judgements.

Criterion-related validity is investigated by comparing test or scale scores with one or more external variables or criteria. A test of sporting aptitude might be checked against outcomes to see whether those who scored high on the sporting aptitude scale, after training, turned out to be good athletes.

Construct validity is investigated by generating a network of theories regarding the way in which the hypothesised construct operationalised by the scale may be expected to relate to other constructs or measures. Such hypotheses can be empirically tested on real data. Construct validity is a theoretically rich way through which scales can be developed and tested..

Reliability

The concept of reliability in everyday life is similar to the concept of reliability in social science measurements. In everyday life reliability refers to consistency. The reliable car starts under all circumstances. The reliable test produces the same scores on different occasions. If you administer a reliable scale to John on Wednesday and then return a month later and ask him to fill in the same questions, unless there have been major changes in him or in the environment, we should expect a very similar score to be attained. Another way putting this is to say that a perfectly reliable scale correlates[3] perfectly with itself when administered on two separate occasions.

If a scale performs in this way, then we may be confident that it is measuring something stable. If we measure how far Jane can throw a tennis ball and then return a month later, unless she has been practising, we would expect there to be little difference in the distance obtained. And a reliable tape measure would verify this. If the tape measure stretched, all kinds of false readings would

---

[3] See C4 of this unit for a much fuller explanation of correlation.

occur. Thus the reliability of a social science scale depends upon an underlying and stable construct and on a consistent measuring instrument. Ideally, to test the reliability of a social science scale we would administer it to the same sample twice and correlate the scores. Although this procedure can be followed, it is time-consuming and sometimes impracticable. Consequently reliability is calculated for scales by an ingenious alternative. With split-half reliability, two halves of the scale are correlated with each other, perhaps all the even numbered items are correlated with all the odd numbered items. The statistic favoured by many researchers, however, is the alpha coefficient developed by Cronbach (1951). This is a model of internal consistency based on the average inter-item correlation. All the items are correlated in turn with each other. The average inter-item correlation is known as the alpha coefficient. A high alpha coefficient indicates that the scale operates coherently, pointing to a psychological or sociological construct, related to the meaning of the items, underlying the scale.

The construction of a scale is carried out by looking for the combination of items that produces the highest alpha coefficient for a scale of a given length. Longer scales by their nature tend to produce a higher alpha, so a shorter scale with a slightly lower alpha is likely to be preferable to a long one with a slightly higher alpha.

Activity C1

What dangers might arise from a poorly drawn sample? Why are levels of measurement important and how can you be sure that the questionnaire items you are using are valid? How might you select items statistically?

Comment on activity C1

Essentially, a poorly drawn sample gives misleading information about the population. If the sample is too small it will fail to reflect the variability within the population. If the sample is not randomly drawn, it may reflect only a certain part of the population. For instance, questionnaires involving pupils at school often under-represent the least able pupils since these are the ones who have most difficulty in understanding and completing the questionnaire. Levels of measurement are important since the use of statistical tests presumes that variables have certain properties. Nevertheless tests intended for 'lower level' variables (such as at nominal level) will apply to 'higher level' variables (such as at interval level) though they will be less sensitive in picking up associations and differences. Conversely, because of violation of underlying assumptions, it is often unwise to use 'higher-level' analyses on 'lower-level' variables. You can make sure that questionnaire items are valid by using all three types of validity and by pilot testing these items and examining the statistics they generate. Some items, for example, may show patterns suggesting that they are misunderstood by younger pupils and others may be answered in such a way as not to discriminate between members of the sample. For example, the question, 'Do you ever sleep?' is likely to be answered 'yes' by 100% of any sample of British schoolchildren. Such an item, endorsed by everyone, is of little use.

C2 Attitude measurement

Psychological literature distinguishes between opinion and attitude. Opinion is focused on individual issues and measurement of it might be derived from a single question like, 'What do you think about the single European currency?' Attitude, by contrast, is considered to apply to broader, often underlying, psychological constructs that include evaluative and affective (or feeling-based) components. An attitude to the European Community would include a predisposition to be in favour of or against the single currency but would also include a range of other relevant judgements and feelings. Because it is broader, and in practice accessed through a set of items and not just one item, an attitude is less likely to fluctuate than an opinion and therefore has more enduring value.

Likert scaling

Attitudes have been discussed in psychological literature since the 1920s and measured in a variety of ways. The unifying idea about measurement is that statements relating to the attitude to be measured are presented to people and their responses are recorded and added together. Provided that the statements are valid in the sense defined above and provided that responses to each statement are recorded on an interval level format, then attitudes can be scaled. The most common type of response to items within attitude scales was developed by R.A. Likert (Likert, 1932). He showed two things. First, that each item could be responded to positively or negatively with a midpoint between positive and negative responses. Typically, the Likert format makes use of five points, 'agree strongly', 'agree', 'not certain', 'disagree' and 'disagree strongly' though a seven point version is also perfectly feasible. Second, he showed that disagreement with a negative item may be equivalent to agreement with a positive item. Thus, if you disagreed strongly with the item, 'I dislike the European Community' you are saying something very similar to what you would be saying if you agreed strongly with the item, 'I like the European Community'.

If a five point format is used and the items are scored in the direction of favourability so that high scores equal a positive attitude to the concept in question, then, if there are ten items in the scale, the most positive score would be 50 and the least positive would be ten. In practice, once the items have been selected using content validity, their statistical properties are assessed on one or more pilot samples. For instance, while testing items in this way Francis (1976) found that younger children have difficulty in dealing with negative items and fail to see that disagreement with a negative is the same as agreement with a positive. Similarly, it is important to ensure that people for whom the scale is intended register responses to each item across the full range of the Likert format and that all the items contribute to the scale more or less equally. This is done by calculating the correlation between each item and the total scale score. Finally, the alpha coefficient is utilised as a general test of the coherence of scale.

Semantic differential

It is also worth drawing attention to a method of assessing attitudes developed by Osgood, Suci and Tannenbaum (1957) and known as the semantic differential. This method operates with several pairs of opposing adjectives arranged with numbers between them like this:

good.   3   2   1   0   1   2   3   bad

strong 3   2   1   0   1   2   3   weak

Respondents might be presented with a concept like 'religious education' and then asked to rate it using the adjectives. The advantage of this method is that a profile of different concepts can be drawn up using the same set of adjectives. We could test religious education against physical education to see where differences lay. If might be, for instance, that pupils found both to be relatively strong but that one was deemed to be good and the other generally bad. Kay (1996) was able to show how religious education and school worship were differently assessed by pupils on the important-unimportant adjectival pair, though very similar in other respects. Nevertheless, despite its usefulness, the Osgood system has been criticised because of the ambiguity inherent in the midpoint or zero. It might mean either uncertainty or neutrality as between the two adjectives.

Finally, if a coherent set of adjectival pairings are used (perhaps all have an aesthetic dimension - beautiful-ugly, harmonious-discordant, etc.) then the scoring system can be adjusted after the questionnaire has been completed. A 3 on the positive side can be scored as 7 and a 3 on the negative side can be scored as 1 and the other points adjusted in between so that each pairing is turned into a seven point format. The scores on each pairing can then be added up and an attitude measurement calculated. In this way, for instance, we might find out what sort of aesthetic attitude existed towards several art objects.

Activity C2

Compare the Likert and Osgood methods of attitude measurement. What are the strengths and weaknesses of each? Illustrate your answer with examples.

Comment on activity C2

The Likert system for measuring attitudes is simple and intuitively obvious. It is well-established, having been in existence for more than 60 years, and the interpretation of scale scores is relatively easy. The method can be put to use for the construction of scales on every conceivable topic. Only the imagination of the researcher imposes limits to the possible content of Likert scales. In addition, the alpha coefficient provides an important objective measure of the reliability of scales constructed by this method. On the negative side, the statements put into a Likert scale need to be carefully chosen, statistically examined and balanced between positive and negative items. Moreover, though the interpretation of scores derived from the Likert system is easy, it is not always clear what low scores mean. Does a low attitude score to the European Community mean that someone is against the Community or simply that they are lukewarm about it? In other words, if items are scored in the direction of favourability can we interpret a lack of favourability as antipathy?

The Osgood system is also relatively well-established and simple and can be shaped towards particular research ends. The researcher has control over the choice of adjectival pairs and so can select emotional or cognitive pairs or a combination of these just as seems most suitable to the project in hand. The particular strength of the method is that it allows profiles to be generated using the same set of adjectival pairs. This allows discriminating comparisons to be made between different concepts. Negatively, the problem of each midpoint in the Osgood pairs is difficult to resolve. Moreover, whereas we could make a comparison between attitudes to two concepts explored by two Likert scales, this would be more difficult with the Osgood method since the adjectival pairings are likely to vary between research projects. Thus, though we might be able to correlate attitude to football and attitude to school using two Likert scales, this is likely to be more difficult using the Osgood method because of the problem of finding adjectival pairings that apply equally well to football and school. Finally, the alpha coefficient can only with difficulty be applied to an Osgood scale; most researchers would not attempt to do so.

C3 Calculating basic statistics

Central tendency and dispersion

The *mean* of any set of numbers is also called the average. It is calculated by adding together all numbers in the set and then dividing by the size of the set. Imagine, for example, that you had the following set of numbers: 1, 8, 12, 19, 44, 44, 45, and 51. There are 8 numbers in this set and they add up to 224. The mean is therefore 224 divided by 8, or 28. The mean has many uses in statistical analysis, but the most obvious use is that it allows a set of numbers, however large, to be summarised by one number.

We might also summarise numbers in a different way, simply by looking at the number which occurs most often. In this case it is the number 44 since this occurs twice and all the others only occur once. The number 44 in this set is called the *mode*.

There is one other common way of summarising a set of numbers and this is to select the number that divides the data set in half, so that 50% of the observations lie on one side of this point and 50% lie on the other side. If there are an odd number of observations in the set, the middle number is easy to find. If there are an even number of observations in the set, then the middle number is halfway between two numbers. In the example above, as there are 8 numbers in the set, the halfway point is between the fourth and fifth numbers or 31.5. This is called the *median*.

The most often used summarising statistic is the mean, but to describe any set of numbers more completely we also need to know how dispersed they are from the mean. For example, suppose we have the following set of numbers 1, 2, 3, 4, 18, 18, 28 and 150. Like the first set of numbers, the mean is 28 but this set of numbers looks very different from the first set because of the 150 at the top and the group of small numbers at the bottom. So we need a way of showing how the numbers are dispersed about the mean and it might seem that the simplest method of doing this is to subtract every number from the mean and to take an average of these figures. The trouble with doing this is that some of the differences will be positive and some negative and very large differences from the mean will tend to predominate. To remove the negative numbers the simplest procedure is to square the differences, since all squared numbers are positive. Once we have squared the differences we can add them up and take the average of them and then take the square root of the average (to undo the effect of squaring). This number is called the *standard deviation* and gives you an estimate of the average distance of the observations from the mean value. In the first set of numbers the standard deviation is just over 19, but in the second set the standard deviation is just over 50. The second set is much more spread out than the first set, which is why the second standard deviation is higher than the first standard deviation.

How do you calculate the standard deviation? An example given in table 1 and using the second set of numbers will make this clear.

- First calculate the total: 1+2+3+4+18+18+28+150=224.
- Then calculate the mean: 224/8=28

Table 1: calculating a standard deviation

X	X-mean	$(X-mean)^2$
1	-27	729
2	-26	676
3	-25	625
4	-24	576
18	-10	100
18	-10	100
28	0	0
150	122	14884

The numbers in the first column, headed X, are the original data. The middle column is each number minus the mean. The right hand column is these differences squared.

Add up the figures in the right hand column. They come to 17,960. There are 8 numbers in the table but for reasons to do with the relationship between the standard deviation and other statistics, the total in the third column (called the sum of squares) is divided by one less than the number of figures in the set. Thus 14884/7=2527 and the square root of 2527 is 50.27, which is the standard deviation.

While we look at the standard deviation, there is one other term that is associated with it. The *variance* of a set of numbers is the standard deviation squared. It is another way of referring to the amount of variation in the figures and is spoken of in connection with correlation and regression, as will become evident later in this unit.

T-test

Very often we will be interested in the difference between the scores recorded by two distinct groups, perhaps between males and females, between younger and older pupils, or between pupils educated in different parts of the country, in different schools or by different methods. We may want to make comparisons between these two groups to discover whether the differences between them are merely as a result of sampling variation or whether the differences are significant, that is, they would not have come about by chance more frequently than five times in a hundred.

So, when comparing figures derived from two groups we are interested in two pieces of information. What are the means of the two groups and what are the standard deviations from these two means? In practice calculations about the significance of differences between the means are dependent on the standard deviation (or variance) and, as we shall see, when these calculations are made using statistical packages the figures are produced twice, once on the assumption that the variances (or squared standard deviations) within each of the two groups are the same and again on the assumption that the variances are different. The test for comparing the means of two groups is called a *t-test*.

To discover how to compare the means of two samples we have to begin by imagining a known situation. Suppose we had a set of 1000 figures generated randomly by a computer. Suppose we took two samples of 100 from this set of 1000. And suppose we calculated the means and standard deviations of our two samples. If the samples were drawn randomly we would expect the means and standard deviations to be very similar. We would not expect them to be identical because of chance factors in drawing the samples, but we would expect them to be close to each other and close to the true mean of the full set of 1000 figures and its standard deviation.

In effect, we would expect our two samples to be so close to each other that we could conclude that really they belong to the same population. Now, drawing two samples from the same population and comparing means is similar to the problem posed in many research situations. What we really want to know is whether our two samples can be thought of as belonging to one big population or whether they are really samples that belong to two distinct populations with different parameters.

In the example we are using, the set of 1000 randomly generated figures is a 'population'. Remember that in most statistical analysis we are operating with a sample of some kind, where a sample is a subset drawn at random from a total population that is beyond the reach of our research. For example, we may want to know whether the mean scores from a questionnaire designed to measure extraversion are the same or different for British boys and girls. For practical reasons, we cannot administer the questionnaire to every single boy and girl in Britain! We are forced to make use of a sample and then, from the sample, to infer information about all the young people in Britain as a whole. If the scores recorded by boys and girls on extraversion were different, we would be saying that they belonged to two separate populations, two separate groups whose characteristics were different.

Return now to the idea of drawing many samples from the same known set of 1000 figures. If a hundred samples were drawn, then we would have a hundred means and we could take the mean of those hundred means and compare it with the true mean. If this is done, the mean of means turns out to be very close to the true mean and the standard deviation of all these means is very close to the true standard deviation. Yet, in real-life we cannot draw many samples from the same population. We have to work with the samples that we have obtained. Can we work out the relationship between our samples, whatever they are, and the true figures of the population, even if we do not know exactly what these true figures are?

The answer is that by making use of the kind of illustration given above - where random samples have been drawn from known sets of figures - statisticians can work out precise relationships between samples and the parent populations from which they are drawn.

When numerous samples are drawn and the results plotted in a graph, a normal distribution curve is produced. Very many of the sample means are close to the true mean and then there are gradually declining numbers of means below the true mean and equal and declining numbers of means above the true mean. The normal distribution is also called a Z-distribution and is pictured as the well-known bell-shaped curve. A closely-related (and often graphically indistinguishable) distribution was calculated by a statistician Gosset who published under the pseudonym 'Student' and he called the statistic relating the sample means to the true mean t, which is often referred to as the Student's t distribution. (Statistics often have names given to them by the statisticians who discover them just as planets often have names given them by the astronomers who discover them. Statisticians have the right to name their statistics anything they like and by convention they often name them after letters of the Greek alphabet, though Gosset was an exception[4].) It is the symmetrical characteristics of the t distribution that we take advantage of when using the t-test.

How accurate is a sample mean? In other words how close is it to the real mean (the mean of the population) that we do not know? Here we make use of the concept of 'standard error'. The standard error may be thought of as the

---

[4] W.S. Gosset (1876-1937) applied statistical methods to problems in chemistry and biology and later became head brewer for Guinness!

standard deviation of sample means of many samples from the same population. The standard error enables us to make use of the mean and standard deviation calculated from a sample and then assess how likely this is to be the true mean. The standard error is calculated as follows:

- $SE = SD/\sqrt{n}$
- where SE = standard error; SD = standard deviation; n = size of sample

If you look at the formula you can see that as the standard deviation goes down or the size of the sample goes up, or both, the standard error will also go down. The smaller the standard error the closer the sample mean will be to the true mean.

The formula used to calculate the significance of the difference between two means is simply the difference between those means divided by the difference between their standard errors. This ratio has a t distribution and the larger the t value, the more likely the means are to be significantly different (drawn from different populations). The calculation is as follows:

- $t = m1-m2/SEm1-SEm2$;
- where m1 is the mean of group 1 and m2 is the mean of group 2; SE m1 is the standard error of mean 1 and SE m2 is the standard error of mean 2.

The example in table 2 should make this clear. First it is easiest to calculate the standard error of the differences between the means and then to substitute this result in the equation above.

Take these two sets of numbers, set A and set B.

Table 2: Calculating t

A	(x-mean)	(x-mean)^2	B	(x-mean)	(x-mean)^2
4	0	0	3	0	0
5	1	1	1	-2	4
3	-1	1	5	2	4
2	-2	4	2	-1	1
6	2	4	4	1	1

Mean of A = 4; sd of A = 1.58

Mean of B = 3; sd of B = 1.58

SE of A = sd/$\sqrt{n}$ = 1.58/$\sqrt{5}$ = .705; SE of B = 1.58/$\sqrt{5}$ = .705

$SE_{a-b} = \sqrt{(.705)^2 + (.705)^2}$

$= \sqrt{.994} = .997 = 1.00$ (rounded)

t = (mean of A-mean of B)/ SE mean of A-SE mean of B

= 4-3/1 = 1/1 = 1

Since this measure of difference is no greater than the measure of error, it is obvious that it is not significant. And the t value, being low, when checked against the appropriate statistical tables, confirms this.

Activity C3

What is the mode of this set of figures: 3, 4, 5, 5, 8, 2?

What is the mean of the same set of figures?

What is the median of the same set of figures?

What is the standard deviation of this set of figures: 5, 8 , 11, 9, 8, 6, 8?

Here are parameters belonging to two sets of figures. Calculate the t value.

- Set A: the mean is 10.12, the sd is 5.40 and the number of cases is 73.
- Set B: the mean is 6.61, the sd is 4.69 and the number of cases is 217.

Comment on activity C3

If you use the examples given above and substitute the figures given here in the equations you should have no difficulty in coming to the solutions given below.

- The mode is 5 (the most common number).
- The mean is 27/6 = 4.5.
- The median is also 5 (the half way number).
- The standard deviation is 1.95.
- The t value is 4.95.

Chi-square

T tests are designed to show whether the differences between mean scores on the same variable by members of two groups are significant. Despite their usefulness, t-tests have limitations. The first of these is that they can only cope with two groups at the time. If you wanted to compare three groups simultaneously, you would be unable to use the t test. Of course, you could test group 1 against group 2 and then group 1 against group 3 and then group 2 against group 3, but this still would not solve your problem of a simultaneous test and it would become increasingly cumbersome if you have a lot more than three groups that you wished to compare. The second limitation of the t test is that it deals with continuous variables like height, weight, attitude scores,

scores on personality tests, and so on, but it cannot deal with categorical variables like religious affiliation, place of residence or marital status.

To discover whether there is an association between two or more groups and two or more categorical variables it is necessary to use a *crosstabulation* (also called a contingency table). The basic idea of the crosstabulation is very simple. It is easiest to understand with two categorical variables. Imagine that we have a hundred people and that 80 of these have dark hair and 20 have fair hair. Imagine also that 60 of the dark haired people have brown eyes and 20 of them have blue eyes. Of the fair haired people suppose 15 have blue eyes and 5 have dark eyes. The crosstabulation lays out the relationship between these categorical variables in a table (see table 3) where each variable has its own row or column.

The point where rows and columns intersect is a *cell*. Once the cells are filled it is possible to see the relationship between hair colour and eye colour more easily. Notice also that the cells are filled with numbers of people (rather than scores of some kind) and that the total given in the bottom right hand corner of the table must be the number of people in the sample.

Table 3: Crosstabulation example

	Brown Eyes	**Blue Eyes**	**Total**
Dark Hair	60	20	80
Fair hair	5	15	20
Total	65	35	100

Notice the way the so-called marginal totals are added to a table so that it is possible to see column and row totals at a glance. Notice, too, that it would be possible to calculate what percentage of brown-eyed people have dark hair (60/65*100) or what percentage of fair haired people have brown eyes (5/20*100). In other words we can inspect the numbers of people in each cell in relation to rows or columns, or both. (Incidentally these figures are completely invented for purpose of this example and should not taken as real statistics.)

Now, for purpose of calculation, take table 4 which is designed to show how a die (the singular of dice) fell after being thrown 120 times. If the die were true we should expect that each of the numbers on its face would turn up exactly 20 times so that in the 120 throws the single spot 1 would appear 20 times, 2 would appear 20 times, 3 would appear 20 times, and so on. In this example the die has not landed equally often with each number face upward. The number one has appeared 16 times and the number five 23 times. But for each number the expected appearance was 20 times, and that is shown in the bottom row of the table.

Table 4: Example with a die

Number of spots	1	2	3	4	5	6
Observed number of times landing face up	16	19	27	17	23	18
Expected number of times landing face up	20	20	20	20	20	20

The question we face is whether the numbers produced by these throws of the die are significantly different from what would happen if the die were completely true. We could simply subtract the expected number of times a one is thrown from the observed number of times a one is thrown (16-20) and then add up all differences between expected and observed frequencies. But the problem with this is that if we add these figures up they reach zero, and they always reach zero in this kind of problem. It is more satisfactory to square each difference and then to add the resulting squares of differences. This always yields a positive number and this number is larger when the deviations of observed from expected frequencies are larger. However just to leave the matter there would be unsatisfactory. And this is why.

In the example of the die that is thrown 120 times, the sum of squared differences is $(-4)^2 + (-1)^2 + 7^2 + (-3)^2 + 3^2 + (-2)^2 = 88$. In table 5 in a different example where much larger numbers were used, where for instance we might still have a squared sum of differences of 88 but we would be right to assume that the difference between expected and observed frequency of 4 (between 460 and 464) was rather less significant than a difference of 4 between 16 and 20, and so on through the rest of the set. So what we have to do is to relate the size of the squared difference to the size of the expected frequency. When we add together the square of the observed frequency minus the expected frequency in relation to the expected frequency for each cell of the table individually we have calculated the chi square statistic. Formally it is written

$$X^2 = \text{sum of}$$

$$\frac{(\text{observed count in each cell-expected count in each cell})^2}{\text{expected count in each cell}}$$

and would be calculated for the table of die throws in table 6.

Table 5: Example figures

	1	2	3	4	5	6
Observed number in cell	460	449	307	297	453	498
Expected number in cell	464	450	300	300	450	500

Table 6: Calculating Chi square

N spots	Ob	Ex	Ob-Ex	$(Ob-Ex)^2$	$(Ob-Ex)^2/Ex$
One	16	20	-4	16	0.80
Two	19	20	-1	1	0.05
Three	27	20	7	49	2.45
Four	17	20	-3	9	0.45
Five	23	20	3	9	0.45
Six	18	20	-2	4	0.20

Note: Ob = Observed; Ex = Expected.

The items in the last column add up to 4.40, which is the value of X^2

The chi-square statistic, as we have seen, was designed to deal with categorical variables. Other statistics derived from chi-square more recently have been designed to extend the use of the technique to ordinal level variables but where continuous variables exist. For example, where people were rated on scores between 0 and 100, the table would simply become too large and cumbersome to print out and inspect. There is a better way of dealing with continuous variables. This is by using the *correlation coefficient*.

Correlation

Table 7 gives a set of hypothetical figures relating 12 people's income to the value of their car. Correlation refers to the idea of association between variables and the simplest, though most impressionistic, way of looking at the relationship between variables is to construct a scatterplot. In the example given here it is clear that as one set off variables goes up (those measured along the horizontal axis) so the other set of variables also goes up (those measured along the vertical axis). The more precisely the points on the graph align themselves into a sloped straight line, the clearer the correlation. If the line of points goes up on the right-hand side of the graph, then the correlation is positive; if the line of points goes up on the left-hand side then the correlation is negative. If the points simply cluster around in a random way, then there is no correlation between the two variables.

Table 7: Income and price of car

Income	Car price
10	6
7	4
12	7
12	8
9	10
16	7
12	10
18	15
8	5
12	6
14	11
16	13

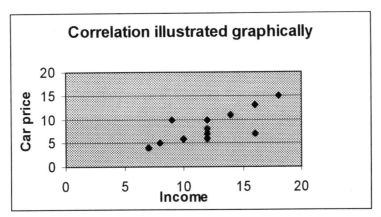

The graph presented above is based on the two sets of figures in table 7. While the graph is useful for providing a general sense of the relationship between two continuous variables, it is not precise enough for most purposes. We need a single figure that can express the relationship between the two sets of figures in a standard way. The correlation coefficient does this. It ranges between -1 and +1. The correlation of +1 would indicate a perfect positive match between the two sets of figures such that the highest figure in the first set was related to the highest figure in the second set, the second highest figure in the first set was related to the second highest figure in the second set, and so on. In other words in the example given here the person with the highest income would own the most expensive car and there would be a perfect correspondence between income and car value in the rest of the set. If, however, the highest income were related to the cheapest car, and so on through the rest of the set, then the relationship is reversed and a perfect negative correlation is recorded. Negative correlations occur between such variables as the number of cigarettes smoked in a day and life expectancy. As the number of cigarettes increases, life expectancy decreases. If there is no relationship at all between two sets of figures, the coefficient works out as 0.

In practice perfect positive and perfect negative correlations are not normally found. Moreover there are different kinds of correlation coefficient since sets of numbers can be correlated by rank rather than by the actual score recorded, and this is preferable if the scores are not distributed normally. But if the correlation deals with figures like those in table 7, then a Pearson coefficient can be calculated. Pearson's coefficient is designated by the letter r in lower case. If ranks are being considered then the Spearman rank order coefficient is the one to use[5]. Spearman's coefficient is designated by the Greek letter rho (ρ).

Before seeing how to calculate the Pearson correlation it is important to realise another property of correlation coefficients[6]. Clearly there must be some kind of relationship between correlation coefficients and the size of the sample from which they are drawn. This relationship can be expressed like this: large correlation coefficients between small samples are as significant as small correlation coefficients between large samples. This is intuitively obvious. Imagine you have a group of 5 six-year-old pupils and wished to correlate their heights and weights. If you had two pupils in the group who happened to be either very tall and thin or very short and fat, the overall positive correlation between height and weight would be masked. But if you took 1000 pupils and compared height and weight, the occasional unusual person would not affect the overall relationship between the figures. Only a slight association between height and weight would be needed to indicate a trend. Just as statisticians have worked out distributions of t and chi-square, so also they have worked out critical values of correlation coefficients in relation to different sample sizes. These values show, to take one example, a Pearson's r of .63 with a group of 10 people is as significant as an r of .20 with a hundred people, where significance means what it usually means in statistical terms: that the finding would have come about by chance less frequently than five times in 100. For this reason SPSS generates correlation coefficients, the print-out gives their significance levels and the sample size on which they were computed.

To give you a sharper idea of Pearson's correlation, the example below demonstrates how the calculation is carried out. The value of r =

$$\frac{n(\Sigma xy) - (\Sigma x)(\Sigma y)}{\sqrt{[n * \Sigma x^2 - (\Sigma x)^2][n * \Sigma y^2 - (\Sigma y)^2]}}$$

where Σ means 'the sum of'.

---

[5] C.E. Spearman (1863-1945) was Professor of Psychology in London, 1928-31.

[6] Karl Pearson (1857-1936), mathematician and biologist, became Professor of Eugenics in London, 1911-33.

Table 8: calculation of Pearson's r

x	y	x^2	y^2	xy
10	6	100	36	60
7	4	49	16	28
12	7	144	49	84
12	8	144	64	96
9	10	81	100	90
16	7	256	49	112
12	10	144	100	120
18	15	324	225	270
8	5	64	25	40
12	6	144	36	72
14	11	196	121	154
16	13	256	169	208
146	102	1902	990	1334

Substituting in the equation above

$$\frac{12*1334 - (146*102)}{\sqrt{[12*1902 -(146)^2]*[12*990 - (102)^2]}}$$

$$= \frac{16008-14892}{\sqrt{[22824][11880]}}$$

$$= \frac{1116}{\sqrt{2225808}}$$

$$= \frac{1116}{1491.9}$$

= .748, which is the value of Pearson's r

C4 Using SPSS

SPSS or Statistical Packages for the Social Sciences have been in existence for at least thirty years. The packages, or software as they would now be called, began on large main frame computers in the days of punched cards and have been steadily revised and adapted not only to give better options on main frame machines but also to run on desktop computers. The relationship between the packages run on main-frame and desktop computers is made explicit by the possibility of transferring data between the two kinds of computer so that, for instance, data can be prepared on a main-frame machine but then, using a floppy disk, transferred to a desktop machine.

Moreover, desktop machines linked by e-mail can exchange SPSS files without difficulty. The greatest advantage of the desktop versions of SPSS, however, is that it can be integrated into other software, and output from SPSS can be pasted into word processing programmes or spread sheets. Ideally a researcher can carry a large database on the hard disk of a desktop machine, analyse data, and then transfer output from the analysis directly into documents without having to re-type or re-format the figures.

Because SPSS has developed over many years some of the commands have changed and some of the commands used for mainframe analysis are different from commands to carry out the same functions on desktop computers. Be aware of slight differences between SPSS versions, therefore. The comments made below will relate to SPSS 8.0 which was produced in 1998 and runs on Windows operating systems. The main refinements of the later versions of desktop SPSS appear to be related to their enhanced graphics capabilities and to the redistribution of the same statistical procedures into different SPSS modules. SPSS 8.0 is sold as a Base version which contains basic statistics but more advanced statistical routines have to be purchased separately (though they are provided on the same CD-ROM as contains the Base version). This means that earlier versions of SPSS *may* contain statistical routines for which extra payment is required in the later versions. Because of these complexities it is impossible to explain exactly how you should use SPSS on your computer but some of the principles showing how the system works do also apply to earlier desktop versions including the DOS based version 5. This said, the Base version provides an excellent variety of statistical procedures and the only serious omission for social science or practical theology researchers appears to be in the Reliability routine for calculating the alpha coefficient used in the construction of scales.

SPSS carries an excellent help facility and animated tutorials as well as clear and comprehensive manuals[7]. The desktop package also carries several sample databases that you can practise on and which are used as examples in the manuals. New users should not be afraid of launching in to what it has to offer. This overview should simply make the learning process more rapid.

The first things to notice when booting up the SPSS package on a desktop computer is that it operates using three separate windows. The third window (see below) is opened only when the command language is being directly viewed or edited. The *first window*, or data editor window, contains the data file itself. This is a file that is presented like a spread sheet with rows and

---

[7] The website is on http://www.spss.com/uk.

columns. Most of the cells in your data sheet will contain numbers, mainly because that is the kind of data most commonly collected and because computers can process numbers more easily than other kinds of information (such as text). The rows represent cases, one row to each case. The case is a unit of the sample. In research using questionnaires the row represents a single questionnaire, or one person. The columns represent their answers to the questions in the questionnaire and, for the sake of example, assume that column five gives information about the age of respondents. If you let your eye run down column five you will see listed all the ages of the people who responded to your survey.

It is possible to edit the data file even after the data has been entered into the computer and it is also possible to create new variables and these will be added to the data file at the end of each row. It is not feasible to give details here of how to set up the data file except, briefly, to say that the data file can begin its life as an ordinary text file produced by WordPerfect, Word or as a spread sheet, for example from Excel or dBASE or, if the data has been coded straight into SPSS, then the file is created immediately without an intermediate stage.

The *second window*, or output viewer, will contain output from any computer run that has been undertaken. This output will contain tables, charts and any other features that have been produced by the necessary commands. The output from any SPSS session can be saved as a separate file with its own name. This means that chunks of output for work in progress can be saved in separate files or, alternatively, an old file can be opened and new output can be added to it.

SPSS has invested a considerable amount of ingenuity in allowing users to modify the tables that are produced in the output file. By double clicking on a table the 'pivot tables' commands become available. This allows a table to be altered in a way appropriate to your analysis. For instance, rows and columns can be made to swap round or chosen columns or rows can be hidden.

The *third window*, or syntax editor window, will contain the syntax, or sets of commands, that produce the output from the open data file. New users of SPSS often fail to appreciate the value of the syntax system. SPSS introduces users to the menu-driven capabilities of the system. Menu-driven programmes are, like most word processing programmes, sets of commands which are kept in the tool bar at the top of the screen and you can then scroll down at the click of a mouse. When one of these menus unscrolls the user can select a particular command. The menus group together commands in logical categories so that commands relating to files or commands relating to tables are all on the same separate menus. The trouble with using a menu-driven system is that the user may forget what steps he or she took to arrive at a particular outcome. This is one reason why the syntax system is helpful; it can be used as a record of commands which can be saved and kept and reused[8].

To produce syntax it is helpful to begin by using menus and selecting the particular options one is interested in and then pressing the 'paste' command on the menu. This allows you to view the command language that drives each of the dialogue boxes, by pasting the syntax into a syntax editor window. Once syntax and output are saved with similar names it is possible to see which syntax produced which output and, since much analysis requires the repetition of commands (for example a series of the tests might be carried out on different sets of data) the same syntax can be re-run with minor alterations to produce the necessary coverage of all analytic possibilities. We would certainly recommend users to become familiar with the syntax system and to be ready to save syntax files with suitable names related to the document that is being written.

In addition the saving of syntax allows the user to group together any temporary commands making modifications of the data and to store these without having to alter the data file itself. To activate any piece of syntax it is necessary to select it first using the usual highlighting procedure with a mouse. Hold the left-hand mouse button down and drag the cursor over the area which is to be highlighted. Once this has been done click on the arrow head on the tool bar at the top of the syntax window. The new output, responding to the syntax that has been run, will be visible in the output window.

Finally, notice that the menus, and therefore the syntax, contain many options. Extra statistics can be generated, labels can be added, special conditions can be set. When you run a particular command, it is always sensible to look at the possibilities available to you.

Means and standard deviations

Means and standard deviations, if requested, are produced by almost all SPSS commands found under the Summarise sub-menu. The most obvious command to use, though, is 'frequencies'. This is available in the data editor window by choosing: statistics, summarise, frequencies. In the frequencies menu select 'statistics' and then tick the boxes for 'mean' and 'standard deviation'. Press 'continue' to return to the frequencies menu and then put the variables whose mean and standard deviation you want into the variables box. If you press

---

[8] If you fail to operate from the syntax, then, when you generate output with menus, there is also a 'log' section which is, by default kept hidden, but contains the syntax you used. The syntax in the log can be copied into the syntax window and run from there. There is also an SPSS journal file (spss.jnl) made for each SPSS session and that also contains the syntax you have used. Be careful, though, because the spss.jnl file is overwritten by each session. To preserve it, you need to change its name between sessions. This file will normally be placed in C:\windows\ temp.

'paste' you will open the syntax window but not generate the output. If you press 'ok' you will generate the output but not preserve the syntax. Suppose you press 'paste'. You should see syntax something like this[9]:

FREQUENCIES
  VARIABLES=a3 a4
  /STATISTICS=STDDEV MEAN
  /ORDER ANALYSIS .

where a3 and a4 are the names of the variable you are interested in. Notice the general shape of the syntax with the basic command (VARIABLES=) at the beginning: and then after a forward slash the statistics you have selected (/STATISTICS=). The last line deals with the presentation of the information on the output (/ORDER). Notice that it is necessary to end the syntax with a full stop. The full stop is an important piece of punctuation since it indicates the end of a particular group of commands. If you do not use a full stop you are likely to receive an error message in the output.

The mean and standard deviation are printed out in a table that also contains the number of cases on which these statistics were computed and the number of missing cases. A record of missing cases is given because in any larger data sets it is almost inevitable that there will be certain items that people have left blank. Statistics would become misleading if blank responses were included as if they were zeroes. Consequently the cases that have missing values are excluded from that particular computation and adjustments are automatically made. In computing a mean the total is divided by the number of valid cases rather than the total number of cases. SPSS deals with this difficulty by dropping cases that have missing values but you need to be careful with the interpretation of statistics on data files that have large amounts of missing data since you can find yourself dealing with a small and unrepresentative portion of the data set.

T- test

SPSS offers you three t-tests. These are the 'independent samples t-test' (which we have discussed already and which compares the means between two groups), the 'paired samples t-test' and the 'one sample t-test'. The paired samples t-test is used when the two groups are made up of readings from the same people on separate occasions. For example, supposing you were comparing heart rate before and after eating a heavy meal, the t-test would compare each person's heart rate on two different occasions. The other t-test

---

[9] In all the examples of syntax given in this unit, you should be aware that your own syntax will look different because your variables will not have the names used here and because the various choices available for each basic command are reflected in extra lines of syntax.

is used to compare the mean of a group with a chosen figure which is added to the appropriate menu during the command sequence. The usual test, though, is the independent samples t-test.

To use this, select from the menu 'statistics', 'compare means', 'independent samples t-test'. Then in the dialogue box put the variable that is being tested in the box labelled 'test variable(s)' and the grouping variable into the lower box. Once you enter the grouping variable, the 'define groups' option is activated and you need to select the values that correspond with the groups you want. Suppose sex is coded 1 for male and 2 for female, then you would select the gender variable and put the number 1 in the first group box and 2 in the second group box. When you run the test males and females are compared. If you had a variable that had four categories in it (for example, church attendance weekly, monthly, yearly, never) and wanted to compare the two ends of the scale you could enter 1 and 4 in the 'define variables' boxes and these would be the ones used in the t-test.

The output shows you the means and standard deviations of the two groups and the number of cases in each group. Underneath this is a separate table showing you in the second and third columns an F statistic based upon a test of the variances of the two groups and a p value in a box entitled Sig. (that is, is less than 0.05). If the p value is not significant then you can safely assume the two variances are the same and read the t value in the higher row in the fourth column and its associated p value in the fifth column. Otherwise use the lower t value. Syntax looks like this:

```
T-TEST
 GROUPS=a1(1 2)
 /MISSING=ANALYSIS
 /VARIABLES=a3
 /CRITERIA=CIN(.95) .
```

Chi-square

Again, use 'summarise' and then go to 'crosstabs' where you will be given a series of choices. Choose which variable is to go in the row box and which to go in the column box and then, if you wish, you can also use the layer box to produce tables for two different groups in your sample. For example, you might put age in the column box and marital status in the row box and then gender in the layer box. In this way you would generate tables of age by marital status separately for males and females.

After you have selected the variables for columns, rows and possibly layers you have three more choices to make. There is a 'statistics' menu available to you and from it you can choose 14 different statistics of which chi-square is the top of the list. The others are grouped so as to allow you to choose statistics appropriate to nominal or ordinal level variables. Press 'continue' once you have chosen the statistic you want, presumably chi-square, and then go to the 'cells' menu where you can choose to have observed and expected frequencies displayed and also row, column or total percentages and different kinds of residuals. The residuals are designed to help you interpret the table more precisely. The adjusted residuals allow you to see which cells are most extreme in the departure from expectation. Before looking at the chi-square, note that there is a danger of misinterpreting the association if many of the cells are empty or have very low figures. Check to see whether this is so. If there *are* empty cells or cells with very little in them in the table, you may be able to solve the problem by dropping some of the sparsely represented categories.

The print out gives you Pearson's chi-square and shows you its significance as well. If chi-square is significant then a measure of association between the column and row variables is established. Syntax looks like this:

CROSSTABS
 /TABLES= mstatus BY age
 /FORMAT= AVALUE TABLES
 /STATISTIC=CHISQ
 /CELLS= COUNT row column.

Correlation

Again go to 'statistics' and then select 'correlation' where you were given the choice of 'bivariate' or 'partial'. Normally you expect to choose the bivariate correlation. This allows you to enter as many variables as you want and to select either Pearson's or Spearman's correlation or both and to have the significance of the correlation printed out. The two-tailed option is the default for this and simply ensures that where a significance is calculated it is not done on the basis of any predicted direction. If you are able to predict the direction of the correlation (that is, predict that it would be positive or negative) then a smaller value (that is, less than 0.025) is required for the correlation to be significant. The syntax looks like this:

CORRELATIONS
 /VARIABLES=ducks rabbits
 /PRINT=TWOTAIL NOSIG
 /STATISTICS DESCRIPTIVES
 /MISSING=PAIRWISE .

If you choose the partial correlation you will be able to enter a factor whose variance will be removed from the correlation between the other variables you have selected. Suppose you correlate the number of ducklings on the canal with the number of rabbits in the field, you find a significant correlation and might think that ducklings in some way produce rabbits or vice versa, but if you partial out temperature (that is, if you choose 'partial correlation' and put temperature in the 'controlling for' box in the menu) you discover the correlation dwindles to near zero and that the number of ducklings and rabbits only correlate because both are related to the warmth of the weather. There are many examples where a third factor correlates with two others and partialling out (or controlling for) the effect of this third factor provides a much clearer picture of the relationship between the other two.

One-way analysis of variance

Analysis of variance is a method of making comparisons between the means of two or more groups[10]. However, as the name suggests it works not primarily with means but with variances (the square of the standard deviation). Imagine you have three groups: boys in primary school, boys in secondary school and boys in higher education, and suppose you test the reading speed for each group. Each group's reading speed would have a mean and a standard deviation. The analysis of variance compares the variance of each individual group with the variance of group means, from the mean of all the boys taken together as one big group. If the means are far apart relative to the variance of each group, then the F statistic, which describes this relationship, becomes large[11].

Like the other statistics mentioned earlier, the distribution of the F ratio, which is the statistic associated with analysis of variance (or ANOVA for short), has been worked out for all permutations of samples. As a result a significant F ratio shows that there are differences between the groups, but it does not show exactly which group means vary significantly from each other. The standard print-out routinely calculates group means and standard deviations so it is usually easy to see which groups are especially high or low. But there are procedures within the 'analysis of variance' commands that allow for more refined and statistically sensitive testing using the 'post hoc' options in the menu.

SPSS places 'analysis of variance' under 'statistics', 'compare group means' and then gives a choice of which variable to put in the 'dependent list' and which to put in the 'factor' boxes. In the example given above we would put 'reading speed' in the dependent list and 'boys' in the factor box. The syntax looks like this:

---

[10] An analysis of variance for two groups produces an F value that is the square of the t statistic produced by a t-test.

[11] The F statistic is named after R A Fisher (1890-1962) who described it.

```
ONEWAY
  rspeed BY boysage
  /STATISTICS DESCRIPTIVES HOMOGENEITY
  /MISSING ANALYSIS .
```

Two-way analysis of variance

In the previous example we looked at three groups of boys at different ages to discover the effect of age on reading speed. Suppose we had a more complicated problem. We might wish to investigate the use of two maths schemes by two teaching methods. The two maths schemes might be an old and a new one and teaching methods might be formal and informal. Using a two way analysis of variance we can simultaneously investigate the effects of these factors on the maths progress of pupils. Notice that there are now four possibilities: old maths scheme taught formally, old maths scheme taught informally, new maths scheme taught formally and new maths scheme taught informally. The two way analysis of variance will explore the effect of these factors and also what is called the interaction between them. Interaction refers not just to the effect of the maths scheme on its own or the teaching method on its own but to the combined effect of the two things at once. We can imagine a situation where the informal teaching on its own did not appear to make much impact on the progress of pupils and where the new maths course also did not make much impression but where, when the new method and the new course were combined, a considerable impact was made.

It is too complicated to try to provide a worked example of this sort of analysis, but the general principle is similar to a one-way analysis of variance. It is just that the groups are drawn up twice, once for the maths scheme and once for the method of teaching. SPSS carries out two way analysis of variance in the 'general factorial analysis of variance' which is on the 'statistics' menu under 'general linear model'. In the example we have given we would enter a measure of pupils' maths progress in the 'dependent' box and then the two factors, maths method and maths course, in the 'fixed factor(s)' box. We would select a 'custom' model and then put the two main effects into the box, and also the interaction term which is indicated by an asterisk between the two main effects. The syntax looks like this:

```
UNIANOVA
  mathprog  BY mathype metheach
  /METHOD = SSTYPE(3)
  /INTERCEPT = INCLUDE
  /PLOT = PROFILE(mathype*metheach)
  /EMMEANS = TABLES(mathype*metheach)
  /PRINT = OPOWER
  /CRITERIA = ALPHA(.05)
  /DESIGN =  mathype*metheach.
```

Multiple regression

Multiple regression analysis is, mathematically, an extension of correlation[12]. With a simple correlation two variables are associated with each other. This relationship is expressed by Pearson's r or Spearman's rho. Once the coefficient has been calculated, then the knowledge of one variable can help to predict scores on the other variable. If you know someone's weight, then you can predict their height and, of course, the accuracy of the prediction is dependent upon the strength of the coefficient.

Remember, however, that correlation first was detected by means of a graph. When we are looking for correlation we are looking for a straight line graph, whether it represents a negative or a positive coefficient. Unfortunately, however, in real-life some variables are related to each other in a curve. If you plot a graph of job satisfaction against age, you may end up in some cases with a J curve such that satisfaction is high to start with, drops off in middle life and then rises again towards the end of the working life, presumably once a certain position of seniority has been reached. Curved relationships between variables considerably complicate correlational analysis which assumes a linear association between the variables. This danger needs to be borne in mind when considering more complex analysis[13].

The idea of bivariate correlation can be extended greatly by employing a large number of variables and correlating them all with one variable, the so-called *dependent variable*[14]. Again, an example helps to make this clear though, as we shall see, it does not reveal the rich variety of applications that this technique offers. Imagine you had access to a large database containing information about a great number of pupils and that, within this database, was a measure of the artistic ability of pupils. You might wish to discover which combination of variables helped predict artistic ability best so that you could understand it more fully. Suppose, further, that age, gender, personality and poetic ability correlated with artistic ability. The multiple regression equation would be calculated and the four *independent variables* would be regressed against (in a way correlated with) artistic ability, the dependent variable. This equation could show us three things.

First, we could see the total correlation between all five variables, a figure that behaves like Pearson's r (except that it only varies between 0 and 1) but is written in upper case. This R would almost certainly be larger than the

---

[12] The basic equation is $y = c + b1x1 + b2x2$ etc. Y is the predicted value of the dependent variable, b is the regression coefficient and x1 and x2 are the values of independent variables. C is a constant. You can take this equation and calculate what a value of y would be for any combination of values in the independent variables.

[13] Variables can be transformed mathematically, for instance by computing the log of a set of values, to solve this problem. The SPSS manual explains how to do this.

[14] The dependent variable is the one variable that is being correlated with all the others in a multiple regression procedure. It is the 'dependent' variable because it depends on or is determined by the other variables being correlated with it.

individual correlations between artistic ability and the four independent variables. So, to the extent that high correlations are useful for prediction, the equation would have achieved what could not be achieved using bivariate analysis, or one variable against another, one at a time.

Second, the R helps to indicate how much variance in the dependent variable can be accounted for by the independent variables. Normally R^2 is thought of as a measure of the percentage of variance which can be accounted for. If R^2 were .2503 we would say that 25% of variance had been accounted for by the regression equation, or that 25% of the variation in inartistic ability could be explained by the age, gender, personality and poetic ability of the individuals.

Third, we could see the relationship between the independent variables and the dependent variable together. It might be, for example, that gender correlated strongly with artistic ability but that, when personality was entered into the regression equation, the individual correlation between gender and artistic ability disappeared. In other words, the effect of gender was partialled out by personality. The regression equation could show us that we had been misled into thinking that artistic ability was a particularly, say, feminine attribute but learn that it was an attribute associated with, say, introversion. Indeed in a real-life example investigation into attitudes to religion and gender indicated that more positive attitudes were held by females. This finding was accepted without modification until a study was carried out that included personality as well as gender among the independent variables. In the first step of the regression equation, gender did indeed correlate significantly with attitude to religion but, when personality was entered into the regression equation, the gender relationship disappeared showing the crucial factor lying behind attitude to religion was personality not gender (Francis, Pearson, Carter and Kay, 1981).

The multiple regression equation can allow us to partial out a great number of intervening variables so as to allow for testing of the relationship between the one crucial independent variable we are interested in and the dependent variable. By putting all the intervening variables into the equation first so that they can account for the maximum amount of variance available to them, we can then put the variable we are interested in last and see whether it has any effect. A piece of research on the impact of Agreed Syllabi on the attitudes of children to religion was carried out in this way (Smith, 1999). Attitude towards religion was the dependent variable and into the equation were put school characteristics, age, gender, social background and other variables that the researcher had collected and then, last of all, the variable representing the Agreed Syllabus was put into the equation. The reasoning here was that if the Agreed Syllabus could be shown to be influential, even after all the other variables had been taken into account, then the Agreed Syllabus was indeed relevant to the attitudes of pupils. This particular piece of research, because it used different Agreed Syllabi, had to collect data from different local education authorities so, in effect, what was partialled out was all variability due to the extraneous factors associated with differences between schooling in the local authority areas. If this had not been done, then the differences that were detected might have been due to some other feature of the schooling, perhaps social class of pupils or the religious background of the home. By removing the effects of these features first, the impact of Agreed Syllabi could be identified and measured.

There is one further feature of multiple regression and this is its ability to contribute to path models, also called path analysis. In essence a series of multiple regression equations are calculated. Perhaps variables 1 and 2 are treated as independent and variable 3 is treated as dependent, then variable 3 is treated as independent along with variable 4 while variable 5 is treated as dependent. In this way the effects of variables 1 and 2 mediated through variables 3 and 4 on variable 5 can be assessed.

Because multiple regression can be carried out in various ways and used for various purposes the output from the regression command is very full. Briefly, we will mention how the equation might be set up. If we are interested in an example like the one above about the Agreed Syllabi, we could arrange to enter all the intervening variables in a single step or block first before we entered the variable representing Agreed Syllabus. Thus the order in which variables are entered into the equation can be controlled by the researcher and the output will provide statistics relating to each stage of the process. But we might be interested simply to discover which variable, out of a group of variables, was most influential on the dependent variable and so, in this case, we would enter all the variables together in one block.

For a two-step equation the syntax looks like this. The dependent variable in this example is a9 and there are two steps in the equation. First a3 is entered and then together a1, a2 and a4.

```
REGRESSION
 /MISSING LISTWISE
 /STATISTICS COEFF OUTS R ANOVA
 /CRITERIA=PIN(.05) POUT(.10)
 /NOORIGIN
 /DEPENDENT a9
 /METHOD=ENTER a3  /METHOD=ENTER a1 a2 a4  .
```

The output first gives a summary of the two models. R and R^2 are shown. Following this an ANOVA table indicates whether each equation as a whole is significant. If it is not, there is no point in proceeding further with the analysis. Then the output gives a series of coefficients for each of the different variables and shows their individual significance. A so-called B coefficient is given, then a beta coefficient (which is a standardised version of the B), then a t value and then a significance level. The t value is the B coefficient divided by its standard error. The beta coefficient is what the B coefficient would be if all scores were so-called standard scores (a score less its mean divided by the standard deviation of that variable). Effectively the beta coefficient provides a way of seeing how the variables operate when they are measured in the same units. Beta coefficients are used in path analysis. The significance of the t value is the significance of the correlation of that particular independent variable with the dependent variable.

Before carrying out a multiple regression analysis it is wise to inspect the relationship between the dependent variable and each of the independent variables to see whether they relate together in a linear fashion. Multiple regression is a robust procedure and is able to cope with departures from linearity but, ideally, the independent variables should be inspected either using scatter plots or tested using the analysis of variance programme and then selecting the linear option under 'contrasts'. If the independent variables do not relate to the dependent variable in a linear way, then their categories can be conflated or alternatively they can be broken down into dummy variables[15].

After the analysis it is sensible to look at the diagnostic outcomes from the regression analysis. Most of these are based upon the notion of comparing the predicted value of the dependent variable as calculated from the regression equation, with its actual value. These diagnostic statistics are helpful as a check on the validity of the regression procedure but, with large samples, multiple regression works well even when there are minor violations of the assumptions on which the test is predicated. There is one other difficulty that can arise if a large number of independent variables are used and if these variables intercorrelate strongly. The problem is known as (multi)collinearity. SPSS offers a test of this. The usual solution is to drop one of the offending variables and allow it to be represented by one with which it strongly correlates.

Reliability

Reliability has been discussed in C1. All that needs to be noted here is that the statistical routine for reliability is only offered in the professional module of SPSS.

---

[15] Dummy variables are created by taking a variable with several categories (such as religion divided into Catholic, Protestant and Jewish) and making the smaller two categories a dummy variable. The dummy variable which is created by an 'if' statement in the syntax uses the mean of the relevant group within the regression equation.

Factor analysis

Factor analysis is used when a large matrix of correlations needs to be simplified into a smaller number of variables. If you had distributed a questionnaire containing 100 items about school to children and correlated all the items with each other, you would produce a matrix with 450 different correlations in it. Trying to interpret a dataset of this size is daunting. But factor analysis is a tool that enables a simplification of the matrix to be achieved. Essentially factors are 'extracted' from the matrix and the 'loading' (or correlation) of items in the questionnaire with the factors shows how groups of items belong together. In the questionnaire about school, we might discover that 15 of the items load onto a factor by themselves and this factor relates to homework, and that ten other items load onto another factor that relates to sport. Quite quickly a pattern within the matrix can be found.

There are interpretative problems about the meaning of some factors and there are mathematical choices to be made about the number of factors that can be extracted from any individual matrix, and about the method by which this extraction should take place. Factor analysis requires a 'feel' for the data and is not an automatic procedure for generating meaning but, this said, it has proved itself to be useful over many years and, moreover, once the factors have been identified, they can then be turned into the scales and used to measure attitudes or other psychological constructs. The syntax looks like this.

```
FACTOR
  /VARIABLES b1 to b50
  /MISSING LISTWISE /ANALYSIS b1 to b50
  /PRINT INITIAL EXTRACTION
  /CRITERIA MINEIGEN(1) ITERATE(25)
  /EXTRACTION PC
  /ROTATION NOROTATE
  /METHOD=CORRELATION .
```

Activity C4

Consider the strategies and tactics you might use to discover what factors influence pupils' attitudes towards bullying. To help you in your research assume that you have been given access to a database containing information about the opinions of pupils to many aspects of school life. In addition assume that the database contains measures of teacher effectiveness, the type and place of training received by teachers, type of school in which pupils are located, details of school catchment area, the age of pupils, and the Eysenck Personality Questionnaire for assessing pupil personality. The database has been collected using a proper sampling procedure and is free of many missing values.

Comment on activity C4

In attempting to find out the answer to your research question, you begin with a study of the literature on the subject to discover what previous studies have found, and to see whether any of the variables in your database may be similar to those used previously. Having made this search of the literature, you are ready to turn your attention to your database. First, you want to get a 'feel' for your data and very often the simplest way to do this is to print out the frequencies of many of the variables in the dataset. This allows you to see the characteristics of your sample, how many boys and girls there are, how old they are, what sort of personality scores they return, what their opinions are on the numerous items in the questionnaire they filled in, information about the number of schools attended by the pupils, the relevant catchment areas, the types of school attended (some may be 11 to 16 and others 11 to 18) and also to look at the variables relating to teachers that will show you how old they are, the mix of males and females and perhaps give you information on their qualifications and place of training.

You now need to begin to try to make sense of the mass of information before you, bearing in mind that you are specifically interested in attitudes to bullying. You may choose to try to construct an attitude scale towards bullying from the numerous items filled in by the pupils. We will assume that the items have all been filled in using the same format. You could pick out items that appear to refer to bullying and correlate them with the rest of the items in the questionnaire and see which items correlate significantly with the bullying items. This set of items, correlating significantly with the bullying items you have picked out, could become the basis for your scale.

However, you may decide that you want to use an alternative strategy and to factor analyse your matrix to see whether any factor emerges which might be relevant to bullying. The advantage of this procedure over the first one is that you may end up with a scale that includes items which did not, on the face of it, appear to have much relationship with bullying. So by exploring the whole matrix through factor analysis, but without preconceptions, you have let the data speak to you more freely.

In practice, though, it may well be that the two methods produce similar results. Once you have identified the items that appear to measure bullying you need to carry out reliability analysis on them to demonstrate that the items form an acceptable scale. We will assume that the items have been completed using the Likert format. You will be looking for a high alpha coefficient in the scale items without making the scale excessively long (up to 12 items should be ample). As a further refinement, once you have selected the items for a scale, you might carry out a factor analysis of these items on their own to see whether they all loaded onto one factor, or nearly so (see also van der Ven, 1993). This would be a further safeguard of the properties of the scale you are constructing.

Once you have constructed the scale, you are in a position to see which factors correlate with it. Your previous literature research should have given you ideas about what to look for so that the explorations you make are not haphazard. Suppose your reading leads you to believe that teacher effectiveness, the catchment area of the school and the personality of pupils are likely to be relevant to attitudes to bullying. Suppose, too, that the teacher effectiveness variable is provided by inspectors working to uncertain criteria so that some teachers are rated on a ten point scale, others are rated A to E and yet others have no rating at all although you have information about where they trained. Clearly, you have a choice: you can either try to put all the teachers in your sample onto one scale of your own invention, or you must try to work with some subset of teachers. For example, you might be able to show that the ten point scale and the rating A to E could be conflated so that a score of A might be equated with a score of 9 or 10, B with 7 or 8, etc. Perhaps you could make use of a chi-square test of association between rating and place of training. If you were able to do this then, if you only knew place of training of a teacher, you might be able to make an assessment about what sort of rating they would have obtained if they had been rated.

If the catchment area of the school also provides some clues about attitudes to bullying then you would expect to find associations between different aspects of the area and pupils' attitudes. It is unlikely that all the variables describing the catchment area would be of the same kind and you might find it necessary to carry out some data transformations in order to make them compatible or, alternatively, you might look for associations between catchment area variables and pupil attitudes (perhaps testing using analysis of variance since the catchment area variables might be categorical rather than continuous) and then use the best variables in a later and fuller equation.

The personality variables are good quality data. The Eysenck Personality Questionnaire will usually give you normally distributed data suitable for use in correlations. Initially, you might correlate the different personality dimensions with your attitude to bullying scale and then, perhaps, partial out age or gender in the correlations to see whether the associations remained. You might expect to find a negative correlation between introversion and attitude to bullying and a positive correlation between tough-mindedness and attitude to bullying. You might also wish to use a t-test to compare two groups of pupils in their attitude to bullying, perhaps taking older and younger pupils or pupils with different socio-economic backgrounds.

To complete your analysis you might attempt to put together the personal variables relating to pupils with the school and catchment area variables and the teacher variables in a single multiple regression equation.   The dependent variable would be attitude to bullying and the other variables would be independent.   Before putting the multiple regression equation together, you might test for linearity between the variables you were using and attitude to bullying and, if necessary, adjust your variables by creating dummy variables to ensure linearity existed.   You would only expect to use the variables that had already been shown to have an association with attitude toward bullying.

Probably you would enter the variables in the equation in three separate blocks in this order, one corresponding to school and catchment area, one corresponding to teachers and one to pupils.   In doing this you would, of course, partial out the variance caused by the school and teacher blocks so that the pupil block would only be significant if it contributed variance over and above that of the other blocks.   Your analysis, on this model, would be on the assumption that pupil variables were crucial to attitude towards bullying.   Yet, it is possible that your reading of the research literature might have suggested to you that pupil variables were less important than school variables, in which case you might enter the block of school variables last.

This consideration of the activity should have shown that although research methods provide precision and 'hard' evidence, they also require imagination and flexibility in their application.   There is rarely only one way to solve a research problem though, admittedly, in the discussion here, a variety of techniques have been deliberately employed to give you a better idea of the possibilities inherent in the whole process.

Readers

Examples of statistical analyses of relevant data are provided in L.J. Francis, W.K. Kay, and W.S. Campbell (eds) (1996), *Research in Religious Education*, Leominster, Gracewing.   Further information about SPSS procedures are provided in M.J. Norusis (1998), *SPSS 8.0: guide to data analysis*, Englewood Cliffs, New Jersey, Prentice-Hall and A. Diamantopoulos and B.B. Schlegelmilch (1997), *Taking the Fear out of Data Analysis*, London, Thomson Business Press.

Bibliography

Cronbach, L.J. (1951), Coefficient alpha and the internal structure of tests, *Psychometrika*, 16, 297-334.

Francis, L.J. (1976), An enquiry into the concept 'Readiness for Religion', Unpublished Ph.D dissertation, University of Cambridge.

Francis, L.J., Pearson, P.R., Carter, M. and Kay, W.K. (1981), The relationship between neuroticism and religiosity among English 15 and 16 year olds, *The Journal of Social Psychology*, 114, 99-102.

Kay, W.K. (1996), Religious education and assemblies: pupils' changing views, in L.J. Francis, W.K. Kay and W.S. Campbell (eds), *Research in Religious Education*, Leominster, Gracewing, pp 267-277.

Kerlinger, F.N. (1973), *Multiple Regression in Behavioral Research*, London, Holt, Rinehart and Winston.

Likert, R.A. (1932), A technique for the measurement of attitudes, *Archives of Psychology*, 140, 1-55.

Osgood, C.E., Suci, G.J. and Tannenbaum P.H. (1957), *The Measurement of Meaning*, Urbana, University of Illinois Press.

Peers, I.S. (1996), *Statistical Analysis for Education and Psychology Researchers*, London, Falmer Press.

Smith, D.L. (1999), What does religious education achieve? An investigation of the effect of secondary pupils' experience of religious education on their attitude to religion, Unpublished PhD dissertation, University of Wales.

van der Ven, J.A. (1993), *Practical Theology*, Kampen, The Netherlands, Kok Pharos.

Index of names

Index of subjects